Coastal California

John Doerper
Photography by Galen Rowell

COMPASS AMERICAN GUIDES
An Imprint of Fodor's Travel Publications, Inc.

Coastal California

Copyright © 1998 Fodor's Travel Publications, Inc.
Maps copyright © 1998 Fodor's Travel Publications, Inc.

LIBRARY OF CONGRESS CATALOGING-IN-PUBLICATION DATA
Doerper, John.
Coastal California/John Doerper; photography by Galen Rowell
p.   cm. —(Compass American Guides)
Includes bibliographical references and index.
ISBN 0-679-03598-2
1. Pacific Coast (Calif.)—Guidebooks. I. Rowell, Galen A. II. Title.
III. Series: Compass American guides (Series)
F868.P33D63 1998   98-9229
917.94'0453--dc21   CIP

10 9 8 7 6 5 4 3 2 1
First published in 1998

Editors: Kit Duane, Deborah Dunn,
  Michael Oliver
Managing Editor: Kit Duane
Creative Director: Christopher Burt
Lodging & Restaurants Editor: Julia Dillon

Designers: Christopher Burt, Deborah Dunn,
Map Design: Mark Stroud, Moon Street
Cartography
Produced by Twin Age Ltd., Hong Kong
Printed in Hong Kong

Compass American Guides, 5332 College Ave. Suite 201, Oakland, CA 94618, USA

The Publisher gratefully acknowledges the following individuals and institutions: Bancroft Library, Berkeley pp. 21, 22; The Berkshire Museum, Pittsfield, MA. p. 155; Buffalo Bill Historical Center, Cody, WY pp. 60-61; Dr. & Mrs. Edward Boseker p. 26; California Historical Society, Title Insurance and Trust Photo Collection, USC Library, Los Angeles pp. 285, 329; James Doolin/Koplin Gallery, Los Angeles p. 265; Joann Irvine Smith Fine Arts, Irvine pp. 166, 289; Fleischer Museum, Scottsdale, AZ pp. 194, 295; Garzoli Gallery, San Rafael, CA pp. 38-39, 168; The Pat Hathaway Collection of California Views, Monterey p. 183; Hearst Castle/Hearst San Simeon State Historical Monument, photo by John Blades p. 204; Huntington Library, Pasadena p. 149; International Surfing Museum, Newport Beach, photo by Elmar Baxter/Images Inc. p. 284; History Collections, LA County Museum of Natural History p. 190; Harry Mayo, Santa Cruz p. 176; National Archives p. 230; Oakland Museum p. 24; Peter E. Palmquist, Eureka pp. 129, 146, 150, 158; San Francisco Maritime NHP p. 29 photo by Gabriel Moulin #J7 23, 649n1, p. 47 photo by O.V. Lange #A12 152n; Santa Barbara Mission Archive Library p. 25; courtesy Santa Catalina Island Co. p. 281; Dr. Albert Shumate p. 64; Square Books, Santa Rosa, hand-tinting by Ann Rhoney p. 31; Sunkist Growers, Inc. and The Villa Park Orchards Association p. 7; Westphal Publishing, Irvine p. 278. Additional photography was supplied by Sean Arbabi pp. 12 (bottom) 210, 221, 239, 252, 322; Adam Ballachey pp. 316, 317 (both); Kerrick James pp. 40, 41, 48; Susan Scheding p. 273; Mark Wexler p. 277; and Michael Yamashita pp. 50, 55, 80. Also thanks to Adam Ballachey for essay on pp. 316-317, Jill Bell for essay on page 273, readers Barry Parr and Bill Burden, Ellen Klages for proofreading, Lesley Bonnett for research, Bara Bonnett for fact-checking, and Julie Searle for the index.

To Victoria, my favorite beach buddy.

C O N T E N T S

Literary Extracts

Topical Essays

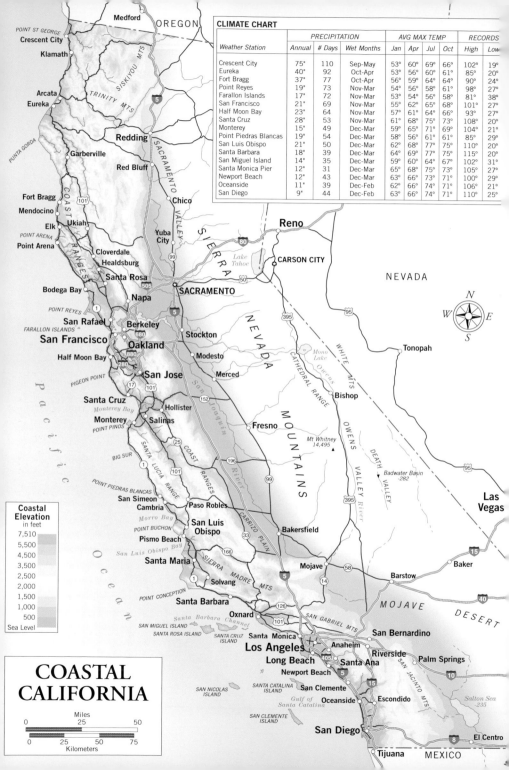

CLIMATE CHART

Weather Station	PRECIPITATION			AVG MAX TEMP				RECORDS	
	Annual	# Days	Wet Months	Jan	Apr	Jul	Oct	High	Low
Crescent City	75"	110	Sep-May	53°	60°	69°	66°	102°	19°
Eureka	40"	92	Oct-Apr	53°	56°	60°	61°	85°	20°
Fort Bragg	37"	77	Oct-Apr	56°	59°	64°	64°	90°	24°
Point Reyes	19"	73	Nov-Mar	54°	56°	58°	61°	98°	27°
Farallon Islands	17"	72	Nov-Mar	53°	54°	56°	58°	81°	38°
San Francisco	21"	69	Nov-Mar	55°	62°	65°	68°	101°	27°
Half Moon Bay	23"	64	Nov-Mar	57°	61°	64°	66°	93°	27°
Santa Cruz	28"	53	Nov-Mar	61°	68°	75°	73°	108°	20°
Monterey	15"	49	Dec-Mar	59°	65°	71°	69°	104°	21°
Point Piedras Blancas	19"	54	Dec-Mar	58°	56°	61°	61°	85°	29°
San Luis Obispo	21"	50	Dec-Mar	62°	68°	77°	75°	110°	20°
Santa Barbara	18"	39	Dec-Mar	64°	69°	77°	75°	115°	20°
San Miguel Island	14"	35	Dec-Mar	59°	60°	64°	67°	102°	31°
Santa Monica Pier	12"	31	Dec-Mar	65°	68°	75°	73°	105°	27°
Newport Beach	12"	43	Dec-Mar	63°	66°	73°	71°	100°	29°
Oceanside	11"	39	Dec-Feb	62°	66°	74°	71°	106°	21°
San Diego	9"	44	Dec-Feb	63°	66°	74°	71°	110°	25°

COASTAL CALIFORNIA

Coastal Elevation
in feet

7,510
5,500
4,500
3,500
2,500
2,000
1,500
1,000
500
Sea Level

Miles
0   25   50

0   25   50   75
Kilometers

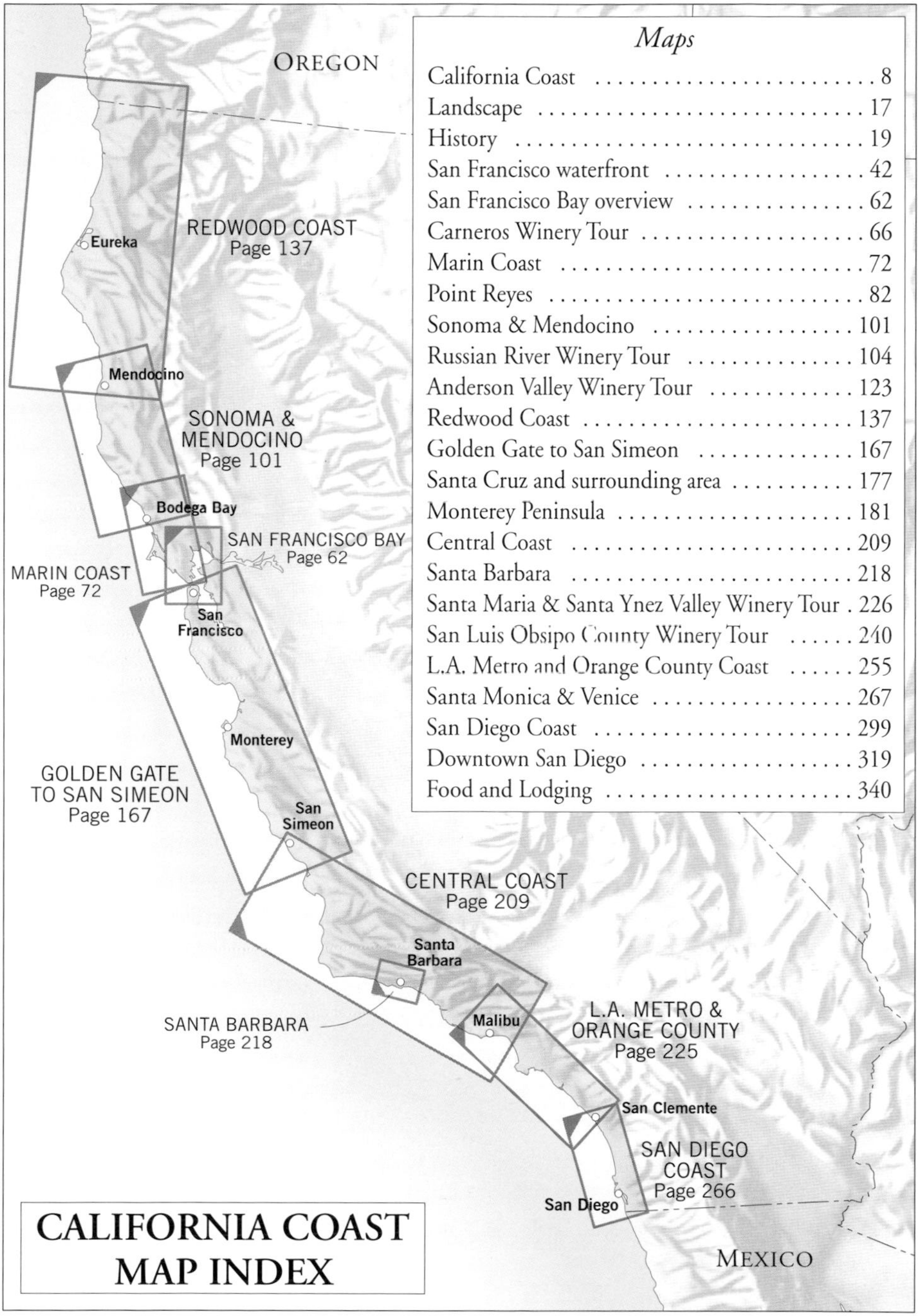

OREGON

CALIFORNIA COAST
MAP INDEX

MEXICO

Eureka

REDWOOD COAST
Page 137

Mendocino

SONOMA &
MENDOCINO
Page 101

Bodega Bay

SAN FRANCISCO BAY
Page 62

MARIN COAST
Page 72

**San
Francisco**

Monterey

GOLDEN GATE
TO SAN SIMEON
Page 167

**San
Simeon**

CENTRAL COAST
Page 209

**Santa
Barbara**

Malibu

SANTA BARBARA
Page 218

L.A. METRO &
ORANGE COUNTY
Page 225

San Clemente

SAN DIEGO
COAST
Page 266

San Diego

Maps

O V E R V I E W

HOW TO USE THIS BOOK:

To long-distance drivers, the California coast is a 1,200-mile ribbon of highway running from Oregon to Mexico. But to most visitors, it's a beautiful stretch of shore within easy reach of their home city or of a major airport. Since most Californians live in one of the state's three great coastal metropolitan areas—San Francisco Bay, Los Angeles/Orange County, and San Diego— we have taken each of the metropolitan areas as a departure point, providing guides for an easy exploration of the coast by car from San Francisco, Los Angeles, or San Diego.

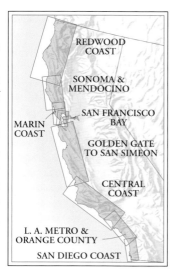

REDWOOD COAST

SONOMA & MENDOCINO

SAN FRANCISCO BAY

MARIN COAST

GOLDEN GATE TO SAN SIMEON

CENTRAL COAST

L. A. METRO & ORANGE COUNTY

SAN DIEGO COAST

■ SAN FRANCISCO BAY
This hill-girt bay is one of America's most important ports as well as California's largest estuary. The restaurants, theaters, museums, and charming neighborhoods of its urban areas have a counterpoint in beautiful, undeveloped Angel Island, bayside state parks, and rocky cliffs. This magnificent bay is so large, it is hard to grasp in just one visit. You can explore it by ferry, or walk along its coastside trails. At the northern extension of the bay lies the famous Carneros wine district.

■ MARIN COAST

From the cliffs of the Marin Headlands to the magnificent sweep of Point Reyes and the fishing boats of Bodega Bay, this is an awesomely beautiful area. Rolling hills rise above rocky headlands and offshore sea stacks. Coves, sea caves, and long, sandy beaches are perfect places for exploring on foot or by kayak. Along the way are comfortable inns and excellent restaurants.

■ SONOMA TO
   MENDOCINO

A wild and rural coast, with comfortable inns and restaurants catering to the needs of the body, while the galleries and theaters of Point Arena, Fort Bragg, and Mendocino stimulate the mind. Vineyards thrive in sunny coastal valleys.

■ REDWOOD COAST

Only a few towns brave the wildness of this lonely stretch where steep coastal mountains merge with sandy shores. Along the rivers which flow into the ocean here grow the world's tallest trees—the most magnificent of California redwoods. These silent woods are perfect for contemplative walks. Small towns and villages like Shelter Cove, Ferndale, and Trinidad invite visitors to relax a while. Humboldt Bay, California's second largest estuary, is a perfect place for watching birds from the shore or from a kayak.

■ GOLDEN GATE TO
SAN SIMEON
South of San Francisco, along the San Mateo coast, lie a rural landscape and wide views of an indigo sea. At Monterey, the Santa Lucia Mountains push to the sea forming rocky coves that face green and turquoise waters. CA 1,

which runs along seaward cliffs of the Big Sur coast, is one of the most beautiful— as well as hair-raising—drives in the world. Elkhorn Slough and other estuaries make for great birdwatching. Santa Cruz, Monterey, Pacific Grove, and Carmel cater to travelers. Hearst Castle at San Simeon is a cultural showcase of a different kind—a monument to a nouveau riche fascination with European antiquities.

■ CENTRAL COAST RIVIERA
Long, sandy beaches, the largest sand dunes in North America, rocky cliffs, monolithic Morro Rock, and warm ocean waters are highlights of this scenic coast. The old mission town of Santa Barbara, the most beautiful on the coast, adds a touch of Mediterranean elegance. Pismo Beach and Avila Beach are old-fashioned beach towns with splendid beaches and lots of sunshine. Morro Bay's compact waterfront has shops and restaurants; its beaches and those of Cayucos to the north are perfect for walking, watching birds, and surfing.

■ L.A. METRO
AND ORANGE COUNTY

The West Coast's largest metropolitan area is known for its beach culture, warm waters, and effervescent, *au courant* lifestyle. A large crescent of sandy strand curves from the shores of Malibu past culturally sophisticated Santa Monica, friendly, down-to-earth Manhattan Beach, folksy Redondo, and the flower-bedecked bluffs of the Palos Verdes Peninsula. From Newport Beach south, rocky shores with pocket beaches dominate the coast before giving way to more sandy beaches that run south through San Clemente. This is a shore of sand, sun, palm trees, and extensive development.

■ SAN DIEGO COAST

With its rocky shores, quiet coves, sandy beaches, and warm ocean waters, San Diego County is the Mediterranean shore of California. State-protected coastal lagoons add a touch of wildness, as do surfers who brave the breaking waves at some of the West's most famous surfing beaches. Gardens of subtropical flowers bloom all year long, and graceful palm fronds wave in the sea breeze. Along the Coast Highway lie chic, sophisticated La Jolla, expensive Del Mar, and the historic sights of the city of San Diego. Mexico, just a few miles away, profoundly influences the area's music, cuisine, economy, and political life.

INTRODUCTION

THE CALIFORNIA COAST, with its wide, sandy beaches, flower-bedecked bluffs, surf-washed cliffs, and wild mountain ranges, is one of the most scenic places of the world. It is both rugged and urbane, with wilderness abutting the West Coast's most cultured cities.

Since most of California's people live near the coast, you'll find it easy to switch back and forth between wilderness and civilization, following up a beach picnic of fresh oysters with dinner at an elegant restaurant; bird-, seal-, or whale-watching with a night at the opera; a day of hiking lonely trails with a stroll along an urban boulevard.

One unique aspect of this coast is the climate: In summer, when inland valleys and mountains swelter in the heat, the coast is cool; in winter, when inland areas are cold—even frosty—the coast is delightfully mild. Even if the weather is too cool for swimming or sunbathing, it's rarely wet enough to make beachcombing or hiking unpleasant.

The color of sky and ocean vary with the seasons; sometimes with the time of the day. The sea can be a deep royal blue or indigo, battleship gray, a translucent green, turquoise, or a reddish brown like redwood bark. The sky can be intensely cerulean, pale golden, or glaringly white with the intense light of the summer sun or pearly gray with fog. For most of the coast, the horizon is a long dark line broken only now and then by the outline of a fishing boat or freighter, but off the Southern California coast, islands, previously hidden by haze, appear out of nowhere, and the outlines of offshore oil rigs and passing ships may be etched sharply into the sky.

The California coast is as much a state of mind as it is a place. Its people, and the stories and myths they have woven around this magic coast, are as captivating as the spectacular scenery.

This book introduces you to many of these: it will tell you what the beaches are like and whether they are good for sunbathing, swimming, surfing, diving, or beachcombing; it will take you on scenic trails and into quiet backwaters; it will visit villages and towns and tell you where to find the best food and most comfortable lodging; and it will take you on winery tours. Anecdotes and historical stories will introduce you to the people of the coast and to their way of thinking, because this coast is as filled with interesting things to do as it is with natural beauty.

Spring wildflowers carpet the Marin Headlands.

LANDSCAPE & HISTORY

IMAGINE YOURSELF ABOARD a Manila galleon, one of the Spanish treasure ships that, once every year in the mid-1700s, made the trip from Manila across the wild Pacific Ocean on the prevailing westerly winds, then scooted south to Acapulco on the California Current and favorable winds.

Storms have driven you a bit north of the standard route. As the galleon turns south you catch glimpses of a rocky, surf-washed shore overtowered by huge conifers. The pilot turns the ship's bow out to sea, for he sees whitewater and spume ahead, indicating that a reef runs far out into the ocean from the shore, posing danger to the galleon. Soon the water turns muddy, and huge driftwood logs, with roots as big around as whales, bob in the waves. You suspect that large rivers flow into the ocean here. You want to land at an estuary to take on fresh water, but the pilot counsels against it, reminding you that several galleons have sunk off this coast since the Manila trade began.

Suddenly a huge headland emerges from the fog. Cape Mendocino. You're back on the regular galleon route. Steep mountains loom forbiddingly off the starboard bow. A few leagues further south, cliffs give way to sand dunes—still overtowered by those huge trees, some of which you estimate must be more than 50 *brazos* tall.

After you pass a large sandy hook reaching far into the ocean (later named Point Arena) the galleon once again runs along a shore of rocky cliffs. Sea otters watch you from the safety of kelp beds and sea lions bark from offshore rocks. You pass a rocky headland sheltering a secure harbor (later to be known as Bodega Bay) and shortly after sail past Point Reyes, with its white cliffs (that were likened to the cliffs of Dover by that notorious pirate, Francis Drake). Just south you note a muddy discoloration of the water. Surely a large river must flow into the ocean through a gap in these steep headlands, but the pilot points to the unbroken wall of cliffs and a white line of the surf and says it's impossible. He refuses to risk the ship by sailing closer to shore. Yet it is here that in 1769 a land expedition led by Gaspar de Portola discovers San Francisco Bay, the greatest harbor on the coast, and in 1775 your acquaintance Manuel de Ayala will brave the entrance and moor in the vast protected waters off beautiful Angel Island.

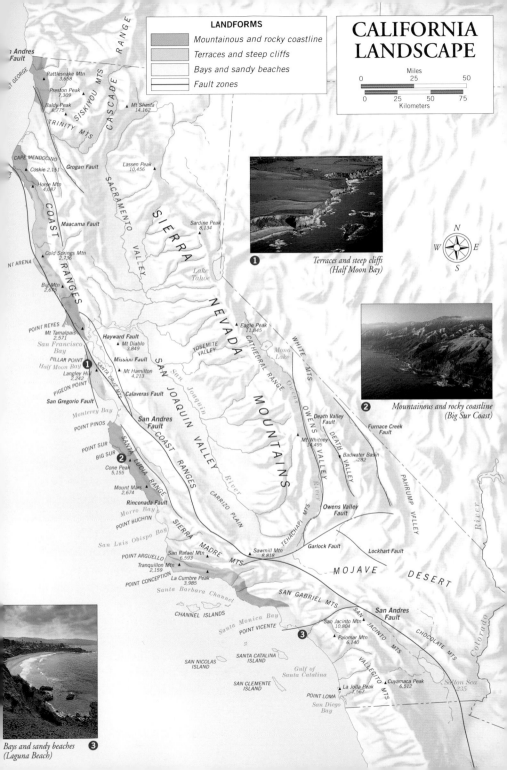

LANDFORMS

- Mountainous and rocky coastline
- Terraces and steep cliffs
- Bays and sandy beaches
- Fault zones

CALIFORNIA LANDSCAPE

Miles
0   25   50

0   25   50   75
Kilometers

San Andres Fault

ST GEORGE

RANGE

Rattlesnake Mtn
3,658

Presfon Peak
7,309

Baldy Peak
6,775

SISKIYOU MTS

CASCADE

TRINITY MTS

Mt Shasta
14,162

CAPE MENDOCINO

Coskie 2,151

Grogan Fault

Lassen Peak
10,456

Horse Mtn
4,087

SACRAMENTO

Maacama Fault

SIERRA

COAST

Cold Springs Mtn
2,736

Lake
Tahoe

NEVADA

PT ARENA

Big Mtn
2,672

VALLEY

Sardine Peak
8,134

① Terraces and steep cliffs
(Half Moon Bay)

POINT REYES

Mt Tamalpais
2,571

San Francisco Bay

Hayward Fault

Mt Diablo
3,849

Eagle Peak
11,845

WHITE MTS

RANGES

PILLAR POINT

Half Moon Bay ①

Langley Hill
2,242

PIGEON POINT

Mission Fault

Mt Hamilton
4,213

YOSEMITE
VALLEY

CATHEDRAL RANGE

Mono
Lake

San Gregorio Fault

Calaveras Fault

San Joaquin

MOUNTAINS

Owens

② Mountainous and rocky coastline
(Big Sur Coast)

Monterey Bay

POINT PINOS

San Andres
Fault

Death Valley
Fault

Furnace Creek
Fault

POINT SUR

BIG SUR ②

Cone Peak
5,155

SANTA LUCIA RANGE

COAST RANGES

VALLEY

River

Mt Whitney
14,495

Badwater Basin
-282

DEATH
VALLEY

PAHRUMP VALLEY

Mount Mars
2,674

Rinconada Fault

Morro Bay

POINT BUCHON

CARRIZO PLAIN

Owens Valley
Fault

River

San Luis Obispo Bay

SIERRA

Sawmill Mtn
8,818

TEHACHAPI MTS

Garlock Fault

Lockhart Fault

POINT ARGUELLO

San Rafael Mtn
6,593

MADRE

Tranquillon Mtn
2,159

POINT CONCEPTION

La Cumbre Peak
3,985

MTS

MOJAVE   DESERT

Santa Barbara Channel

SAN GABRIEL MTS

San Andres
Fault

CHANNEL ISLANDS

Santa Monica Bay

POINT VICENTE

③

San Jacinto Mtn
10,804

SAN JACINTO MTS

CHOCOLATE MTS

Palomar Mtn
6,140

Colorado

SAN NICOLAS
ISLAND

SANTA CATALINA
ISLAND

Gulf of
Santa Catalina

VALLECITO MTS

SAN CLEMENTE
ISLAND

La Jolla Peak
1,567

Cuyamaca Peak
6,512

Salton Sea
235

POINT LOMA

San Diego
Bay

③ Bays and sandy beaches
(Laguna Beach)

Now, the forest-clad mountains retreat from the shore. Coastal terraces are covered with meadows of lush grass, studded with oaks, pines, and cypresses. Occasionally, you spot herds of deer and elk. Lagoons, marked by swarms of waterfowl and shorebirds, interrupt a grim line of cliffs.

South of Point Año Nuevo, where huge elephants seals loll on the beaches, the shore recedes at "Santa Cruz" to form a vast bay with a long crescent of sandy beach. At its southern end a rocky headland, covered with pines and cypresses growing almost to the water's edge, shelters the bay. The sand here is so white you think at first it must be snow. Surely this must be the port of Monterey described in his logs by Sebastian Vizcaino 150 years ago.

South of this bay there is no safe anchorage for a hundred leagues or more. Tall mountains rise straight from the sea, their southern slopes covered with meadows and oaks. As the galleon scuds ahead of the wind, every sail set and drawing well, the mountains give way to rolling hills. You see miles of sand dunes, a few almost as high as mountains, before you reach Point Conception, the most notorious cape on the coast, a place of fogs and storms. But you're lucky and have the wind and current on your side. Racing past the dreaded rocks, you suddenly find yourself in a changed world. A golden sun shines above a cobalt-blue sea, highlighting the white sands and tawny hills of the shore and setting off the chain of Channel Islands in dark relief against the sea. You can clearly see the large domed huts of the natives on the bluffs. As you sail past San Miguel Island (where Juan Cabrillo, the explorer, died and was buried more than 150 years ago) the natives approach the galleon in their canoes, hoping to trade fruit and meat for fish hooks and trinkets.

Sailing between the islands and the shore, you note that the landscape becomes drier, more barren; scrub and chaparral rather than forest cover the seaward slopes of mountains rising from the sea. The air is warm, the light fine and clear. A large plain opens up to the east. Grass and cactus dominate the vegetation of the coastal terraces, but here and there copses of oaks and pines interrupt the open prairies.

Every few leagues, the line of cliffs is broken by freshwater lagoons. From the heaving deck of the galleon, you can just make out the tops of the tule and willow thickets, and see the line of thick-trunked sycamore trees marching down to the sea along stream and river banks.

Soon you sail past Point Loma and stop for a few days at the sheltered harbor of San Diego with its long sand spit. Rumor has it that this will be the sight of Alta California's first presidio and mission to be established by the Viceroy of Mexico.

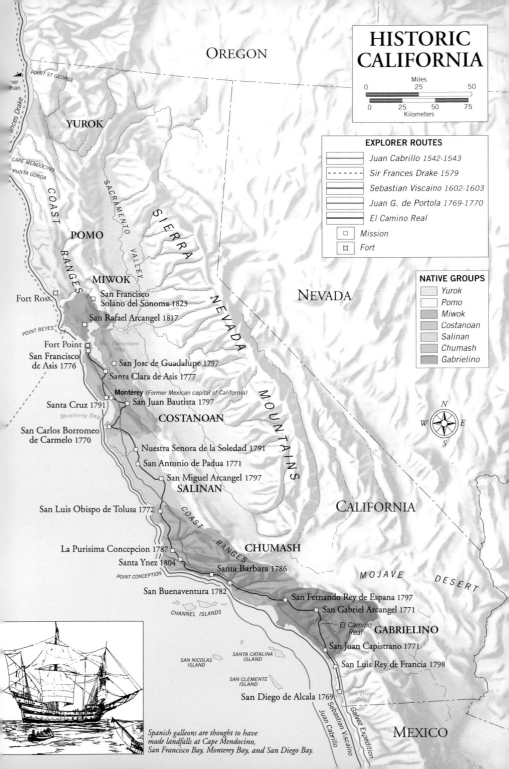

HISTORIC CALIFORNIA

Miles
0   25   50

0   25   50   75
Kilometers

EXPLORER ROUTES

Juan Cabrillo 1542-1543
Sir Frances Drake 1579
Sebastian Viscaino 1602-1603
Juan G. de Portola 1769-1770
El Camino Real
□ Mission
⊡ Fort

NATIVE GROUPS
Yurok
Pomo
Miwok
Costanoan
Salinan
Chumash
Gabrielino

OREGON

POINT ST GEORGE

YUROK

ances Drake

CAPE MENDOCINO
PUNTA GORDA

COAST RANGES

SACRAMENTO VALLEY

SIERRA

NEVADA

POMO

MIWOK

Fort Ross □

San Francisco
Solano del Sonoma 1823

San Rafael Arcangel 1817

POINT REYES

Fort Point □ San Francisco Bay

San Francisco
de Asis 1776

San Jose de Guadalupe 1797

Santa Clara de Asis 1777

Monterey (Former Mexican capital of California)

Santa Cruz 1791 □ San Juan Bautista 1797

Monterey Bay

COSTANOAN

San Carlos Borromeo
de Carmelo 1770

Nuestra Senora de la Soledad 1791

San Antonio de Padua 1771

San Miguel Arcangel 1797

SALINAN

San Luis Obispo de Tolusa 1772 □

COAST RANGES

La Purisima Concepcion 1787 □

Santa Ynez 1804

POINT CONCEPTION

CHUMASH

Santa Barbara 1786

San Buenaventura 1782

CHANNEL ISLANDS

NEVADA

CALIFORNIA

MOUNTAINS

MOJAVE DESERT

San Fernando Rey de Espana 1797

San Gabriel Arcangel 1771

El Camino
Real GABRIELINO

San Juan Capistrano 1771

SAN NICOLAS
ISLAND

SANTA CATALINA
ISLAND

San Luis Rey de Francia 1798

SAN CLEMENTE
ISLAND

San Diego de Alcala 1769

San Diego Bay

N
W ✦ E
S

Sebastian Viscaino

Juan Cabrillo

Galvez Expedition

MEXICO

Spanish galleons are thought to have
made landfalls at Cape Mendocino,
San Francisco Bay, Monterey Bay, and San Diego Bay.

Just south of here, the pilot tells you, the land turns very dry. You've reached the desert shores of the California Peninsula, and the pilot turns the galleon's bow seaward. From here to Cabo San Lucas you will sail far out to sea, to avoid the hidden reefs of this arid shore. And then, 2,000 miles south of San Diego you will reach Acapulco with your treasure ship.

■ FIRST IMMIGRANTS

The shape of the land has determined the human history of the coast. Access was easiest from the valleys and forests of the Pacific Northwest, and by 9,000 years ago settlers had edged down into California. From every other direction access was difficult. Deserts and the Sierra Nevada defined its eastern and southern boundaries. Its western coast, in many places rocky and rough, faced 1,200 miles of ocean.

The individual tribes and tribelets who reached California began to settle into a stable way of life sometime between 7,000 and 5,000 years ago, enjoying a staple diet of wild grains, flower seeds, acorns, small and large game, fish, and shellfish.

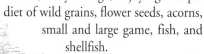

While most of the coastal tribes collected shellfish from tidal rocks, only a few native people developed seaworthy boats. The Tolowa and Yurok in the far northwest used their sturdy redwood dugouts to visit the offshore sea stacks; the Chumash of the Central Coast

Indians surf fishing off coast of Mendocino. (Harper's Monthly, 1861)

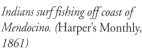

*In 1806, these California Indians were drawn by Wilhelm von Tilenau, a German artist with
a Russian exploring expedition.(Bancroft Library, University of California at Berkeley)*

also built large canoes (a technology they shared with the neighboring Gabrielinos) in which they paddled across the Santa Barbara Channel to the Channel Islands, where a large part of the tribe lived.

It was a peaceful life, with little or no warfare. Battles might be fought, but the
action consisted mostly of shouting and threatening gestures with hunting
weapons.

According to anthropologist Alfred Kroeber, the Indians of the Northern California coast were not pressed for food. He noted that there were almost no references, either in myth or tradition, to famines.

■ SPANISH GALLEONS AND BRITISH BUCCANEERS

Navigator Juan Rodriguez Cabrillo was the first European explorer to touch the
California shore. In September of 1542, he sailed into San Diego Bay (which he
named "San Miguel") and took possession for Spain, hoping that on this voyage
north he'd find gold. He found none, but was the first to report on the seafaring

In this DeBry etching Indians welcome Sir Francis Drake to California in 1579.
(Bancroft Library, University of California at Berkeley)

Chumash of the Santa Barbara Channel. He did not return from this voyage, dying of an injury he received while disembarking on the rocky shore of one of the Channel Islands on January 3, 1543. Cabrillo's crew continued exploring the coast after their captain's demise, but with little success. Because they found no gold, their reports were filed away and forgotten.

The pride of the Spanish colonial fleet were the great Manila galleons which sailed between the port of Acapulco, in Mexico, and Manila, in the Philippines. Once a year, large well-armed galleons, loaded with silver, wafted west from Acapulco by favorable trade winds. In Manila, the silver was traded for silks, porcelain, pearls, rubies, sapphires, and assorted knickknacks, as well as nutmeg, cinnamon, and other spices at reasonable prices. Which means the goods could be transshipped in Acapulco, sent across the Atlantic, and sold in Europe at fabulous profits.

Galleon captains soon discovered that the quickest way back from the Philippines

SAFE HARBOR ALONG THE COAST

In 1603, Sebastian Vizcaino, under commission of the Viceroy of Mexico, set out to map and explore the California coast, with three ships and 200 men. Although navigator Juan Cabrillo had first described Monterey some 60-odd years before, Vizcaino was the first to map the area and describe it carefully.

*A*mong the ports of greater consideration which I discovered was one in thirty -seven degrees of latitude which I called Monterey. . . . It is all that can be desired for commodiousness and as a station for ships making the voyage to the Philippines. . . . This port is sheltered from all winds, while on the immediate coast there are pines from which masts of any desired size can be obtained, as well as live oaks and white oaks, rosemary, the vine, the rose of Alexandria, a great variety of game, such as rabbits, hares, partridges, and other sorts of species found in Spain . . .

This land has a genial climate, its waters are good, and it is very fertile—judging from the varied and luxuriant growth of trees and plants; . . .

—Sebastian Vizcaino, Publication of the
Historical Society of Southern California, from ship's logs of 1603

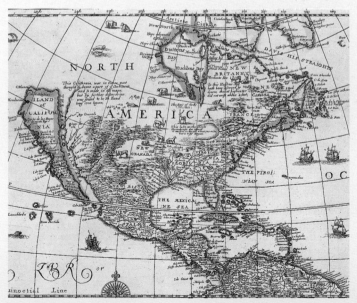

Based on information pieced together from navigators and merchants, European cartographers began to illustrate California as an island beginning in 1620. This theory persisted for a century before further exploration corrected the error.

to Mexico was along a northern route, which brought the ships to the coast of California, at about the latitude of Cape Mendocino. Here the galleons picked up the California current and sailed south on the prevailing northerly winds. The Spanish tried to keep their lucrative trade route secret, but the news was quickly learned by British buccaneers who intercepted the galleons off the California and Mexican coasts. None other than Sir Francis Drake, English man-about-town and buccaneer, was the first to challenge the Spanish supremacy in what was then known as the South Seas.

In 1577, Drake sacked and pillaged unprotected Spanish settlements all along the west coast of the Americas. Off Lima, Peru, he captured the treasure ship *Cacafuego,* his richest prize. He sailed as far north as 48 degrees, but after failing to find the elusive Northwest Passage (which would haunt sailors for another 200 years), he sailed south. Because his ship the *Golden Hind* needed major repairs, he hauled her out in a protected bay on the Northern California coast, of which he took possession for Queen Elizabeth and called New Albion (New England), bestowing that name decades before the Pilgrims appropriated the appellation.

Drake's descriptions of the bay where he landed are vague, though they make it quite clear that the natives of the region were central California Indians, most likely Coast Miwok, and not tribes to the north or south.

"We came here to serve God, and also to get rich."
—Bernard Diaz del Castillo, 1576.

■ SPANISH MISSIONS; RELUCTANT INDIANS

By the 1770s the Viceroy of Mexico, under the direction of the Spanish crown, had embarked on a three-pronged approach to colonize California: missions, military presidios, and pueblos along the coast. The first mission and presidio were established in San Diego in 1769, followed by a missions and presidio at Monterey in 1770. In roughly 50

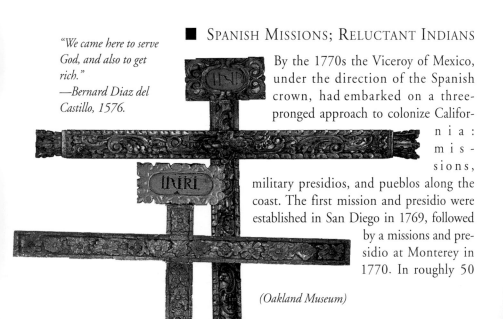

(Oakland Museum)

Mission San Gabriel *in San Gabriel, east of Los Angeles, was painted by Ferdinand Deppe in 1832. (Santa Barbara Mission Archive Library)*

years, Franciscans built a total of 21 missions, planted grapes for sacramental wine, and introduced olives, corn, and other useful plants. Adventurers and idealists, they believed they were bringing salvation to the heathen, but in the end they converted few and unwittingly, by carrying contagious diseases, they contributed to the destruction of the people they meant to help.

Mexico gained its independence from Spain in 1821, and in 1833, the missions were secularized. When the Americans took over in 1848, they returned many of the churches and cloisters to the Catholic Church.

■ RANCHO ERA

After a number of missions, pueblos, and presidios (military forts) had been established, settlers began to make the arduous journey north from Mexico and to spread over coastal hills and plains. The vast grasslands of coastal California (just in from the sea) proved ideal for raising livestock—a Mexican gentleman's preferred way of making a living. Land for the ranchos was obtained by government grant. By the time Americans occupied California, some 8,987,000 acres had been granted. California had become a land of vast cattle ranches (some of them several hundred square miles in area). The cattle needed no feeding and no care, and they were rounded up only for the annual branding of the new calves and for the periodic *matanzas,* or slaughters.

The ranchos had *vaqueros* skilled with rawhide *reatas,* who could not only subdue the semi-wild cattle with ease, but would "just for sport" lasso wild grizzly bears and drag them to town. There were even tales that more than one love-struck swain, distressed that a rival in love was serenading the woman of his heart, caught a grizzly and released it next to the guitar-strumming rival, to chase him off. Such a ploy might have worked or not, for the *caballeros* were known to charge the bears with their swords as the only weapons.

California's Rancho Period was idyllic for the Spanish, despite frontier living conditions and few cultural diversions. There were fiestas, dances, weddings, and lengthy visits to friends. These were peaceful times, when travelers could ride the length of El Camino Real, from San Diego north to San Francisco, without having to fear for their safety. Nor did voyagers have to worry about food or lodging, for ranchos and missions alike welcomed all visitors, entertained them free of charge, and even gave them provisions and a fresh horse to continue their journey.

Mexican Cattle Drivers in Southern California by William Hahn, 1883.
(Collection of Dr. and Mrs. Edward H. Boseker)

■ Yankee Traders and American Settlers

While the Spanish controlled California, settlers could only trade with the mother country and its colonies. Russians established an outpost at Fort Ross (west of Healdsburg) beyond the reach of the Spanish, but they were not allowed to barter for goods in San Francisco Bay. When Count Nicolai Rezanov sailed through the Golden Gate in 1806 hoping to buy food for the starving Russian settlement at Sitka, he was politely refused by the presidio's comandante. However, in the course of many hospitable dinners at the presidio, Rezanov and the comandante's daughter fell in love, and while the marriage was deferred, Rezanov did in the end manage to buy the food he needed.

Trade with Americans was carried out through smuggling, by surreptitiously landing goods on the Channel Islands or in hidden coves.

After Mexico gained its independence from Spain, trade was permitted, and Yankee traders, skilled at navigating the turbulent North Pacific in their solidly built, fast ships began to call on the coast at regular intervals.

Bostonian Richard Henry Dana, who shipped out as a common seaman in 1835, wrote in his *Two Years Before the Mast* that his ship supplied:

> . . . spirits of all kinds (sold by the cask), teas, coffee, sugars, spices, raisins, molasses, hardware, crockeryware, tinware, cutlery, clothing of all kinds, boots and shoes from Lynn, calicoes and cottons from Lowell, crapes, silks; also shawls, scarfs, necklaces, jewelry and combs for the ladies; furniture; and in fact everything that can be imagined, from Chinese fireworks to English cartwheels—of which we had a dozen pairs with their iron rims on.
>
> Things sell on an average at an advance of nearly three hundred percent upon the Boston prices.

The Californios had little money to pay for these goods—what silver they had went into decorating their elaborate saddles and horse trappings—but they had plenty of cowhides, which the Yankees were willing to take in trade. Soon these hides became known as California bank notes.

The loading of the hides onto the ships was done by the sailors because, strange for a people living on the coast, the Californios had no boats, not even at Monterey, the capital and official port of entry. William H. Thomes, who visited the coast in 1843 as a ship's boy, reported, "wonderful as it may seem, the port officers of Monterey did not own a boat for the purpose of boarding vessels that traded with the people." Nor were there piers: all the trade goods as well as the hides, had to be taken through the surf by ship's boat. This could be wet work, especially in places where the surf was heavy. "The beach at Santa Cruz did not appear inviting, as we surveyed it from aloft. The surf was breaking heavily, and it looked as though some of us would get ducked the next morning, when we landed, and our predictions were true . . . ."

Americans played a prominent role in Mexican California as settlers, rancheros, and even as politicians. Most converted to Catholicism (leaving their conscience at Cape Horn as a popular saying had it), married the daughters of prominent Californios, and obtained land grants from the government. In 1835, the United States tried to buy California from Mexico but bungled the deal. On October 19, 1842, Commodore Thomas ap Catesby Jones of the U.S. Navy captured Monterey, believing the U.S. and Mexico were at war. When he learned otherwise, he lowered the American flag, apologized, and sailed south to San Pedro, where he was entertained by the local rancheros.

Four years later, on June 14, 1846, several American settlers proclaimed California's independence, captured the "fortress" of Sonoma, and took military commander Mariano Vallejo captive. This time, as it turned out, the U.S. and Mexico were actually at war. On July 7, Commander John D. Sloat raised the American flag at the Monterey customs house and formally declared California a possession of the United States. The Californios were not that willing to concede, but several months—and skirmishes—later, on January 13, 1847, the Californios capitulated at Rancho Cahuenga in Southern California. Mexico formally ceded California on February 2, 1848, in the Treaty of Guadalupe Hidalgo. On September 9, 1850, President Fillmore signed an act of Congress admitting California as a state into the Union.

■ GOLD, VINEYARDS, AND RAILROADS

Until the Americans acquired California, much of its history happened near the coast, where most of the settlements were. But after gold was found at Sutter's Mill in the Sierra Nevada foothills on January 24, 1848 (nine days before Mexico officially ceded California), the action shifted inland. By 1849, hundreds of sailing ships were bringing prospectors from all over the world up the coast, and the town of San Francisco roared to life as the state's first important city. So many sailors

The barque Star of Shetland *was one of many ships to sail into the booming port of San Francisco. (Photo by Gabriel Moulin, courtesy of the S. F. Maritime Nat'l Historic Museum)*

jumped ship in San Francisco between 1849 and the 1880s that ships' captains routinely sent out thugs to "shanghai" young men and force them to travel the China trade.

After the Gold Rush, California's political and economic focus shifted back to the coast (and has remained within 75 miles of saltwater ever since). As veins of ore gave out, many of the miners turned to other pursuits: they established farms and orchards in coastal valleys, logged the redwood forests, and built boats to exploit the bounty of the sea. Vineyards and orange groves began to replace cattle pastures. William H. Thomes, visiting the coast from 1843 to 1845, talked about eating ripe grapes straight from the vine, and commented in 1884, that California raised "enough grapes to manufacture a sufficient supply of wine and brandy to supply the whole of the United States, and part of Europe."

Northern California's population swelled after railroads connected it with the

East Coast in 1869, but Southern California remained largely a backwater until a direct rail connection was established in 1885. By the 1930s, as farmers from the dust bowl came to pick California fruit, the state's population topped five million.

■ MODERN TIMES

During World War II, California not only became one of the major staging areas for the war in the Pacific, but war-related industries infused the state's largely agricultural economy with manufacturing. Soldiers who had gone through basic training at Ford Ord, Camp Pendleton, Fort Roberts, or other military bases near the coast, or who had been stationed at the naval bases on San Francisco Bay, in Long Beach, or in San Diego, liked what they saw and stayed on after the war. The Cold War spawned both massive defense as well as aerospace production, attracting ever more workers to the Golden State and its magnificent coast. Coastal towns soon had world-class hotels and restaurants, theaters, opera houses, and museums. It is also significant that the state's early universities were established near the coast (and that today, most campuses of the far-flung state system are within easy driving distance of beaches and surf).

Nor are the modern centers of California far inland. Hollywood and its foster child, Culver City, are an easy drive from the beaches—where Hollywood has shot many of its movies and TV serials; Silicon Valley is but a clam toss from southern San Francisco Bay. On the coast, 20th-century pleasures have been unabashedly sybaritic—an outlook on life enhanced by real estate advertisements, the songs of the Beach Boys, a score of surfer movies, and newspaper and magazine gossip columns commenting on the life of the movie stars living near (or even on) the beaches.

A dynamic economy and a mild climate were the engine behind California's population growth. By the end of World War II, San Francisco's population numbered 750,000; L.A.'s more than two million. By 1950 there were 10.5 million people living in California; 35 million at the end of the 20th century.

As California's population continued to grow by leaps and bounds, real estate developers tried their best to get their hands on all of the coast—even some of the parks protecting the most scenic spots. In the 1970s, an ally, then-governor Ronald Reagan, even talked of turning as idyllic a spot as Leo Carrillo State Park into a coastal Disneyland. In the meantime, housing developments began to appear on once pristine bluffs and the lagoons so essential to migratory birds on the Pacific Flyway were being drained and filled. Actions like this (and fear of runaway development) led to a counter-revolution among environmentally minded Californians, who realized that their greatest treasure, the natural beauty of their coast, was rapidly disappearing under concrete and subdivisions. In November of 1972, California voters passed Proposition 20, the Coastal Initiative, which protected much of the coastline that was as yet undeveloped.

The coast is a beautiful, if unstable place, where beaches and cliffs fall victim to the ever-gnawing surf, while tectonic forces raise old sea bottom to the height of marine terraces. The works of man, too, have shown a tendency of being very temporary—some 19th-century logging ports and towns, for example, have already reverted to nature, making a landscape once well populated again seem half-empty. Let's hope that, no matter how much the physical appearance of the coast fluctuates, that the snowy plover, willets, pelicans, gulls, ospreys, egrets, sea otters, elephant seals, sea lions, and whales will be able to survive, and that we will continue to have an opportunity to enjoy the mysterious power and beauty of marine animals and birds, marshes and lagoons, and wild, surf-washed beaches.

One of the great engineering feats of its time, the Golden Gate Bridge
was built between 1933 and 1937. (From Square Books, hand colored by Ann Rhoney)

SAN FRANCISCO BAY

■ HIGHLIGHTS

Ferry Trips on the Bay
Alcatraz
Angel Island
Telegraph Hill
North Beach
Embarcadero
Golden Gate Bridge
Sausalito
Carneros Wine Region

■ TRAVEL OVERVIEW

San Francisco Bay is set inland from the Pacific Coast, stretching north and south some 50 miles and embracing a region of over six million people. The city of San Francisco sits at the head of a peninsula, the surging Pacific Ocean marking its western boundaries. Across from San Francisco's northern shore (where most of its historic areas are located) are some of the most interesting places to visit in the Bay Area: Alcatraz and Angel Islands, Sausalito, and the southern Sonoma and Napa wine region, the Carneros.

Urban pleasures are to be enjoyed here: San Francisco's hillside neighborhoods and fine architecture, its majestic bridges, good food, and leisurely walks. But along the shores of the bay itself are rural islands, historic parks, and to the north, excellent wineries.

■ TRAVEL BASICS

Getting Around

The bay can be seen by ferry; its shores walked on several coastal trails; its towns or sights visited by car.

Climate

The shores of San Francisco Bay enjoy a Mediterranean climate with a pronounced wet season (November to March) and dry season (May to October). June is apt to be sunny but in July and August a cool fog usually hugs the immediate coast and often drifts through the Golden Gate into the bay at night, only to recede again in the late morning. Temperatures can vary wildly as a result. While it averages 60 degrees coastside during the summer, the temperatures in Vallejo or San Rafael may well be in the 90s. August days at Ocean Beach are foggy 66 percent of the time; at Civic Center in San Francisco, 44 percent of the time.

September and October are the warmest months of the year coastside, when offshore winds push the fog seaward and temperatures often rise into the 70s and 80s under crystal clear skies. This is when the Bay Area is at its best. Winter brings relatively mild temperatures, 40s to 60s, with rainy spells lasting two to three days. **Water Temperature:** San Francisco Bay's water temperature is too cold for all but the hardiest swimmers, averaging between 50 to 60 degrees year-round. San Francisco's oceanside beaches are even colder than those in the Bay, and are known for riptides and big winter surf. Although some very sturdy swimmers swim every day at Aquatic Park, we can't recommend it.

Food and Lodging

Ever since Alice Waters of Berkeley's Chez Panisse restaurant declared that fresh was it—and created a culinary movement known as "California Cuisine"—the Bay Area has been at the center of excellence and creativity in the creation and presentation of food. Local purveyors have a knack for importing the best from abroad. Ethnic markets and restaurants add variety and spice to local menus. San Francisco, Marin County, and Berkeley have some of the best, as well as the most famous restaurants in the country.

Lodging ranges from the plain but serviceable to the utterly luxurious; rates run the gamut from affordable to exorbitant. (**Lodging and restaurants listings** can be found on pages 339-390.)

■ FOG AND FERRY BOATS ON THE BAY

The sky is gray and San Francisco Bay is a bit choppy, with light-gray crests, as we pull away from the ferry dock at Fisherman's Wharf. A sea lion raises its head from the water and stares at the bow of our boat, and executes a smooth dive as we close in on him. A dozen sea gulls and two brown pelicans follow in our wake, mistaking us for a party boat.

All of San Francisco Bay's landmarks are clearly visible in the crisp morning air—the Golden Gate Bridge to the west, its paint coat of international orange looking a bit dull this morning. Mount Tamalpais rises to the northwest, high above the Marin Headlands, and the windows of Sausalito beneath it flash like signal mirrors in the early sun. The rock of Alcatraz and bucolic Angel Island lie straight ahead; and to the east, the Bay Bridge glimmers silver above Yerba Buena Island.

As I walked to the pier this morning, the air carried the aromas sent into the morning breeze by crabs boiling in huge outdoor cauldrons, the heart-warming smell of garlic, slowly sautéing in olive oil, the tang of barbecued pork, soy squid, and glazed duck at a Chinese take-out place, the bite of fresh chiles wafting across the street from a neighborhood taqueria, the nose-tingling lure of freshly baked sourdough bread.

This special San Francisco air has been proposed as one of the reasons why San Franciscans are so fond of good food and wine—the air allows them to appreciate their aromas to the fullest. The marine tang increases and the land aromas fade as we run out into the bay, and the boat heels slightly as it feels the impact of the flood current rushing through the Golden Gate.

The Golden Gate marks the dividing line between the two worlds of San Francisco, the world of the Pacific Ocean and the world of the bay, between the chill, windswept oceanside of the peninsula over whose very tip the city spreads, and the calmer and warmer bayshores where most of the city's business, dining, and entertaining takes place.

The bay provides a focal point for the city, much in the same way the Seine does for Paris and the Thames does for London. Yet, in all truth, it's more splendid than either of these famed waterways. Its primal beauty draws me whenever I return to San Francisco. It orients me (as also do the hills) and it ever serves as a resting place for my eye, reducing the tall office buildings and awesome bridges to a proper perspective. When I look around me—at the rows of houses climbing the steep sides of the bayside hills, and at the old business edifices which survived the 1906 earthquake—I'm reminded that this cosmopolitan city did not grow up along the windy shores of the Pacific, but along the inland shores of a sheltered bay, 50 miles long and several miles wide, rimmed by grassy and wooded hills. It is no gray, chill city by the sea but, as newspaper columnist Herb Caen once observed, a many-splendored Baghdad-by-the-Bay. As you stand atop one of the city's hills and look out over the bay and the cities lining its shore, it can be hard to believe that the Bay Area is indeed populated by more than six million people.

On a sunny morning, with the waters of the bay sparkling in the silver light, I board a ferry at the Larkspur Landing in Marin County for a scenic trip to San Francisco. Now, the famous San Francisco fog is creeping in through the Golden Gate. It coils and swirls like a dragon (or if you're in a more prosaic mood, like

INCIDENT ON THE BAY

The hero of the Jack London novel from which this quote is taken, a smug intellectual, is crossing from San Francisco to Sausalito on a ferry doomed to collide in the fog with another ferry. Here are some of his observations just before the crash:

I fell to dwelling upon the romance of the fog. And romantic it certainly was—the fog, like the gray shadow of infinite mystery, brooding over the whirling speck of earth; and men, mere motes of light and sparkle, cursed with an insane relish for work, riding their steeds of wood and steel through the heart of the mystery, groping their way blindly through the Unseen, and clamoring and clanging in confident speech while their hearts are heavy with incertitude and fear.

Then everything happened, and with inconceivable rapidity. The fog seemed to break away as though split by a wedge. . . . I could see the pilot-house and a white-bearded man leaning partly out of it, on his elbows. . . . As he leaned there, he ran a calm and speculative eye over us, as though to determine the precise point of the collision, and took no notice whatever, when our pilot, white with rage, shouted, "Now you've done it!"

—Jack London, *The Sea-Wolf,* 1904

(following pages) The city's famous fog encircles the San Francisco skyline.

whipped cream squirted from a can), and covers the bay and the low-lying parts of the city in no time at all. I'm beginning to understand how Noah must have felt in his Ark.

With the shores veiled in mist—but the islands and hills still rising above the fog—it is almost possible to imagine how this bay must have looked in August of 1775 when the first Spanish mariner to sail through its narrow entrance, Juan Manuel de Ayala, anchored his ship in the Angel Island cove that now bears his name. Around him the bayshore was lined with small villages, some of them rising on top of huge shell mounds—which were as large as 600 feet long and 30 feet high. Ohlone Indians lived to the east and south; Coast Miwok to the north. The gentle climate made for easy living; the waters of the bay provided abalones, oysters, mussels, and fish, the marshes teemed with ducks and geese.

The Golden Gate (Looking In) *by Raymond Dabb Yelland, 1880.*
(Courtesy of the Garzoli Gallery, San Rafael)

But back to reality . . . . My ferry is approaching Pier 41, and though the fog has entered the bay itself, it hesitates at Angel Island. As the boat docks, I watch the city and its hills come into focus again. Perhaps no neighborhood is more emblematic of its early days than Telegraph Hill, with its wooden, pastel houses, its intimate gardens, its steep slopes and sheer rock faces, and at the top, the white column of Coit Tower.

In 1849, the bay lapped the edges of Telegraph Hill, and ships moored right below it. I can't help but wonder what it must have been like to arrive here aboard the first truly "gold rush" ship—the mail boat *California*—which left New York harbor in October of 1848 with seven passengers. Rounding Cape Horn, the ship picked up another 150 passengers off Peru. By the time it reached Panama, news of the California gold strike had been announced by President Polk. Heavily

armed Americans demanded to be taken aboard, and 350 passengers soon jammed the decks. When the *California* docked below Telegraph Hill, the crew and everyone else aboard headed for the hills.

In fact, the hill gets its name from the fact that, in the early days, a semaphore signaling station stood here, which alerted the citizens of Gold Rush San Francisco to the arrival of ships entering the Golden Gate.

In early 1848, 800 people lived in San Francisco; a few months after gold was discovered the population had grown to 25,000 people. During the next 10 to 20 years the dusty adobe village on the bayshore grew into a vital, youthful city, where men outnumbered women two to one. Some of the houses sitting up on that hill date from those years; and it's even possible that some were built with gold dust taken from those dry Sierra foothills some hundred miles to the east.

■ TELEGRAPH HILL

Rising steeply above the bay and the Embarcadero, Telegraph Hill rewards visitors with some of the most marvelous views anywhere in the Bay Area. At the top of 284-foot hill, the bay spreads out before you like a life-size topographical map, and you realize that San Francisco sits indeed at the very tip of the peninsula which separates its bay from the Pacific Ocean.

You can get a more panoramic view—360 degrees—from the top of 180-foot-tall Coit Tower, supposedly made to look like the nozzle of a firehose and built with money donated by socialite Lily Hitchcock Coit, who adored fire engines and firemen. (Be sure to stop and look at the WPA murals inside the 1933 tower.)

❖

There are many ways to reach the top of the hill. From North Beach, you can drive up Lombard, but parking is scarce and traffic moves at a snail's pace. Far better is to walk, either from the west on Greenwich or Filbert, or up the steep steps from Sansome Street, on the east.

*From its perch on Telegraph Hill, Coit Tower overlooks
"The Rock"—Alcatraz. (Photo by Kerrick James)*

Patrons relax in the sun at the Cannery in Fisherman's Wharf. The cafes of North Beach are short walk from here. (Photo by Kerrick James)

Whenever I meander up Telegraph Hill, I first fortify myself with a cappuccino-to-go at one of the small cafes in North Beach, or a few squares of focaccia from Liguria Bakery on Stockton. Then I stroll up the steep blocks slowly, enjoying the unique, old houses and apartment buildings, and the views across the city that come up unexpectedly at every turn.

The last time I took in the view from Coit Tower was one of those beautiful, clear mornings, when the cerulean sky above San Francisco Bay was streaked with fair-weather cirrus clouds, and house finches were singing in the shrubbery of tiny city backyards. The ascending sun had tinted everything with a sheen of gold—the clouds and the sea gulls preening on lamp posts.

To the west, the towers of the Golden Gate Bridge glowed like huge orange candles, and every nook and cranny of the Marin Headlands to the north of the bridge was highlighted in the angled light. The rising sun brightened the massive shoulders of Mount Tamalpais, lit up the windows of Sausalito, and poured liquid platinum over the choppy waters of the bay where Angel Island, Alcatraz, and Point Richmond rose from the water. To the east beyond Treasure and Yerba Buena Islands and the Bay Bridge, the white, chateau-like buildings of the Claremont Resort were visible in the green hills of the East Bay.

That day, after soaking up an invigorating dose of the view, I followed the Greenwich Street stairs leading down the eastern cliff of Telegraph Hill to the Embarcadero. The shape of this rocky escarpment is not natural, but was created by a quarry which once operated right smack in the center of the city. Too much noise, dust, and the damage done by rock blasting finally got the city to close it down. Today, this side of the hill has some beautiful cliff-hanger homes. Because this face of Telegraph Hill is so steep, Greenwich Street and nearby Filbert Street are served by stairs. Enjoy the views of the waterfront as you walk down and take a look at the beautiful flower gardens to the right and left of the stairs. The flats below Telegraph Hill are occupied by old warehouses and factories now converted into offices, blocks of flats, and the Embarcadero (see page 46).

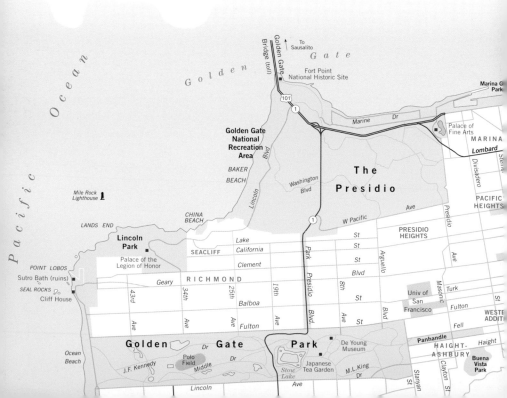

If you walk to the top on a chilly day, you may want to head down the hill on the west side and wander into the warm embrace of the North Beach neighborhood—the *Rive Gauche* of San Francisco.

■ NORTH BEACH

The valley nestled between Telegraph Hill and Russian Hill is known as North Beach, but don't look for a beach. There is none. The cove and beach were filled in back in the 1870s. Once a thriving Italian immigrant neighborhood, it still has some of its old flavor, although it is no longer, alas, saturated with the heady aromas of fermenting *must* that each fall wafted from the Italian homes. This scent was lovingly described by Margaret Parton in *Laughter on the Hill*:

*I*t was autumn now in San Francisco, and wine-making time on the hill. As I walked down Union Street toward the streetcar I could smell the

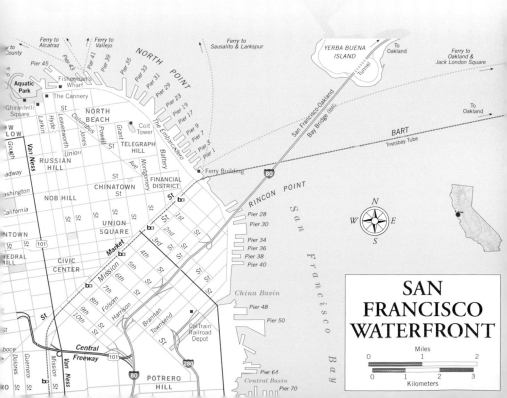

SAN
FRANCISCO
WATERFRONT

purple grapes hanging rich and heavy in the hidden arbors behind the bare white fronts of the Italian flats. Great wooden barrels, scoured for the wine to come, began to appear in front of every doorstep, and one day there was the stained old wine press starting its yearly journey from the houses at the top of the Hill down to the late harvesters at the bottom. Each day as I passed, it would be moved a little further down, its heady smell mingling with the warm air from the basement bakeries, the odors of Provolone, salami, and black olives from the dim Italian groceries, the acrid reek of the dark, male-frequented alleys, the salt wind from the Pacific.

Back in my college days, when friends and I visited the city, we would always make our first stop at poet Lawrence Ferlinghetti's **City Lights Bookstore**. Located near the intersection of Broadway and Columbus (and set at the southwest corner of North Beach), City Lights remains an important part of San Francisco today. As the nation's first paperback bookstore, City Lights always has a good selection of virtually unknown authors and books from small presses (and is still the best place for stocking up on the works of Jack Kerouac and other Beat authors).

I still come here, then head across Columbus and up Grant a few blocks to stop at one of the neighborhood's many Italian bakeries for freshly baked bread. I'll stop at **Washington Square** to enjoy the life of the neighborhood—a big Italian wedding party emerging from Saint Peter and Paul's Church; or the huge groups of middle-aged Chinese practicing T'ai chi in the morning. Artists set up their paintings for sale, locals come out of their apartments to sit on the grass and read their newspapers.

Nearby is **Club Fugazi**, where *Beach Blanket Babylon,* one of the funniest revue shows anywhere, has been playing to sell-out audiences for longer than anyone remembers. At Washington and Mason, you'll find the **cable car barn** where spinning wheels and whirring cables provide the power to drive all of the city's remaining cable cars. For some reason the place has always reminded me of a huge candy factory.

One of my favorite haunts is **Vesuvio Cafe** at 255 Columbus (across the alley from the City Lights Bookstore), one of the classic old bars—and one of poet Dylan Thomas' favorite places in the City. Jack Kerouac got drunk here back in 1960, when he was supposed to be on his way south to meet Henry Miller at Big Sur. He couldn't tear himself away and never got to meet Miller.

Vesuvio is unique. Even though most of the beat poets are gone, interesting characters still drop in. Perhaps they're lured by the sign that proclaims, "Don't Envy Beatniks . . . Be One!" There's always a big and happy crowd here as well as at Tosca and Specs, both across the street. I remember one night when a patron brought a pet rabbit into Vesuvio, which became the most petted rabbit in the city before the night was old. Just goes to show what a friendly place Vesuvio is. (More recently, a man carrying a knapsack with several rabbits was seen at Specs, and apparently is often to be found hanging out at one of the local bars!)

The **Tosca Cafe**, next door to Specs on Columbus, is another old-time hangout, where Bob Dylan was once evicted, along with Allen Ginsberg and Lawrence Ferlinghetti, because a friend they had brought misbehaved. The place is still a hangout for writers and musicians, most of them making a lot more money in a year than most beat poets made in a lifetime.

There's an embarrassment of riches here—so many good and interesting small restaurants, you'll probably want to eat at all of them—Caffe Puccini, Cafe Michelangelo, Caffe Stella, Cafe Greco, Cafe Roma, Rose Pistola.

If you're in need of picnic food, stop by **R. Iacopi & Co. Meats**, 1460 Grant at Union, which has traditionally cured pancetta and prosciutto; **Molinari's** on Columbus, famous for its cheeses and sausages; the **Liguria Bakery** at 1700 Stockton for focaccia. **The Italian French Baking Co. of San Francisco** at 1501 Grant also has a great selection of baked goods. If you're thinking of getting some wine to go with it, try an Italian Chianti Classico, or perhaps a California sangiovese or barbera. Molinari's sells wine and North Beach Liquor (Columbus and Union) has a pretty good selection.

■ AMBLING THROUGH CHINATOWN

South of City Lights Bookstore and along Broadway and Grant begins one of San Francisco's most historic—and lively—neighborhoods, Chinatown, which is now expanding into North Beach.

The last time I came to San Francisco, I approached it, not from North Beach, but from Nob Hill, leaving a friend's apartment at the break of dawn and strolling down California Street toward the bay as the gray towers of the Bay Bridge emerged from the gloom. Turning north on Grant, I wandered into Chinatown, just as it was coming alive. Big men unloaded double-parked refrigerator trucks that restock the Chinatown larder: crates of exotic fruits, herbs, and vegetables, fish so fresh they wiggled on the ice, whole hog carcasses, and loads of fresh flowers. Vans brought cages of chickens and chukar partridges, and bins filled with huge green frogs and fresh-water turtles. Merchants were just starting to set up crates of produce outside their shop, while cooks began to prepare the savory take-out dishes which would be displayed in the shop windows, and started up the bar-becue ovens. Soon the delectable tang of barbecued pork, soy squid, and glazed duck wafted down Stockton and Grant, intermingling with the fragrances of flowers and exotic spices.

As the sun rose, I headed east again along Kearny Street, and my pace quick-ened—out of necessity really—as I entered the Financial District, where on this workday thousands of people were rushing energetically to work. But I had my eye on the Ferry Building and the newly spruced up Embarcadero.

■ EMBARCADERO

Earthquakes now and then do something good. The last one so destabilized the Embarcadero Freeway (which cut off downtown from the bay shore) that it was demolished and the waterfront is once again integrated into the city. A new wide sidewalk runs along the bay, backed by sycamores and palm trees (which may seem a bit odd to dyed-in-the-wool San Franciscans, but they look nice, and remind the locals that, yes, indeed, they're part of California, despite the frequent fog). The re-moval of the freeway has brought renewal to the strip between Telegraph Hill and the water. There's a great deal of new, architecturally interesting housing here and those who live in it jog and walk along the waterfront, past the old Ferry Building and past the tugboats moored near the Bay Bridge. On Saturdays residents walk down from Telegraph Hill or out of the Embarcadero apartments to shop or eat at the farmers market by the Ferry Building—one of the best big-city farmers mar-kets on the West Coast. Not only is the produce extraordinary: huge strawberries, thin-stemmed asparagus, etc., but several excellent local restaurants sell food here at booths, and set out tables, chairs, and awnings. The view, while you're sitting there sipping your cappuccino, is of the Bay Bridge, the Tuscan-style Ferry Build-ing, and the tall office towers of the Financial District; plus, of course, Telegraph Hill.

The busy Embarcadero of San Francisco in 1894.
(Photo by O. V. Lange, courtesy of San Francisco Maritime National Historic Park)

The venerable **Ferry Building** (next to Pier 1), which survived the big 1906 earthquake, was used only as an office building for many years after the bridges replaced the cross-bay ferries. But in recent years commuter demand has brought passenger ferries back to the bay, and the Ferry Building's tall tower once again watches the multitudes clamber onto outgoing ferries and rush off the incoming boats. You can choose from several ferry trips across the bay.

The ferry to **Jack London Square** across the bay in Oakland takes 20 minutes and passes Yerba Buena Island, which author Henry Richard Dana visited in 1836, and its adjacent landfill, Treasure Island, before you pass between the silver towers of the Bay Bridge. After steering up the Oakland estuary, the ferry docks right between a massive bookstore and a waterfront hotel. The square, where Jack London once toted cargo, is now a motley collection of shops and restaurants. *For ferry information call 415-705-5555.*

The ferry to **Larkspur Landing** is used by Marin County commuters who work in San Francisco's financial district. This is an enjoyable way to see the bay and the area is less crowded than Pier 39 near Fisherman's Wharf. *For ferry information and reservations call 415-923-2000.*

■ FISHERMAN'S WHARF

During the day, Fisherman's Wharf is a touristy place. Locals denigrate it, but kids love it. Pier 39, adjacent to the big ferry landing, is an amusement park of sorts atop an old shipping dock. Sea lions squat on several yacht floats north of the pier. Here you'll find a wind-up-toy store, a store selling sea shells from all over the world, a great national parks book store (right where you look at the sea lions) and a store for left-handed people only. A baseball store sells trivia items for every

imaginable team. On nearby Jefferson Street is a Ripley's Believe It Or Not and a Guinness Museum of World Records.

To the west, seafood restaurants can be found both on and off the water, and with or without views of the bay or the fishing boats. (Few San Franciscans eat at Fisherman's Wharf.). You can buy a freshly cooked, ready-to-eat crab. While it won't be from San Francisco Bay—most "local" crabs are brought in from Eureka, the Pacific Northwest, and Alaska—it will still be very good. Prepare to pay about $10 per crab; one feeds about two people.

Crab vendor Tony Cresci is a fixture at Fisherman's Wharf. (Photo by Kerrick James)

Along the working part of Fisherman's Wharf, fishing boats still tie up. On a back pier, half-hidden by waterfront restaurants, is a small chapel honoring fishermen and catering to the spiritual needs of the rugged men and women who draw their sustenance from the turbulent waters off the Golden Gate.

You should visit the wharf at least once in the gray light of early morning, when it looks like a scene from a French *noir* movie. Brown pelicans have discovered not only that the tops of pilings make for perfect (and very secure) preening places, but that it's perfectly safe to hang out at the ends of the docks as well. Sometimes you can get surprisingly close to these big birds. And don't be startled when somebody barks at you from the water. Sea lions seem to be everywhere along the San Francisco waterfront.

The Cannery *(2801 Leavenworth)* was one of the country's first brick factories to be converted into a shopping mall. Like the former chocolate factory at nearby **Ghirardelli Square**, it's had its ups and downs, but there's usually something interesting to see, plus a few good shops and restaurants.

Parking at Fisherman's Wharf is unbelievably expensive—costing about $30 for five hours. Avoid the high cost by walking, by parking down the Embarcadero, riding a Muni bus or a cable car, or taking a ferry from Oakland or Marin. The majority of shops and restaurants of the Wharf stretch along the Embarcadero, including Pier 39 and the ferry dock on Pier 41, where boats depart for Sausalito, Alcatraz, and Angel Island. There are several sailings daily; *415-705-5555.*

■ ALCATRAZ ISLAND

You can see the former island fortress-prison, known to prisoners as "The Rock," which old-time San Francisco columnist Herb Caen once called San Francisco's "Chateau D'ifficult," from almost any point along San Francisco's northern shores and from the north-facing slopes of its hills. I love taking the short ferry ride from Fisherman's Wharf to Alcatraz, because I think of it less as a prison than as a former citadel. I can walk past the bomb-proof barracks (with 10-foot-thick walls) whose casemates still have the old embrasures and square gun ports designed for muzzle-loading cannons, up the old ramps below the high fortress walls from the 1850s, and through the well-defended 1857 fortress gate (which once had a moat and drawbridge, and still looks like something straight out of a European romance).

Besides Fort Point, Alcatraz is San Francisco Bay's other pre-Civil War fortress. Designed as a fortress to protect the entrance of the bay from enemy ships, the island had no human habitations before the first citadel was built here between 1853 and 1859, but was the abode of seals, sea lions, and pelicans (*alcatraz* means "pelican" in Spanish). The island's life as a citadel was short; the Rock became, in turn, a prison for locals who sympathized with the Confederacy during the Civil War, a military prison, and a notorious federal penitentiary, where such evildoers as Machine Gun Kelly, Al Capone, Alvin "Creepy" Carpis, and Robert Stroud, the Birdman of Alcatraz, were incarcerated in the large cell block on top of the island. Supposedly, men on Alcatraz could hear the voices of party-goers at the San Francisco yacht club on quiet evenings—which made their punishment even harder to bear. Alcatraz is now administered as part of the Golden Gate National Recreation Area. Rangers give tours and tell stories of famous prisoners who tried to escape into the cold water and wild currents of the bay.

But Alcatraz is also a strangely beautiful place, with green lawns, trees, and flowers (planted on soil shipped in from the mainland). If you visit, you will be rewarded with spectacular views of the city, the bay, the Golden Gate, and the Marin

The Alcatraz wall of infamy, from left to right: Machine Gun Kelly, Al Capone, Robert Stroud (the Birdman of Alcatraz), Meyer "Mickey" Cohen, Alvin "Creepy" Carpis, and Arthur "Doc" Barker. (Photo by Michael Yamashita)

THROUGH THE GOLDEN GATE

*A*t three o'clock in the afternoon, we saw right ahead of us Alcatraz Island, looking like a variegated marble, with the deposits of sea birds, and the air full of shrieking and quarreling gulls, while off on the rocks were a hundred or more old sea lions, whose roars, as they fought or struggled for good places, were enough to chill the blood of those who did not know that the animals were harmless, unless attacked and brought to the bay. Off our larboard bow was a beautiful island, wooded and green, even to the water's edge. This was Angel Island, in those days as lovely a spot as the eye needed or rest on. Off the starboard bow was the presidio, or fort, to guard the entrance of the Golden Gate, and containing two pieces, but, as neither was mounted on a carriage that was capable of sustaining a discharge, it was evident that they were intended more for ornament than use.

—William H. Thomes,
On Land and Sea, or California in the Years 1843, '44, '45

and Contra Costa shores. Look for seals, sea lions, and sea birds hauled out in the small sandy coves or on the rocks below. During my last visit, I even saw brown pelicans roosting on their eponymous island. A two-and-a-half-hour ferry ride/guided tour leaves daily from Pier 41 on Fisherman's Wharf; *415-705-5555.*

■ ANGEL ISLAND

This beautiful, rocky island rising straight from the blue waters of the bay wears a robe of classic California flora that gives off a rich aroma: a fragrant blend of dry summer grasses, bay trees, and pine. In spring, the island is verdantly green and covered with wildflowers. Wild white and purple iris bloom on the top of Mount Livermore. If you would like to have a picnic in the country while staying in San Francisco, walk to Fisherman's Wharf and take the ferry to this magic island.

On sunny weekends, hundreds of people disembark with their bikes and picnics at Ayala Cove. From the cove's green lawn and sandy beach you look across Tiburon Strait to the wooded island of Belvedere, to the peninsula of Tiburon, and the forested hills rising behind it.

Follow the signs and walk the road that circles the island for marvelous views.

In some coves the water is an almost tropical emerald green. As you turn east you'll pass a former immigration and quarantine station, the "Ellis Island of the West" from 1910 to 1940, that served as an entry point for Asian immigrants. Because they had to prove they were related to an American citizen and carried no communicable diseases, some had to wait here for weeks, even months, before they were allowed to enter the country. The walls of the old dormitory still carry poems scribbled by frustrated detainees. *Island*, by Him Mark Lai, Genny Lim, and Judy Yung gives a good account of this period. One of the interned wrote: "This place is called an island of immortals, when in fact, this mountain wilderness is a prison. Once you see the open net, why throw yourself in? It is only because of empty pockets I can do nothing else." (*Island*, poem # 23.)

❖

In spring, the island meadows are covered with wildflowers; and you may see black tailed deer and their spotted fawns. Look for oystercatchers and turnstones on the rocky shores, and for ospreys on branches or snags overhanging the water. By the

Angel Island rests off Tiburon Peninsula in San Francisco Bay.

time the day is done, you'll agree that Angel Island is a perfect place for spending a day away from the city without having to drive, for enjoying the views, the trees, and the flowers, and for musing on the beauties of nature.

Angel Island ferry leaves from Pier 41; 415-705-5555. You can avoid paying the horrendously high parking fees near the pier—about $30 for five hours—by walking to the wharf, or by driving north across the Golden Gate Bridge to Tiburon and taking the ferry from there.

■ HYDE STREET PIER AND AQUATIC PARK

Hyde Street Pier, just west of Fisherman's Wharf, serves as permanent moorage for a number of historic ships, all of which are open for visiting (although occasionally one or another is being restored). They include: the *Eureka,* a paddle-wheel ferry which made the last run to Sausalito; *C. A. Thayer,* a three-masted lumber schooner—one of two surviving schooners of the vast fleet that once rode the waters of the Northwest; and the *Balclutha,* a full-rigged ship that once sailed between San Francisco and Britain and later worked the Alaskan fishing trade.

Looking across the bay from Aquatic Park, with its sandy beach protected by a curved pier, you can conjure up much of the maritime history of the bay—Spanish navigator Juan Manuel de Ayala's ship coming to anchor in 1775, the steamers and clipper ships carrying passengers to San Francisco during the Gold Rush, the Italian fishermen in their sleek, Mediterranean-style lateen-rigged fishing boats, the lumber and sealing schooners, and the great ocean liners which once sailed from San Francisco to Hawaii and East Asia. **The San Francisco National Maritime Museum's** collection of ship models augments the historic ships you have visited at the Hyde Street Pier and gives you a sense of the bay's maritime history. Nearby is the Dolphin Club, whose members come to swim in the icy bay every morning and evening, and who kayak from here around the bay. The pier to the west was once the embarkation point for the federal prison on Alcatraz Island.

The **Golden Gate Promenade,** which you can walk all the way to Fort Point underneath the Golden Gate Bridge, begins here. It's very popular with joggers who love running along the bayshore with its beautiful views and bracing breezes.

■ FORT MASON AND MARINA GREEN

Fort Mason, a former Army bastion, now houses a number of cultural institutions. Drop by Green's restaurant, which serves vegetarian haute cuisine; try the restaurant or pick up food from the to-go counter. Walk out with a delicious chili or soup to sit on the benches by the pier and watch the bay.

Continue along the shore to the Marina Green, a bayfront greensward that has great views of the Golden Gate Bridge and of the yacht harbor. Early in the day women perform T'ai chi exercises; at other times of the day it's filled with kite-flyers, joggers, and dog walkers. On the city side, the Marina Green is faced by elegant, California-style houses.

The Wave Organ, on a tip of the harbor breakwater, is a sculpture that transmits the sound of bay waters.

The Palace of Fine Arts (a short detour down Baker Street, two blocks south of Marina Boulevard) was built for the Panama Pacific International Exposition of 1915 and designed by architect Bernard Maybeck. It's a faux palace with huge stucco pillars topped by female figures dressed in togas, who face away from all viewers. When the fair ended, San Franciscans could not part with this supposedly temporary structure. In 1962, a Marina resident donated money to have the decaying "palace" restored. It is surrounded by a large reflecting pool and is one of the most popular places in San Francisco to get married. Behind the rotunda is the **Exploratorium,** dubbed the finest science museum in the country.

■ FORT POINT

This brick and granite pre–Civil War fort is especially impressive on a foggy day, as its tall walls rise into the mist. The huge south arch of the Golden Gate Bridge looms overhead.

Constructed between 1853 and 1861, according to a pattern familiar from such East Coast fortresses as Fort Sumter, this massive citadel is the only defensive structure of its kind on the West Coast. Its guns—three rows of casemated 42- and 32-pound muzzle loaders and a rooftop tier of 8-inch shellguns—never fired a shot in anger. Fort Winfield Scott, as it is officially known, has an entrance gate constructed of heavy oak. It's large enough for teams of horses to drag through the huge cannons which once armed the fort and protected the Golden Gate.

The Palace of Fine Arts was originally constructed for the Panama Pacific International Exposition of 1915. (Photo by Michael Yamashita)

The passage inside the gate is protected by "murder holes," gun ports through which the defenders of the fort could shoot invaders trapped between the inner and outer doors. Inside, arched casemates open onto a courtyard on the seaward side of the fort, living quarters border the landward side. There's a mysterious air about this citadel, perhaps because its pattern of construction goes back to Elizabethan times, when guns were first used to defend castles. When fog wafts through the courtyard and veils the wide-yawning openings of the casemates, you can imagine all sorts of strange and mysterious happenings taking place here.

Rangers in Civil War garb give tours and lectures and may draft you into a gun crew and teach you how to load and fire a Civil War cannon. From the top gun tier and from the promenade surrounding the fort you can enjoy some truly great views of the Golden Gate and the Marin Headlands.

■ WALKING ACROSS THE GOLDEN GATE BRIDGE

A walk across this bridge (two miles one way) is a spiritual and bracing experience in any weather (dress warmly). You can really appreciate the height of the towers, which rise 746 feet above the water. Don't worry if the bridge sways: it's designed to sway 27.5 feet from east to west in strong winds or earthquakes.

From the bridge deck and from the overlook north of the Golden Gate Bridge, you get a good view of the city as it rises on its hills, the towers of the Financial District poking their tops above Russian Hill, the Marina District, and the Presidio. And, of course, of the bridge as it sweeps across the Golden Gate to the green hills of the Presidio.

Remembering that the early nautical explorers along this coast missed the entrance to San Francisco Bay for several hundred years, I recently asked a bay tugboat captain at what point, when out on the ocean and looking from his pilot house toward the east, he could tell that he was entering a bay instead of piling up on a rocky shore. He answered that he hadn't thought about it before; he just follows a prescribed course. But without reference to the Golden Gate Bridge and other man-made structures, he said, you had to wait till you got to Land's End before you could tell the opening led into a bay. Which explains perfectly well why the early explorers sailed past the bay without seeing it—Land's End is awfully close to disaster for an old-fashioned galleon, and its crew wouldn't have dared to sail in that close without knowing that the sheer rock walls they saw from their pitching deck would open and a passage would lead to a safe anchorage.

A bridge painter toils at his never-ending task high above the Golden Gate.

■ PRESIDIO

The 1,480-acre Presidio, a military reservation until 1995, was founded by the Spanish in 1776. It served as an American military reservation after California fell to the U.S.; today, it is administered by the National Park Service. The reserve, which borders both the Golden Gate and the Pacific Ocean, has San Francisco's largest expanse of forest —all of which was planted by the army. Old officers' houses are tucked among the trees, as is a national military cemetery, hidden gun emplacements, tree-shaded roads, and miles of hiking trails.

One of four such fortresses established in California, the Presidio served as Northern California's social center during the Spanish period. It was here that Russian Count Nicolai Rezanov arrived on an American ship, the *Juno*, in 1806 hoping to buy food to feed the starving Russian colony in Sitka, Alaska. The Spanish, who had closed their ports to foreigners, did not allow the Russians and Americans to land. Rezanov not only won them over though, he also won the heart of the Presidio comandante's beautiful 15-year-old daughter, Concepcion (Concha) Arguello. The middle-aged widower proposed marriage and was accepted, but, because he was a member of the Russian Imperial family, he had to return to Russia to ask the czar's permission. After loading much needed food aboard the *Juno* and dropping it off in Sitka, he set out for St. Petersburg. But he died on the arduous overland journey through Siberia. Concha Arguello waited for him until she learned of his death; then she entered a convent in Benicia, where she lived out her final days.

❖

The Spanish also established a mission in San Francisco, under the leadership of Franciscan friar, Father Junipero Serra. Mission Dolores, located at the corner of 16th and Dolores Streets in the Mission District, is the oldest building in San Francisco. Since its construction in 1791, it has withstood numerous earthquakes, but is as sound as ever. The small, enclosed cemetery holds graves of pioneers—as well as those of several thousand Indians.

■ BAYSIDE TO THE PACIFIC

One of the most beautiful of the Presidio's trails is the **Coastal Trail,** which starts south of the Golden Gate Bridge toll plaza. (If you're coming from the city, take the last exit before the toll plaza and follow direction signs to the Presidio. This will take you through a tunnel under the bridge approaches. Follow signs directing you to the trail and park your car in the dirt parking lot west of the road. If you come from the north, turn right on the first road after the toll plaza.) The Coastal Trail winds its way south along the clifftops through groves of eucalyptus and cypress in the Presidio, past abandoned batteries, and along Lincoln Boulevard and El Camino del Mar.

Rising from a Lincoln Park hilltop is the spectacular **California Palace of the Legion of Honor,** an art museum devoted mainly to Continental, especially French art. The museum houses a varied collection from the sculptor Rodin, including the original bronze casting of "The Thinker." During the next several years, it will also be the main venue for traveling art exhibits, as the de Young Museum is brought up to earthquake safety standards.

From **Lincoln Park** the Coastal Trail descends on steps to **Land's End,** the most rugged stretch of shoreline in San Francisco, with some truly great ocean views. Be careful if you leave the main trail, perhaps to take a spur down to little pocket beaches. The surf can be treacherous. There's also been a lot of erosion in recent years, and trails (and even part of El Camino del Mar) have fallen into the ocean.

At the northern end of Ocean Beach stands the **Cliff House,** one of San Francisco's most famous landmarks, and one of the city's first tourist attractions. It was originally built in 1863 by real estate tycoon Charles Butler. In 1881, Adolph Sutro bought the property and turned it into a family resort, bolstering business with a huge bathhouse next door, known as the **Sutro Baths.** The wooden castle burned in 1907. The present incarnation of the Cliff House, built in 1908, is a restaurant more popular with tourists than locals. Relaxing in the bar, with its expansive view of the ocean and wildlife on offshore rocks, is a wonderful way to spend a quiet hour or so. Nearby paths lead down to the ruins of the Sutro Baths, which burned in the late 1960s.

The Golden Gate Bridge from cliffs above Baker Beach.

■ BEACHES OF SAN FRANCISCO

■ Baker Beach

In the Presidio, a road winds through the woods down the cliffs to Baker Beach, where you can walk out onto the four-mile-long beach and look back at the Golden Gate Bridge and across the frothy waters of the Golden Gate to the rugged, brown cliffs of the Marin Headlands. On rare warm days families from throughout the city set up their picnic lunches on the southern portion of the beach. Towering above them are magnificent houses set into the cliffs. Further north along the beach, toward the Golden Gate Bridge, the San Francisco experience is more sybaritic: clothing optional sunbathing.

■ China Beach

South of the Presidio, the road takes you past the beautiful mansions of the Seacliff neighborhood. China Beach's name is from a Chinese fishing village that once stood here. This beach is unusual for San Francisco's oceanfront, because it's safe for swimming. Though the water is abominably cold, many people swim here anyway. Brrr!

■ Ocean Beach

San Francisco's Ocean Beach (more commonly reached by driving through Golden Gate Park) is apt to be a chilly, wind-swept, sandy waste in the summertime, when it is socked in with fog 66 percent of the time. In fall and winter it's clear and clean, and on a sunny day, packed with sunbathers. Children laugh as they chase each other and scream as they make mock runs at the surf. Joggers and kite-fliers are out in force. The beach glistens in the sun, and the spindrift sparkles like diamonds. Even the sea gulls are smiling. The surf, however, is dangerous.

When the surf is rough at Ocean Beach, there will be surfers at the Taraval Break. This crowd is usually lead by Doc Renneker, the "Surf Doc"—made famous by an article in *The New Yorker* magazine. His fellow surfers on this wild break are apt to be local celebrity/singer Chris Isaak; lead singer of the rock band Third Eye Blind, Stephan Jenkins; and surf writers Daniel Duane and Matt Warshaw.

If you're looking for a place to stop for hot tea or a meal, drop by the newly restored Beach Chalet at the west end of Golden Gate Park. It's where the locals come, and it's worth it.

Buffalo Bill's Wild West Show came to Ocean Beach in 1902. Sutro's incarnation of the Cliff House is visible in the background. (Buffalo Bill Historical Center, Cody, Wyoming)

■ GOLDEN GATE PARK

With its 1,017 acres, Golden Gate Park is the largest cultivated park in the country and the only one to border the Pacific Ocean. It was designed by William Hammand Hall in 1871, after he took on the seemingly impossible task of landscaping the largest stretch of sand dune on the California coast.

An aerial view of Golden Gate Park extending down to Ocean Beach.

The western end of the park borders the Great Highway which runs parallel to Ocean Beach. The western half of Golden Gate Park is far quieter than the busy eastern half. Here, during the week, a stroller on Speedway, Marx, or Lindley Meadows or along the Chain of Lakes, meets few passers-by. Holding down the westernmost corners of the park are two windmills from Holland, installed at the turn of the century to irrigate the park. The Queen Wilhelmina Tulip Garden blooms in spring at its foot.

■ BAYSIDE MARIN COUNTY

■ MARIN HEADLANDS

For the most spectacular views of San Francisco Bay, drive north across the Golden Gate Bridge, take the first Sausalito exit, and double back under the freeway following the signs that direct you to the Marin Headlands. As you drive up narrow, steep Conzelman Road, hugging the cliffs, the Golden Gate Bridge will seem close enough to touch. People stop all along this road and get out to marvel at the view. With the bridge to your left (east) and San Francisco's hills and houses sparkling in the sun, it's one of the most beautiful places in California. Here, too, are miles of windswept hiking trails. Continue on the winding road over the headlands to reach **Point Bonita** and its spectacular cliff-hanging lighthouse (only open to the public Saturdays and Sundays 12:30 P.M. to 2:00 P.M., weather permitting).

■ SAUSALITO

Today Sausalito can once again be reached by ferry, although most people drive here, taking the exit from US 101 on the north end of the Golden Gate Bridge. If you do come in by ferry from San Francisco, look for sea lions and seabirds in the blue waters below the red and ochre bluffs of the Marin Headlands. As you approach the town, Angel Island lies to the east, and the serried rows of white and pastel-colored Sausalito houses rise above the shore to your left, sharing the steep hillsides with flowers and trees. Sausalito is a very popular destination and can be a bit touristy at times.

It's along the waterfront that most of Sausalito's chic shops and restaurants are located, but what makes Sausalito special are the cliffs and the flowers, some of the latter cascading down steep rock faces, and the steps up the cliffs to hidden backroads, which are a delight to explore, even if some natives have a sour attitude toward visitors straying off the well-beaten tourist paths. The locals avoid the bars and restaurants along Bridgeway when they go out to drink and eat, heading instead for Caledonia Avenue, a street whose cafes and bars are not prominently listed in tourist brochures.

If you plan to spend more than a day, there are several hotels up high on the bluffs with great views of the bay and San Francisco. From Mikayla, the cliffside restaurant at Casa Madrona, where the windows are opened and the roof is pulled back on warm evenings, you can feel the sea breeze on your cheek as you sip wine and watch the sailboats move briskly around the point. Or you can go to the Alta Mira

Hotel with its huge deck and a fabulous view of the bay. If you come for Sunday brunch you may see one or two Japanese brides having their pictures taken. Japanese couples come here on special package tours, marry in the nearby chapel, and are feted on the deck with champagne.

■ CHINA CAMP

To reach China Camp, turn east off US 101 onto North San Pedro Road at the Marin County Civic Center. The road curves through a suburban development before winding through marshes and headlands to a pristine landscape of meadows, low cliffs, and quiet coves. Point San Pedro (whose bulk keeps the fogs at bay), still shelters San Francisco Bay's last Chinese fishing village, which has been preserved in China Camp State Park.

Near the cove are shacks and other vestiges of the Chinese settlement which flourished here from the 1870s to the 1950s. The men who lived here harvested San Pablo Bay shrimp, which was (and still is) considered the caviar of shrimp by Asians. China Camp was one of 27 Chinese fishing villages that prospered in the

Chinese Fishing Village *by Frederick Butman. (Courtesy of Dr. Albert Shumate Collection)*

area, and sent 10 million pounds of the dried shellfish to Asia.

Most Chinese villages were villages of men, but China Camp was unique in having families, a school, and gardens. Chinese exclusion laws and others against the use of funnel nets closed some of these camps, but by the 1950s all but China Camp was gone because the shrimp population had been virtually wiped out. This happened after dams built upstream on the Sacramento River caused the salinity of San Pablo Bay waters to vary so widely that shrimp were unable to survive in large numbers.

Today, at China Camp's pier, you'll find a small store owned by Frank Quan, whose grandfather also ran a store here. You can stop by for a shrimp cocktail or for sandwiches and soft drinks on weekends, when the store is open. Quan still shrimps occasionally, and group of insiders who know him well seem to find out immediately when he comes in with a big catch (about two or three times a year); they arrive in droves and buy shrimp in five-pound bags.

The shores and hills surrounding the village have become a pleasant state park, with some of the sunniest weather in the Bay Area. On a sunny day at China Camp, sunbathers lie shoulder to shoulder on the narrow beach like sardines in a can, while children splash in the warm water of the cove. Rock music drifts from the family picnics on the low bluffs, with lyrics in Cantonese.

■ CARNEROS WINERY TOUR

The Carneros District, an American Viticultural Appellation established in 1983, stretches across the cool, lower reaches of Sonoma and Napa Counties at the northern reaches of San Francisco Bay (known as San Pablo Bay). Grapes were planted here before Prohibition, but the Carneros wine boom did not take off until the 1970s and 1980s, when winemakers discovered that the relatively cool climate of these often foggy vineyards put complex flavors into the grapes and gave the wines character and backbone. Vineyards experienced a major expansion in the 1990s, as more and more cattle and sheep pastures were plowed up and planted with vines. Some recently planted vineyards come so close to tidewater that you can almost pick grapes from a boat.

The wines made from Carneros grapes are unique. They have better acids and more subtle fruit than the grapes grown in the Wine Country's hot valleys. Even

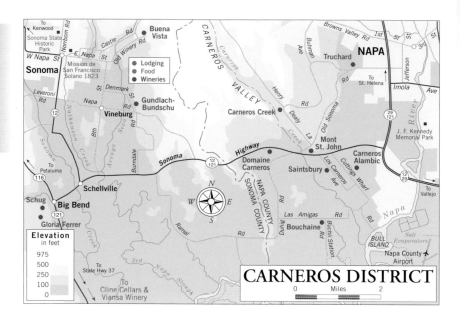

warm-climate grapes like cabernet sauvignon and merlot ripen well in favored lo-cations. Yet zinfandel may not ripen at all, and chardonnay needs shelter. Surprisingly, the fickle pinot noir ripens well on exposed, windy slopes, making excellent wine of great complexity and depth. It and the chardonnay grown here also make superb sparkling wine. While chardonnay and pinot noir are generally considered the area's top grapes, merlot and cabernet sauvignon from Carneros vineyards are also excellent.

The Carneros district is the wine region most easily reached from San Francisco, less than an hour's drive from the city. Head north on US 101, turn east onto CA 37 in Novato, and then turn north on CA 121 (Carneros Highway) at the Sears Point Raceway.

As you drive along CA 121, a two-lane highway that sometimes carries an astonishing amount of traffic as it winds through the rolling green hills north of San Pablo Bay, you'll soon begin to spot wineries. Some of my favorites are listed on the following pages.

■ **Viansa Winery & Marketplace**

On the east side of a low rise, you'll come upon Viansa Winery & Italian Marketplace. Built in the style of a Tuscan country house, the winery overlooks the lowlands and marshes of lower Sonoma Creek. This winery has become a pioneer in exploring such Italian varietals as nebbiolo, sangiovese, and muscat canelli. There are also experimental plantings of vernaccia and malvasia. The Sebastianis, who run Viansa and are one of the oldest wine-growing families in the area, believe in the marriage of food and wine—thus the Italian Marketplace in the name. The marketplace sells a wide variety of Italian-style food products and tasty dishes such as focaccia sandwiches, pasta salads, and torta rustica—a sort of Italian quiche. Visitors are encouraged to use the picnic area, which is shaded by olive trees and overlooks a wetland (administered by Ducks Unlimited), where turtles, river otters, and more than 60 species of birds—including herons, egrets, ducks, and golden eagles—have been spotted. *25200 Arnold Dr./Hwy. 121, Sonoma; 707-935-4700.*

■ **Cline Cellars**

You can really feel the famous Carneros winds, with their ocean chill, at the grounds of Cline Cellars. As you taste the wines you will encounter some unusual but very pleasing flavors. The marsanne tastes quite unlike any other California white, and the mourvèdre is quite different from the more familiar cabernet sauvignon. Be sure to taste the Cotes d'Oakley, a blend of red Rhône grapes, as well as the vin gris white, made with red mourvèdre grapes. There are also semillon and zinfandel for more traditional palates. *24737 Arnold Dr. /Hwy. 121, Sonoma, 707-935-4310.*

■ **Gloria Ferrer**

As you drive north from Cline, look for a winery to your left, up against the gentle slopes of the hills, that looks sunny even on a gray Carneros day. This is Gloria Ferrer Champagne Caves, built in 1982 by the Spanish sparkling-winemaker Freixenet. The winery is named for the wife of José Ferrer, the company president. The sparkling wines made here under the direction of winemaker Bob Iantosca are truly superb, but also be sure to taste the chardonnay and pinot noir made by Iantosca. Both have that elusive Burgundian quality California winemakers strive for but seldom achieve.

Sitting on the deck at Gloria Ferrer on a warm, sunny afternoon, sipping sparkling wine as you look out over the vineyards and listen to the birds sing, is one of the Wine Country's happiest experiences. *23555 Hwy 121, Sonoma; 707-996-7256.*

■ Domaine Carneros

After Big Bend, the Carneros Highway runs west, passing through a landscape of fields, pastures, and dairy farms before coming to the next winery, on the Napa side of the district. A large French chateau to the right side of the highway is Domaine Carneros, established in 1987 by the champagne house Taittinger and American partners. The sparkling wines made here are very austere, the perfect accompaniment for fresh Tomales Bay or Point Reyes oysters, or for caviar from farm-raised Sacramento Valley sturgeon.

There's a reason why Domaine Carneros

looks like an authentic French chateau: it is a copy of the Château de la Marquetterie, an 18th-century mansion owned by the Taittinger family in Champagne. *1240 Duhig Rd., Napa; 707-257-0101.*

■ Mont St. John Cellars

If you have some time to extend your visit, go to Mont St. John Cellars, at the junction of CA 121 (the Carneros Highway) and the old road leading from Napa to Sonoma across the Carneros hills. They offer good-value, estate-grown chardonnay, muscat di canelli, gewürztraminer, white riesling, and pinot noir from the Madonna Vineyard, which straddles the Napa/Sonoma County line along the west bank of Huichica Creek. *5400 Old Sonoma Rd., Napa; 707-255-8864.*

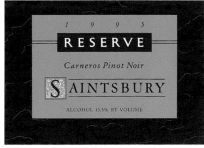

■ Saintsbury

You'll have to call ahead and make an appointment to visit Saintsbury, a small winery that has gained renown for the quality of its pinot noir, but it's worth the effort. *1500 Los Carneros Ave., Napa; 707-252-0592.*

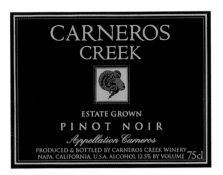

complexity as well, as Truchard Vineyards has amply proved. (The winery's pinot noir is also in a class by itself.) Be sure to call ahead for an appointment at this small winery. And don't miss the zinfandel and cabernet sauvignon. *3234 Old Sonoma Rd., Napa; 707-252-8864.*

■ **Carneros Creek Winery**

To visit a truly pioneering winery, drop in at Francis Mahoney's Carneros Creek Winery, a bit up the hill off Old Sonoma Road. While other wineries—most notably Louis Martini—established earlier Carneros vineyards, it was Mahoney's winery, opened in 1972, which proved that cool-climate pinot noir can be very complex indeed. *1285 Dealy Ln., Napa; 707-253-9463.*

■ **Truchard Vineyards**

Not only do chardonnay and pinot noir grow well here, merlot reaches surprising

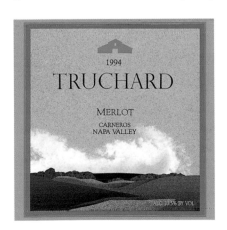

■ **Bouchaine Vineyards**

Bouchaine Vineyards, on the south side of the Carneros Highway, is rather close to tidewater, between Carneros and Huichica Creeks and the tidal sloughs of San Pablo Bay. The alternately breezy and foggy weather has a special effect on the fermenting wine. Call ahead and make an appointment to taste the chardonnay and pinot noir, which are surprisingly Burgundian, as well as the gewürztraminer, which has a definite Alsatian character. *1075 Buchli Station Rd., Napa, 707-252-9065.*

M A R I N   C O A S T

■ HIGHLIGHTS

Marin Headlands
Muir Beach and Muir Woods
Mount Tamalpais
Stinson Beach and Bolinas
Point Reyes National Seashore
Bodega Bay

■ TRAVEL OVERVIEW

The shoreline from the Golden Gate north to Bodega Bay in Sonoma County is one of the most scenic stretches on the West Coast. It is a landscape of great variety: rocky shores alternate with sandy beaches, reedy inlets and estuaries are overtowered by tall cliffs. Deep river canyons, where sea fog lingers even on hot summer days, shelter groves of tall redwoods.

Hills are brown and gold in summer and fall, and thick with green grass and wildflowers in the late winter and spring. Trees—mostly oaks, California bays, Bishop pines, and Douglas firs—stand straight and robust along the ridgetops; or they hug the bottom of small valleys where creeks run in the wintertime.

■ TRAVEL BASICS

Getting Around
North of San Francisco two-lane CA 1, the Coast Highway, curves slowly in

and out of draws and then rides high along the cliffs above the ocean. It's beautiful, but if your time is limited, you can take faster US 101 to points north and cut over to the coast on sideroads; see map, page 72.

Climate

The weather along Marin County's coastline is enormously variable. It ranges from cold, windy, foggy days, to days so pristine they make your eyes water. The coast is consistently cool year-round, and often foggy in summer when inland valleys and cities swelter in the heat. Between July and August, however, there can be clear, warm days, especially on south-facing beaches such as Stinson. September and October are the most pleasant months. Winter brings rainfall of varying intensity. During spring, days are generally pleasant and mild, but expect a stiff breeze. **Water Temperature:** Swimmers in wet suits, hardy children, and surfers enjoy the fine but cold water at Stinson Beach, but for the most part this coast is not suitable for swimming. It is a good place for long, barefoot walks in the surf.

Food and Lodging

Most villages and small towns have homey cafes with extremely good coffee, and there are many superb restaurants and bakeries. Oyster farms can be found in protected inlets, dairies in green valleys, and cattle ranches on the drier upland slopes. Some of the dairies milk goats and sheep to make exquisite, flavorful cheeses. Wines from Napa, Sonoma, Carneros, the Russian River, and the Anderson Valley are some of the world's best and readily available. Most local grocery stores stock fresh vegetables and fruits from valleys just inland: in short this is a fine place to picnic, and with a little discrimination and inquiry along the way, an outstanding area in which to dine out.

This coast is dotted with small inns—perfect places for holing up to read by a blazing fire after wandering over the bluffs above the sea thinking about the meaning of life. (For **lodging and restaurant listings** see pages 339-390.)

MARIN COUNTY

Miles
0   5   10

Kilometers
0   5   10   15

Elevation
in feet

2,571
2,500
2,000
1,500
1,000
500
Sea Level

Westside Regional Park
Bodega Bay
Bodega Head
Doran Regional Park
Bodega Bay
Bodega
Occidental
Graton
Valley Ford
Sebastopol
Tomales Point
Dillon Beach
Fallon
Cunningham
Bloomfield
Laguna de Santa Rosa
McClure's Beach
Tomales
Rohn Park
Two Rock
Cotati
Kehoe Beach
Marshall
Walker Creek
Penngro
Abbotts Lagoon
Tomales Bay State Park
Oyster Farm
Schooner Bay
Inverness
Pt Reyes Lighthouse
Point Reyes
Drakes Estero
Kenneth C Patrick Visitors Center
Drakes Bay
Petaluma
Limantour Beach
Point Reyes Hostel
Pt Reyes Station
Bear Valley Visitors Center
Olema

Point Reyes
National
Seashore

See map page 82

Nicasio Reservoir
Nicasio
Novato
Forest Knolls
Black Point
Woodacre
Samuel P Taylor State Park
Kent Lake
Laguntas Creek
Audubon Canyon Ranch
Fairfax
Bolinas Lagoon
Bolinas
Santa Venetia
China Camp State Park
Duxbury Point
Bolinas Bay
Alpin Lake
San Anselmo
Kentfield
SAN RAFAEL
Stinson Beach
Mt Tamalpais State Park (elev 2,571)
Larkspur
Corte Madera
Richmond Bridge
San Pablo Bay
Muir Woods National Monument
Mill Valley
Muir Beach
Marin City
San Pablo
RICHMOND
Pt Bonita Lighthouse
Sausalito
Tiburon
ANGEL ISLAND
Angel Island State Park
El Cerrito
Mile Rock Lighthouse
Golden Gate
Golden Gate Bridge
ALCATRAZ ISLAND
SAN FRANCISCO

SAN ANDREAS FAULT ZONE

■ HEADING NORTH FROM SAN FRANCISCO

Today is very special, because for the first time in years, I have enough time to spend several days ambling along the shores and uplands of Point Reyes and other splendid places of this beautiful coast. I have left San Francisco early in the morning and crossed the Golden Gate Bridge just as the sun cleared the Berkeley hills to the east of San Francisco Bay, casting long slants of light westward, and lighting up the bay in a silver and almost translucent blue. As commuters wind slowly south, I leave the US 101 freeway and drive west on CA 1, through Mill Valley up to a spur of Mount Tamalpais and then down the coastal slopes to Muir Beach. Near the top of the ridge a road leads north to Muir Woods (a grove of ancient redwoods in a deep creek canyon some three miles from here) and continues to Stinson Beach.

Another road runs north to **Mount Tamalpais** (2,571 feet) with its miles of hiking trails and grand views of bay and ocean. The winding road to Muir Beach (CA 1) leads down a steep-sloped valley of low treeless hills—thick with green grass during late winter and spring, golden in summer and fall—toward a blue Pacific Ocean. The road turns and twists till it comes upon a eucalyptus grove and a turnoff for Green Gulch Farm run by the San Francisco Zen center. This retreat has a small Japanese style inn, where people interested in attending lectures or meditations spend the night, drink tea, and wander through the beautiful farm and gardens down to Muir Beach. At the bottom of the hill, the road reaches the pastures of a horse farm and a spur road turns toward the beach.

At the entrance to this road stands the **Pelican Inn,** a perfect re-creation of an English pub, with flowers and a green lawn out front. Here you can warm yourself with a hearty meal, enhanced by a pint of stout ale.

■ MUIR BEACH

Several unmarked trails lead from the paved parking lot through a marsh to a beach of dark sand, past ducks dabbling in the waters of the tidal lagoon. A great blue heron waits for the movement of a minnow or amphibian. The pocket beach is quite small, even for a North Coast beach, hemmed in as it is by steep headlands, and it usually has a somber, lonely, and bracing quality to it, but it is warm today, shielded by the cliffs from the chilly northwesterly breeze.

(following pages) Mount Tamalpais, popular hiking terrain for locals, rises above the ocean and the Marin Headlands. The Farallon Islands and downtown San Francisco are often visible from its slopes.

Most strollers walk south on the beach, but some cross the narrow strip of rocks to the north of the parking lot and come out in a perfect little cove, a fine place to swim if you can take cold water, and if you don't mind, or want to join, nude bathers. The scene is less than erotic, as most people baring themselves to the sun are of the 60s generation. (For the most part, in Northern California, younger people don't *do* this kind of thing.)

North of Muir Beach, a vista point just off the highway has a splendid view of the ocean, with the headlands of the Point Reyes Peninsula jutting into the sea to the northwest, and the Farallon Islands, prime haven for breeding seabirds, looming up on the western horizon. To the south spreads glimmering San Francisco.

■ STINSON BEACH

Over a ridge and a few switchbacks to the north of Muir Beach, and at the base of the west flank of Mount Tamalpais, sits the village of Stinson Beach, and one of the finest beaches in Northern California. Traffic slows to a halt along the two-block-long main street where there's a kayak rental and not surprisingly, a surf

An egret pauses in the glow of a Marin coastal sunset.

shop, as well as a few small restaurants. The Parkside Cafe (just off the main drag) is the popular local hangout (the menu is augmented by hamburgers from a takeout stand in summer), and there's also a good market uphill from the Coast Highway. It has evolved from a country store to a place where you can buy local wines, roasted chickens, imported cheeses, fresh breads—in fact everything you need for a picnic. Stinson Beach Books (half a block north) advertises itself as the only bookstore located directly on the San Andreas Fault.

Ron Kauk, rock climber par excellence, tackles "Endless Bummer," an overhang at Stinson Beach.

Facing south and shielded by Point Reyes from the northwesterly sea winds and much of the fog, this beach gets quite toasty. This is a wonderful place for a long barefoot walk through white sand. Mornings and evenings the ocean is often calm and reflects the colors of the sunrise or sunset. Birds are everywhere—marbled godwits and dunlins probe deep in the wet sand for edible invertebrates. Sanderlings rush about in busy groups, first following the receding waves, then running from the surf wash, snatching up any morsels dislodged by the swirling waters. These tiny (blackbird-sized) shorebirds move their legs so quickly, they look like mechanical toys on wheels. Willets probe more deliberately. They look like washed-out, plain gray birds until they are disturbed and flash dramatically black and white wings during take-off.

Even though the ocean here has dangerous riptides and can be quite cold, some people swim at Stinson. (If you can rent a wet suit at the surf shop, do it.) It is also a popular surfing spot. On the Fourth of July surfers have a famous bonfire in which they burn all the old wood and furniture they can collect plus some old surfboards, and then pray to the god of surfing, asking for a good year!

■ BOLINAS LAGOON AND BOLINAS

Just beyond Stinson Beach, the two-lane Coast Highway runs along the eastern shore of Bolinas Lagoon, a tidal inlet that has been silting up very rapidly and is in the process of becoming a salt marsh. The silted-up channels are a paradise for shorebirds, who congregate here in great numbers in fall, winter, and spring. Great blue herons, egrets, and cormorants can be seen at all seasons. Harbor seals and their pups haul out on a sandbank near the eastern shore.

■ AUDUBON CANYON RANCH
A bit further north, east of the highway, is a bird refuge with a heron and egret rookery in one of its redwood canyons. It is most exciting to visit in February and March when the great blue heron and snowy egret chicks hatch in nests high up on top of the redwood trees. From a trailside viewing platform with stationary binoculars, you can look down upon the nests and watch the chicks wait for their parents to return with minnows or frogs from Bolinas Lagoon; *415-868-9244*.

■ BOLINAS
Unless you look carefully, you can easily miss the turnoff to the village of Bolinas because it is unmarked. (Residents tear down any direction signs the state or county put up.) The center of the village is comprised of two narrow streets, with side roads leading to houses tucked away into craggy nooks above the ocean and all along the Bolinas plateau. Both commercial streets dead-end on narrow beaches; parking spots by the beach itself are almost non-existent. From the westernmost of these beaches, you can walk to the tidepools of Duxbury Reef, which are very popular with marine biologists because of their varied intertidal marine life. Bolinas's

■ Birds of the Coast

Black-necked stilt

Sandpiper

Egret

Brandt's cormorant

Western grebe

American avocet

main road runs down to the outlet to the Stinson-Bolinas lagoon and has a few docks for boats. The channel is so shallow that the boats sit on the mud at low tide.

The last time I visited, I found a place to park my car and walked to the Bolinas Bakery and Cafe. Some Bolinas folk are wary of strangers, but less so if those strangers walk, wearing bland smiles, as though they've see it all before. I also carried my sketch book. It almost always breaks the ice, and it worked this time, especially after I executed surrealistic sketches of other visitors, giving them fish heads, crab claws, and octopus legs. I struck up a conversation with the long-bearded men sitting out front, watching the world go by. They've seen it all. "Before satori, I sit and drink coffee. After satori, I drink coffee and sit." We had a good talk about the channels silting up and the effect that will have on the seasonal wildlife, animal and human.

Across the road from the bakery lies Smiley's Schooner Saloon on Wharf Road, the oldest tavern on this section of the coast, and a relic from the days when schooners carried redwood lumber from the Bolinas Wharf to San Francisco. William Tecumseh Sherman, of Civil War fame, was once shipwrecked on Duxbury Reef, walked to Bolinas and took a schooner bound for San Francisco, but the ship foundered in the high swells of the Golden Gate. After being rescued

A local dog makes himself at home in Bolinas. (Photo by Michael Yamashita)

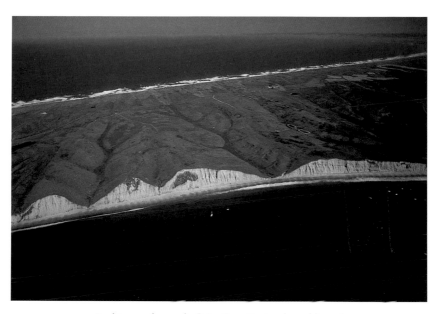

Looking north over the Point Reyes Peninsula and beyond.

for the second time in 24 hours, Sherman finally reached San Francisco by rowboat.

■ POINT REYES NATIONAL SEASHORE

The crown jewel of this coast is Point Reyes, the large, roughly triangular peninsula jutting out from the beautiful coast north of San Francisco. It has been called an "Island in Time," because it is part of a landmass that has moved north over the millennia, and because it is separated from the mainland by a narrow rift valley which is filled with water at Bolinas Lagoon to the south and Tomales Bay to the north.

The rocks and vegetation of Point Reyes differ from that of the mainland, and give the National Seashore a special magic. Visiting Point Reyes is like stepping away from the everyday world with its cares, and entering a different one where time has stood still. And in many ways it has. Most of the National Seashore has been preserved in its natural state, which bestows a timeless aura on its cliffs and beaches, meadows and forests, valleys and hills, and saltwater inlets.

There are not many signs of man in this pristine landscape: a few roads, visitor centers and dairy farms, a lighthouse, an oyster farm, and the small villages of Inverness and Inverness Park on the Tomales Bay side, and Bolinas at the southern tip. A narrow road winds for 21 miles from the Inverness entrance to the lighthouse; spur roads lead to beaches, mountaintops, and to the long rocky finger of Tomales Point at the northern end of the peninsula. Miles of trails lead through woods and meadows to beaches and marshes.

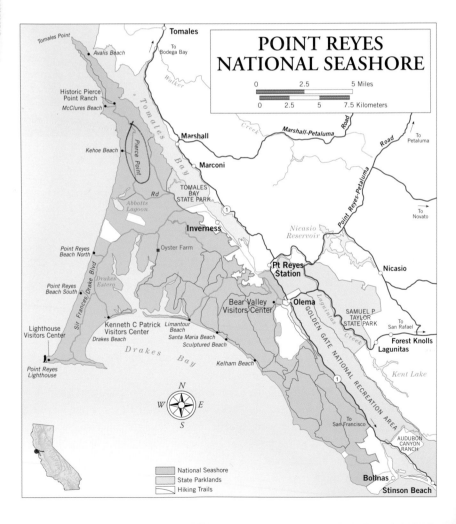

🚗 **Getting to Point Reyes from San Francisco**

Option 1: From San Francisco along scenic Highway 1, take the Stinson Beach exit from US 101 and follow the signs north.
Option 2: Take US 101 north to Lucas Valley Road and travel west to the town of Point Reyes Station. (See map page 82.)
No entry or day use fees are charged at Point Reyes National Seashore. Camping is permitted only in four hike-in campgrounds; fee. Call *415-663-1092,* Monday–Friday, 9:00 A.M. to noon, for reservations.

■ BEAR VALLEY ENTRANCE
From the Bear Valley Road at Olema, you enter the central section of the National Seashore. Don't let the landscape confuse you. You cannot see the ocean from any point in this narrow valley, because Douglas fir–clad Inverness Ridge to the west blocks the view. Stop at the **visitors center** to pick up a detailed map of the seashore and get a quick update on what's happening.

Kule Loklo
You might want to take the short but beautiful walk to the meadow where the bark-slab houses, sweathouse, and shade ramadas of a reconstructed Coast Miwok village rise from the dewy grass. Look for red-capped, black-and-white acorn woodpeckers which chatter noisily as they sit atop the fence posts parting the trail from the meadow where the rangers pasture their Morgan horses. The village looks alive, as fog drifts in and out among the trees and slab houses, or as the sun heats the grass and water vapors rise like smoke from native campfires.

The short earthquake trail begins on the east side of the parking lot (look for a prominent marker). This trail straddles the San Andreas Fault, which is explained by markers with photos, rock samples, and plaques. You can see the spot where the peninsula moved 16 feet north in the 1906 earthquake and where a cow (albeit legendary) cow was swallowed whole, leaving only its tail protruding from the crack.

Bear Valley Trail
This 4.1-mile-long trail is well graded and mostly level, with a slight rise and drop to and from Divide Meadow. The trail runs through laurel, oak, Douglas fir, and alder woods along the banks of creeks to the coast and has a sea arch where Coast

Creek enters the ocean. The trail has many rustic benches (cut from huge logs) for weary travelers to rest their limbs, as well as a picnic area in Divide Meadow. Odd trees and flowers growing along the trail and in the meadow remain from old cabins and a former hunting lodge. The latter has also left behind herds of exotic Asian axis and European fallow deer. The axis deer are reddish brown and have whitish spots year-round (only the fawns of native black-tailed deer have spots); the fallow deer come in a variety of colors, including pure white. No, you're not hallucinating if you see a white deer stepping from the woods.

■ LIMANTOUR BEACH

Farther north on the Bear Valley Road you reach the turnoff for Limantour Road, which winds over the spine of the peninsula to Limantour Spit, Estero, and Beach. West of Inverness Ridge, many of the magnificent native Douglas fir forests fell victim to the great fire of 1995. While blackened tree trunks still rise against the skyline, the area's non-woody vegetation has recovered quickly. In the spring, wildflowers densely cover the burned slopes; white-headed cow parsnips, and multicolored lupines grow five feet tall. The **Point Reyes Hostel** charges the most reasonable lodging rates in the region. In spring the ground around the hostel, a former farmhouse, is dense with yellow daffodils.

The road ends, almost with a question mark, in a rather rough parking lot on a gentle slope above the lagoon. From here an easily walkable paved trail leads down the slope to a causeway across Limantour Estero, which here consists of a series of ponds and marshes connected by sluggish creek channels. To the east of the causeway upstream is a pond where coots and their odd-looking, black-and-red chicks putter in spring. Listen for the piping calls of a black rail from a reedy thicket on the far shore.

Along Limantour Spit

At different seasons, you can watch dowitchers probe the shallow mud as they walk along in tightly packed flocks, moving their heads up and down in unison in a stitching motion; or you can watch long-billed curlews daintily stepping across the marshy ground as they reach forward with their long, downward-curved bills, picking unsuspecting insects off reed and grass culms. Or you might come across a yellowlegs rapidly stalking through the shallow water of the marsh, jabbing at

Arch Rock, at the end of Bear Valley Trail, in the Point Reyes National Seashore.

animals on or below the surface of the water. Then again, you might hear the high-pitched trill from a flock of least sandpipers emerging from the salicornia (pickleweed) margin of the marsh, picking and probing for tiny crustaceans among the fleshy joints of the succulent plants. Sparrow-sized least sandpipers are the world's smallest shorebirds, yet they often crouch to get closer to their prey, getting their legs and belly feathers quite muddy in the process.

You can't miss the white egrets (both "snowy" and "great"). They stand quietly in marshy nooks, fly overhead, and may race through the shallow water, chasing a frog, fish, or garter snake. Merlins look for prey on the wing by slipping low over the edge of a bluff, then soaring high on an updraft, before dropping down to repeat the maneuver. Turkey vultures gently rock their wings as they soar overhead.

The estero is a shallow fresh and saltwater lagoon which spreads between the bluffs of the peninsula and the sand dunes and beach of sandy Limantour Spit. The path ends on the western shore of the estero, but the low dunes are easily crossed on informal trails.

Beyond the dunes, a wide, sandy beach beckons. In spring, harbor seals haul out here with their pups (it is illegal to disturb the seals or the pups). At all seasons, even in summer when they're supposed to be breeding in the arctic or on the shores of upland lakes, shorebirds probe the wet margin of the sand. World-weary willets poke their beaks listlessly into the sand, while dunlins, startled by the human intruder, dash into the air, where they twist and turn, alternately exposing their grayish brown backs and wings and their white bellies—at one moment they flash like a bright signal, the next moment they seem to have vanished from the air as they blend into the dun background color of the bluffs; then the flock suddenly turns and flashes another white signal. Back on the beach, the dunlins settle down to the serious business of extricating worms and crustaceans from the mud of the estuary and the wet sand of the beach, by moving as a solid phalanx, head down, as they probe the ground.

As you approach a flock of sanderlings resting above the high-water line, watch their curious behavior. Like other shore birds, sanderlings puff up their feathers and pull up one leg under the warm covers to preserve body heat. As you come closer, the whole flock may hop away from you—instead of flying off—on one leg. It seems that sanderlings can hop around on one leg as easily as they can on two, so why waste any extra motion.

If you visit coastal beaches and marshes in winter, you may wonder why most of the birds appear to be sleeping through the day instead of foraging actively. That's because in winter the lowest tides—the ones during which the birds gather most of their food—occur at night.

■ INVERNESS

From Highway 1, Sir Francis Drake Boulevard takes you first to the village of Inverness Park and then to woodsy Inverness on the shores of protected Tomales Bay, with its shops, restaurants, and inns.

Stop at the well-stocked grocery store for a bit of local color and to stock up on picnic supplies. Across the street is Vladimir's, a Czech restaurant, where locals enjoy eating cabbage rolls and apple strudel. Just north of town is Manka's Inverness Lodge, a classic, and quite old, local inn, set back under trees on a winding wooded lane. The lodge has a comfy sitting room with a fireplace—and a pricey restaurant.

Sir Francis Drake Boulevard runs close to the shore in Inverness. You can see the boats bobbing out in the bay and an old yacht club building on stilts with a large white sign that proclaims "Launch for Hire."

At the north end of the village, the road turns west to climb **Inverness Ridge**, the rocky spine that runs along the back (the east side) of the peninsula. After passing through chaparral (look for the creamy blooms of ocean spray in early summer) and fir and pine woods, it opens to a different landscape east of the crest—green pastures and windswept fells where the Douglas fir and pine woods huddle in sheltered draws, and lonely dairy farms are protected by windbreaks of dense cypress trees. These aren't the tall, columnar Mediterranean cypresses, however, but highly irregular trees stretching out long, thin mats of dark foliage that look like banshees in fog or wind. You can easily tell the prevailing wind direction—all of the trees point away from it. Hawks, conditioned by countless days of fog, swoop low over the land, barely clearing the pasture fences in their relentless pursuit of prey.

■ THE ROAD TO DRAKES BAY

Just west of the ridge, Sir Francis Drake Boulevard veers off to the left, into a wooded glen, while Pierce Point Road branches off to the north toward Tomales Bay State Park, McClure's Beach, and Pierce Point Ranch. A mile down Sir Francis Drake is the turnoff for the Mount Vision Overlook (1,282 feet) and Point Reyes

Hill (1,336 feet), which have sweeping views of all of the Point Reyes Peninsula—in clear weather. (The winding road to the overlook is three miles long.)

Schooner Bay and the Oyster Farm

At Schooner Bay, an arm of Drake's Estero, a road runs south along the water to **Johnson's Oyster Farm**, a great place for stocking up on oysters and clams. Be sure to bring an oyster knife if you plan to buy oysters and open them at a picnic. Like all oyster farms, this place, with its weathered shucking sheds and piles of oyster shells, has a somewhat bleak air about it, but don't let that distract you from the oysters. They're delicious. *17171 Sir Francis Drake Boulevard; 415-669-1149.*

In the wild, oysters grow on tidal mudflats and rocks. But the substrate can impart an indelicate flavor to the oysters, while twice-daily exposure to the air during low tide can stress the oysters and make them less succulent. Like many modern oyster farms, Johnson's grows its oysters by a process known as "rope culture." Young oysters (spat) are attached to ropes which are suspended from floats in deep water. The ropes keep the oysters in the nutrient-rich water 24 hours a day while, at the same time protecting them from predators crawling over the ground (like oyster drills, a marine snail, starfish, or boring worms).

Toward the Lighthouse

After you return from the oyster farm, turn left onto Sir Francis Drake Boulevard. The road soon rises from the valley onto the moor-like western spine of the peninsula which runs almost at a right angle to Inverness Ridge. To the left lies sheltered Drake's Bay, to the right, surf-beaten Point Reyes Beach North and South. All have well-marked access roads, parking lots, and wind-sheltered restrooms. Past the turnoffs, the road narrows and becomes more twisted as it winds past dairy farms and past occasional copses of cypress trees to the headlands. Drive slowly. On foggy mornings, a common occurrence at this sea cape, animals often emerge mysteriously from the whiteness—a doe and her fawn, a harrier swooping low over a patch of bulrushes, a lost heifer mooing despondently, or a turkey vulture rocking past on stiff wings.

Seen from above, the headlands look like the head of a hammerhead shark, and the road splits near a sea lion overlook. The main road continues to the left, toward the lighthouse; a narrow (but well-marked) side road branches off to the east just beyond the corrals of a dairy farm. Automobile access ends at a small parking

The great horned owl is one of many magnificent wild animals to be seen at Point Reyes.

lot above the fish dock and the old lifeboat station, both of which you can reach by walking downhill to the beach. The southern end of the beach has some good rocky tidepools, where you can see (but not touch) sea snails, limpets, hermit crabs, sea anemones, and tiny (and very camouflaged) sculpins.

From the parking lot, a narrow trail (clearly marked by signs) leads to **Chimney Rock,** the easternmost point of the headlands.

Point Reyes Lighthouse

This lighthouse is very popular—so popular that the park service runs a free shuttle bus from the Drake's Beach parking lot to the lighthouse during the height of the winter whale migrating season. On foggy days, there isn't much of a view from this viewpoint (Point Reyes gets an average of 2,700 hours of fog annually), but when the fog lifts, the views are spectacular: far out to sea in the west, south to the Farallon Islands, and southeast along the coast to the Golden Gate. If you're lucky, you can see murres clinging to the sheer cliffs or watch porpoises, dolphins, and whales swim past.

*Point Reyes Lighthouse. (*Harper's Magazine, *1874)*

Three hundred steps lead *down* to the 1870 lighthouse, which is 294 feet above mean sea level. It's a steep climb down, but the climb back up seems even steeper (there are rest platforms for those who can't take the steps at a straight run). Between November and March, when the California gray whales swim south past the point, their huge bodies rising from the water, sending up vapor clouds of air as they exhale, and cresting before they dive, these platforms are perfect for watching the huge marine mammals.

The **visitors center,** in the old keepers' quarters atop the bluff, has a collection of stuffed seabirds and an excellent selection of local history and natural history books. *415-669-1534.*

Drakes Beach

If all this hiking and wildlife watching has made you hungry, now is the time for a picnic. If the day is too windy for a blufftop meal, drive back (east) on Sir Francis Drake Boulevard to the Drake's Beach turnoff, turn right and take the road to the parking lot at the foot of the bluff. A picnic area sheltered from the wind by willows borders a lagoon on the north side of the parking lot. But you're in luck if you forgot to bring your meal. **The Drakes Beach Cafe** (in the Drakes Bay Visitor Center complex) serves some great food. When I stopped by recently, I expected to get a hamburger, maybe, or fish 'n chips, but the cook told me she had fresh local halibut and salmon. Since I had seen the fleet of trollers just inside the point, I took her word for it—and I'm glad I did. The salmon was wonderful: perfectly fresh, lightly sauteed, and accompanied by a dill sauce (with little bits of fresh dill). Even the fries tasted homemade. It was one of the best meals I'd had all summer (and the best salmon I've had south of Seattle).

Drakes Beach got its name because some historians believe that Sir Francis Drake careened and repaired his ship, the *Golden Hind,* on this beach or in Drake's Estero in the summer of 1579, after the English explorer had captured Spanish treasure ships off the Latin American coast; others believe he hauled out in Bodega Harbor or in the cove between Tiburon and Belvedere Island in San Francisco Bay. We may never know for certain because the only tangible proof, the ship's log, has never been found. In 1936, a banged-up brass plate found near Point San Quentin claimed to mark the shore where Drake landed and careened his ship. But the plate had supposedly been found even earlier at Point Reyes by a chauffeur, who later discarded it. In the 1970s, the British Museum declared the plaque a fake and a metallurgist determined that the brass was less than a hundred years old. So there goes another myth and we still don't know where exactly Drake landed. My guess is as good as anyone's, and I'll opt for Bodega Harbor.

Sir Francis Drake's Point Reyes

*O*ur general called this country *Nova Albion,* and that for two causes: the one in respect of the white banks and cliffs which lie toward the sea, and the other because it might have some affinity with our country in name, which sometime was so called. There is no part of earth here to be taken up wherein there is not a reasonable quantity of gold and silver.

At our departure hence our general set up a monument of our being there, as also of her Majesty's right and title to the same, namely a plate nailed upon a fair great post, whereupon was engraved her Majesty's name, the day and year of our arrival there, with the free giving up of the province and people into her Majesty's hands, together with her highness's picture and arms in a piece of sixpence of current English money under the plate, whereunder was also written the name of our general.

It seems that the Spaniards hitherto had never been in this part of the country, neither did ever discover the land by many degrees to the southward of this place.

—Richard Hakluyt, *The Principal Navigations, Voyages and Discoveries of the English Nation,* 1589

The mouth of **Drake's Estero,** east of the beach, the seashore's largest tidal inlet, also changes constantly—one month there may be sandbars or small islands where sea lions haul out, the next it may be wide open with nothing but smooth water

MARIN COAST

ALONG PIERCE POINT ROAD
Pierce Point Road runs north from Sir Francis Drake Boulevard along the triangular rocky headland that forms a sort of peninsula on a peninsula as it reaches north toward Bodega Bay. To the right lies Tomales Bay State Park with its campground, bayfront picnic areas, and the sheltered cove and warm sands of Hearts Desire Beach, which is often sunny when the rest of the peninsula is socked in.

Abbotts Lagoon
On the ocean side of the peninsula (two miles beyond the state park turnoff), this long expanse of blue water can be reached by a mile-long trail from a parking area. It's a great spot for watching dowitchers and godwits probe the mud for food, and watch whimbrels pick any tidbits off the surface that may have escaped the voracious feeders. In winter, canvasback, redhead, and other ducks congregate here. Look for a herd of "wild" goats on the hill behind the lagoon.

Kehoe Beach
Kehoe Beach, two miles farther up the road, marks the end of the long, sandy beach that sweeps up the west coast of the peninsula. It can be reached by a half-mile-long (often muddy) trail from a small parking area.

McClure's Beach
About nine miles north of Sir Francis Drake Boulevard, is about as rough a place as Point Reyes beaches get. A steep, and often muddy, trail leads down to this mile-long sandy beach that is cut off at both ends by steep granite cliffs. Cormorants, murres, and other seabirds roost offshore on Elephant Rock and other sea stacks. It's easy to tell the murres from the other birds—they most look like penguins (though they are not closely related and, unlike penguins, can fly).

The point north of the McClure's Beach parking lot is accessible only by trail. The white-washed buildings beyond the trailhead belong to the Pierce Point Ranch, a 19th-century cattle ranch that has been preserved as an outdoor museum. A self-guided tour with numerous plaques explains farm operations.

En route to the trailhead, you encounter a tall fence designed to keep dairy cattle apart from the peninsula's herd of Tule elk. These dwarf elk (about the size of a mule deer, but with huge racks of antlers) were once common throughout lowland California, but were almost wiped out by market hunters during the 19th century. A small herd has been maintained by the state in the Owens Valley to assure the survival of this species. Two bulls and eight cows from this herd were moved to Point Reyes in the late 1970s; today their offspring number more than a hundred.

To reach the very tip of Tomales Point you have to hike north some five miles through rolling clifftop fells where wildflowers bloom profusely in spring.

■ TOWN OF POINT REYES STATION

To head north along the coast follow Sir Francis Drake Boulevard to the Coast Highway (CA 1), then turn left into **Point Reyes Station**. This small town at the head of Tomales Bay has preserved its atmosphere from the time when it was a butter-and-egg stop on the local narrow gauge railroad line. True to the town's dairying tradition, a recording played at noon and six P.M. "moos"; and the favorite local hangout is the Bovine Bakery, which claims its products are "udderly divine." The retail store of the Point Reyes Oyster Company sells organically grown oysters and mussels *(415-663-8373)*; Toby's Feed Barn caters to the needs of farmers with hay, feed, seeds, garden plants, and fresh local fruits and vegetables and to the needs of visitors with arts and crafts produced by West Marin artists.

■ ALONG TOMALES BAY

Beyond Point Reyes Station, the highway runs along Tomales Bay. Look for signs marking parking areas and trails along the shore. Tomales Bay is a shallow, flooded rift valley atop the San Andreas Fault. The road runs along the shore past oyster farms and past the boatyard, cafe, and houses of **Marshall.** Oysters from the Hog Island Oyster Co. *(Friday-Sunday, 9:00 A.M. to 5:00 P.M., 20215 CA 1; 415-663-9218)* and the Tomales Bay Oyster Co. *(daily, 9:00 A.M. to 5:00 P.M., 15479 CA 1; 415-663-1242)* are delicious. Hog Island makes a few picnic tables available to its customers (bring your oyster knife!), or you can shuck these delectable mollusks wherever you plan to enjoy your al fresco repast.

Also near Marshall is a kayak rental shop for those would like to explore the wild spots along the bay.

(following pages) Tule elk were once common throughout California. These survivors live on the Point Reyes Peninsula.

MARIN COAST

■ TOMALES TO BODEGA BAY

■ TOMALES

Before reaching the mouth of the bay, Highway 1 runs inland past the picturesque village of Tomales, along a stretch of plush green hills, where contented dairy cows produce lushly rich milk. In town is an excellent bakery, an old fashioned grocery store and, up on the hill, a small white Presbyterian church that is on the National Historic Register. At Christmas service, most attendees are ranchers.

From CA 1 in Tomales, the Dillon Beach Road leads to wide, windy Dillon Beach and its rather prosaic town. If you take the toll road at Lawson's Landing you can take the Clam Clipper on low tide weekends to the Tomales Bay clam beds. *For boat trips and campground reservations call 707-878-2443.*

■ BODEGA AND BODEGA BAY

The small country town of **Bodega** (not to be confused with Bodega Bay), just north of Highway 1 as it crosses into Sonoma County, was the setting for Alfred Hitchcock's 1963 thriller *The Birds.* (The schoolyard scene was shot in Bodega, but the harbor and cafe are actually in Bodega Bay.)

The highway returns to the coast at **Bodega Bay,** just south of Doran Spit which protects the harbor from the southeasterly gales of winter. The narrow strip of land between the highway and the tideflats is lined with fishing boat docks, marine supply shops, fish processing plants, and restaurants. The most popular of these is Lucas Wharf, which also has a seafood market selling freshly caught local fish. Lots of fresh seafood is landed at Bodega Harbor, which is the largest fishing port between San Francisco and Eureka.

A hundred years ago, Bodega Bay was better known for its red potatoes than for its fish. The potatoes, as well as other produce grown in the hinterland, helped keep Gold Rush San Francisco supplied with fresh food. Agriculture in Bodega Bay was started by Russian fur traders who settled here in 1812, half a decade before the Spanish founded Mission San Rafael north of the Golden Gate (1817) and more than a decade before Padre Jose Altmira established Sonoma Mission (1823). The Russians raised cattle and hogs on the coastal slopes, as well as vegetables. They grew grain inland, in the Freestone Valley. But the Russians were hunters and traders, not farmers, and their farms did not prosper.

I've spent the night in Bodega Bay at the Inn at the Tides, and enjoyed a simple meal while looking across the bay at Bodega Head—I'd picked up bread at the bakery in Tomales, and a Camembert at the Marin French Cheese Company *(707-762-6001)* on the Red Hill/Petaluma–Point Reyes Road (from Petaluma take D Street until it becomes this road). At the market in Point Reyes I'd bought sweet sheep's milk cheese from Bellwether Farms, a local sheep dairy, and I had a bottle of Russian River pinot noir which I'd bought at Gourmet au Bay *(913 CA 1; 707-875-9875)*, an excellent little wine shop in town on Highway 1 just north of Tide's Wharf.

Bodega Head

Bodega Head, a rocky promontory jutting out into the Pacific Ocean, is even more windswept and bleakly beautiful than Point Reyes, perhaps because it does not have as many visitors crowding its trails.

Narrow dirt trails lead to headlands, hidden coves, and into vast stretches of sand dunes. Chaparral-covered Bodega Head is a great place for watching both sea and land birds. Sea lions hang out on offshore rocks. It is also a great place for watching fishing and pleasure boats wind their way through the mudflats of the harbor on a narrow channel.

Sun and fog meld together to create a distinctly North Coast sunset.

SONOMA & MENDOCINO

■ HIGHLIGHTS

Jenner
Russian River Winery Tour
Fort Ross
Point Arena
Anderson Valley Winery Tour
Mendocino

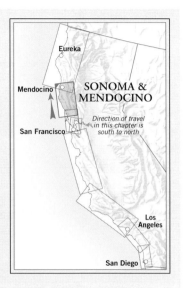

■ TRAVEL OVERVIEW

This beautiful coast of scenic, surf-splashed headlands, sandy beaches, and quiet coves can be surprisingly lonely, but it's not at all primitive. Away from the sea, lovely valleys hide foggy redwood dells, sunny vineyards, and fragrant apple orchards—many of them perfect for picnics or strolls. Restaurants and inns in the small villages dotting the shore are among California's best.

■ TRAVEL BASICS

Getting There
This rugged stretch of coast has no freeways. US 101, the closest four-lane highway, runs far inland along the valleys lying between the two main north/south ridges of the Coast Ranges. CA 1, a narrow, twisty, two-lane road runs along the coast from Marin County north to Mendocino County. The road is most difficult to drive at the southern and northern stretches, where it crosses the spine of the coastal mountains, and between Jenner and Fort Ross, where a spur of the mountains pushes west into the sea. This is not a road for travelers in a hurry.

There are two inland valleys where we encourage you to linger, not because the road is difficult, but because all along them are vineyards and wineries to visit.

To drive more quickly to an area described in this chapter, follow US 101 north of San Francisco and take a side road across to the coast (see map on page 101).

Climate

Summer days here can be sunny and warm, but more often they are windy and cool, or foggy and cold. Yet, just inland up the coastal valleys, it can be dramatically warmer, the hills burned a golden brown and the air filled with the aromas of bay trees, redwoods, and coyote bush. Fall is warmer and sunnier. Winters are wet and wild with rainfall increasing from 20 inches at Bodega Bay to 40 inches in Mendocino. Yet, it's fair to say that many winter days along this coast are brilliantly sunny. **Water Temperature:** Cold year-round (50 to 60 degrees) and unsuitable for swimming, except in a wet suit.

Food and Lodging

There are many places on this beautiful coast where you could bring a picnic basket and a tiny portable stove, clamber down a steep, sandy trail to a wild beach, and settle down on the lee side of a small cove. Here you can grill local oysters while pulling apart a loaf of freshly baked bread from a local bakery, and sipping wine from the coastal vineyards of the Russian River or Anderson Valley.

The Sonoma and southern Mendocino coasts are just west of some of the most fertile and interesting farming areas in California. You'll find organic farms, apple orchards, fresh cider, fine wines, and in summertime, succulent tomatoes of every color and taste. Fine cheeses are made here and in many restaurants care is taken with cooking. Expect some surprisingly good food.

This coast has many small, comfortable inns and B&Bs sitting high on coastal bluffs with magnificent views, or tucked into tiny, protected coves or into the quiet back streets of coastal towns and villages. (For **lodging and restaurant listings** see pages 339 to 390.)

■ SONOMA COAST BEACHES

North of Bodega Harbor, Highway 1 winds from Bodega Bay to the mouth of the Russian River and beyond. The beaches along the way are very popular, but they are rarely crowded, and the majority of visitors come for only a few hours, to lie in the sun or watch the surf. There are more than 40 parking areas with beach access along Highway 1 (most of them free).

The best of these beaches is **Goat Rock,** just south of the Russian River mouth, which is connected to the shore by a low spit (that is, unfortunately, topped with a parking lot). Sweeping views up and down the coast more than make up for the uninspired shore facilities. Murrelets, cormorants, and gulls coast above the surf and seals haul out on sandbars. Arch Rock, a few hundred yards offshore, supports a colony of cormorants, gulls, and other seabirds. Even though the gray-green water is considered unsafe for swimming, on warm summer days many intrepid folk of all ages brave the surf (and not just surfers in wet suits either). Perhaps they're inspired by the way those tiny murrelets and auklets roll with the breaks.

■ JENNER

The village of Jenner clings to the cliffs of the north bank of the Russian River. Jenner, once a bustling bedroom community for local loggers, is best known today for its cliffside restaurants and inns. East of Jenner, Highway 116 and River Road lead to the vineyards and wineries of the lower Russian River Valley, which are well worth a short detour.

Schooners loading from apron chutes at Mendocino Harbor in 1865.

Giant redwoods once grew densely on the Russian River floodplain and along the coastal bluffs north to Oregon. From the 1850s on, the trees were cut and shipped to San Francisco on small sailing schooners from tiny ports known as "dog holes" because they were "barely large enough for a dog to turn around in and chase its tail." Because storms on the North Coast are too fierce to allow long piers to survive, ships had to be loaded by more creative means—usually by some Rube Goldberg–type contraption of poles and wires that ran the logs from the shore to the frail schooners waiting offshore.

The schooners, of course, were only as good as their skippers—most of whom were of Scandinavian Viking stock, undaunted by such minor disturbances as storm-tossed, rocky shores, invisible underwater rocks, and riptides. Usually the names of mariners from the skipper to lowliest sailor were Scandinavian: Ahlstrom,

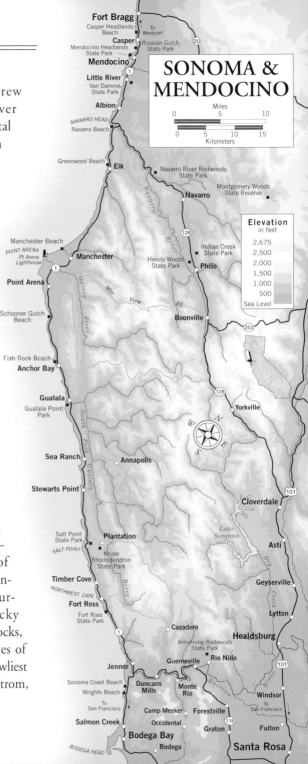

SONOMA & MENDOCINO

Miles
0   5   10

0   5   10   15
Kilometers

Elevation
in feet
2,675
2,500
2,000
1,500
1,000
500
Sea Level

Bellesen, Bergmark, etc. By 1900, Finns were the largest foreign-born group in Mendocino County. Today, Americans of Scandinavian descent own many of the farms on the North Coast. There are still redwoods in the valleys, though in reduced numbers. But even in prehistoric times not all of the coast was covered by redwoods. Many headlands had meadows and groves of pines and cypresses (as you can judge by the size and age of those trees). The pines and cypresses survived, because they produced inferior lumber. Their windswept, gnarled forms add a dramatic touch to the coastal landscape.

SONOMA & MENDOCINO

■ RUSSIAN RIVER WINERY TOUR

Northern Sonoma County is going through a boom of vineyard planting in the valleys and on the ridges near the coast, often just above the fog belt but within reach of cooling sea breezes. (Wine giants Gallo and Kendall Jackson are both planting grapes near the Sonoma coast.) Look for some exciting wines to come from the Sonoma coast as the vines reach maturity.

(preceding pages) Dairy farms are a common feature of the landscape along the coast of northern Sonoma and southern Mendocino Counties.

The Russian River enters the ocean at Jenner, but you'll look in vain for vineyards on the grassy seaward slopes. Summer days are simply too chilly here to properly ripen grapes. You'll have to drive inland and upriver, through the redwoods to where the valley widens into a rolling mini-plain, to visit the Russian River vineyards. Even though this valley can get quite warm in summer, it is cooled by fogs rolling up the Russian River as far east as Healdsburg. This combination of hot and cool summer days and nights puts lots of complex flavors into grapes and favors such cool-climate varieties as chardonnay and pinot noir. But cabernet sauvignon and sauvignon blanc ripen well on the higher slopes, above the fog belt, and zinfandel produces elegant and complex wines as well.

On your drive upriver on Highway 116, you'll pass through the riverside resort towns of Monte Rio and Guerneville, where Highway 116 turns south and crosses the Russian River on its way to Sebastopol. Don't take that turn; continue straight through town on River Road to Rio Nido. Just east of Rio Nido, the valley opens up and you'll see your first winery, Korbel Champagne Cellars, on your left. You can stop here now, or bypass Korbel for the time being. It will make a great end to your trip. Don't plan to stop at more than three wineries in one day.

———•◆•———

■ Korbel Champagne Cellars

This winery is a visitor's delight, with its 19th-century buildings, including a tower built to house a still, and extensive rose gardens in the beautifully landscaped grounds. The tour—considered by many to be the best in Sonoma County—will give you a very good idea of how sparkling wine is made. It includes a display of wine memorabilia and old photographs. In 1977, the winery added a microbrewery and deli (west of the tasting room) to its complex. Korbel's deli is a great place for a snack before you drive back to the coast. *13250 River Rd., Guerneville; 707-887-2294.*

❖

If you're planning to have a picnic, the deli

counter at Speer's Market has all the fixings you'd ever want, plus a great selection of local wines. *A few blocks off River Rd. at 7891 Mirabel Rd.; 707-887-2024.*

❖

Return to River Road and turn right. Turn right again at Trenton Road and then left at the T and follow Laguna Road to Martini & Prati.

■ Martini & Prati

Martini & Prati is the last old-fashioned Italian "redwood winery" in Sonoma County, and it's the last winery where you can have a jug of red wine filled from a cask. Modern health department regulations make this a bit more complicated than it was in the old days, when you could just bring your own container and fill it with wine from a barrel. You'll buy a jug at the tasting room, which you'll take to the winery's only stainless steel cask (it's made from sturdy, air-proof steel to allow the remaining wine to stay fresh under nitrogen pressure as jugs are siphoned off). This jug wine is a bargain for the price. If you're planning a long trip, you might want to fill several jugs from the cask and take them along for picnics (store them in the trunk of your car). The winery has a "museum" tour of its old facilities—old screw-operated wine presses, open-top concrete fermenting vats, and redwood aging barrels of the kind you no longer see at other wineries. Outdated as this equipment now seems, keep in mind that most wineries once used them, and that it was the wine made in old-fashioned wineries like Martini & Prati that first put California wines on the map. *2191 Laguna Rd., Santa Rosa; 707-823-2404.*

■ Joseph Swan Vineyards

By retracing your steps on Laguna Road, you'll find this winery started by the legendary Joseph Swan who made some of the first world-class pinot noirs in California, as well as superb chardonnays and zinfandels. It is now run by his daughter and son-in-law. The wines are as good as ever and well worth a stop. The zinfandels can be more complex and have greater depth than first-rate Bordeaux reds. *Open weekends only; 2916 Laguna Rd., Forestville; 707-573-3747.*

■ Mark West Estate

Return to River Road and cross it. Continue on Trenton-Healdsburg Road. A short drive will bring you to this winery on a knoll to the left of the road, where Kerry Damsky, formerly of the Gauer Estate Winery, makes the wine. There are some fine chardonnays and pinot noirs to taste here, as well as excellent gewürztraminers. Call for hours. The winery borders on Mark West Creek and has a beautiful picnic area, plus a deli where you can stock up on food to enjoy with your wine. California Carnivores, a unique collection of flesh-eating plants tucked into a greenhouse behind the winery buildings, is a must-see, especially if you've brought your kids along. *7010 Trenton-Healdsburg Rd., Forestville; 707-544-4813.*

GEWÜRZTRAMINER
RUSSIAN RIVER VALLEY
VINTAGE 1996

Turn left after leaving the winery and drive to the junction of the Trenton-Healdsburg and Eastside Roads. Turn right, then left at the junction with the Old Redwood Highway. You'll see two wineries on the left just after the turn: J Wine Company and Rodney Strong.

1994 Estate Bottled

FOPPIANO
Vineyards

Petite Sirah
Russian River Valley
ALC. 13.5% BY VOL.

■ **J Wine Company**
This winery makes some exquisite bubbly. *11447 Old Redwood Hwy., Healdsburg; 707-431-5400.*

■ **Rodney Strong Vineyards**
Started by former ballet dancer Rodney Strong as "Sonoma Vineyards" in 1961 and renamed in 1984, this vineyard is known for its beautifully landscaped grounds and well respected for its chardonnay, cabernet sauvignon, and reserve pinot noir. *11455 Old Redwood Hwy., Healdsburg; 707-433-6521.*

■ **Foppiano Vineyards**
Up the road from J stands one of the area's oldest and most respected wineries. Owned and operated by the same family since 1896, Foppiano is a pioneer—and master—of California petite syrah. It also produces other excellent reds, including cabernet sauvignon. *12707 Old Redwood Hwy., Healdsburg; 707-433-7272.*

■ **Healdsburg: Town and Restaurants**
Continue north on the Old Redwood Highway to US 101. Take the freeway north to the next exit, Healdsburg Avenue, and follow that street into Healdsburg, a good place to break for lunch. Several excellent restaurants are on or near the plaza. Best of all, you'll get to choose from a great variety of foods. You can enjoy rustic, hearty fare at the Bear Republic Brewing Co. (345 Healdsburg Ave.) elegantly prepared food at Bistro Ralph (109 Plaza St.), or the recently opened Oakville Grocery (124 Matheson), which is not only a deli but also has take-out food and a patio dining area. See "LODGING & RESTAURANTS," page 351-352 for more details.

Drive back (south) on Healdsburg Avenue to Mill Street, which turns into Westside Road after it crosses under the US 101 freeway. Immediately after the freeway underpass look for the sign on the left (south) side of the road directing you to Alderbrook.

SONOMA &
MENDOCINO

■ **Alderbrook Winery**

This small winery is surrounded by chardonnay vineyards, from which it produces an excellent estate wine, but in recent years it has also become well known for its sauvignon blanc, cabernet sauvignon, and zinfandel. Alderbrook has an excellent culinary program, designed to match wine and food (inquire at the tasting room). *2306 Magnolia Dr., Healdsburg; 707-433-9154.*

❖

Return to Westside Road and turn left. Westside Road is one of the Wine Country's prettiest drives, as it winds its idyllic way along the western slopes of the Russian River Valley, past oak woods and vineyards. From here to where the road runs into River Road at Hacienda, just east of Rio Nido, you're rarely out of sight of vineyards. One stretch of hilly cow pastures has just been planted with vines by Gallo. Wineries, too, are strung out along this road (well marked by signs).

■ **Armida**

This winery has a beautiful hilltop location, with great views of the Russian River Valley. The wines— chardonnay, merlot, and pinot noir—match the view. *2201 Westside Rd., Healdsburg; 707-433-2222.*

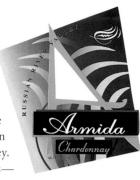

■ **Rabbit Ridge Vineyards**

This small winery, owned by Belvedere winemaker Erich Russell, produces a large variety of different wines, and most of them are well made, especially the "Super-Tuscan" reds and the chardonnay. *3291 Westside Rd., Healdsburg; 707-431-7128.*

■ **Belvedere**

This winery is known mainly for its Russian River and Alexander Valley chardonnays and its Dry Creek Valley zinfandel. *4035 Westside Rd., Healdsburg; 707-433-8236.*

■ Hop Kiln

A unique feature of this small winery, founded in 1973 by Dr. Martin "Marty" Griffin, is that it was built in and around a historic hop kiln without destroying any of the kiln's equipment. Thus you'll find wine stored in the old ovens (kept cool by their thick stone walls) and strange pipes and railroad tracks running through the winery. The wines are mostly estate grown and include such rare varietals as valdiguié and verveux. Your best bet for a picnic on the winery's sunny grounds is a wine appropriately called Marty Griffin's Big Red. *6050 Westside Rd., Healdsburg; 707-433-6491.*

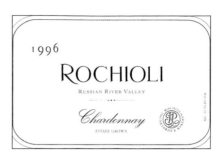

■ Rochioli Vineyards & Winery

The small parking lot of Rochioli is immediately west of Hop Kiln, on the same side of the road. The Rochiolis became winegrowers in 1933, when they took over vineyards planted in the 19th century and planted new vines of their own on gravelly benchlands above the Russian River. After decades of selling their grapes to local wineries, the Rochiolis started making their own wine in 1982. Production is small, but the wines are worth stopping for. Considering their farm background, it is not surprising that Joe and Tom Rochioli believe in letting the vineyard determine the quality of the wine (of course, they know they have just the right vineyard for this). Because of the cool growing conditions, the flavors of their pinot noir, cabernet sauvignon, chardonnay, and sauvignon blanc (from old vines) are intense and complex. The tasting room patio, shaded by roses, is a great place for sipping wine and enjoying the view across the Russian River vineyards. *6192 Westside Rd., Healdsburg; 707-433-2305.*

■ Davis Bynum

From the road, this place looks more like a summer retreat in the woods than a serious winery, but once you've made it past the white entrance cottages and tasted the wines, you'll agree that this winery's reputation is well-deserved. The winery was founded by Davis Bynum in 1965 in an

SONOMA & MENDOCINO

Albany storefront and moved to its present location in 1973. Bynum was the first to make pinot noir exclusively from Russian River grapes and has championed local grapes ever since. Quality has kept up with the expansion of production. Besides pinot noir, be sure to taste the merlot, the zinfandel, the fumé blanc, and the gewürztraminer. *8075 Westside Rd., Healdsburg; 707-433-5852.*

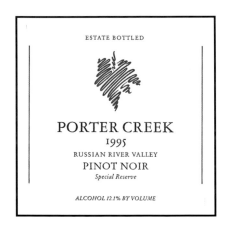

ESTATE BOTTLED

PORTER CREEK

1995

RUSSIAN RIVER VALLEY

PINOT NOIR

Special Reserve

ALCOHOL 12.1% BY VOLUME

■ **Porter Creek**
You'll have to look closely to find this tiny winery on the north side of the road. Watch for the inviting sign after a sharp bend near the new Gallo vineyard plantings. If there weren't an inviting sign out front, you might never take this place for a winery. It's a very small family farm that also happens to make very good wine. All the grapes are estate grown. Compare the hillside pinot noir with the creekside pinot noir to taste which one you prefer. The chardonnay is made from hillside grapes

only and has a very Burgundian character. *8735 Westside Rd., Healdsburg; 707-433-6321.*

Follow Westside Road to its end and turn right (west) where it merges with River Road in a grove of redwoods, and you'll shortly be back at the winery you passed on your drive up the valley, Korbel Champagne Cellars.

Other Russian River wines to look for, from wineries too small to be open to the public, include **Acorn, Williams-Selyem,** and **Bannister Wines** (a tiny winery with superb chardonnay, from Russian River grapes and zinfandel from Russian River and Dry Creek grapes). Look for these wines in local stores.

If you don't return to the coast, consider having dinner (and a comfortable stay) at Guerneville's Applewood Inn & Restaurant (see page 350), just south of the Russian River on Highway 116. The food here is great: Chef David Frakes, who learned his craft from Gary Danko (of San Francisco's Ritz Carlton fame), has been gaining high praise ever since he took over the inn's kitchen in early 1997.

Applewood is close enough to the coast to allow you to have dinner here and still take a leisurely drive back to the seashore. Owner Jim Caron is also exceptionally knowledgeable about Russian River wines. Ask him for his recommendations and you can't go wrong.

School outing at Fort Ross.

■ FORT ROSS

The Russians established their largest settlement in California, Fort Ross, north of the Russian River in 1812, to grow food for their Alaskan forts and to hunt sea otters with the help of Aleut hunters who had been brought south with their *bidarkas,* the first sea kayaks on the California coast. The sea otter was almost exterminated by the mid-1800s. They started making a healthy comeback in the 1930s.

Fort Ross saw many ups and downs, even after it became a state park. At one time, Highway 1 ran right through the middle of the fort. The road was diverted, and the fort enclosed by a palisade, after arson destroyed the fort's Russian-Orthodox chapel. Today it has been fully restored. In summer, rangers demonstrate aspects of Russian life on the coast in the early 19th century.

■ TIMBER COVE TO SALT POINT

The highway runs almost straight over the coastal terraces north of **Timber Cove,** which once was a dog hole port but now has a well-weathered lodge with a restaurant that's a local favorite. The Timber Cove Inn is also noted for its 85-foot-high concrete and mosaic statue of *Peace* (1960) the last finished work by noted Bay Area sculptor Beniamino Bufano.

North of Timber Cove, the coast turns quiet and rustic. **Salt Point State Park** south of Gualala is one of my favorite places on the coast. It's a great expanse of wildflower meadows, beaches, cliffs, and forest, with some of the coast's most spectacularly sculpted Bishop pines and fascinating tidepools. It is a hiker's, artist's, and diver's paradise. Be sure to reserve campsites well ahead of time; this state park is very popular, especially in summer.

More than any other place on the coast, it reminds me of an ancient Chinese garden with its combination of rocks and pines, secluded coves (which have the feel of seaside courtyards), and seasonal flowers. This feeling is heightened by the moldering signs of a "lost civilization," as the remnants of this once booming mill town and lumber port (at Gerstle Cove and elsewhere in the park) are being slowly reclaimed by nature.

This is a place for sitting quietly in a meadow, or dangling your feet over a bluff, or listening to the shrill cries of oystercatchers rising above the roar of the surf; it's a place to contemplate the meaning of life—and the ridiculous frailness of the human existence.

If you see men (mostly older men) clambering over rocks, carrying short poles which they poke into nooks and crevices, you are watching a local sport called "poke poling." Critics might call it the pursuit of the "unspeakable edible," for the object of the hunt is the monkey-faced eel, a rather homely blenny that actually tastes rather good when properly prepared. Poke poling, a custom which appears to be restricted to the California coast, may be encountered from the central coast north, but on these rocky shores it is practiced the most.

Beyond Salt Point the Coast Highway winds its way north past the Sea Ranch development and the town of Gualala to a wilder area of coastal terraces, meadows, and steep cliffs, with the ever-pounding surf to the west, and wooded slopes to the east. Farmhouses and weathered barns, half-hidden by climbing pink roses or multi-hued flower gardens, break the lulling wave pattern of the meadows. Hawks circle overhead or sit on fence posts, waiting for road kill to happen. There is some beach access at Sea Ranch and at the Gualala River, more at Arena Cove. These

Highway 1 along the North Coast affords spectacular views of the rugged coastline.

vast grasslands were the northernmost Mexican land grants on the coast, made just before California was taken over by the United States.

Eventually the highway emerges from a draw, and you find yourself on the narrow, busy main street of **Point Arena,** a small farm town that turns its back to the sea. Point Arena has not changed much over the last decades, except for an influx of artists who could no longer afford the ever-rising rents of the artist colony of Mendocino. But Point Arena is much more sophisticated than you'd expect a simple farm town to be: it has an excellent restaurant (Pangaea), a coffeehouse, bookstore, theater, and several excellent art galleries.

A narrow, one-mile-long road runs from the south end of town to the Arena Cove wharf. Just off the short beach, murres fish in the surf. When I last ate lunch there, at The Galley, I was lucky enough to snag a window table. The view is limited by the steep rock walls of the cove, but between watching the fisherman on the wharf and the offshore birds, it's quite interesting. My meal was superb—fish 'n chips made with fresh local rockfish. I could also have enjoyed my fish sauteed in garlic butter, poached in broth, or blackened Cajun-style.

The cove also has a pizza parlor (Cosmic Pizza, "it's out of this world") and an inn. A charter outfit at the wharf offers full-day and half-day rockfishing excursions.

Curiously, Point Arena, two miles west of town, was named by British explorer George Vancouver who noticed the sandy spit jutting out into the ocean and decided to give it a Spanish name, since the area was controlled by Spain at the time (*arena* means "sandy" in Spanish). It seems almost hard to believe that inconspicuous Point Arena, with its lighthouse, is one of the westernmost points in the contiguous United States.

■ Manchester State Beach

Sand is certainly in evidence at Manchester State Beach. The parking area is surrounded by sand—in the form of drifts and dunes. It's only when you get to the edge of the dunes (past the signs that say DANGER, GO BACK) that you realize the dunes are sitting on low bluffs above the beach. Figuring out how enough of the beach sand got to the top of the bluffs to form dunes seems easier at times than figuring out how to get down to the sandy beach. But there are surf fishermen

SONOMA & MENDOCINO

down there, so you know it can be done. Fishermen can't fly. Eventually, the trail, which becomes more sandy as you trudge along (and the sand gets deeper), winds all the way down to the beach. Once you're on the beach you may have problems deciding whether it's more fun to watch the fishermen perform an esoteric dance in which the deliberate motion of their fishing pole tips appears to play a ceremonial role; or the sanderlings, as they dash in and out of the waves; or the sea lions sleeping just offshore, beyond the surf line, one flipper lazily reaching for the sky. You half expect a sanderling or fisherman to be swept off by a wave, or for a sleeping sea lion to wash up on the shore, but it won't happen. All the performers in this nature ballet are too much in control. They forestall their impending doom with the flap of a flipper, the beat of wings, or a quick dash to dry ground to avoid an oncoming wave. In the midst of all this excitement, willets slowly prod the sand into giving up edibles.

You wouldn't want to swim (or even surf) at this rough beach with its nasty northern exposure, but you can take long walks, all the way out to the sandy point to the south, or north to the mouth of the Garcia River.

At the sandy beach below the bluff, several black oystercatchers, who seem to have forgotten that the field guide clearly states that oystercatchers hang out on "rocky shores," perform courtly dances that seem to have come straight from the court of Louis XIV, before taking to the air with shrill, raucous cries that would do any street urchin proud. On the gravelly part of the beach, a pair of ruddy turnstones, in black and gray off-season coloration, do what they are expected to do: they turn over flotsam and jetsam in search of food. One will flip a beer can looking for a beach hopper to gobble; another will flip a piece of Styrofoam twice its size high into the air and devour the amphipods hiding on its shaded side.

■ ELK AND NAVARRO BEACH

Elk, a weather-beaten clifftop hamlet, has been turned into a rustic B&B strip mall by urban refugees eager to exchange the daily drudgery of office work for the weekend drudgery of serving breakfasts and changing sheets. They have to work much harder than innkeepers to the north and south because the scenery just isn't that spectacular and there aren't many hiking trails.

Nearby **Navarro Beach** is a "real place," quiet, despite its proximity to Highway 1 and to Highway 128, the main connector road from US 101 at Cloverdale to

the coast, and despite the presence of a couple of dilapidated motorhomes, a run-down VW bus, and a beat-up pick-up camper. You can reach it by a narrow (and unmarked), paved road that branches off Highway 1 just south of the Navarro River bridge. The beach has primitive campsites, bluffs splashed with colorful wildflowers, offshore sea stacks with seabird colonies, and flocks of goldfinches which feed on thistle seeds and almost settle on your shoulder as you hike along the base of the bluffs. Despite a touch of grunginess, this is the kind of down-home neighborhood beach you could once find up and down the California coast.

The people camping here are civilized. They might drink a bottle of Husch gewürztraminer with their dinner of grilled fish. Which serves as a reminder that a short side trip up the Navarro River will take you through redwood groves to the Anderson Valley wine country (see page 122).

■ MENDOCINO RIVIERA

After Point Reyes, the Mendocino Riviera, which starts north of the Navarro River, may well be the most beautiful part of the North Coast. This wildly sculpted stretch of rocky headlands, sea stacks, sea caves, blowholes, and sandy beaches looks in places as though Coyote, the creator, had enjoyed a few too many bottles of wine as he went about his work. This stretch of coast gets more sunshine than the parks farther south because the fog banks tend to stay a mile or so offshore, making local beaches pleasantly warm. For this reason it is also very popular with urban escapees and can be quite crowded in summer. Be sure to make inn and campsite reservations well ahead of time.

After winding around rocky headlands and in and out of deep gulches, the Coast Highway runs on top of gently undulating sea terraces all the way to the Ten Mile River north of Fort Bragg. Most of the creeks are spanned by bridges, making for easy, relaxed driving without forcing you down into dank gullies (as the highway sometimes does on the Sonoma coast).

The day draws to a close on a Mendocino beach.

■ ALBION

Today, there's little to tell that this hamlet was a major mill town during the height of the redwood timber boom. The Albion River Inn, north of the river, on the ocean side of the highway, has great food and great views, as it did in the old days, but it's a safe bet that it has a lot less excitement than it did in those rowdy times of steam schooner skippers and loggers with caulked boots.

■ VAN DAMME STATE PARK

This small, sandy cove, where the Little River (one of several coastal rivers with that name) empties into the ocean, once had several shipyards where coastal schooners were turned out assembly-line fashion right on the beach. Now, there are campgrounds and miles of hiking trails up the creek, where a large lumber mill once stood. No traces remain of this 19th-century industrial glory, except for a mooring bolt in an offshore rock. This beach is very popular with scuba divers and has an annual abalone festival. For information call the Van Damme State Park Visitor Center at *707-937-4016.*

The view from the Albion River Inn extends out over the coast.

The quaint town of Mendocino is a favorite weekend getaway.

■ MENDOCINO

Whenever I approach this picturesque clifftop village, I'm beguiled anew by the pleasing view: the bridge over the river set off by a wall of dark conifers and the broad sandy beach at the mouth of the Big River. Above the flower-bedecked bluffs spread the green meadows of the headlands, overtowered by a finely crafted white church with a pointed steeple. On one side stands the large "goat lady's" house, where well into the 1970s a local woman lived and kept a flock of goats. Behind the church are the false-fronted business houses of Main Street. Nothing expresses the spirit of this place more than the fact that they look out to sea across an expanse of wildflowers, past cliffs where gnarled Bishop pines appear to rise straight from the sea.

Mendocino was founded in 1852, as a lumber town. After the local mill closed down in the 1930s, Mendocino fell into an economic slumber, which helped preserve its old buildings and water towers. It was rediscovered in the 1950s by artists looking for pretty scenery and low housing prices. By the 1960s and 1970s, the village was being invaded by weekend travelers, many of whom liked the community so much they wanted to settle down. But the new generation of "locals," worried about exchanging their newly discovered rustic lifestyle for yet another Sea Ranch–style version of exurbia, forestalled a major development on the headlands by having the meadows and bluffs surrounding the village turned into a state park. Since its establishment in 1974, **Mendocino Headlands State Park** has attracted almost a million visitors a year. Even so, its miles of cliffside trails are rarely crowded. Wildflowers cover the bluffs in spring; gray whales swim past the headlands in fall and spring, on their annual migration; the birdwatching is great the year-round. Several small but high offshore islands serve as refuges for cliff-dwelling shore and seabirds like cormorants, murres, murrelets, storm-petrels, oystercatchers, turnstones, and gulls.

I have fond memories of Mendocino, because I showed my artwork at galleries here back in the early 1970s, when I sketched most of the village's venerable pine trees, cypresses, and homes. What attracts artists is the beauty of the scenery and the special quality of the light. The color of the water can be extraordinary, ranging from indigo and turquoise to silver, slate-gray, and even brown; the headlands can change from golden to dark purple to deep red to pale ash almost in the blink of the eye. Only the black oystercatchers and their bright scarlet bills never change—they look the same whether they probe dark beach rocks for mussels and limpets, or whether they are sitting out a particularly vicious high tide on the upper edges of the headlands cliffs.

While many of the artists who made Mendocino famous have escaped the steady crush of visitors by moving south to Point Arena or north to Fort Bragg, the **Artists Co-op of Mendocino** (Main near Woodward) is still the best place for buying local art. The workshops and classes taught at the **Mendocino Art Center** are very popular; *45200 Little Lake Street; 707-937-5818.*

❖

Mendocino provides one of those relaxing environments where you relish reading a good book in a comfortable inn, then pulling on a heavy coat and wandering the bluffs. The headlands, with their meadows and cliff-edge trails, are quite definitely the place to go for a long thoughtful stroll. On a clear night, you can sit at the edge of a meadow, admiring the brilliance of the stars. (Take a star chart to learn what exactly you're admiring.) Even in the fall, when the grass on the headlands is a silvery brown and blows back and forth in the wind like ruffled bear fur, you can still find a flower or two blooming in its hidden depths—like earthly stars lighting up a hidden world.

Many of the old homes have been converted to B&Bs, with varying degrees of luxury and with generally great breakfasts. Most of the local inns have their own coffee blends, put together by a local roaster. All of them are within easy walking distance of the village's core, with its shops and restaurants. There are some great restaurants here, of which Cafe Beaujolais, the Mendocino Hotel, and the McCallum House may be the best known, but the Mendocino Cafe and the Bay View Cafe are the local favorites.

I've stayed at the Whitegate Inn in the center of the village and at the Agate Cove Inn perched above the rocky cliffs to the north (at breakfast, an osprey perched in a pine outside the dining room window). (Also see pages 358-359.)

Along the quiet streets are a number of historic buildings: the **Temple of Kwan Ti** (1852), the oldest Chinese temple on the North Coast; the **Kelley House** (1861), now a museum (45007 Albion Street); the **Ford House** (1854) on Main Street which now houses the Headlands park headquarters and a historical museum; the **Masonic Lodge** (1866) topped by a sculpture of "time and the maiden" carved from a single redwood log; and the **Mendocino Presbyterian Church** (1868) whose spire rising above the cliffs of the cove is a Mendocino landmark. Trails lead from the back of the church down to Big River Beach. On sunny days, this beach is popular with sunbathers and volleyball players.

Twenty years ago, I paddled up the Big River for the first time, past ancient redwood stumps. Ever since, I've returned to glide upstream in my kayak; nothing much has changed, except that the second-growth trees have grown bigger. Ospreys and kingfishers still sit on snags, herons still wade in the shallows, and the quacking of mallards sounds from a clump of reeds and willows.

Curiously, Mendocino is the only coastal town between San Francisco and Eureka with a large population of street people.

SONOMA &
MENDOCINO

■ ANDERSON VALLEY WINERY TOUR

When you drive up or down the coast on Highway 1, and cross the narrow estuary of the Navarro River, you don't even suspect that there's a sunny valley a few miles upstream where some of California's best wines are made.

Driving inland, on Highway 128, along the north bank of the Navarro River, where tall redwoods grow, you might think this a very quiet, pastoral valley, but Highway 128 is also the main route from the San Francisco Bay Area to the Mendocino Riviera, and traffic can be very hectic. Drivers in a hurry can be exceptionally pushy. But don't let that bother you. Pull over, let the speed freaks pass, and enjoy the idyllic beauty.

The redwoods along this stretch of river are all second-growth (the original trees were cut long ago and floated downstream to waiting schooners), but that doesn't make the trees less beautiful. They've had time to grow up, and the forest cover—dense carpets of green and golden mosses, dark-green clumps of sword ferns, and emerald-green willows—carpets the open spaces between the big trees and lines the streamsides. Look for kingfishers and ospreys in riverside boughs. In season, the river may be thronged with human fishermen as well, when silver salmon and steelhead run upstream.

The **Paul Dimmick Wayside Campground** is in a pretty redwood grove bordering the Navarro River. It's not only a good place for camping in summer (it floods in winter) but has some perfect picnic spots as well. If you want to walk in the shade of more impressive redwoods, head upriver to the wine country, where the virgin redwoods of **Hendy Woods State Park** rise tall above the river. They seem like an anomaly here, because this is a warm part of the valley, but the same fog that creeps upriver to sustain these majestic trees also cools the valley enough to put flavor and complexity into grapes. Ask the rangers to point out the locally famous fallen redwood stump where an eccentric known as the Boonville Hermit used to live.

Coastal redwoods (as opposed to the *Sequoia gigantea* of the Sierra Nevada) can only thrive where sea fogs penetrate inland. Northwest of Boonville, Highway 128 cuts through a low ridge, which is just high enough to impede the sea fog creeping up the Navarro River. North of here the land is much cooler than the southern valley—making it perfect for redwoods, apples, and grapes. The Anderson Valley's best vineyards lie between Philo and Navarro, near the redwoods. Philo, where Rancheria, Anderson, and Indian Creeks merge to form the Navarro River, has long been the center of an apple-growing region—primarily of Gravensteins, which need a cool climate to give their best.

Bob Thompson writes in *The Wine Atlas of California and the Pacific Northwest* that grapes were first planted high on the ridges of the Anderson Valley at the turn of the century, primarily by Italian grape growers, or by farmers making wine for home use. Zinfandel found a unique home here. To quote Thompson: "At their best they are like none other from the variety: dark, lean, firm, balanced, and intensely berry-like in flavor." But these plantings were only known to a few. While some winegrowers, like Ukiah's Parducci family, slowly expanded their Anderson Valley holdings over the years, the valley's wine boom dates only from the early 1970s, when Tony Husch of Husch Vineyards and Ted Bennett of Navarro Vineyards planted gewürztraminer vines in what they considered to be the perfect climate for this finicky Alsatian grape—the cool part of the Anderson Valley. But chardonnay and pinot noir grew even better here—and sold better, so most of the vineyards today are planted with these varieties.

❖

The first winery we'll visit is south of Navarro and on the west side of Highway 128. From there we'll travel south of Philo to **Scharffenberger Cellars**, and then turn around, head back

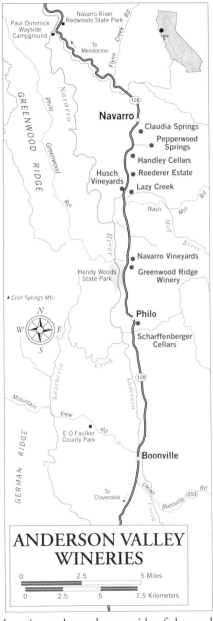

north toward the ocean, and visit the other vineyards on the east side of the road (which we by-passed on our way up-valley).

■ **Husch Vineyards**

Among the top wineries along this route is Husch Vineyards. It's still family-owned—albeit by a different family, the Oswalds, who bought the winery from Tony Husch in 1979. The estate-grown gewürztraminer is about as good as it gets anywhere, and the pinot noir has a distinctly Burgundian structure—as well as that elusive aroma and flavor. *4400 Hwy. 128, Philo; 707-895-3216.*

HUSCH
ESTATE BOTTLED

1994
MENDOCINO
CHARDONNAY

GROWN, PRODUCED AND BOTTLED BY THE H.A. OSWALD FAMILY
TALMAGE, CA, ALCOHOL 13.5% BY VOLUME

■ **Greenwood Ridge**

Because this ridge high above the Anderson Valley (the winery is 1,200 feet above sea level) is the place where Italian vintners planted zinfandel and other red wine grapes early in the 20th century, we expect this winery to produce excellent cabernet sauvignon and merlot; but what's surprising is that it also makes excellent riesling. Look also for sauvignon blanc, zinfandel, and chardonnay. *5501 Hwy. 128, Philo; 707-895-2002.*

■ **Scharffenberger Cellars**

John Scharffenberger firmly placed Anderson Valley among America's top producers

in 1981, and so impressed the French with his bubbly that the champagne producer Roederer moved in next door in 1982, instead of settling in the Napa Valley as other French wine entrepreneurs had done. In 1989, Scharffenberger sold a controlling interest in his winery to another French champagne maker, the house of Pommery. Today, the sparklers of these neighborly wineries consistently rank among the top

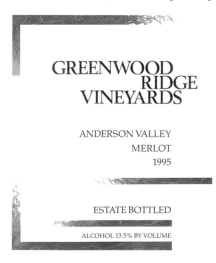

GREENWOOD
RIDGE
VINEYARDS

ANDERSON VALLEY
MERLOT
1995

ESTATE BOTTLED

ALCOHOL 13.5% BY VOLUME

half-dozen produced in North America. The success of the sparkling wines called attention to the excellence of other Anderson Valley wines. *8501 Hwy. 128, Philo; 707-895-2957.*

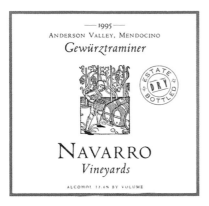

■ **Navarro Vineyards**
Gewürztraminer is the show wine here (the Anderson Valley has amply proved that it can make wines of great class from this difficult grape) and is well worth seeking out. But don't let that tempt you into neglecting the chardonnay and pinot noir, which are also excellent. *5601 Hwy. 128, Philo; 707-895-3686.*

■ **Lazy Creek**
This small winery makes a very drinkable chardonnay, excellent gewürztraminer, and a delightful pinot noir. *4610 Hwy. 128, Philo; 707-895-3623.*

■ **Roederer Estate**
The Roederer Champagne folk from Reims, France, came to the Anderson Val-

ley in 1982 because they had tasted the local sparkling wines and were impressed by the quality. These French-made sparklers are as good (or perhaps even better) than the Champagnois hoped for. *(See also* Scharffenberger, *page 124). 4501 Hwy. 128, Philo; 707-895-2288.*

■ **Claudia Springs**
This small winery makes good chardonnay, pinot noir, and zinfandel from Anderson Valley grapes. Call for directions, open weekends; *Philo; 707-895-3926.*

SONOMA & MENDOCINO

■ **Pepperwood Springs**

There's some very good pinot noir and chardonnay from this winery on the northern slopes of the Anderson Valley. *1200 Holmes Ranch Rd., Philo; 707-895-2920.*

■ **Handley Cellars**

This winery makes not only classic sparkling wines but also highly enjoyable chardonnay, sauvignon blanc, and gewürztraminer, and has been a pioneer in matching local foods to local wines. *3151 Hwy. 128, Philo; 707-895-3876.*

The Anderson Valley is also known for the high quality of fruit it produces. One of the best places for buying locally grown apples and produce and freshly squeezed cider is **Gowan's Oak Tree**. Apples from the orchard; cider made from their own apples; Gowan's ships anywhere in the United States. There's a family picnic area where visitors may linger. *6600 Hwy. 128, Philo; 707-895-3353 or 707-895-3225.*

Nearby **The Apple Farm** sells wonderful chutney, jam, cider syrup, organic apples, and cider, and offers cooking classes taught by Sally Schmitt, who together with her husband, Don, founded the French Laundry in Yountville. The classes are given year-round, and emphasize seasonal ingredients. Call for reservations. There's also a guest room available. *18501 Greenwood Rd., Philo; 707-895-2461.*

By now, you're quite close to the magnificent giants of **Navarro River State Park**. Its cool glades are perfect for a post-prandial stroll. *1810 Hwy. 128, Philo; 707-895-3000.*

■ **Boonville Sights**

If you have the time, you don't need to turn around at Philo, but can continue up-valley to the country town of Boonville, which was once so isolated, locals developed their own dialect, known as "Boontling."

Highway 128 ended Boonville's isolation, and Boontling was soon a "forgotten" language of interest mainly to anthropological linguists, but it still shows up in some local shop signs, like "Horn of Zeese" for "coffeeshop." Boonville has, in fact, become a rather civilized place in recent years, due to the wineries down-valley, several excellent restaurants, and even a microbrewery (with restaurant, of course). The Boonville Hotel and Restaurant is run by John Schmitt (Sally Schmitt's son), whose cooking has a loyal following from diners as far away as San Francisco. The hotel is also living up to its name by having rooms for rent. (See page 342).

What's surprising for a town as small as Boonville, however, is that it has not just one good restaurant but two. The Buckhorn Saloon sits across the highway from the hotel, atop its own brewery, the Anderson Valley Brewing Company (see page 342). The food here is as good as the beer. Boonville's other claims to fame are the annual Apple Show and Sheep Dog Trials held in October. It attracts dogs from all over the state.

To return to the coast from Boonville and the Anderson Valley, follow Highway 128 north all the way to Highway 1.

■ RUSSIAN GULCH AND JUGHANDLE RESERVE

A few miles north of Mendocino is **Russian Gulch State Park,** known for the blowhole through which seawater blasts skyward during storms. It also has wildflower covered bluffs, a cliffside picnic area, and a quiet sandy beach in a rocky cove. Trails lead into the redwood forests of the shady canyon.

❖

A few miles to the north lies **Jughandle State Reserve,** a largely unspoiled slice of coast and mountain. I always enjoy walking out onto the headlands where wildflowers hang over the edge of the bluffs, and cormorants can be seen nesting on an offshore sea stack. Gnarled spruces, pines, and Douglas firs lie at odd angles, broken apart by winter storms. A steep trail leads down to a small beach and another leads up the hill into a landscape known as an "ecological staircase"—a series of five marine terraces which were uplifted over the millennia, with a surprisingly even spacing of about 100,000 years between each uplift, making the lowest terrace—the one with the wildflower meadow and the cliffs—some 100,000 years

Ice plants, which thrive in the coastal fog, turn brilliant colors in the spring.

SONOMA &
MENDOCINO

old and the highest terrace (about 650 feet above sea level) some 500,000 years old. The trail ends at a **pygmy forest**, a dense stand of trees dwarfed by highly acidic soils. Among the unusual trees growing here is the endemic Bolander pine. A two-foot-tall Bolander pine with a trunk one inch in diameter may be 40 or 50 years old; ancient trees may top out at a height of only five or six feet. Carry water when going on this hike—all that uphill climbing makes for a mighty thirst.

■ FORT BRAGG

This very pleasant small town, which started as the headquarters of the short-lived Mendocino Indian Reservation, was, until recently, a major mill town. In the 1990s, Fort Bragg turned itself into a haven for artists, writers, and retirees.

Noyo, the fishing port on the banks of the Noyo River at the south end of town (turn right after the bridge), is about as authentic a gunkhole port as you'll find anywhere. It's all business, with little space devoted to visitor amenities. A couple of seafood restaurants and a motel overlook the river and the docks. Charter boats cater to fishermen. I often stop at a seafood shop here to stock up on the excellent smoked sablefish, salmon, and albacore—the perfect picnic food. Fort Bragg is a town made for walking.

Skunk Train

At the foot of Laurel Street, one block west of Main and a short walk from the North Coast pub, is the terminal for the California Western Railroad "Skunk" Train. It got its name from a smelly gasoline car used in the early years of operation. But now the train has a steam locomotive and an open excursion car. The tracks wind inland above Pudding Creek and the Noyo River, above marshes and through meadows and redwood forests. It's an exhilarating, scenic ride. There's a stop at North Spur, while the engine is switched to the other end of the train and fills its water tank at an old-fashioned railroad water tower. Here, passengers can catch the train across the mountains to Willits, or they can refresh themselves with drinks and snacks. The return trip is even more exhilarating than the journey out; *707-964-6371.*

Redwood logs are transported from the woods using the Excelsior Redwood Company railroad in 1892, near Mendocino. (Courtesy of Peter E. Palmquist, Eureka)

■ MACKERRICHER STATE PARK

In its heyday, the local lumber company had a private haul road which ran from the mill north to the Ten Mile River. This road, as well as the eight miles of cliffs, meadows, and beaches lying between it and the ocean, is now part of the state park—the main entrance and campgrounds are about three miles north of Fort Bragg. The road now serves as a foot and bicycle trail. I like to walk it from the beach beneath the old Pudding Creek trestle on the north end of town. This sandy beach borders the favorite local swimming hole, because the shallow waters of the creek get quite warm by afternoon. If I have time, I wander along the bluffs to Laguna Creek where trails lead down from a series of low cliffs to tidepools and small sandy beaches.

The last time I visited, I stood watching oystercatchers perform their courtship flights, and I let a killdeer believe that I was fooled by its feigned injury. I looked carefully where I trod, because killdeer eggs look so much like rocks, it's easy to accidentally step on them. Birds were everywhere that evening. As I dawdled along, the sun began to set, and the sky and the land turned golden. Soon the entire landscape was clothed in pure gold—the bluffs, the surf, the pines, and the birds. But I could still distinguish the species by their shape and song: black oystercatchers on the rocks and on the sand of a pocket beach, little killdeer running along the surf line, mourning doves on the trail, and white-crowned sparrows in the shrubbery. A hawk circled overhead before gliding off to a copse of tall cypress trees. At Laguna Point, even the harbor seals had taken on a golden sheen. I took the raised wooden boardwalk (which makes the Point wheelchair accessible) to the parking lot and walked back to my lodgings in the deepening gold of the sunset.

A sandy beach stretches north from Laguna Point toward the Ten Mile River. Here and there, the broad strand is interrupted by rocky outcroppings and backed by sand dunes. Harbor seals and their pups loll on the rocks, utterly unafraid of the presence of man.

Before entering the Pacific, Laguna Creek passes through Lake Cleone, a large, reedy pond popular with fishermen.

■ WESTPORT

Westport is the last village on this stretch of coast. The once-bustling town now consists of little more than a store, a post office, and a few houses clustered around a wide spot in the road. A few miles farther north, **Westport-Union Landing State Beach** allows for beach access and primitive camping atop the windswept bluffs west of the highway. The water here is too cold and turbulent for swimming, but the beach makes for great fishing and beachcombing. During spring and summer, fishermen catch spawning surf smelt here with A-frame dipnets.

Somehow this beach seems wilder, more raw than beaches to the south or north —perhaps because it is always swept by winds or fog, or perhaps because offshore rocks look sharp, like the giant fangs of some sub-littoral monster. Yet it is beautiful, in an austere, almost feral way, like a place the ancient Gaelic bards might have sung about.

A few miles north of the state beach, the final stretch of Highway 1 veers inland before it dumps into US 101, cut off from the shore by tall cliffs rising straight from the sea.

California poppy is the state flower and is common along the state's entire coast.

SONOMA &
MENDOCINO

REDWOOD COAST

■ HIGHLIGHTS

Sinkyone Wilderness
Lost Coast
Eel River Delta
Humboldt Bay
Trinidad
Patrick's Point State Park
Redwood National Park
Klamath River
Crescent City
Lake Earl

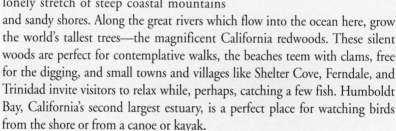

REDWOOD COAST

Direction of travel in this chapter is south to north

Eureka

San Francisco

Los Angeles

San Diego

■ TRAVEL OVERVIEW

Only a few towns brave the wildness of this lonely stretch of steep coastal mountains and sandy shores. Along the great rivers which flow into the ocean here, grow the world's tallest trees—the magnificent California redwoods. These silent woods are perfect for contemplative walks, the beaches teem with clams, free for the digging, and small towns and villages like Shelter Cove, Ferndale, and Trinidad invite visitors to relax while, perhaps, catching a few fish. Humboldt Bay, California's second largest estuary, is a perfect place for watching birds from the shore or from a canoe or kayak.

■ TRAVEL BASICS

Climate

Rainfall along this section of the coast averages from just under 40 inches per year at Fort Bragg and Eureka to almost 80 inches near the Oregon border and along the Lost Coast near Shelter Cove. Summers are almost perpetually foggy and cold—the temperature has rarely exceeded 75 degrees during July in Fort Bragg and Eureka. Fall is the clearest and warmest season, but the rains begin sooner and end later than they do below Mendocino, and even October and May can be very rainy months. Tremendous winter gales lash the coastline between November and April. **Water Temperature:** Water is frigid year-round (45–60 degrees).

Food and Lodging

California's northwestern corner is blessed with a bountiful supply of natural foods. You can buy fresh rockfish, salmon, shrimp, and Dungeness crab from bay and ocean at waterfront seafood markets in Eureka, Trinidad, or Crescent City. Cultivated oysters from Arcata Bay are for sale along the Eureka waterfront.

The land, too, will tempt you with its seasonal bounty: strawberries in spring; blackberries, raspberries, and huckleberries in summer; cranberries and apples in autumn. Wild hazelnuts grow in streamside thickets and moist woods. Mushrooms are plentiful in the woods in the wet seasons, but leave the picking to the experts. It's better to buy them at a local farmers market than to be sorry (many poisonous varieties are difficult to discern from edibles.)

Cows munch contentedly on the lush green pastures of the Eel and Mad River estuaries— which in turn makes their milk uncommonly rich and puts an extra morsel of flavor into the cheeses produced locally at the Loleta Cheese Factory. But goats, too, thrive in the mild coastal climate, as the tangy goat milk cheeses from Cypress Grove in McKinleyville amply prove.

All of the small and large towns of the region have bakeries where you can buy fresh bread to go with your fruit, cheese, or seafood. Many restaurants have a knack preparing the best and freshest of the region's foods.

Lodgings in this region tend to be comfortable rather than luxurious (though this coast, too, has its gaggle of overstuffed B&Bs). But what you lose in luxury, you more than make up for in spectacular views and in quiet walks through the woods. But camping is king here, and you'll find plenty of places to pitch a tent. (See **lodging and restaurant listings** on pages 338-390.)

REDWOOD COAST

REDWOOD COAST

■ LAND OF MIST AND WILD SCENERY

Sea gulls cry as they wheel above the surf, which seems to have the consistency and color of thick cream on this calm morning. The sun, muted by the shroud of fog clinging to the jagged ridge of the coastal hills to the east, lightens up the shore and sea with deeply golden rays, making the gulls and the surf spray look almost supernaturally bright against the dull indigo of the ocean. To the south, coastal terraces and low hills spread as far as the eye can see; to the north, steep cliffs and tall mountains—their seaward side still cloaked in gloom—rise straight from the Pacific. The piercing cries of black oystercatchers rise from the tidal rocks below my vantage point, as the scarlet-billed birds probe the rough, kelp-swathed surface for mussels and limpets.

I have pulled off the road to look at the spectacular scenery where CA 1, the Coast Highway, turns inland, away from the shore. Fog swirls past rocky outcroppings and precariously poised patches of trees, alternately veiling and baring the mysterious faces of the rugged sea cliffs. Looking north along the rocky escarpment, it's easy to see why, so far, no more than a narrow dirt road has penetrated the wilderness ahead. The mountains are too steep, and the cliffs, their bases constantly gnawed by the surf, are too unstable.

This coast looks like a different land from the gentle coastal terraces and river bottoms of the Mendocino Riviera, which stretches from the Navarro River north to Fort Bragg. It looks like a lost world—and in many ways it is.

Called the Lost Coast because it is so remote and difficult to access, the 100-mile stretch of shore between Rockport and the mouth of the Eel River is the loneliest stretch of coast in California. It is bypassed by both US 101 and CA 1 and is touched by paved roads in only a few places—at Shelter Cove; at the mouth of the Mattole River; along a four-mile stretch of beach south of Cape Mendocino; and at Centerville Park west of Ferndale.

Don't, by the way, look for the place called "Rockport" shown on your map. It no longer exists, but persists on maps because it conveniently marks the place where the Coast Highway leaves the shore.

Mist spun from an offshore fog bank rises with an onshore breeze into a transparent pastel pallette of sky along the California coast.

■ LOST COAST

The northern Mendocino County coast, from Rockport to just south of Shelter Cove, is a beautiful, albeit almost impenetrable, wilderness of steep-sided gorges, roaring creeks, burbling brooks, dense forests, razorback ridges, sheer cliffs, and quiet sandy and rocky beaches.

The 7,312-acre stretch from Usal Creek north to Whale Gulch, the former fishing and hunting ground of the Sinkyone Indians, has been set aside as the Sinkyone Wilderness State Park.

A **hiking trail** runs from the mouth of Usal Creek, through very rough country, north along the 16.7-mile strip of park land to Orchard Creek, where it connects with the King Range National Conservation Area trail system (call the BLM at *707-986-7731* for information), and with Black Sands Beach, near Shelter Cove, which stretches north to the mouth of the Mattole River. You will need a wilderness permit to hike in these areas. Call the Sinkyone Wilderness State Park in Whitethorn for permit, campground, and road information; *707-986-7711.*

Other trails cross the King Range. Hiking through the region, you feel at times like you're on an archaeological expedition as you stumble upon house foundations and bits and pieces of abandoned pilings, and perhaps a weather-beaten shack or two. During the heyday of local logging, this region was much more heavily settled than it is now. When the logging companies left, they not only took the mill machinery with them, but sometimes the company towns as well. Today, the backcountry is sparsely settled, the coast virtually not at all. For a good insight into the region, read Ray Raphael's *An Everyday History of Somewhere.*

The southern end and western edge of this wilderness are accessible from CA 1 via the unpaved Usal Road (No. 431) which turns north near Rockport at milepost 90.88 (slow down; the sign is hard to see and there's a sharp uphill turn). Jack London and his wife took this road back in 1911 in the conveyance best adapted to its ruggedness—a team and wagon. The road is passable for automobiles to the campground at the mouth of Usal Creek for most of the year, and to the north in the dry season. It connects with the Briceland Road (No. 435) near the north end of the Sinkyone Wilderness. If you can get through, you can drive from here, via Chemise Mountain Road, to Shelter Cove. If not, you have to return and take CA 1 to US 101, head north and take the (marked) road from Redway to Shelter Cove. The road into Shelter Cove is very steep and puts tremendous strain on brakes. Use low gear!

■ SHELTER COVE

Shelter Cove is one of those odd places that has, you might say, a lot of charm in spite of itself. First developed as a community of fancy getaway homes for Southern Californians with airplanes of their own, this very isolated seaside community of 300 people has never really taken off. But, because of the spectacular scenery and the good fishing, it has attracted families with summer homes and a small population of year-round residents—retirees, fishermen, and artists.

The coast south of **Point Delgada** (about the center of town) has some interesting tidepools where you can watch sea anemones try to snag small fish, where hermit crabs scurry about, and tiny fronds of kelp wave in the current. If you're lucky, you may see a small abalone crawl among the limpets, mussels, and sea snails. Watch oystercatchers pry open mussels with their flat beaks. And look for black turnstones—the black and white birds that turn over rocks as

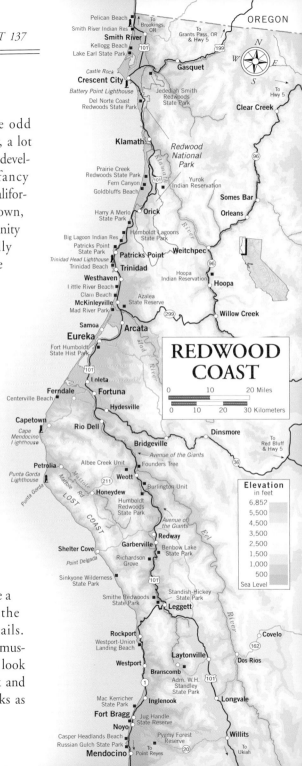

well as all sort of flotsam and jetsam washed up by the tide—as they gobble up crabs and other small animals hiding underneath (and not fast enough to make a quick getaway). The tidal rocks are also very popular with poke polers (see page 112). The sandy beaches north of Point Delgada are great for long walks and hikes and for beachcombing.

The main cove in "downtown" Shelter Cove (at the end of Machi Road) has a public boat launch where you can also rent a boat or go on salmon charters if there are salmon—increasingly uncertain. Abalone, which have attracted divers to the cove in the past, are also becoming scarce.

Shelter Cove doesn't have fancy restaurants (the ones that open here periodically seem to vanish quickly), but you can get good food from the small store/cafe at the campground near the boat ramp. While you eat, be sure to strike up a conversation with the owner, who has lived here for a long time, or with other residents who come for their daily coffee and chat.

Here I learned, over a lunch of some of the best fish 'n chips I've had anywhere, that one reason the place didn't take off is because the airport is fogged in for much of the year. Of course, it was foggy that day, too.

But never mind the fog, the beaches are particularly beautiful on foggy days, capturing your imagination with their stillness, the heightened sound of the sea, the indiscernible shapes looming in the mist.

■ SHELTER COVE TO MATTOLE RIVER HIGHWAY

The Kings Peak and Wilder Ridge Roads, which connect Shelter Cove to the Mattole River Highway at Honeydew, are paved, but that does not at all make them easy to drive, because they are narrow and wind their way in and out of steep-sided canyons on countless switchbacks. (I had blisters on my hands by the time I got back to US 101.) But the scenery is wildly beautiful and makes the drive well worthwhile, though you're miles from the ocean. In spring, the meadows are red, white, blue, and golden with wildflowers; in summer the roadway may be all but covered with the cream-colored flowers which have dropped from red-trunked madrone trees overhanging the road, and at all times of the year, a deer or cougar may step from the roadside woods. California quail forage for seeds along the

Starfish and octopus cling to tidepool rocks during the lowest tide of the month.

Cougars inhabit coniferous forests and chaparral-covered foothills in the coastal mountains.

banks, goldfinches flit across this-tle patches, and golden eagles soar overhead.

At Honeydew, you'll pick up the Mattole Road, CA 211, which runs from US 101 through Hum-boldt Redwoods State Park, west to Honeydew along the Mattole River and then north to Petrolia, Cape Mendocino, and Ferndale. It reconnects to US 101 south of Humboldt Bay, between Fortuna and Loleta.

■ HUMBOLDT REDWOODS

At this point we need to take some time out for redwoods. While there are small groves of redwood trees tucked away in the canyons of the Lost Coast, chances are you will not see them unless you plan to do some major hiking. Even so, these trees are not comparable to the giant redwoods of the Eel River Valley and of the forests north of Humboldt Bay. You will have driven beneath giant redwoods near Redway, if you took the road from US 101 to Shelter Cove. If you continue north on the US 101 freeway toward Eureka, you will shortly come to signs directing you to the "Avenue of the Giants." These are groves of ancient redwoods growing in the Eel River bottom along (two-lane) Old US 101, which mostly runs below the freeway, but periodically rejoins it where the canyon becomes too narrow for two roads. All along the Northern California coast, redwoods grow in canyons penetrated by sea fog in summer, which explains why you'll encounter isolated redwood groves as far as 60 miles from the sea.

Note that the surrounding hillsides are covered with live oaks, tan oaks, bay trees, chaparral, and meadows and are, by contrast, quite dry.

If you're not planning to explore the Sinkyone Wilderness and Shelter Cove, drive north on US 101 to Humboldt Redwoods State Park, which lets you take in some of the most beautiful of the giant trees as well as the scenic drive on Mattole Road to the coast at Cape Mendocino. Be sure to bring a picnic. If you don't want to take time out for a meal under the giant trees, you'll want to do so at the mouth of the Mattole or in the lee of Cape Mendocino.

Rockefeller Grove in Humboldt Redwoods State Park.

■ MATTOLE RIVER ROAD AND BEACH

CA 211 is a state highway, but this scenic road isn't much wider or straighter than the roads you've taken north from Shelter Cove. But never mind that. You have lots of time, and the mountain landscape is even more beautiful here than it was to the south. The valley of the Mattole is a painter's dream.

From **Honeydew,** the road winds its way slowly downriver toward the coast, passing through a beautiful river valley that's green even at the height of a hot and dry summer. There are very few homes, farms, or ranches on this narrow road which winds and twists its way through these fractured mountains. But little birds—warblers, flycatchers, sparrows—keep you company as they flit through the roadside shrubbery, catch insects on the wing, or scratch for seeds by the side of the road.

The main highway turns right across the Mattole River just before you get to Petrolia. If you continue straight downriver on Lighthouse Road, toward the wild and lonely **beach at the mouth of the Mattole,** you'll reach a sandy strand cowering beneath steep bluffs. Beyond the marsh and low dunes to the north you can just make out the bulky mass of Cape Mendocino. The primitive campsites are shielded from the sea wind by huge driftwood logs. You can park your car here (or camp) and walk south three miles along the beach to the abandoned lighthouse at Punta Gorda. Or you can hike along the beach all the way to Shelter Cove (about 24 miles one way).

❖

Petrolia is reached by driving back to the intersection with CA 211 and turning north. The village got its peculiar name when oil was discovered here in the 1860s, leading to California's first commercial exploitation of the sticky black liquid. But the boom quickly proved a bust, and Petrolia has been snoozing ever since. During one visit, things were so quiet in mid-morning that I spotted a covey of California quail who were strolling down Mattole Road in downtown Petrolia—and the quail didn't mind posing for a photo.

■ CAPE MENDOCINO

West of Petrolia, Mattole Road emerges from the mountains and runs on a low bluff above the ocean for four miles. On the west side of the road are several beach and dune access points. These lonely beaches are great places for birdwatching.

You can't miss the big bulk of Cape Mendocino rising to the north. This sizeable hunk of rock poking into the Pacific is not, as guidebooks often claim, the westernmost point in the contiguous United States. If you doubt this, check your atlas. It will tell you that Cape Flattery, Washington, is at W 124 degrees, 43 minutes, 90 seconds; Cape Blanco, Oregon (another place for which the westernmost claim is often made) is at W 124 degrees 34 minutes, and Cape Mendocino at W 124 degrees 24 minutes, 55 seconds. Case closed. But who cares. The cape is a spectacular sight no matter how far west it stands.

For centuries, this cape has been an important landmark for mariners—it got its name in the 16th century when the Spanish Manila–Acapulco galleons used it as a marker to tell them when it was time to turn south and catch a ride home on the California Current. It is also an important weather divide. North of here, chances are that you'll get rain instead of fog (even in summer); south of here summer fogs prevail.

It is an immensely scenic spot where the surf seems to be charged with special potency. Sea birds and Steller sea lions breed on Sugarloaf Island and Steamboat Rock just offshore. I'm not surprised when the earth moves. It's not the surf, but an earthquake. The cape lies near the junction of three very active tectonic plates.

❖

Above the Bear River Valley, the road winds through some very rugged mountains as it heads north toward Ferndale. The landscape is exquisitely beautiful, a series of high, soft-shouldered green-grass ridges where wild roses bloom in roadside thickets

The wilder areas of Humboldt County are home to many black bears.

and goldfinches flit across the road. Be sure to pull out before you reach the first ridge and look back. Below you, west of the pastures and white-washed farm buildings of the Bear River Valley, you can see the surf break on a sandy beach through a narrow gap in the green hills.

As you continue on this very narrow, winding road, keep your eyes on the pavement and away from the deer browsing on roadside brush, where the road drops over a ridge and the vista opens to truly spectacular scenery.

■ FERNDALE

Mattole Road drops from the mountains quite literally into Ferndale on a series of very steep switchbacks. Ferndale, a pleasant, well-preserved 19th-century village is known for its Eastlake and Queen Anne–style Victorian houses, which are virtually unchanged since the 1890s, except for a bit of earthquake damage now and then. The town is, in fact, so well preserved, it's on the National Register of Historic Places. If you're into Victoriana, this is a good place to stop and wander around, browsing in the shops. A side trip along Centerville Road takes you to a sandy beach south of the Eel River mouth.

■ EEL RIVER DELTA

North of Ferndale, the road runs through the flat Eel River delta. To the north and northeast, the delta is separated from lower Humboldt Bay by a low ridge that starts at Table Bluff on the ocean and curves southwest, past Loleta to the river.

The land between the ridge and the river is taken up by green pastures. Here, placid black and white cows contentedly munch on lush grasses and transform them into first-class milk. Many delta farms were settled by mid-19th century Portuguese whalers who gave up the hazardous hunt for the giant mammals, but enjoyed a view of the sea from the parlors of their farmhouses. Near the ocean, freshwater sloughs teem with ducks and other bird life.

Many roads run through the delta and cross the sloughs on bridges. You can scout the sandy and sedgy edge of the **Eel River Slough,** a long, much-branched lagoon and marsh, by walking north along the sandy beach from Centerville Park

A madrone tree stands sentinel over Eel River country in Humboldt County.

or south from Table Bluff. There's also a parking lot and an unimproved county park at the end of Cannibal Island Road, west of Loleta, from which you can hike north along the sandy edge of a slough.

■ LOLETA

Loleta is a small, very pleasant dairy town, where time seems to have stood still. It sits high on a slope above the Eel River delta whose pastures provide the town with its economic sustenance.

Loleta has homes and stores, a creamery, and the **Loleta Cheese Factory** at 252 Loleta Drive, which has some of the best foods produced in this region. The factory makes some truly great cheddar and jack cheese, as well as several specialty cheeses. I have found wine here made from grapes grown in Humboldt County.

To reach **Table Bluff** from Loleta, take Copenhagen Road west to Table Bluff Road, then turn left. The beach at the foot of the bluff runs south to the mouth of the Eel River (tides permitting) and north for several miles along the south spit of Humboldt Bay to the south jetty of the bay entrance. The rough waters near Table Bluff are very popular with local surfers. To return to US 101, just follow Table Bluff Road north past the Humboldt Bay National Wildlife Refuge (where there's more great birdwatching in the bayshore marshes) to the freeway.

From Loleta to Eureka, US 101 runs between a bluff and the bay and through dairy pastures on low, gently undulating slopes.

You can't miss Eureka. It's the largest town on the North Coast, and you know you're getting near when the four-lane highway suddenly sprouts stoplights and shopping malls.

■ EUREKA

Eureka is known for its elaborate Victorians—of which the Carson mansion, a private club that looks like a giant wooden fruitcake, is the most ostentatious.

A bit too grimy for its beautiful setting, Eureka wears smudges on its potentially pretty face. Ugly malls along the waterfront have not helped. Downtown has a few interesting old business buildings, a working waterfront and oyster plant, and a couple of decent restaurants, but unfortunately it's not safe after dark.

An ocean kayaker passes the fishermen's monument which stands above Eureka Bay.

■ HUMBOLDT BAY

Humboldt Bay, a large estuary, is California's second largest enclosed bay, after San Francisco Bay. It is divided into two sections, South Bay south of Eureka and Arcata Bay to the north. Humboldt Bay is separated from the ocean by two long, sandy spits, aptly called South and North Spit. North Spit has been heavily industrialized for more than a hundred years and is still covered with pulp mills and other lumber-related plants. The long spit running from Arcata south to **Samoa** became one of California's earliest industrial sites. Samoa's claim to fame today is the Samoa Cookhouse, which once catered to loggers and mill workers and their giant appetites. It's the only cookhouse in the West still operating, and still cooking up the same kind of hearty food it served a hundred years ago.

Eureka in 1895.

The city square of Arcata is the focus of town life.

■ ARCATA

Arcata was founded in the 1850s as a supply point for the northern mines but was soon overtaken by Eureka, which has the bay's deepwater harbor. Arcata has an industrial past, like other bayshore communities, but is doing its best to clean up its ill effects. Locals have done a great job with cleaning up the upper bay (so that today commercial oyster farms once again prosper—Arcata Bay supplies about 45 percent of California's oysters). They have restored a formerly degraded 65-acre salt marsh by cleaning it up and replanting it with native vegetation. The **Arcata Marsh and Wildlife Sanctuary** is now home for fish and more than 150 species of birds. (The Audubon Society sponsors nature walks; *707-826-6918.*)

Arcata, the home of **Humboldt State University**, is a wholesome, funky college town with a pretty plaza surrounded by beautiful old buildings. In this area are health food shops, organic grocery stores, stores selling driftwood lamps and brown candles. Some houses up on the hill are fine old Victorian mansions. You'll find lots of surfers here, inhabited vans parked along streets, and (white) college kids wearing dreadlocks.

Redwood Park east of downtown has picnic tables, lawns, and 600 acres of redwoods. The great event of the year is the annual (Memorial Day) **Great Arcata to Ferndale Cross-Country Kinetic Sculpture Race.** The "sculpture" should be weird enough to please the crowds and it must float as well, in order to move across Humboldt Bay; information: *707-839-3231.*

The coast north of Arcata looks more like the Pacific Northwest than California, an illusion that is heightened by the fact that the first major beach you get to is called **Clam Beach** and actually has clams free for the digging. (You will need a license. I always check with a local tackle or bait shop to see what licenses I need, what limits or seasons apply, and where in the sands most clams have recently been spouting.) The beach is a county park and a great place to stop even if it looks, at times, like an RV parking lot.

■ TRINIDAD

One of the prettiest villages on the California coast, Trinidad has come a long way from the days when the WPA guide to California (1939) described it as a place where "small straggling homes, windows broken and boarded, fringe the empty offices, refineries, and vats of the California Sea Products Company, a whaling firm." Trinidad Head, which shields the harbor from storms, rises above a rocky coastline and pocket beaches. Trinidad was founded in 1850 as a supply point for the gold mines of the interior, and it once had a population of more than 3,000 people. It was the North Coast's first "American" settlement.

But before the first white men arrived, Trinidad was the site of a Yurok village more than 5,000 years old. It is also the place where European explorers first set

Indian Village, Trinidad, *by J. G. Bruff, ca. 1850 illustrates the plank siding used in Yurok construction. (Huntington Library, Pasadena)*

A. W. Ericson's photographs depicting the life of Indians in North America are in the anthropological collections of many major museums. In this photograph, an Indian spears for salmon near the village of Hoopa. (Courtesy of Peter E. Palmquist)

foot on the far northern shore, when the Spanish explorers Heceta and Bodega erected a cross here in 1775. Peter Corney, a Northwest Company trader, came by in 1817 and described the people he met there, the Yurok, as warlike. They seemed a bit surprised when the ship's crew took the sort of precautions they'd learned on the Northwest Coast, tricing up boarding nets and disarming anyone coming aboard to trade. Corney sadly reported that women would not board the ship, even though the crewmen offered them blankets and axes. "This is the only place on the coast where we could not induce the females to visit the ship." Perhaps it was the Yurok's warlike nature and natural reticence that kept them alive as a tribe. Today the Yurok are among the few California natives to still occupy many of their original village sites.

Trinidad's small harbor is a beautiful, romantic treasure. If you come at lunchtime try Seascapes, a pleasant restaurant with a view of the pier and the rocks. This delightful, very friendly place is where the locals mingle with visitors, and where they bring their visiting friends. The seafood is very fresh, and there's wonderful smoked fish available. During my last visit, one regular customer couldn't get a crab sandwich because they hadn't cooked the crab yet—it had just come in on a boat. I enjoyed a delicious shrimp and cheese sandwich, accompanied by a microbrew from Eureka.

■ PATRICK'S POINT STATE PARK

A back road runs from Trinidad to Patrick's Point State Park (also directly accessible from the US 101 freeway), another one of the truly great places on the California coast. Patrick's Point has it all: forests, meadows, bluffs, sandy beach, rocky shores, tidepools, and great campsites. But I've come to spend some time in a very special place, a reconstructed Yurok village.

The Patrick's Point **Yurok Village** is a reconstruction, but a very authentic one. Houses of redwood planks, fronted by stone platforms, are partially set into the ground; only low walls and the heavy redwood slab roofs rise above a meadow in which strawberries and daisies are in full bloom. There is also a sweat house and a few finished and half-finished canoes lying next to the houses, just as they might in a real village.

■ LAGOON COAST

Right after Patrick's Point, as you drive north on US 101, you pass **Big Lagoon**, the first of several bodies of fresh water separated from the ocean by spits of sand. The park at **Dry Lagoon** includes a marshy lake rapidly turning into a meadow, and the spit separating **Stone Lagoon** from the ocean, with one of the best walking beaches on this coast. At Stone Lagoon, US 101 turns away from the coast for a short stretch. **Freshwater Lagoon** is a beautiful sandy driftwood beach popular with surf fishermen. All of the beaches fronting the lagoons are also great for long, meditative walks.

At the beach north of Freshwater Lagoon, you can't miss the **Redwood Creek Beach Picnic Area** and **Redwood National Park Visitors Center** just west of US 101. The national park itself stretches along this coast for miles. The visitors center has a great bookstore and friendly rangers. This may well be the most user-friendly place of its kind on the entire California coast. This is the place to pick up one of the limited permits issued each day for seeing the world's tallest tree, a redwood 368 feet tall and 14 feet in diameter.

North of the visitors center, US 101, which has reverted from a freeway back into a rural two-lane highway, turns inland to Orick, an odd little town—a mixture of tourism savvy and backwoods orneriness in the redwoods. Both sides of US 101 are lined with redwood sculptures, for Orick is the chainsaw redwood sculpture capital of the world. Now, if they'd just import a few artists and show them how to use a chainsaw . . . . If you can't afford one of the large sculptures, or have no room, you can console yourself with a redwood burl. Orick is also the redwood burl capital of the world.

■ PRAIRIE CREEK REDWOODS STATE PARK

A few miles north of Orick, look for the turnoff to Davidson Road, which runs across the coastal mountains to **Gold Bluffs Beach** and **Fern Canyon**, within Prairie Creek Redwoods State Park, on the west side of the highway. Also look for elk. During a recent visit, there was a traffic jam at this intersection, because several elk were grazing in a roadside meadow and visitors pulled their cars off the road to take photos.

As soon as the pavement ends, you'll begin to notice the erosion caused by winter rains (especially in an El Niño year, when California gets a lot more than its usual share of the wet stuff). The clay-dirt road from Berry Glen to the ocean can be very slick; and along the beach beneath the towering Gold Bluffs, it may be cut by creeks in several places. When the bluffs above the road and beach are wet, they look top-heavy, as though they might collapse at any moment. Be prepared, in wet or dry weather, to ford several creeks en route to Fern Canyon. You should make it with a bit of sliding and much splashing. If you don't, there's likely to be a fellow traveler or ranger to pull you out.

Because Fern Canyon is narrow and steep-walled, and the creek meanders back and forth between the cliffs, rangers install foot bridges during the summer. But don't expect bridges in the off-season. Be prepared to get your feet wet, or bring rubber boots or waders.

Fern Canyon is is one of the most serenely beautiful places in the West, with row upon row of five-finger ferns reaching out from the steep 50-foot vertical walls, wafting to and fro in the sea breeze. Lady ferns, deer ferns, and chain ferns add variety to the texture of this natural tapestry.

If you walk onto the beach, watch out for Roosevelt elk. Males have huge racks of antlers, stand more than five feet high at the shoulder, and can weigh as much as a thousand pounds. Even the smaller females look about the size of a Jersey cow. Elk, which should more properly be called wapiti, since the English term originally referred to the European moose with its shovel-like antlers, are now considered to be conspecific with the European red deer—the stag hunted by royalty as well as by Robin Hood and his Merry Men.

After you return to the road, US 101 once again assumes freeway status. Look for the exit taking you to Old US 101, which takes you through a thick redwood grove, a beautiful drive that, at times, seems like a narrow canyon road. Except that the road is not hemmed in by cliffs but by huge trees—some of them more than 300 feet tall. A large fenced meadow near the park headquarters usually holds a herd of elk, allowing you to take a good look at the size and majesty of these magnificent beasts.

Ask the rangers to point you to the trail running along the banks of Redwood Creek—one of the most peaceful walks anywhere in the West.

A lot of things magically come together in the Prairie Creek redwood forest to make this a truly special place: a wide, clear stream, meadows with wildflowers in season, elk that are singularly unafraid of human visitors, huge redwoods, and lanky rhododendrons blooming in the understory. Here, where the redwoods stand on fairly level, easily accessible ground, you recognize what magnificent trees they are.

■ THE MAGIC OF THE REDWOODS

Redwoods are simply the tallest trees known. The tallest redwood has been measured at a height of 367.8 feet; there are hundreds of trees more than 300 feet tall, but the average height is about 200 feet. Trunks can reach a diameter of 15 to 20 feet at (human) chest level. The bark contains no resin and may be as thick as 12 inches. Redwoods have surprisingly shallow roots for such huge trees—they go only about four to six feet down but may spread as far as 80 to 100 feet from the trunk. Redwoods live to an age of several thousand years. The oldest redwood has been authenticated at 2,200 years old, meaning it was a seedling when the Great Wall of China was built, when Hannibal marched on Rome, and when Central America's Mayan civilization began its meteoric rise. Redwoods may be the only immortal beings, since a cut or fallen tree will send up sprouts that are genetically

FROM SONG OF THE REDWOOD TREE

California Song

Farewell my brethren,
Farewell O earth and sky, farewell you neighboring waters,
My time is ended, my time has come.

Along the northern coast,
Just back from the rock-bound shore and the caves,
In the saline air from the sea in the Mendocino country,
With the surge for base and accompaniment low and hoarse,
With crackling blows of axes sounding musically driven by strong arms,
Riven deep by the sharp tongues of the axes, there in the redwood forest dense,
I heard the mighty tree its death-chant chanting;
The choppers heard not, the camp shanties echoed not,
The quick-ear'd teamsters and chain and jack-screw men heard not,
As the wood-spirits came from their haunts of a thousand years to join the refrain,
But in my soul I plainly heard.

—Walt Whitman, *Leaves of Grass,* 1876

Giant Redwood Trees of California *by Albert Bierstadt, 1874.*
(The Berkshire Museum, Pittsfield, MA)

identical to the parent and thus rejuvenate it. Early American settlers did, however, manage to kill redwoods by burning the stumps and killing the shoots. Little direct light can penetrate the dense foliage of a redwood grove, but plant life thrives in clearings left by fallen trees and along rivers and creeks.

Continue north on Old US 101 to the US 101 freeway, which is uncommonly scenic for such a high-speed highway, running north through alder, oak, and redwood forests and along hillside wildflower meadows, which sparkle in the sun. Look for the turnoff to scenic, eight-mile-long Coastal Drive in Redwood National Park, a rough, and periodically paved clifftop road (not recommended for motorhomes or cars with trailers) that runs north to the mouth of the Klamath River. The Carruther's Cove Trail leads from the southern end of the drive to secluded Carruther's Beach.

■ KLAMATH RIVER AND KLAMATH

You can't miss the Klamath because the bridge entrances are marked by gold-painted sculptures of bears. Here ends the last and northernmost strip of the US 101 freeway. The Klamath is California's second largest river (after the Sacramento), and once had great runs of salmon; but stocks have lately suffered from over-fishing. The days when fishing boats were packed so tightly next to each other that you could cross the river on them are long gone. Local smokehouses still sell smoked salmon—commonly made with salmon imported from Alaska, since commercial fishing is not allowed on the river.

A spur road leads to **Requa Overlook** on the northern cliffs above the mouth of the Klamath River. The overlook has picnic tables, interpretive plaques, and offers great views of the Lower Klamath River valley and the coastline. The four-mile Coastal Trail runs north along the cliffs to Lagoon Creek (see Yurok Loop Trail, following).

■ LAGOON CREEK AND YUROK LOOP TRAIL

US 101 descends to the ocean at **Lagoon Creek Fishing Access** near False Klamath Rock. There's a former millpond here, now stocked with rainbow trout and brightened by yellow water lilies. Look for ducks, herons, egrets, and river otters. The self-guided half-mile Yurok Loop Trail winds through willows, alders, and over bluffs with some truly spectacularly sculpted Sitka spruces. The "look" of this landscape is one that Chinese landscape painters of the past would have found familiar.

I've set up my easel on the cliffs at the seaward side of the trail several times in the past, but one visit was especially memorable. It was one of those special, quiet, soft mornings when the air was filled with the chirping of sparrows, with the distant roar of the surf, and with the delicate, yet surprisingly audible, tingling sounds water makes as it drips off leaves. The water came from fog, not rain. The day promised to be beautiful, as the golden rays of the sun began to pierce the curtain of fog.

As I looked down onto the foggy beach north of the trail, I tried to imagine what it was like when a Yurok village stood here, before white men came to this coast. As a ribbon of fog swirled across the sand and through the trees, it was easy for my mind's eye to turn driftwood logs into redwood-planked lodges (like the ones at Patrick's Point; see page 151) and hand-carved canoes. Sea stacks, barely visible in the mist, loomed offshore, just as they did in the old days, when every one of these monoliths was owned by families who had inherited rights to the bounty of their intertidal zones—to the mussels, barnacles, and algae growing on the rock, and to the sea snails, limpets, abalones, and sea cucumbers crawling over their rough surfaces or hiding in their crevices.

I took the half-mile trail uphill, through an alder and willow thicket, and past tall grasses and ferns. Where the trail curves to the south, I stood high up on a cliff, above the breakers roiling in from the far reaches of the open Pacific. Suddenly, without warning, a dark specter loomed supernaturally large on the offshore fog bank. Had I trespassed on sacred ground and raised a spirit? Of course not. The sun broke through the low clouds, throwing the shadow of a gnarled Sitka spruce onto the wall of white fog.

I did, however, wonder how a Yurok would have reacted to the apparition. For the Yurok believed that the material world is closely intertwined with the spiritual, and that all places and objects, even this humble trail, had their spirits. Therefore, a Yurok, walking where I had just trod, might have asked permission of the local spirits to trespass. And he might have rested his load and waited until he felt sure that it was all right to go on.

Seeing or imagining spirits is easy on this wet coast, where the land and the sea, the shore and the tall redwood trees bleed into each other in the misty air. The spirit of the Indians who first settled on this coast is still very much alive today.

The jumping (or redheaded woodpecker) dance was performed by Indians of Weitchpec, California. (Humboldt County Collection, Humboldt State University)

The traditional jumping dance is still held, and the daughter of friends of mine recently put on a traditional flower dance that had not been performed for more than a hundred years.

■ NORTH TO CRESCENT CITY

North of Lagoon Creek, the highway runs along sandy Wilson Creek Beach for a short stretch before climbing up along the sheer sides of the cliffs. Soon giant redwoods crowd in on all sides at Del Norte Coast Redwoods State Park, and the road narrows. In almost no time you will be deep in a primeval forest of ancient redwood trees. Pull over at one of the many turnouts and take a short walk into this cathedral of trees, where green huckleberry leaves, pink-flowered native rhododendrons in full bloom, and patches of blue sky provide an illusion of stained glass windows suspended from the boughs. And don't be afraid to gawk—everybody does, in the presence of such natural majesty. Occasionally, through gaps between the tall tree trunks, you can spot patches of dark blue or gray ocean.

As the road leaves the forest, it drops down to a sandy crescent of beach,

Crescent Beach in Redwood National Park, the very beach from which one of California's oldest cities takes its name.

■ CRESCENT CITY

Crescent City was founded in 1852 as a supply depot for the Trinity River mines; the following year it got its first lumber mill for cutting beams and planks from local redwood trees. Today, Crescent City is a small, pleasant harbor at the northwest end of the long, sandy beach. The downtown doesn't look its age, because much of the old business district was washed away in April of 1964 by a *tsunami* generated by the big Alaskan earthquake. Today, a breakwater of more than 1,600 concrete tetrapods, weighing 25 tons each, appears to be doing a good job of protecting the port during storms.

Crescent City shows two faces to the world: a public, not particularly appealing face along the US 101 business strip; and a private face that is among the most beautiful on the California coast.

The "public face" includes the fishing port and the waterfront along grassy Beach Front Park, where you can take a look at one of the strangely shaped giant concrete anchors (on display just south of Front Street).

The "private face" starts west of the harbor, and north of the lighthouse, which sits on an island and is, with its museum, only accessible at low tide. Crescent City's pretty seaside promenade is reached by driving straight west where US 101 turns north. If it were further south, in warmer climes, its beaches would be thronged with sunbathers on a sunny day like today. But here, where the fog may roll back in at any time, everybody stays well bundled up. But that does not mean people aren't enjoying themselves. Children, watched by their mothers, explore tidepools; old men, watched by their wives, poke-pole for monkey-faced eels; and beachcombers, turnstones, gulls, and oystercatchers check out the tidal rocks for edibles and other interesting objects.

Castle Rock, northwest of town, has the second largest breeding population of seabirds on the California coast; only South Farallon Island off of San Francisco has more. With a good set of binoculars, you can easily make out the shapes of common murres, cormorants, and gulls. Occasionally, you can also spot Cassin's auklets, Leach's petrels, pigeon guillemots, and tufted puffins. You can always count on seeing a few fork-tailed storm petrels fluttering above the surf, and pairs of black oystercatchers working over mussel clusters.

Halfway up the shore is a monument and memorial park dedicated to the drowned crewmen and passengers of the sidewheel-steamer *Brother Jonathan,* which sank in 1865 on St. George reef, seven miles off shore. Rumors have been widespread that the steamer was carrying a fat payroll up to Portland. In the 1960s, a team of treasure hunters were scouring the sea floor for the gold when, overnight, the crew and ship disappeared without a trace. Many locals believe they found what they were after, and promptly split with the booty.

If you follow the road along the bluffs, as it winds north, you'll come to Point St. George, a grassy promontory that looks like a place straight out of a Scottish or Irish tourism brochure. As you walk out toward the cliffs on the greensward in spring, you will be surrounded by wildflowers; in summer, you may be serenaded by band-tailed pigeons which appear here in great numbers; in fall, you will stir up flocks of sandpipers. On a clear day, you can just make out the faint shape of the St. George reef lighthouse, seven miles offshore.

■ LAKE EARL AND POINTS NORTH

Unlike the wide-open headland of St. George, nearby Lake Earl is a mystical place. Drive to the parking area at the end of Lakeview Drive, park your car, and sit quietly on a snag. Meadow-like patches of reeds grow far out into the shallow lake. Blending with the morning mists, they obscure the boundaries between land and water, and land and sky, blending all into a marriage of the solid, the liquid, and the ethereal. And then, just as this mystic mood is threatening to draw you into its vortex, you're brought back to reality by the exuberant quacking of mallard ducks and by the crowing of farmyard roosters from lakeshore homesteads.

During the fall and spiring migrations, Lake Earl is home to more than 250 species of birds; at all times of the year, look for deer, brush rabbits, river otters, red-tailed hawks, ospreys, peregrine falcons, and an occasional bald eagle.

❖

North of Crescent City along US 101, the forests recede from the coast and dairy pastures spread across the lowlands. A short detour will take you to **Jedediah Smith Redwood State Park** in the lower valley of the Smith River along US 199 (the two-lane highway running from the coast east to Grants Pass, Oregon).

The beaches along the few miles of California coast north of the Smith River are not the best in this area, but there is good beachcombing after winter storms.

(Left) The snow-covered Siskiyou Mountains form a backdrop for this aerial view of Crescent City. (Following pages) A grove of redwoods at Prairie Creek State Park where the trees stand 200 to 300 feet tall.

G O L D E N   G A T E
T O   S A N   S I M E O N

■ HIGHLIGHTS

Point Año Nuevo
Santa Cruz
Monterey
Carmel
Big Sur
San Simeon

Eureka

Mendocino

San Francisco

GOLDEN GATE TO SAN SIMEON

Monterey

Direction of travel
in this chapter is
north to south

Los Angeles

San Diego

■ TRAVEL OVERVIEW

South of San Francisco suburbs and malls give way to rolling hills, wide open spaces, and unobstructed views of the blue Pacific. Along the spine of San Francisco's peninsula, the rugged Santa Cruz Mountains raise their stony shoulders to the sky from marine terraces dropping off sharply to the ocean in cliffs and bluffs.

Along Monterey Bay large stretches of the sandy shores are preserved as public beaches. At the southern end of the bay, spurs of the Santa Lucia Mountains encroach on the beaches, forming the Monterey Peninsula, with its spectacular rocky headlands, sandy coves, and turquoise and indigo sea.

South of Carmel, mountains edge up to the sea, and the pines and cypresses of Monterey give way to grassy slopes. The mountains drop into the surf at an even steeper angle south of the Big Sur River and do not give way to gentler shores until the mountains recede from the coast south of Gorda.

The cities along this coast, most notably Santa Cruz, Monterey, and Carmel, are small urban microcosms, providing all the amenities of metropolitan areas with a fraction of the urban sprawl and congestion.

■ TRAVEL BASICS

Driving

You may wish to begin a drive south to the Monterey Peninsula and Big Sur by traveling the faster inland roads, then cutting west over to the coast. If you choose to follow the Coast Highway out of San Francisco, you'll begin at Ocean Beach, described in "SAN FRANCISCO BAY" on page 60. Roads along the coast from San Francisco south to San Simeon—with the exception of two stretches of freeway near Santa Cruz and Monterey—are for the most part beautiful and rural but two-lane, making for slow driving on weekends and during the height of the summer travel season.

Climate

Expect some wind and fog in the summer, although many days will be clear and warm by noon. Spring and fall are brisk and clear. Winter can be rainy and damp with daytime temperatures in the 50s. Remember that if you travel inland a few miles, it's usually warmer. A mild climate is the rule along the entire coastline. Monterey is the driest coastal location north of Los Angeles with only 15 inches of rain per season, whereas Santa Cruz across Monterey Bay is the wettest with 28 inches. Summer (June through August) temperatures along the shore rarely rise above 70 degrees but are commonly in the 90s a short distance inland. Heavy winter (November to March) storms often cause mud slides along CA 1. Fall is magnificent, with warm temperatures and clear skies. **Water Temperature:** Cool year-round (50 to 60 degrees).

Food and Lodging

Santa Cruz and Monterey are in the heart of a culinary wonderland. The sea provides fresh seafood year-round. The Salinas Valley is the salad bowl of America. Local wines, made from grapes grown in the region's valleys and mountains, enhance the local dishes.

A number of unusual and very comfortable inns are tucked away in coastal towns and sunny valleys. (See **lodging and restaurant listings** pages 339–390.)

■ OVERVIEW OF A RURAL COASTLINE

From San Francisco's Ocean Beach (see page 60) south, suburbs and sprawl line the coast road for about 20 miles, but once the highway passes Pacifica, one of the prettiest pastoral landscapes in California begins. Hillside meadows alternate with groves of wind-twisted pines, sandy beaches give way to steep-sided bluffs, and in places, tall mountains push right up to the edge of the sea. Lichen-covered fences line the spring-green pastures, and weathered old barns raise their frayed roofs from seaside draws. On clear spring days the colors are bright enough to dazzle an impressionist painter: a translucent sky arches over a steely-blue ocean pounding the pale shores with creamy surf; darkly green pines and cypresses make the brightness of the green grass appear even brighter; and fields of golden-yellow mustard flowers are offset by the spiky gray-green fronds of artichoke plants. All of this is swathed in a light mist, which makes distant headlands seem near, and rocky coves beneath your feet vanish in a wisp of fog. Above all hangs the constant hum of the surf, punctuated by the chirping of white-crowned sparrows and the trill of meadowlarks and red-winged blackbirds.

Cypress at Monterey *by impressionist painter Mary DeNeale Morgan.*
(Courtesy of Joan Irvine Smith Fine Arts, Irvine)

GOLDEN GATE
TO SAN SIMEON

■ PACIFICA

Directly south of San Francisco's Ocean Beach, bland buildings line the road, but as the two-lane highway descends steep hills toward Pacifica there are some fine views of the ocean. The town itself is an uninspired suburb that creeps from the northern cliffs into lowlands bordering beaches and east into wooded hills. Pacifica has several narrow beaches, one of the most popular being the southernmost, San Pedro Beach, called Linda Mar by the locals because it's at the end of Linda Mar Boulevard. The grungy parking lot (immediately to the west of the highway) is usually full of young men and women getting in and out of wet suits—so many, so often, that the city of Pacifica has passed an anti-nudity law.

Unlike other surfer beaches, this is a generally friendly beach, and very democratic—local beach bums mix with young, professional San Franciscans trying desperately to learn to surf. This is *the* learners' spot. Boogie boarders (a boogie board is a short styrofoam board that you don't stand up on but ride flat on your belly) ride the whitewater. Surfers near the shore can find themselves

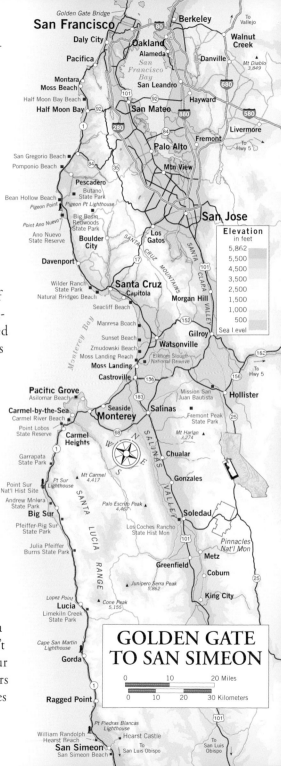

GOLDEN GATE TO SAN SIMEON

Elevation in feet
5,862
5,500
4,500
3,500
2,500
1,500
1,000
500
Sea level

riding the waves between a hydrophilic dog and a curious seal checking out the human scene. People walk their dogs along the strand, beachcomb, sunbathe, and drop by an old wooden house on the beach with a Taco Bell inside. If the tide isn't too high, walk along the upper edge of the beach, toward San Pedro Point. The brown pelicans put on a spectacular show here, flying low over the water in a loose skein and, one by one, suddenly plunging into the water. Others soar high before diving headfirst into the sea. Their eyes must be able to penetrate the surface glare of the waves, for they get their fish every time.

❖

Discovery of Bay of San Francisco by Portola *painted by Arthur Frank Mathews, 1896. (Courtesy of the Garzoli Gallery, San Rafael)*

Walking this beach, I often find myself thinking of a Spanish exploratory expedition that struggled through this area more than 200 years ago. Under the command of Capt. Juan Gaspar de Portola and acting on orders from the Viceroy of Mexico, a small party of soldiers arrived here in 1769 after having traveled by foot and horseback from San Diego. Looking for Monterey Bay—as described in the ship's logs of Spanish navigator Sebastian Vizcaino—the party had passed

GOLDEN GATE TO SAN SIMEON

*In winter, landslides often close the Coast Highway just south of Pacifica along
a stretch of road known as Devil's Slide.*

beside Monterey but not recognized it as such, and had continued north along the
coast, plodding through ravines, along surf-swept beaches, and across rocky ridges
until they wearily stopped at one of Pacifica's beaches. A party of hunters set out
looking for game, and reaching the ridgetops looked east and saw before them a
vast body of water. Jose Francisco de Ortega, later to become the first comandante
of the presidio of Santa Barbara, is said to have been the first of the party to see
San Francisco Bay.

The Portola party was too tired to press further, and they returned to San
Diego. The first European settlements of this peninsula, the presidio and mission
of San Francisco, were not established for another seven years.

Southeast of San Pedro Point, the Coast Highway climbs over a shoulder of Montara Mountain and, after a switchback, emerges high above the sea. The view is
breathtaking, but keep your eyes on the road, because there's a sheer dropoff to the
right—straight down to the surf. This cliff and stretch of highway certainly de-
serve their name of "Devil's Slide."

On the way to Half Moon Bay you'll pass three more beaches worth exploring, if you have time. They are **Gray Whale Cove State Beach, Montara State Beach,** and **West Beach Trail at Pillar Point Harbor.** Three-mile-long **James Fitzgerald Marine Reserve** at Moss Beach is known for its tidepools.

■ HALF MOON BAY

A small Portuguese fishing and farming village just 30 years ago, and a popular hideaway for San Franciscans during Prohibition, Half Moon Bay is now on its way to becoming just another generic suburb. The setting, however, is superb. In summer, flower farms reach far up into the canyons; in autumn, lowland fields are dotted with the orange globes of pumpkins. Families come from all over the Bay Area to pick their favorite jack-o-lanterns. To the west, the small town of **Princeton-by-the Sea,** with its Pillar Point Harbor, remains largely unspoiled.

The coastal bluffs south of Half Moon Bay are bedecked with flowers and wild strawberries in spring, and artichokes and brussels sprouts grow in the fields. The view from the coast road turns rustic. Slopes to the east are covered with grasses

An artist's beach house on Half Moon Bay.

and scrub, offset by copses of pines and oaks and by eucalyptus windbreaks. Roads across the mountains are narrow and twisted—one of the reasons this coast is still largely rural and unspoiled. In late winter and early spring, wildflowers paint the mountain slopes yellow, orange, and blue. Some of this landscape has not changed much since the days when Spanish padres sought converts among the natives and *vaqueros* rode the range.

■ NEAR SAN GREGORIO AND POMPONIO

Along this stretch of road, several attractive, sandy beaches lie to the immediate west of the highway. San Gregorio has a sandy beach and rocky shore right off the highway (the beach is a good place for watching plovers in winter). Pomponio and Pescadero have beaches of soft sand that can be warm and sunny in summer (and are therefore very popular and often crowded on weekends). All three have picnic areas with splendid views of the ocean and of the seals, dolphins, and whales that occasionally swim by. San Gregorio and Pomponio are two of my favorite beaches along this coast.

The inviting **San Gregorio General Store**, a mile inland on Highway 84, sells all sorts of books, clothing, and housewares, and also has a comfortable bar with live music on weekends.

Turn left onto Pescadero Road at Pescadero State Beach. To the left lies the **Pescadero Marsh Natural Preserve**. This miles-long marsh running inland along Pescadero Creek is a prime bird habitat. White egrets are a common sight here, flying low over the water with slow, deliberate wing beats. Red-winged blackbirds sing in the reeds, sparrows flit through the roadside willows, and turkey vultures soar over the golden grasses of the hills, scouring the ground with their dispassionate eyes.

■ TOWN OF PESCADERO

Pescadero is a small, trim village at the head of Pescadero Marsh, surrounded by grassy hills where contented cattle graze. This is a hamlet of a few shops and a bar-restaurant strung out along a main street, plus a few white-washed houses surrounded by well-tended gardens and orchards. Of course, the place and the setting have been compared to New England, like so many pretty places along the California coast. Pescadero not only has the best food, but also the only gas station for miles around. At the gas station is a small Mexican market and taqueria that sells great tamales, Mexican hats, and even a few medicinal herbs.

Duarte's Tavern, a former stagecoach stop, was opened in 1894 by a Portuguese bartender and barber whose family has run it ever since. You can stop here for artichoke or green chile soup (and you can even get them to go). The most prominent place on Pescadero's short main street, Duarte's is a very friendly, homey place that serves excellent seafood and is deservedly popular. The abalone is cooked to tender perfection; rich, flavorful artichoke soup. This normally means long waits; reservations are advised on weekends. (Also see page 364).

■ PIGEON POINT

From Highway 1 you'll see flat, windswept Pigeon Point off to the west, and on it the second tallest lighthouse on the California coast (115 feet high; open Sundays). The beach has some good hiking and tidepooling, and there's a youth hostel in the former keeper's quarters; *650-879-0633.*

■ POINT AÑO NUEVO STATE RESERVE

This flat point of land stretching out into the Pacific, and overlooked by piney hills, is less famous for its natural beauty than for its gargantuan mating scene— one you can witness yourself if you make reservations early enough. What you'll see, stretched out before you in all their hefty splendor, are elephant seals, known to 19th-century sealers as "sea elephants." The popularity of the high-quality oil they produced drove them to the brink of extinction—only one small colony survived on islands off Baja California—but they have made a strong comeback since they were fully protected, and have expanded their range to as far north as Cape Blanco, Oregon.

Male elephant seals, the largest marine mammals to haul out on land, can grow to a length of 16 feet and a weight of three tons. So enormous are they, that occasionally they kill their mates by falling asleep on top of them (females are about the size of a large buffalo).

The elephant seal gets its name from the large trunklike proboscis of older males. Despite their huge size, these seals act like the common harbor seal when

Pigeon Point Lighthouse on the San Mateo Coast.

Bull elephant seals joust for dominance at Point Año Nuevo State Reserve. Researchers have marked the seal on the left for identification purposes.

GOLDEN GATE
TO SAN SIMEON

on land—lolling about on beaches during the day and feeding at night by diving for fish, squid, and rays. In a pinch, they can fast for three months.

Behind Año Nuevo lies a beautiful lagoon with patches of tule reeds where red-winged blackbirds and marsh birds breed. To the west of its sandy beaches, off the edge of the point, is an island with an abandoned lighthouse and keeper's house. Elephant seals have claimed the house as their own and have even been found in the second floor bathtub.

You can visit Año Nuevo during the breeding season (December 15 through April 30) by making a reservation long in advance *(800-444-7275)* or by showing up and hoping for a cancellation. There is a fee and you must take a guided walk.

■ DAVENPORT

Davenport, a hamlet huddled along the cliff-top highway, was once a whaling station and had a rather messy concrete plant in the recent past. Its one street of wooden houses led to a small Catholic church. Now it's a bit larger and all tidied up. There are some great views from the top of the cliffs. The Davenport New Cash Store and Gray Whale Bakery and Cafe have good food.

From the bluff tops, visitors can watch gray whales as they travel south to Baja's calving lagoons in the fall and then north again to Alaska during the spring. It's a sign of progressing civilization that whale watching has replaced whale killing on this coast. In the 19th century, there were whaling stations all along this coast, with lookouts on the headlands, not only at Davenport, but also at Half Moon Bay, Point Lobos, and San Simeon.

As you drive south along the undulating bluffs, you can't help noticing fields of tall, dark-green vegetables. These are the famous (or notorious, depending on your viewpoint) brussels sprouts. Those who don't like eating brussels sprouts cringe when they see the vast acreage devoted to raising this miniature "cabbage," a member of the mustard family. But there's a good reason, as devoted aficionados know: a properly prepared brussels sprout is a toothsome delight. Never boil brussels sprouts and never ever overcook them. A mishandled sprout will release offensive odors and taste like cardboard. Gently steam the sprouts until they are just tender and begin to release a delicately nutty fragrance. Then toss them with butter, salt, pepper, a little nutmeg and crushed hazelnuts, and you'll understand what the excitement is all about. The fields run all the way into the suburbs of Santa Cruz.

■ SANTA CRUZ

🚌 To reach Santa Cruz from San Francisco, drive south on CA 1 or cross from US 101 near San Jose and follow Highway 17 through the Santa Cruz Mountains.

Santa Cruz appears to be as much a state of mind as it is a city. If it looks a bit like Southern California, that's perhaps because it has more sandy beaches and more sun than any place north of Pismo Beach. Because Santa Cruz is so liberal, it does not discriminate against homeless, against those exhibiting alternate lifestyles, or against wayward teenagers. In Santa Cruz some folks carry their fish hooks in their nostrils, ears, or nipples; elsewhere they put them into tackle boxes.

The town's liberal epicenter, by the way, is up the hill on the University of California at Santa Cruz campus, but its professors and students live all over town.

Santa Cruz surfing club, 1941. (Courtesy, Harry Mayo, pictured third from right)

■ SURF CAPITAL

The reliable surf of these shores has brought surfers, making Santa Cruz in particular a surfing capital. Surfing also fosters a special, laid-back lifestyle, since surfing seems to be less a form of recreation than a way of life. Daniel Duane describes a "surf session" in his book *Caught Inside,* as "a small occurrence outside the linear march of time," and explains that:

O̱ne often hears surfing compared to sex; quite a stretch, except perhaps in the unselfconscious participation in a pattern of energy, in a constant physical response to a changing medium—at its best, emptying your mind of past and future.

You see the cars and pick-up trucks of surfers parked all along the coast, from Montara south to Santa Cruz, and you can watch surfers, dark as sea lions in their wet suits, riding every major break, including the huge and dangerous ones further north at Mavericks.

■ SANTA CRUZ SITES

Signs from Highway 1 lead down commercial streets to the interesting parts of town, including a lively downtown and many woodsy neighborhoods filled with gracious houses. Attractive old buildings have been refurbished, and along Pacific Avenue you'll find a great bookstore-cafe, flower sellers, and locally owned shops.

It's a nice town to be in, with a real sense of place. If you need to re-energize yourself, you can take the pick of several first-rate coffee and espresso shops, and on a sunny day, head out to Lighthouse Point, to look at the surfers zooming down Steamer Lane.

Pacific Avenue also leads to one of the coast's earliest amusement parks, the "Boardwalk," erected at the turn of the 19th century. If you're in the mood for a roller-coaster ride, cotton candy, and a corn dog, this is the place to come. The unmistakable Giant Dipper is the only wooden roller coaster left on the West Coast. **Santa Cruz City Beach**, directly in front of the boardwalk is the perfect spot for observing the local wildlife of the human kind—you'll see more Lolitas in bikinis, more teenagers, more punks, and more vacationers in short-shorts than you'll find anywhere else on the coast.

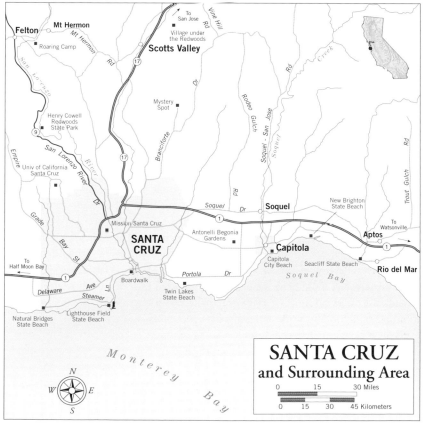

SANTA CRUZ
and Surrounding Area

THAT SPECIAL SANTA CRUZ LIFESTYLE

Santa Cruz is the town with the most alternative lifestyles on the coast, but that's nothing unusual, for the special Santa Cruz lifestyle started quite early, in 1797.

Six years after Mission Santa Cruz was founded, a civilian settlement was established by decree of the Viceroy of Mexico on the east bank of the San Lorenzo River and named Villa de Branciforte after him. Since the viceroy couldn't find any volunteers to populate his new town, he rounded up the sort of folk the government couldn't get along with and shipped them up the coast. The mission priests couldn't get along with them either, even though a river separated them, and they clashed right from the beginning, and constantly thereafter. The first real crisis came in 1818, when the privateer Hippolyte de Bouchard sacked Monterey. He was expected to sack Santa Cruz, too. So the Spanish governor gave orders to abandon the mission and town. The priests fled, instructing the Brancifortians to take care of the mission goods. They did, and they were said to be especially happy when they discovered the padres' stash of aguardiente (brandy).

Had Bouchard actually arrived, he could probably have shanghaied the entire town—without an iota of resistance. When the padres returned, they wanted their goods back, but the Brancifortians replied with the Spanish-colonial equivalent of 'finders-keepers.'

Then, as now, Santa Crucians did not give much of a hoot about religion. After the Mexicans secularized the mission in 1834, it melted away, but Branciforte prevailed, even if it took the older name. The place soon became a hangout for whalers and loggers out for a good night on the town. By the 1860s, the first summer cottages, hotels, and bathhouses popped up. Going to the beaches became popular and Santa Cruz had one major advantage: the water was (and still is) warm enough for swimming, since the town faces south.

Santa Cruz has many comfortable, Victorian-era houses. The downtown, damaged in the Loma Prieta earthquake of 1989, is now rebuilt and very inviting. If the approaches to the city are banal-modern with dull little motels and fast food outlets, the back streets and those along the beach areas are lined with charming small cottages and gardens. It's never been a tourist mecca; it's always been a place for local tourists, people from San Jose, or the farming valleys or the peninsula towns. A few rich people built mansions on the bluffs, and one of these, James D. Phelan, opened his home to writers and artists like Gertrude Atherton (who appears to have had a quiet affair with Phelan), Ambrose Bierce, Isadora Duncan, Jack London, and Joaquin Miller. It set the tone for things to come.

The **Municipal Wharf,** a few feet up the bay, served primarily as a commercial fishing wharf until about 1960, when it was converted to restaurants and shops.

From the Boardwalk drive north to West Cliff Drive and find your way to **Lighthouse Point**—one of the best places anywhere to watch surfing. Backed by a grassy park-like area with big trees, the blufftop sidewalk is a great place for a stroll, or to sit on one of the benches and read the Sunday paper. Off the cliffs is Steamer Lane,

Spectators observe surfers from Steamer Lane.

GOLDEN GATE
TO SAN SIMEON

where a large contingent of Northern California's best surfers can be found any day the surf is up. It's best in the wintertime and the biggest surf begins way out at the end of the point. An expert surfer will begin out there and cruise in toward the beach. In summer the surf is low, and you'll see surfers cutting up little waves close to shore. There's also a sort of temple of surfing, the **Santa Cruz Surfing Museum** in the lighthouse replica on West Cliff Drive.

■ SOUTH OF SANTA CRUZ ON MONTEREY BAY

Other pleasant, sandy, and often sunny beaches in the Santa Cruz area include: **Seabright Beach, Capitola City Beach** (backed by shops), **New Brighton State Beach, Sunset State Beach,** and **Palm Beach.**

At **Aptos,** east of Santa Cruz, **Seacliff State Beach and Pier** has a sandy beach with campsites and trailer hookups right on the sand. A fishing pier runs out to the rear section of a peculiar relic, a concrete, 435-foot World War I supply ship, which once served as an amusement pier with a dance floor on the deck (take Aptos-Seacliff exit on CA 1).

Once past the cluster of beachfront villages south of Santa Cruz, the road traverses a rustic landscape of dairy farms and artichoke fields.

Marked by a tall-stacked power plant are Moss Landing and **Elkhorn Slough.** The latter is a great place to go birding in a canoe or kayak.

Just beyond Moss Landing, pull off at a roadside stand and stock up. This is the lower Salinas Valley, the very heartland of American artichoke production. Or take the short side road into **Castroville,** the "artichoke capital of the world," and stop at the Giant Artichoke for fresh or deep-fried artichokes as well as for other local farm products. Today, the lower Salinas Valley not only grows artichokes, but is also the lettuce bowl of the nation, supporting a $2 billion annual agricultural economy. The artichoke fields end where the sand dunes start, and while the dunes are beautiful in themselves, they hide much of the shore from the road.

■ MONTEREY PENINSULA

Monterey Bay is impressive both from the land, as you look south or north along the vast crescent of sandy shore, and from the window of an airplane, which allows you to see the beautiful, long, gleaming sweep in one glance. Sandy beaches and dunes dominate the shore between Santa Cruz and Monterey, but at Monterey, at the southern end of the bay, spurs of the Santa Lucia Mountains encroach on the beaches, forming the Monterey Peninsula, with its spectacular rocky headlands.

In the autumn of 1769, a ragtag band of Spanish soldiers and missionaries invaded this area. It was Don Juan Gaspar de Portola and his men, who had traveled north to take possession of the land for the King of Spain. They meant to find Monterey

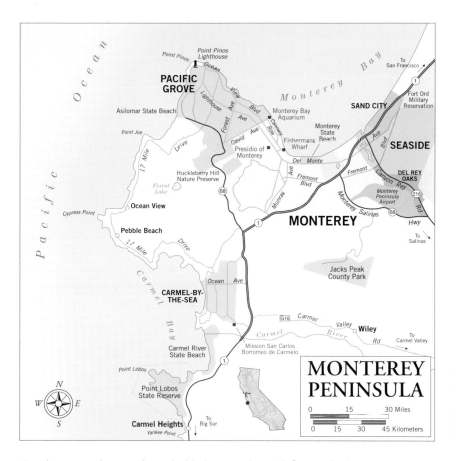

MONTEREY PENINSULA

0   15   30 Miles

0   15   30   45 Kilometers

Bay but missed it, so they plodded onwards until from a lookout point above modern day Pacifica, they saw San Francisco Bay. But they returned to Monterey in the spring of 1770 to found a presidio and mission. Monterey served as the capital of California from 1775 until the American occupation of California in 1848.

There are several ways to reach the Monterey Peninsula. You can drive south from San Francisco on Highway 1, following the route laid out in the previous pages of this chapter, or you can travel from US 101 near Salinas and cross west on CA 68 (until it intersects with Highway 1; *see maps above and on page 167*). The southernmost Monterey exit leads to Cannery Row and the Monterey Bay

Aquarium. Just follow the signs. For easy access to Monterey's historic downtown and the waterfront, you might want to park your car at centrally located Fisherman's Wharf, which has ample (pay) parking.

■ MONTEREY'S FISHERMAN'S WHARF

Monterey's historic Fisherman's Wharf has been spruced up in recent years, but somehow it still works. You'll see more visitors than fishermen, of course (to see the latter, you'll have to go across the harbor to Municipal Wharf No. 2). Seafood restaurants are tucked between fish markets and seashell, T-shirt, and knickknack shops—most of them with spectacular views of the rocky shore, the harbor, or the ocean. Sea lions hang out beneath the piers; brown pelicans may perch on the roofs. (They can be seen roosting on near-shore rocks for most of the year.) You can enjoy decent seafood salads at the restaurants, fresh fish, or deep-fried squid (while looking out the picture windows and watching sea otters frolic in the kelp) or you can order bowls of clam chowder, accompanied by chunks of French bread, or deep-fried artichokes at one of several take-out places.

Fisherman's Wharf sits more or less right in the center of Monterey harbor, a breakwater-protected embayment on the east shore of the peninsula. Its northern end is marked by the Coast Guard Pier, its southern end by Municipal Wharf No. 2, which is where the warehouses are and where boats unload sand dabs, sole, squid, shrimp, salmon, rockfish, anchovies, herring, and sardines (you can drive onto the pier from the south end of the parking lot).

❖

During Spanish and Mexican times passengers and goods were landed by surf boat in the small sandy cove below the harbor's customs house. It got its first pier in 1870. Local fisheries got their start from Chinese fishermen who harvested abalone and squid, then Sicilian fishermen who conquered the huge schools of sardines coursing along the shores.

Carmel poet Robinson Jeffers described the sardine fishery as a beautiful and terrible scene, with the fish caught in the seine wildly beating "from one wall to the other of their closing destiny the phosphorescent water to a pool of flame, each beautiful slender body sheeted with flame, like a live rocket, a comet's tail wake of yellow flame."

■ CANNERY ROW

In the mid 1940s, John Steinbeck wrote:

> Cannery Row in Monterey in California is a poem, a stink, a grating
> noise, a quality of light, a tone, a habit, a nostalgia, a dream. Cannery
> Row is the gathered and scattered, tin and iron and rust and splintered
> wood, chipped pavement and weedy lots and junk heaps, sardine canner-
> ies of corrugated iron, honky tonks, restaurants and whore houses, and
> little crowded groceries, and laboratories and flophouses. Its inhabitants
> are, as the man once said, "whores, pimps, gamblers, and sons of bitches,"
> by which he meant Everybody. Had the man looked through another
> peephole he might have said, "saints and angels and martyrs and holy
> men," and he would have meant the same thing.

Once sardines are caught in great numbers, there has to be a way to process, store,
and market them. Monterey's incipient canneries, which were built to can the local
salmon, were soon converted into sardine canneries and fish reduction plants, creating the effect which Steinbeck so aptly described above in his novel *Cannery Row*
as a poem and a stink.

Boat owners of Cannery Row provide food and beer at this 1937 Sardine Week Celebration.
(The Pat Hathaway Collection, Monterey)

Many of Monterey's citizens failed to recognize the "poetic" aspect of the canneries and heard only the noise, and objected to the stink. Tom Mangelsdorf, in *A History of Steinbeck's Cannery Row,* gives a good synopsis of the battles between citizens, fishermen, and cannery owners. These fights lasted until the sardines, which had been overfished for decades, ran out in the early 1950s. By strange coincidence, the heavily insured canneries began to burn down almost as soon as the fish ran out. But the waterfront was too pretty to be left to rot. In the 1970s and 1980s, new restaurants and hotels sprang up.

To those of us who have read and enjoyed John Steinbeck's novel, the "new" Cannery Row seems like another gussied up "historic" mall. There's none of the old aura (and fortunately none of the old aroma) left. But the removal of canneries has opened up the beautiful shoreline, with its rocks, seabirds, tidepools, and offshore kelp beds where sea otters hang out and where you can, at times, watch white egrets stand *on* the floating kelp, waiting for fish to swim by (a curious sight, since egrets, unlike gulls, pelicans, and cormorants, do *not* swim).

❖

Now, not even the return of the sardines can bring back the canneries of old. And, strange to say, the sardines are returning. This brings us to an ironic footnote: Because canned Monterey sardines were not tasty enough to attract willing buyers, the canneries often made more money from fish reduced to fish oil and meal; but fresh Monterey sardines, prepared by a competent chef are a gourmet's delight.

Today, sardines have made such a comeback they are the second most valuable seafood landed by California fishermen, right after squid.

■ MONTEREY BAY AQUARIUM

The main reason for visiting Cannery Row is the Monterey Bay Aquarium, which is partly tucked into the old shell of the Pioneer Hovden Cannery (immortalized by John Steinbeck as the "Hediondo," i.e., "Stinking Cannery"). This huge aquarium complex, which first opened its doors in October of 1984, is one of the most exciting places to visit on the coast. You'll get an idea of the vastness of the place when you step into the entry hall and see a full-sized *lampara* boat (a Sicilian lanteen-rigged fishing boat that pioneered the Monterey sardine fishery) suspended from the ceiling. A group of life-sized cetacean sculptures—a gray whale, orca, and

Jellyfish at the Monterey Bay Aquarium.

other whales and dolphins—suspended from the ceiling a bit up the hall, are actually dwarfed by the cavernous interior.

There's nothing small about this aquarium, not even the tanks. One has a full-sized, multiple-story re-creation of a kelp forest (it's so big, a scuba diver drops into the tank to feed the fish). In several of the big tanks, the huge swirling mass of fish conveys with vivid immediacy the energy of the ocean.

Monterey Canyon, just offshore, is one of the world's richest marine habitats, and the aquarium allows you to share in the bounty, by bringing fish, shellfish, and sea mammals up close to you, where you can watch them in an almost natural habitat. If the viewing windows of the sea otter tank inside are too crowded, which they often are, just step outside and look for sea otters in the kelp. Free spotting scopes (mounted on columns) bring them very close.

One room has an artificial beach were you can take a long, leisurely look at shorebirds like sanderlings, snowy plovers, black-necked stilts, and phalaropes.

There's even a petting tank for rays and other "touchable" fish. In short, this aquarium gets you as close to the energy and beauty of fish and other sea life in a natural habitat as you'll ever get without donning scuba gear. Needless to say, this aquarium is *very* popular. To avoid long lines plan to visit in the off-season or in

Monterey Bay is home to hundreds of playful sea otters.

midweek; call 831-648-4888. The aquarium also has an excellent restaurant and a first-rate bookstore.

■ PACIFIC GROVE

Pacific Grove starts on the other side of the aquarium and old Cannery Row. This pleasant town spreads over the northern tip of the peninsula, from Monterey all the way to Point Pinos with its ancient (1855) lighthouse—the oldest continuously operating lighthouse on the West Coast—and on to Asilomar Beach.

Lighthouse Avenue runs from Monterey's Cannery Row through Pacific Grove, all the way to the end of the peninsula at Point Pinos. It is one of the most pleasant, old-fashioned main streets on the coast, with small shops, bookstores, and no tourist hubbub. Side roads lead to Lover's Point and other headlands and beaches on the eastern shore of the peninsula.

Several pleasant inns make it possible for you to stay near Point Pinos, with its low rocky cliffs, dunes, and sandy beaches—all washed by a white surf and a turquoise- and indigo-colored sea. You can reach Lover's Point, with its jagged rocks, warm, sandy beach, and tree-shaded picnic area (one of the scenic highlights of this coast and frequented by some of the greediest and most aggressive gulls anywhere) by walking west around the point from Asilomar Beach, or by a number of side streets. From Lover's Point, a very pleasant, landscaped park with many benches for resting your weary limbs, runs atop the cliffs all the way to the Monterey Bay Aquarium. Other trails lead to quiet sandy coves and surf-swept rocky headlands.

Thanks to waters warmed by El Niño, whale-watchers off Monterey had a once-in-a-lifetime experience in January of 1998, when a gray whale give birth north of Point Piños—a highly unusual occurrence since these whales usually deliver their young in the warm, sheltered lagoons of Baja California.

Pacific Grove has an excellent **Museum of Natural History** at 165 Forest Avenue; 831-648-3116; and there's a small museum in the cottage at 222 Central Avenue where John Steinbeck wrote many of his novels.

■ 17-MILE DRIVE

One of the Monterey Peninsula's most popular attractions has a great number of fans as well as detractors. The latter call it glorified real estate with an access fee;

the former love it for its scenic beauty. Decide for yourself. Access by car is easy: just follow the signs from Pacific Grove or Carmel. If you want to walk onto it, park your car at the western end of Asilomar Beach and take the trail that runs on a boardwalk through the marsh at Sunset Avenue, and then through the low dunes and over bluffs and beaches to the Inn at Spanish Bay. (No toll is charged for the trail.) The deer are as plentiful and as friendly as the ones at Point Pinos in Pacific Grove. Who knows, they may be the same deer wandering around from one lea to the next.

The scenery is indeed beautiful and there are some spectacular golf courses here, with links overlooking the surf and sea, plus some very ritzy and expensive inns, as well as the famed "Lone Cypress" on a craggy offshore rock. To play golf at the world-famous Pebble Beach Golf Club, you must be a member or have a room at Pebble Beach Lodge. No one but members or guests plays at the shoreside Cypress Golf Club.

■ CARMEL

🚗 Located at the southern curve of the Monterey Peninsula, and reached by taking Highway 1 along the curve of Monterey Bay, or from US 101 near Salinas via CA 68 which intersects with Highway 1.

❖

Carmel has a manicured, prosperous, careful air. Cars are new yet not ostentatious. If a mongrel dog lives here, it's probably kept hidden in a backyard. Despite the town's staid ambience, it's also a woodsy, artsy place—rather self-consciously so since its earliest days. Carmel's citizens several times elected an actor as mayor. But this being California, he was Clint Eastwood, who perfected the role of the world-weary loner in such Westerns as *The Good, the Bad, and the Ugly* and *Unforgiven.*

Ocean Avenue, the main commercial street, runs straight down to the beach from Highway 1 and is lined with pines and attractive old buildings. In them are expensive shops crammed with people, a great many of them European and Japanese tourists. Shops and galleries invite visitors to browse; restaurants serve square, though pricey meals. The food stores are gourmet, and you'll find plenty in them to bring along on a picnic.

At the end of the street is the lovely white-sand cove of Carmel Beach, one of

(continues on page 192)

A sunset worth applauding at Carmel-By-the-Sea.

CARMEL MISSION, 1786

French navigator Jean François de La Pérouse visited Monterey Bay in September of 1786, as commander of L'Astrolabe and La Boussole, the first foreign vessels to visit Spain's California colonies. Ordered and outfitted by King Louis XVI of France, the ships were to spend four years at sea exploring new lands.

La Pérouse was well received by the priests at Carmel Mission. Following are excerpts from his diaries describing his visit, which occurred two years after the death of the mission's founder, Father Junipero Serra.

*I*t is with the most pleasing satisfaction that I speak of the pious and prudent conduct of these religious men, which so perfectly agrees with the goal of their institution. I shall not conceal what I conceived to be reprehensible in their internal administration, but I must affirm that, by being individually good and humane, they

Mission San Carlos Borromeo de Carmel *by Edwin Deakin, 1895.*
(Collection of the Seaver Center for Western History Research,
Natural History Museum of Los Angeles County)

temper by their mildness and charity the austerity of the rules which have been prescribed by their superiors.

❖

The president of the missions, in his ceremonial vestments and with his holy water sprinkle in his hand, awaited us at the gate of the church, which was illuminated in the same manner as on the greatest feast days. . . .

Before we entered the church, we had passed through a square in which the Indians of both sexes were ranged in a line. They exhibited no marks of surprise in their countenance, and left us in doubt whether we should be the subject of their conversation for the rest of the day.

Indians of Monterey *by José Cardero, 1791.* *(Museo Naval, Madrid)*

The color of these Indians, which is that of Negroes; the house of the missionaries; their storehouses, which are built of brick and plastered; the appearance of the ground on which the grain is trodden out; the cattle, the horses—everything in short—brought to our recollection a plantation at Santo Domingo or any other West Indian island. The men and women are collected by the sound of a bell; a missionary leads them to work, to the church, and to all their exercises. We observed with concern that the resemblance is so perfect that we have seen both men and women in irons, and others in the stocks. Lastly, the noise of the whip might have struck our ears, this punishment also being administered, though with little severity.

—Jean François de La Pérouse, Journals, 1786, excerpts from *Life in a California Mission,* Heyday Books

the prettiest anywhere. On a sunny day the water can be turquoise, and it is rimmed with Monterey pines, sheltered and warm. At sunset on a warm evening as many as a hundred people will gather on the sand facing the setting sun. When it sinks below the horizon, they clap in appreciation of the stellar performance, call to their children and dogs, and head home. In the dusk, the white sand is pocketed with blue shadows and looks from a distance like snow.

If you turn south on Scenic Drive at the end of Ocean Avenue, you follow a pretty drive past cottages and pines. The exquisite white-sand beach below is a lovely place to sit and take in a green and turquoise sea. At the southern end of the beach surfers line up for the low but long and well-formed swells.

❖

Carmel was in fact founded by writers and artists . . . sort of. It may have been a canny real estate promoter who first encouraged artists, suspecting that wealthy investors were sure to follow. In any case, Carmel experienced an artistic renaissance in the early 1900s, when such well-known writers as Jack London, George Sterling, Lincoln Steffens, and Mary Austin lived in the seaside woods, as close to nature as they could manage. At times their lives appeared more like staged productions than a slice of reality. According to the *Carmel Pine-Cone:*

> Picnics such as the ones Jimmie Hopper, Mary Austin, George Sterling, Ferdinand Burgdorf and others frequently organized, were regarded as Bacchanalian orgies. The women danced around the bonfires with bare feet, their long hair flying. A gallon jug of red wine was in evidence and anyone who stumbled upon these seemingly mad, wild gatherings was deeply shocked and went away thinking Carmel was getting to be as wicked as Paris.

Robinson Jeffers was only one of many writers who made their homes in Carmel, but while many of them lived here for just a short time, or came to visit, Jeffers stayed and through his writing helped make the region what it is today. If you're visiting on a weekend, plan to take a tour of Robinson Jeffers's Tor House and tower, which the poet built from stone with his own hands. *26304 Ocean View Avenue between Scenic Drive and Stewart Way; 831-624-1813; by reservation only.*

❖

Carmel Mission, as Mission San Carlos Borromeo de Carmelo at the southern end of town is popularly known, was founded by Father Junipero Serra in June of 1770. It has undergone extensive restoration and is, with its beautiful gardens, one of the prettiest and most restful places on the coast. Today, looking at the irregular, gold-brown contours of the old mission, it's hard to put it all together: the glorious site, the idealistic Franciscans who came north from Mexico, and the lives of the local Indians—whose culture was destroyed, and who, themselves, died in great numbers from diseases brought by Europeans.

The Carmel River, bordered by artichoke fields and sandy beaches, enters the ocean just south of the mission. Some of the beautiful land visible along the river belongs to a ranch donated to the state in 1997 by actor Clint Eastwood.

■ CARMEL VALLEY WINERIES

Up Carmel Valley much of the landscape is as pristine as it was two hundred years ago. Although some unfortunate malls have been built in the past few years, there are still signs by the side of the road alerting you to "Newts Crossing." In the acorn season, you can see wild turkeys gobble up the tasty nuts underneath spreading oak trees; at all times of the year, deer, hawks, woodpeckers, and songbirds are plentiful. The Carmel Valley has several excellent wineries, which are well worth a short detour.

———— •◆• ————

■ Chateau Julien
Because this winery occupies a French-style chateau (just off the highway), it looks the way many people think a winery should look. But it's more than just show. The wines, made from Monterey grapes, are excellent. *8940 Carmel Valley Rd.; 408-624-2600.*

■ Bernardus Winery
This state-of-the-art winery, tucked into the rolling hills southeast of the village of Carmel Valley, makes superb estate wines from its Jamesburg vineyards. If there's one winery that will add the Carmel Valley to the international enophile's itinerary, this is the one. Try the cabernet franc and cabernet

sauvignon, merlot, a lovely blend of reds called Marinus, sauvignon blanc, and chardonnay. Tours and tastings by appointment only. *5 W. Carmel Valley Rd.; 408-659-1900.*

■ Georis Winery
This tiny, up-valley winery makes only merlot—but what merlot. Production is minuscule—only some 500 cases per vintage. If you can't find the wine at local wineshops, look for it at the Casanova restaurant in Carmel (which is owned by winemaker Walter Georis) at 5th Ave. between Mission and San Carlos Sts. *4 Pilot Rd.; 408-659-1050.*

■ POINT LOBOS

Point Lobos, a jagged, surf-swept headland, carved into sandy coves and rocky promontories by the constant pounding of waves, is one of the coast's most spectacularly scenic places. Wind-sculpted Monterey cypresses make their last stand on these cliffs; their ragged foliage and gnarled, salt-bleached trunks add an intensely dramatic accent to the barren cliffs, which rise straight from the white surf. Forests of dark Monterey pine and wildflower meadows cover the back slopes.

This landscape is not as "virginal" as it looks—it has a past. It was once part of a cattle ranch and supported, at different times, a whaling station, a granite quarry, an abalone cannery, and a loading chute for a coal mine. One previous owner even tried to subdivide the point—laying out a townsite with a harsh gridiron of streets.

Today, Point Lobos looks as pristine as any landscape trod by man can ever be. If you see some small (about three-foot-high) people standing in the shadow of rocks or trees, watching you, ignore them. They're the "watchers" and they are said to pop up throughout the Big Sur area. Supposedly they leave you alone if you stick to the trails, but dire things are said to happen if you don't. Some of the folk who have seen the watchers have also seen elves at Point Lobos.

Mist Over Point Lobos *by Guy Rose, ca. 1918.*
(Fleischer Museum, Scottsdale, Arizona)

GOLDEN GATE
TO SAN SIMEON

The dramatic beauty of the Big Sur coast.

■ BIG SUR COAST

While the term "Big Sur" was originally only applied to the valley of the river, it later came to connote the entire coast from Point Lobos to Lucia.

The 90-mile stretch of road from Carmel south along the Big Sur coast has some 30 turnouts with beach or cliff access and spectacular views; the road rises and falls from an altitude of as little as 20 feet to 1,200-foot cliff tops as it winds its way around precipitous headlands and into narrow canyons. In winter, be prepared for washouts, fallen rocks on the road, mudslides, and water over the roadway. In summer, there's usually a fair amount of traffic.

South of the Carmel River, the coast turns rocky, its steepness mitigated only occasionally by the gentler slopes of marine terraces. Here mountains edge up to the sea, and the pines and cypresses of Monterey give way to grassy slopes, brilliantly green during the winter rainy season, dotted with patches of golden poppies in spring, and clothed in a drab tan coat in summer, during the dry part of the year. Lofty bridges span creek chasms where redwoods grow. All along the Big Sur coast—wherever you can get close enough to the water—you should be able to watch sea otters, as the stretch of shoreline from Monterey Bay south to Point San Luis has the largest concentration of these playful mammals in California.

Only one road (G 14) runs east across the Santa Lucia Mountains, but in places the "road" is a mere track.

■ NORTHERN BIG SUR BEACHES AND WOODS

See map page 167

■ Garrapata State Park
Located on the northern Big Sur coast, this beach stretches along four miles of coast. It is still undeveloped but has roadside turnouts for parking and rough trails leading to the water.

■ Andrew Molera State Beach
A trail here leads to the mouth of the Big Sur River, which may be impassable during winter high water. Trails lead to meadows and bluffs; the lagoon has some great birdwatching. The highway runs inland along the Big Sur River and into the redwoods before switching back to the coast. Walk-in campground.

■ Pfeiffer Beach
A truly magic place at the end of Sycamore Canyon Road (one mile south of Pfeiffer Big Sur State Park; not well marked). Crashing waves, sea caves, and arches.

■ Julia Pfeiffer Burns State Park
Wooded, tucked into a canyon above the ocean, a trail leads to an overlook where McWay waterfall plunges 50 feet into the sea. As the surf splashes against the rock,

the water falls back in an arc, creating the illusion of a second, smaller, waterfall. When the sun breaks through the clouds and paints a rainbow onto the sea spray, it's pure magic.

■ Pfeiffer Big Sur State Park
There's no beach here, but redwoods and some great trails into the back country. Over 200 campsites, access to Big Sur River. Check out Pfeiffer Falls and The Gorge.

■ Limekiln State Beach
From here south, much of the beach access is for experienced mountain climbers only; other parts of the beach have steep trails even energetic amateurs can scramble up and down on. Limekiln State Beach takes its name from abandoned limekilns nearby, and is one of the few good camping spots on the Big Sur coast. Jade Cove has pebbles and boulders of nephrite. The state began getting a bit nervous about jade removed from the beach after divers took a 9,000-pound jade boulder, worth $180,000, in 1971.

Julia Pfeiffer Burns State Park.

POETRY AND LIGHT, MYTH AND MADNESS

Rosalind Sharpe Wall, who grew up at Bixby Creek (a canyon best known for the large "Rainbow" bridge spanning it), recalls some of the coast's early history in her book *A Wild Coast and Lonely: Big Sur Pioneers*. Until the coast highway was finished in 1937, only a wagon road penetrated as far south as Big Sur. "There were women," writes Wall, "who had never been to town in their entire lives." The men apparently went to town once a year to sell cattle and farm products.

Novelist Jack Kerouac visited Big Sur in the late 1950s, and stayed at Lawrence Ferlinghetti's cabin in Bixby Canyon (which he calls "Raton Canyon")—and he did almost go mad here, as he claimed in his book *Big Sur*. At night, he hears a noise that ". . . . rises up crashing mysteriously at me from a raging battle among dark things, wood or rock or something cracked, all smashed, all wet black sunken earth danger . . . . ."

Local writer John Steinbeck described the Big Sur backcountry in a short story titled *"Flight"* (from *The Long Valley*). Steinbeck's mother had worked here as a schoolteacher, and claimed to have seen the "watchers." *(See Point Lobos, page 194)*

I first heard about the Big Sur coast from a potter, when I was a college student in Southern California. Several of us sat out in the art studio patio, talking, and the potter mentioned he'd spent the weekend at Big Sur.

"What did you do?"

"Nothing. You don't have to do anything at Big Sur. I sat on a big rock most of the time."

"What did you think about? Did you get any creative ideas?"

"You don't need to think at Big Sur. It will think for you."

"What did it think for you?"

"It makes me want to reproduce the colors of the surf and the cliffs and the grasses and the trees and the fog and the haze in my glazes."

"Will you do it?"

"I can't. No one can reproduce the special light of Big Sur. Photographers have tried and painters and poets, and they've all fallen short. I'm just a potter."

He was right. Because I have tried to capture the Big Sur spirit with brush, camera, and pen, and I have not yet succeeded.

If anyone has come close to catching the spirit of Big Sur, it was Robinson Jeffers, the coast's poet laureate. Jeffers describes the coastal landscape near Sobranes Point as "no trees, but dark scant pasture drawn thin/ Over rock shaped like flame . . . ." *(The Place for No Story),* and states the thesis for which he is perhaps best known, that, "this coast [is] crying out for tragedy like all beautiful places . . . ." *(Apology for Bad Dreams).* Jeffers has been considered a "gloomy" poet, because of his preoccupation with the more tragic events of the lonely Big Sur coast. But Henry Miller understood the truth of Jeffers's poetic vision. He defended him in *Big Sur and the Oranges of Hieronymous Bosch:*

"If Jeffers's narratives smack of Greek tragedy, it is because he discovered here the same physical atmosphere in which the Greek gods and heroes (whose stories he knew well) met their fates. The light here is almost as electric, the hills almost as bare, the community almost as autonomous as in ancient Greece. The rugged pioneers who settled here needed only a voice to make known their secret drama. And Jeffers was that voice.

More than the works of any other writer, in fact more than raw nature itself, his poems provide the visitor with an understanding of hidden forces at work on this mysterious coast."

Rosalind Wall, who knew Jeffers, echoes Miller's sentiment: ". . . without Jeffers, the landscape could never have been voiced the way it was and without the landscape he could never have found his own true voice." Some residents of the coast certainly thought Jeffers went a bit too far in adapting local family histories for his epic poems. One neighbor was so angry with Jeffers, says Wall, "that she talked of suing him."

There is beauty here, too of course, equal to the potential for tragedy. Even Bohemian carouser Jack Kerouac appreciated the beauty of the coast. Of a drive to Nepenthe, the justly famous cliffside restaurant overlooking mountains and the sea, he wrote ". . . . it is beautiful especially to see up ahead north a vast expanse of curving seacoast with inland mountains dreaming under slow clouds, . . ."

His description of Nepenthe reads like a glowing restaurant review and is as true now as it was 40 years ago. Fortunately, some places do not change very much.

(following pages) The southern Big Sur coast where the mountains rise 3,000 to 5,000 feet above the Pacific Ocean.

■ NEPENTHE

Nepenthe restaurant is the sort of place everybody loves, and not because it happens to be one of the few restaurants on the coast, and the only one with a spectacular view. I stopped here last on one of those rare winter days when the pale sun and the weak fogs of winter, and the spindrift of the surf drape the coast in ethereal light. As I sat by the window, enjoying a superb ahi sandwich, I looked south for a long way, past gnarled live oaks, past redwood-filled creek canyons, past Partington Ridge, where novelist Henry Miller lived during the 1940s and 1950s. He wrote:

> *B*ig Sur has a climate of its own and a character all its own. It is a region where extremes meet, a region where one is always conscious of weather, of space, of grandeur, and of eloquent silence. . . . In summer, when the fogs roll in, one can look down upon a sea of clouds floating listlessly above the ocean; they have the appearance, at times, of huge, iridescent soap bubbles, over which, now and then, may be seen a double rainbow.

Miller's memory is kept alive by the **Henry Miller Memorial Library,** founded in the 1960s by Miller's friend, the poet Emil White, in his home. It's about a mile south of Nepenthe, in a sharp curve of the highway, half-hidden under tall redwoods. This shrine for Miller fans is open in the afternoon, but hours may vary, especially in the off-season.

❖

The stretch of coast south of here is about as rugged and beautiful as any part of California gets. The mountains drop into the surf at an even steeper angle than they do north of the Big Sur River. There are hidden waterfalls here, hidden beaches, and splendid cliffs and mountainsides (though a few are messed up by big, ragged clumps of pampas grass, planted to combat erosion). The cliffs and steep mountainsides are covered mostly with chaparral and scrub and a few trees (redwoods in the canyons), and even a few succulents precariously clinging to steep cliff faces. But mostly, it's naked rock. Poet Robinson Jeffers wrote in his poem *November Surf:*

> *L*ike the steep necks of a herd of horses
> Lined on a river margin, athirst in summer, the mountain ridges
> Pitch to the sea, the lean granite-boned heads
> Plunge nostril-under…

*The trail above Julia Pfeiffer Beach is just one
many wonderful places to hike along the Big Sur Coast.*

■ ROAD TO SAN SIMEON

The biggest surprise along the Coast Highway comes on the southern stretch of the road: South of Gorda the mountains recede from the coast. Low marine terraces and gently rolling, grass-covered hills rise from the sea, creating a complete change of scenery.

■ HEARST CASTLE

Hearst Castle rises from the rounded top of a hill southeast of the highway. The castle, officially known as Hearst San Simeon State Historical Monument, is the sort of place art snobs hate and the general public loves. And there's a good reason to hold either opinion. Constructed between 1920 and 1950, as newspaper magnate William R. Hearst's private estate, the monument still contains pieces of Hearst's extensive art collection and herds of exotic animals. And herein lies the clue to understanding this place: Hearst was an eclectic collector (for background information, watch the Orson Welles movie *Citizen Kane*), and it is precisely this

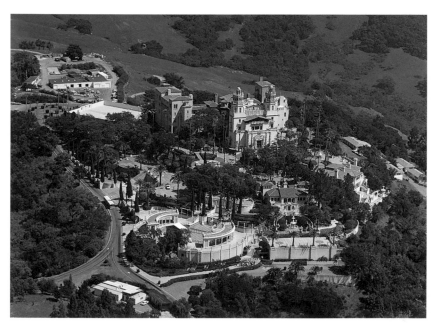

An aerial view of William Randolph Hearst's massive estate.
(Courtesy, Hearst San Simeon State Historical Monument)

eclecticism that makes the castle so popular and qualifies it for folk art status—just like Simon Rodia's Watts Towers in Los Angeles, albeit on a rather larger, more magnificent scale.

But Hearst and Rodia operated in a similar manner. Both collected eclectic objects and incorporated them into their dream structures. Rodia used found objects—glass, metal, bits of porcelain, et al. to decorate his towers. Hearst "found" his objects all over the world and paid big money for them, and instead of designing his pleasure dome bit by bit, he hired a famous architect (Julia Morgan) to arrange the objects for him. The principle is the same, even though Hearst's "found" objects have greater intrinsic value. It's the eclectic assembly that counts and turns the castle as well as the towers into objects of folk art. It's also fair to say that San Simeon is more than the sum of its parts. It remains a classic American nouveau-riche exuberance, beautiful in its own way, and considered a fabulous getaway by the Hollywood stars Hearst entertained there, among them his mistress, Marion Davies, whose career he shamelessly promoted in his newspapers. *750 Hearst Castle Road. For tour reservations, call 800-444-4445.*

For a less famous sample of the same enthusiasm, see Nitwit Ridge in nearby Cambria Pines, an unusual residence built by local contractor Al Beal, also known as "Captain Nitwit." This several-story house, which covers a hillside plot, was built of concrete embedded with bits of seashell, glass, beer cans, auto parts, and other found objects. The home is a California Historical Landmark. *On Hillcrest Drive, off Main Street.*

■ SAN SIMEON STATE BEACH

Sandy San Simeon State Beach runs from Santa Rosa Creek north to San Simeon Creek. William R. Hearst Memorial State Beach has a swimming area that is protected from the worst excesses of the ocean by San Simeon Point and a picnic area in a eucalyptus grove.

 NOTE FOR DRIVERS CONTINUING SOUTH:
The following chapter begins at Point Mugu near Malibu and ends just south of San Simeon on page 248. We hope drivers continuing south won't find it too onerous to switch directions as they read that chapter. Our reason for having done this? The majority of travelers come into the area south of San Simeon by driving north from Los Angeles.

CENTRAL COAST RIVIERA

■ HIGHLIGHTS

Point Mugu State Beach
Channel Islands
Santa Barbara
Winery Tours
Guadalupe Sand Dunes
San Luis Obispo
Morro Bay
Cambria
Missions

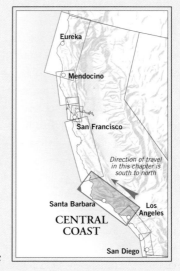

Eureka

Mendocino

San Francisco

Direction of travel in this chapter is south to north

Santa Barbara

Los Angeles

CENTRAL COAST

San Diego

■ TRAVEL OVERVIEW

From Point Mugu north to Ventura, the
Coast Highway runs away from the sea,
through the fertile plain of the Santa Clara River. Offshore lie the wild and
undeveloped Channel Islands, which can be visited by boat provided by the
National Park Service concessionaire (see page 212). North of Ventura the
coastal corridor narrows as the mountains push closer to the sea, leaving barely
enough room between the steep, unstable bluffs and the surf for the highway
to pass through. The pristine landscape of the coast is interrupted only occasionally by a few clusters of homes, oil derricks, and oil pumps.

The town of Santa Barbara is the urban highlight of this trip. Even if you
only have time to get a glimpse of the town as it rises in tiers from the sea toward the mountains, topped by the two-towered facade of the mission, you'll
be impressed by its picture-perfect aspects. Inland from Santa Barbara are several vineyard-laden valleys whose wineries are discussed in this chapter.

Highway 1 and US 101 leave the coast at Gaviota Pass and separate. They
do not return to the coast until they merge again in Pismo Beach and once

again run together inland to San Luis Obispo. To the east is open ranch country; on the coast are towns of charm and interest.

■ TRAVEL BASICS

Climate
The coast from Point Mugu to Santa Barbara and Point Conception enjoys an ideal climate—sunny virtually the year round, with an occasional winter storm between December and March. Summer temperatures average near 80 degrees; winter, 65 degrees. A hot offshore wind, the Santa Ana, occasionally blasts the coastal communities between September and November raising temperatures to extreme levels (115 degrees once in Santa Barbara) and creating danger of wildfires. From Point Conception north to San Simeon the climate is a little cooler and wetter (15 to 25 inches of rain). Water Temperature: From Malibu to Santa Barbara water temperatures average 65 to 70 degrees in late summer and in the low 60s the rest of the year. From Point Conception— which marks the dividing line between a cold northern current and a warmer current coming up from the south—the water is 55 to 65 degrees and unsuitable for swimming.

Food and Lodging
This stretch of coast has some of the most delicious foods found in all of California—fish and shellfish fresh from the sea including tuna, rockfish, squid, red rock crabs, spiny lobsters, and mussels; avocados and other subtropical fruits, including locally raised bananas; and from the Santa Maria Valley, strawberries and winter vegetables. Both Santa Barbara and San Luis Obispo Counties have world-class wineries (see pages 225-228 and 241-242).

Lodging ranges from the comfortable to the sublime. While Santa Barbara seems to foster the utterly sybaritic away from the immediate shore, some of the most comfortable lodgings with a view can be found along San Luis Bay, from Pismo Beach northwest to Avila Beach. In Santa Barbara hotel rooms fill up quickly, especially in summer. Reserve well in advance. (See pages 339-390 for lodging and restaurant listings.)

■ POINT MUGU NORTH

This stretch of coast is at its prettiest on a misty morning, when the hillside houses float above the fog like the temples of a Japanese landscape painting, and when the blue ocean sparkles brightly beneath swirling bands of ocean vapors. Flowers and trees and bluffs look unreal at such times; only sand, the surf, and the water look real, making a visit to the beach seem like you're submerging yourself in a sea of liquid gold.

Point Mugu State Park, bordering the highway, has many sandy pocket beaches, including **Point Mugu Beach**. The last time I visited I saw brown pelicans catching their breakfast, and sea lions and common dolphins offshore. **Mugu Lagoon**, one of Southern California's largest remaining wetlands, lies entirely within the U.S. Navy's Pacific Missile Test Center. A fine view of the lagoon can be enjoyed from the roadside turnout on CA 1, a half mile north of Point Mugu Rock. Mugu Submarine Canyon, half a mile deep and over nine miles long, lies offshore. *Group tours during the winter birding season may be arranged by calling the U.S. Navy's public affairs office at 805-989-8094.*

Due to shore erosion in the Point Mugu area, the coastal highway has been moved inland.

At the mouth of La Jolla Canyon is the 10.8-mile **Ray Miller hiking trail**, a well-graded loop that leads into the coastal foothills, and provides stunning views of the coastline below and, on clear days, the Channel Islands in the distance. There's overnight (permit-only) camping at La Jolla Valley Camp. *For more information, maps, and permits call Point Mugu State Park; 805-488-5223.*

CA 1 curves inland around the missile range, then becomes a freeway cutting through one of the most fertile agricultural areas in the world. To the left of the freeway is a different collection of birds—a display of all sorts of spiky rockets and things designed to kill and maim, but looking surprisingly like an assemblage of oversized spears protruding from the ground.

■ CHANNEL ISLANDS

Seen through the ocean haze of a clear day on the beach, these offshore islands seem to float above the sea like rocky wraiths. They do indeed appear as elusive as ghosts, for on most days you cannot see them at all, even though

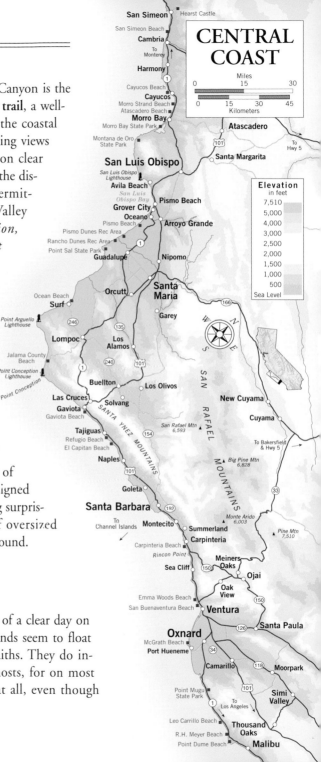

CENTRAL COAST

A sunrise view from East Anacapa Island.
(Photo by Sean Arbabi)

they lie just a dozen or so miles off one of the most populated stretches of the Southern California coast.

They're known as the Channel Islands because they are strung out like a natural breakwater and form the Santa Barbara Channel, which stretches from the northwestern Santa Barbara coast southeast to Ventura County.

Because these islands lie between the cold California Current which rushes south from Point Conception and the warm Southern California Current which flows north along the shore from Mexico, their shores are the battleground of these two clashing ocean streams, and they are often swathed in fog or buffeted by wind. The climatic extremes created by the mingling of cold and warm waters and chilly and hot air, as well as the scarcity of fresh water, drove away most of the early white settlers and may be the reason why these islands have remained virtually unsettled, ever since the last of the native Chumash were carried off to mainland missions 200 years ago.

Though cliffs and mountains dominate the insular landscapes, these islands may look surprisingly intangible even when you approach them on a clear, sunny day by boat and run in right under their surf-swept rocky shores. Rising sheer and straight-sided from the waves, they look like giant ships breasting the ocean, especially on windy days when surf breaks high on the sharply pointed cliffs, making the islands appear like a flotilla of aircraft carriers running out to sea.

But even that is part of the island illusion: these islands are much more than just barren sea rocks. They have sea caves, sandy coves, grassy glens, wildflower meadows, shady forests of oak and pine, and hillsides covered with chaparral and fragrant sage. Dry and golden under the summer sun like most of Southern

CHUMASH MARINERS

The canoe, tomol or tomolo, was one of the glories of the Chumash. . . . The Chumash . . . were mariners; they took to their boats not only when necessity demanded, but daily, so far as weather permitted.
—Anthropologist A. L. Kroeber

If you travel to the Channel Islands today, you can't help but think about the Chumash Indians who came here by canoe or tomol in the 1800s. European explorers described tomols as holding from two to 12 people—one account even says 20. They were made of separate planks lashed together and calked with the tar that abounds on the beach.

Robert O. Gibson writes in *The Chumash* that tomols were usually about 30 feet long and could carry about 4,000 pounds. Using double-sided paddles, rowers could propel a tomol as fast as a person could run.

Possession of a tomol was a sign of high position in Chumash society, and only the members of the upper classes were allowed to own them.

According to Fernando Librado Kitsepawit, a Chumash interviewed by John P. Harrington, there seems to have been a bit of a Catch-22 proposition in Chumash society. Canoes brought wealth, but you could only own a canoe if you were wealthy. To make matters even more exclusive, you could become neither a canoe builder nor owner as an adult unless your parents had enough money to buy you a spot in a canoe society when you were young.

Canoes were essential for travel between the mainland and the Channel Islands, and it comes as no surprise that the islanders, who were the most dependent on these watercraft, were also considered the best canoe builders. Canoes were also used for fishing and for sea lion hunting.

California (despite the frequent fogs), the islands turn lushly green after the winter rains.

❖

When Spanish navigator Juan Cabrillo anchored off Santa Cruz Island in 1542, he found about 2,000 Chumash Indians living here. In the 18th and 19th centuries Spanish and American settlement followed a curious pattern. Because the islands were granted in toto as ranchos, they tended to stay consolidated under single ownership even after the Americans took over. (The one great exception is Santa Catalina Island to the south; see page 278.) They also continued to be used as cattle and sheep ranches. Santa Cruz Island, which was acquired in the 1860s by Justinian Caire, a French settler, became a private fief, self-sufficient in meat, vegetables, grains, and even wine.

Island diversions were few. Cowboys fought their boredom by roping sea lions and selling them to the San Diego Zoo, where they would be trained as circus performers. Other *vaqueros* used their roping skills to procure sea lions for the pet food, seal oil, and hide market.

In 1980, five of the islands were designated as part of a national park. (The Nature Conservancy owns 90 percent of Santa Cruz Island as a private holding within the park.) People come here to observe wildlife and experience natural beauty in a truly wild setting. Rangers lead guided walks along the island trails. Kayakers explore coves and sea caves, watching from the water the sea lions and elephant seals that haul up on the rocky coves, and the gray whales following their migration route to Baja in winter and to Alaska in early spring. Divers and snorkelers find an extraordinary diversity of marine life in the kelp forests surrounding the islands.

Access to the islands is carefully controlled by park rangers. Camping permits must be obtained two weeks in advance; food and water must be brought in by campers.

⌂ GETTING TO THE CHANNEL ISLANDS

Visiting the Channel Islands isn't entirely an easy proposition, but it's do-able. Channel Islands National Park Headquarters is located at the Ventura harbor, *1901 Spinnaker Drive; 805-658-5730.* A concessionaire, Island Packers, offers boat trips year-round to five of the islands; *1867 Spinnaker Drive; 805-642-1393.* You can fly to Santa Rosa Island with Channel Islands Aviation in Camarillo; *805-987-1301.*

■ VENTURA

The city of Ventura marks the northern edge of the L.A. smog belt (though, at times, the smog can reach all the way to Santa Barbara). Ventura hides its priceless setting behind freeway ramps and shopping malls. With its mild, frost-free climate, the city could be a true subtropical paradise. Yet unlike Malibu to the south and Santa Barbara to the north, Ventura lacks a distinctive character. Besides its mission, **San Buenaventura**—the last to be founded (1782) by Father Junipero Serra, and many times rebuilt—and chunks of its aqueduct, Ventura has few mementos of California's Spanish–Mexican period. The two-story **Olivas Adobe,** built from 1837 to 1849, is a good example of what a Mexican rancho of the period looked like; *4200 Olivas Park.*

Ventura does have a splendid **fishing pier,** and its broad, south-facing beaches are sandy and sunny. Local vegetables and fruits are still among the best grown anywhere on the coast.

■ THE BANANA BELT

The stretch of coast between Ventura and Santa Barbara is rightly known as a "banana belt" for even in the coldest winter, temperatures never drop below freezing—and bananas thrive and ripen here. Look for roadside stands set off by dense stands of banana "trees" with their huge, shaggy leaves, or look for locally grown bananas at the Ventura or Santa Barbara farmers' markets.

Some local growers have as many as 40 varieties of bananas, including Ae Ae ("which only Hawaiian royalty were once permitted to grow"), Dwarf Chinese, Green Red ("one of the most beautiful banana fruits in this world with aromatic, cream-colored flesh"), Haa Haa ("delicious fruit"), silvery blue Ice Cream, Jamaican Red ("the pulp is cream orange colored, very aromatic and has a wonderful taste"), Manzano ("apple-flavor"), Mysore ("a favorite Indian dessert banana"), Niño ("tiny, but exquisite taste and texture"), Red Iholena ("pink flesh"), Tuu Ghia ("an intensely flavored Vietnamese variety"), and many others. Quotes are from one growers' catalog.

Before it was turned into a retirement community with its own banana plantation, La Conchita was a bedroom community for oil field workers. You can see signs of their work all along the shore: nodding insect-shaped pumps, tall derricks, and huge, offshore oil rigs.

CENTRAL COAST RIVIERA

OPÉRA BOUFFE BATTLE

An important battle was fought at Rincon Point in 1838—one of the many opéra bouffe civil wars that plagued Mexico. Juan Bautista Alvarado had appointed himself governor. When Don Carlos Carrillo, the governor appointed by the Mexican government, arrived, Alvarado suggested that Carrillo should challenge him by force, adding "I want to go speak with him, to see if he will wait for me or flee to hide with the deer amid the thickets of Baja California." He sent troops under Don Jose Castro down the coast, to head off Carrillo. Castro, by arranging for fresh horses for the soldiers at every stop, reached Santa Barbara in only two-and-a-half days.

Even though it was night, he immediately ordered an advance party to go to the point called El Rincon, a narrow pass between the ocean and the hill, to prevent anyone from crossing. Shortly afterward he left, accompanied by the garrison stationed there and enough artillerymen to handle a well-mounted eight-pound [shot] cannon. Castro succeeded in taking the high point of the ridge which dominates Mission San Buenaventura, where Don Carlos Carrillo had stationed his soldiers. Undetected, Castro had time to position his troops within firing range, and then waited for dawn to break.

Early the next morning, Castro's cannon sounded reveille for the *carlistas*. They were so surprised to be jolted out of their sleep that some of the officers wrestled with the sleeves of their jackets, believing them to be the legs of their pants. Some of them thought that the situation was similar to what happened at Troy, and soon a few began to speak of surrender.

The defenders held out until night. Historian Antonio Maria Osio sets the scene, "Since the nights in that area are typically foggy, they hoped to be able to escape and hide in the mustard fields." But Castro rooted them out: "They searched everywhere, even under the cloak of the great holy teacher and Doctor" [San Buenaventura].

After the men's unconditional surrender, Castro, in typical California fashion, "set the men free and offered apologies." Carrillo eventually left California. Little wonder the president of Mexico, Anastasio Bustamante, said that he did not really care who the governor of California was, and suggested that maybe the Californios should pick one of their own.

■ RINCON POINT

Every time I visit Rincon Point I seem to be munching bananas—I can't drive by the banana gardens in La Conchita without stopping at a local farmers market to buy several (see page 213). I peel skins, eat a new variety, and look out at the view: big combers racing in from the vast reaches of the Pacific Ocean are refracted by a rocky offshore reef at the point, which is sandy below the bluffs on the Santa Barbara County side, and piled high with cobbles on the Ventura County shore. The cobbles were washed down from the mountains during rainstorms. They are also surprisingly stable, because their sides interlock and resist even the biggest waves. To both sides of the point, the mountains come close to the sea. The sun, reflected and muted by the spindrift of the surf, paints the shore with ethereal, other-worldly hues. No wonder this place is so popular with surfers and beachcombers alike, none of whom seem to mind the offshore oil drilling platforms. Because of the unique way in which the waves break on the reef, Rincon Point is considered to be one of the great surfing spots in the West. Depending on the light and weather, the water alternates between shades of green and blue, celadon to aquamarine, and is often clear even when other beaches become muddy after storms.

❖

Long ago, dome-shaped houses of Chumash Indian villages clustered densely along this shore. They used tar they found on the beach in their technology of daily living. Tar served as glue to hold arrow and spear heads to shafts, to glue beads onto bowls, and to hold together the pipes of reed flutes. It was applied as a waterproof coating to baskets, to the thatch of houses, and to the large Chumash canoes, unique artifacts among the native peoples of California.

During Spanish days, the point was a road hazard, since El Camino Real, the "royal" road which ran north from Baja California to the presidios, pueblos, and missions of Alta California, followed the beach. Many of the mudflats were covered at high water, and riders and *carreta* drivers had to carefully coordinate their schedules with the tides. They also had to keep watch for the tar that oozed from natural seeps and springs along the strand and was carried ashore by the surf in big sticky lumps.

🚗 Rincon Point is right off US 101. Take Bates Road to its end on the Santa Barbara County side of the point (county park). Wooden stairs lead down the steep bluff to the beach.

■ From Rincon Point to Santa Barbara

The town of Carpinteria, north of Rincon Point, got its name ("carpentershop") from Spanish explorers who found here a major Chumash boat building center. Sandy Carpinteria State Beach, which has a Chumash Indian interpretive display, is considered the safest beach on the coast, because a shallow offshore reef restricts rip currents.

Nearby Carpinteria Marsh, a coastal lagoon and salt marsh with a narrow strip of freshwater marsh, provides habitat for the endangered light-footed clapper rail which builds a floating nest in cord grass tussocks. The nest is anchored by a ramp that rises and falls with the tide. At least 44 species of birds live in the marsh, including the Belding's Savannah Sparrow (also endangered), a unique songbird that can drink and process seawater.

The state beach is located at the end of Palm Avenue (off Carpenteria Avenue, which runs parallel to US 101). The marsh is reached via Ash Avenue or by walking north along the beach from the state park.

Between here and Santa Barbara the road passes through **Summerland,** with its Yankee clapboard cottages, and through **Montecito,** a wealthy residential community with Spanish-style homes tucked away in elaborate gardens.

■ Santa Barbara

Oh Santa Barbara! You are beautiful, stretched out between the mountains and the sea, with your beaches and blue skies, with your white walls and red roofs, with your palm trees and ever-blooming flowers.

The afternoon sun lights up arches and Moorish windows as I stroll past the partly reconstructed 1788 Presidio at Cañon Perdido and Anacapa Streets. A mockingbird sings in an orange tree, a mourning dove coos in the thatch of a palm, and sparrows chirp in the shrubbery as I head for El Paseo for refreshments.

❖

Even though much of Santa Barbara's Spanish-Mediterranean look was conceived at the turn of the 19th century and implemented after the 1925 earthquake leveled much of the business district, it is based on solid historical perceptions.

The city's Hispanic appearance suffered a bit from 1860 to the early 1900s, when the Yankee spirit reigned supreme and endowed the city with shops, hotels, theaters, and homes in the eclectic architectural styles then in vogue. Historical

Santa Barbara Harbor *by Henry Chapman Ford, 1884.*

photos of that period show a Santa Barbara indistinct from Everytown, U.S.A. Today, these surviving Gothic revival, Eastlake, Italianate, or French Empire edifices do not detract from the city's Spanish-Mediterranean tenor but add a touch of compositional spice.

"Spanish" Santa Barbara felt its first tinge of resurrection in the late 1870s, with calls for the preservation of a large number of solidly built adobes that survived from the Spanish and Mexican period.

■ EXPLORING SANTA BARBARA

Santa Barbara is a city made for walking. Its streets rise gently from the beaches to the mission, posing no major uphill hurdles á la San Francisco. The emphasis on Spanish arches, palm trees, flowering vines and gardens, make Santa Barbara a visitor's delight. Because the city is protected from cold north wind by the Santa Ynez Range (which rises right in its backyard to some 7,000 feet), the climate is so mild that pygmy date palms and bamboo palms, tropical trees grown in greenhouses elsewhere in the U.S, flourish in roadside plantings. Flowers bloom the year round. Most of the city's attractions (with the exception of the Mission District) are in easy walking distance of hotels and motels.

Deposit your car in a parking garage (which might look more like a Moorish palace than like the concrete-slab, layer-cake garages of less enlightened cities) and walk. If you get tired, recover your stamina while sipping coffee or a glass of wine on the patio of a cafe or bistro. Or have a picnic. Fishmongers near the waterfront and on Stearns Wharf sell freshly cooked spiny lobsters and local crab (which they'll crack for you) and crusty bread.

■ WHAT TO DO AND SEE IN SANTA BARBARA

■ Stearns Wharf and the Waterfront

Santa Barbara's waterfront is one long, sandy beach, lined with palms. The lagoon at the east end of the beach encompasses the Andree Clark Bird Refuge. Walk down to the tip of the wharf (at the end of State Street) to watch the sun set over the Pacific, and then return early in the morning to watch the sun *rise* over the Pacific. This is possible, because the coast runs east to west, and the pier runs far out into the water.

■ **State Street**

Closed off from the through-road in recent years, State Street has experienced a renaissance. Car dealerships and repair shops have given way to boutiques, restaurants, and studios; old hotels are being refurbished; and it is now possible to walk between the oceanfront and downtown (or take a waterfront shuttle bus). Earthling Bookshop is a good place to lose track of time. *Take the Garden Laguna Exit off Hwy. 101 and follow the signs to downtown.*

■ **El Paseo**

Back in 1921–1922, the garden of the Casa de la Guerra was turned into El Paseo, the re-creation of a Spanish street. It was the catalyst that set off the conversion of Santa Barbara into a Spanish-style Mediterranean town after the 1925 earthquake destroyed much of downtown.

Today, at the patio-oriented El Paseo Restaurant, the sweet aroma of roasted chilis, hot tortillas, and zingy margaritas hangs in the air. The restaurant puts on an incredible Happy Hour buffet, with the food included in the price of its margaritas. This is what it must have been like to drop in at one of the old Mexican ranchos during dinnertime—except that the rancheros not only wouldn't accept any payment for their hospitality, they even put out plates of silver coins for their guests' use. *10 El Paseo St. (between De la Guerra and Cañon Perdido Sts. and State and Anacapa Sts.).*

Santa Barbara's waterfront.

■ **Paseo Nuevo**

Threats to Santa Barbara's unique ambiance came in the 1990s in the shape of shopping malls, but Santa Barbara builders waxed creative and designed shopping malls in a Spanish image. The best example is laid out as a "new" paseo. The mall's main walkway winds through a city block much like a European shopping street. Despite the fact that the street is lined with the facades of generic mall shops, it conveys—through the use of architectural ornament and copious plantings of palm trees—a pleasant image and houses a number of better-than-average restaurants. *Across State St. from El Paseo.*

■ **El Presidio State Historic Park**

The first comandante of the presidio was Jose Francisco de Ortega, who, on the Portola exploratory expedition of 1769, became the first European to see San Francisco Bay. In 1793, the Presidio was visited by British navigator George Vancouver, who dropped anchor off Santa Barbara.

The old Presidio has badly decayed, except for the old adobe El Cuartel, but the area is being beautifully reconstructed by the state. (Unfortunately, several modern streets bisect the area.)

In this area you'll find the city's oldest adobes. Two of them, **El Cuartel and** the **Lanedo-Whittaker adobe.** Both were sections of the old Presidio's living quarters—built in 1788 and now incorporated into the reconstructed sections of this colonial fortress. Long ago they were surrounded by adobe walls and farmlands, but now they stand at the intersection of two city streets. El Cuartel is the oldest building owned by the State of California.

Four more adobes are within walking distance: The **Santiago de la Guerra adobe** dates back to about 1812, the **Covarrubias Adobe** to 1817. The **Pico Adobe** dates back to 1820, and the **Gonzalez-Ramirez Adobe** to about 1825. The **Hill-Carrillo Adobe** is unique, because it was built 1825–26 by Daniel Hill, an early Yankee immigrant for his bride, Rafaela Luisa Ortega, a descendant of the Presidio's first comandante. The Casa de la Guerra—once the pueblo's foremost mansion—was built between 1819–1827. It is currently being restored. *El Presidio State Historic State Park is at 123 E. Cañon Perdido St.; 805-966-9719.*

■ **Santa Barbara County Courthouse**

Located at the corner of Anacapa and Figueroa Streets, this courthouse seems more like a park than a government building. Often considered *the* public monument of the Spanish Colonial Revival Style in the United States, the offices are broken up into several structures, loosely grouped around a central courtyard. It is quite unlike any other government building, with its dramatic murals, theatrical staircases, sunken gardens, decorative sculptures, and open loggia corridors. As if to emphasize the laid-back Santa Barbara lifestyle, a Roman triumphal arch leads nowhere, but provides great views of Santa Barbara and

The mission at Santa Barbara is among California's most beautiful. (Photo by Sean Arbabi)

the foothills of the Santa Ynez Mountains. The courthouse tower is about as tall as buildings in Santa Barbara can get, since zoning ordinances adopted in 1924 and 1930 restricted the height of buildings. Take time to linger in the garden and to enjoy the aromas of its exotic flowers.

■ **The Fig Tree**
You may notice the huge Moreton Bay fig tree just west of the US 101 freeway at Chapala and Montecito Streets. With huge root buttresses and a spread of some 160 feet, this tree, planted in 1877 by a local girl, is the largest tree of its kind in the nation. In some countries a tree of this magnificence would be considered sacred.

■ **Santa Barbara Museum of Natural History**
This museum has excellent exhibits of regional plants and animal life, geology, and Chumash culture. *2559 Puesta del Sol Rd. (via Mission St. and Mission Canyon Rd.); 805-682-4711.*

■ **Santa Barbara Botanic Garden**
The canyon surrounding the former reservoir of the mission now serves as the Santa Barbara Botanic Garden. Winding Mission Canyon Road leads through the canyon to the garden, an excellent showcase for indigenous California plants growing in a natural setting. Miles of foot trails wind through desert, arroyo, canyon, Channel Island, and redwood plantings above Mission Creek. There's a rock dam and aqueduct,

once part of the mission's water supply system. The ruin of the mission's stone grist mill stands near the mouth of Mission Canyon. *1212 Mission Canyon Rd; 805-682-4726.*

■ **Santa Barbara Mission**
Founded in 1786 on a knoll at the upper edge of the coastal plain, the buildings of the Santa Barbara Mission date from 1815 to 1820 and later, but have undergone much reconstruction, most recently in 1950, when cracks appeared in the church and the entire sandstone facade had to be rebuilt. It is considered one of California's most beautiful missions, and it certainly has the most spectacular view of any of the missions—all the way to the Channel Islands. It also had an almost curiously uneventful history. When Santa Ynez and La Purisima Missions to the north were captured by insurgent Chumash, Santa Barbara Mission basked peacefully in the sunshine (due to the presence of the presidio down the hill); when other missions were secularized, Santa Barbara remained in Church control—which has helped to preserve its gardens and cloisters in perfect shape. An adjacent complex has served as a seminary for the training of priests since the late 19th century. Because this mission never abandoned the faith, it's a great place for soaking up the spirit of Old California. You'll need a car to get there. *Los Olivos and Laguna Sts.; 805-682-4713.*

■ UC Santa Barbara

The modern campus of the University of California at Santa Barbara, 10 miles north of Santa Barbara, is one of the most spectacular centers of higher learning in the country—not because of its ivy-festooned architecture, but because of the setting. It's truly stunning, laid out with the Pacific on one side and the Santa Ynez Mountains on the other. When you approach the campus from the beach, it looks more like a condo development in a tropical paradise than a college campus.

There are the usual lawns and tree-shaded campus walks, and all that, but what makes the place is the view. As is true for all UC campuses, parking is a mess (which is why the majority of students ride bikes). Ask for help. Access is via Highway 217 from US 101.

The university town of **Goleta** offers affordable, though not particularly interesting, lodging. Nearby **Isla Vista** has a slightly trampled but lively look to it, thanks to the thousands of students who make up the majority of the town's population. The main streets are Embarcadero, lined with pizza joints, surf shops, bookstores, and thrift stores, and Del Playa, which runs along the beach and acts as a promenade for the parade of joggers, bicyclists, and in-line skaters.

■ Goleta Point

Three lagoons here provide much needed wildlife habitat. On its shores once stood a village where 1,000 Chumash lived when the Spanish arrived on this coast. In Spanish times, the slough was deep enough to serve as a harbor for small craft. The wreck of one such ship may have given the area its name: *goleta* is the Spanish word for schooner.

Just inside Goleta Point is **Campus Lagoon,** a 25-acre pond where the university's commencement is held each June. The lagoon is fronted by a beach where sea lions haul out. Forty-five-acre **Devereux Lagoon,** on the University of California's Coal Oil Point Reserve, supports populations of egrets, curlews, plovers, cormorants, great blue herons, and black-crowned night herons.

West of Goleta, US 101 runs above steep ocean cliffs on a gently rising grassy coastal shelf. The slopes north of the highway are dark green with avocado orchards. Clusters of tall palms and windbreaks of eucalyptus trees mark homesteads.

To the south, the endless breakers rolling in from the Pacific crash on the rocky shore.

Several nice beaches can be found along the road just north of the point. **El Capitan State Beach,** located at the mouth of Cañada del Capitan, has campsites in the woods lining the banks of the creek and picnic tables on the beach, just above the sand and surf. The almost horizontal, gray-brown mottled trunks of huge native sycamores sprawl over the floodplain, above patches of (non-native) nasturtiums highlighted by clumps of tall white calla lilies. The effect is quite pleasing. A Chumash village called Ahwon or Ajuhuilashmu by the natives once stood near the mouth of the creek.

■ REFUGIO STATE BEACH

Located west of El Capitan, Refugio has a pleasant picnic area and campground shaded by palms; long, sandy beaches where willets, sanderlings, and surfers hang out, and about as much history as any place on the California coast. Refugio became an important stopover place for travelers on El Camino Real after the land was granted to the family of Jose Francisco de Ortega, first comandante of the Santa Barbara Presidio, in the 1780s.

In 1818, the rancho was attacked by the insurgent Argentinian privateer Hippolyte de Bouchard, who arrived on the south coast fresh from the sack of Monterey. Unlike the soldiers of the California capital, who ran away when Bouchard's men landed, the Ortegas put up a fight and captured three of the attackers. Two of these were exchanged for Californios captured by the privateers. The third, a Yankee named Joseph Chapman, claimed he had deserted to get away from Bouchard, who had forced him into serving him. The Spanish authorities accepted this sensible (though untrue) story and sent Chapman to Mission Santa Ynez.

Here Chapman, a carpenter and jack-of-all trades, built a New England–style waterpowered grist mill (whose ruins can still be seen in a field east of the mission). The mill worked so well that governor Sola sent Chapman to San Gabriel to build another. But first Chapman converted to Catholicism, changed his name to Juan Jose, and married Maria de Guadalupe Ortega. He bought a house and planted a vineyard in Los Angeles. By 1830, Chapman and his family had moved back to Santa Barbara where he built an adobe residence. The former raider and itinerant handyman had made it into California society.

In the 1790s and early 1800s, Yankee traders, forbidden by the isolationist government of New Spain to enter California ports, began to defy the ban, and set up a lucrative smuggling trade with ranchos and missions in this area, exchanging California cattle hides for manufactured New England goods. That trade boomed after Mexico gained its independence and allowed Yankees to trade on the coast. But while much of the trade was conducted through legitimate channels, smuggling continued to stay profitable as well, since the Mexicans charged exorbitant import duties, putting trade goods beyond the reach of all but a few wealthy families.

Standing at the overlook of Refugio Beach, I like to envision those intrepid Yankee traders, their brigs, barques, or ships anchored offshore. Facing bluffs, and the coast mountains rising to the east, they rode their longboats through the rough surf, trading with the rancheros and later feasting (the rancheros providing the meat and the skippers providing the libations). Common sailors had to stick close to the boats and got only a view of the coast for their share. But what a view!

❖

Gaviota State Park, just north of Refugio at the mouth of Gaviota Creek, has five and a half miles of shoreline, a fishing pier, and an unimproved sulphur spring. Trails lead into the Santa Ynez Mountains section of Los Padres National Forest.

❖

 North of **Gaviota Pass,** CA 1 leaves the freeway and turns west. On its way to Lompoc, the two-lane highway passes through the rolling cattle country of the Santa Ynez Mountain foothills, and through vegetable and flower fields. Due east, US 101 will take you to Solvang and the following winery tour.

■ Santa Ynez and Santa Maria Valley Winery Tours

In recent years, many vineyards have been planted near the coast of Central and Northern California. Even wine snobs no longer question that wineries in Santa Barbara County and San Luis Obispo (see pages 241-243 for San Luis Obispo winery tours) rival those of Napa and Sonoma to the north in the quality of the wine they produce. While the wines and wineries of this region are becoming more popular with each vintage, the number of visitors are still small enough to allow for a personal touch, yet is big enough to make for lively tasting room discussions. You won't be alone while you're visiting the wineries on these routes, but you won't get trampled to death either.

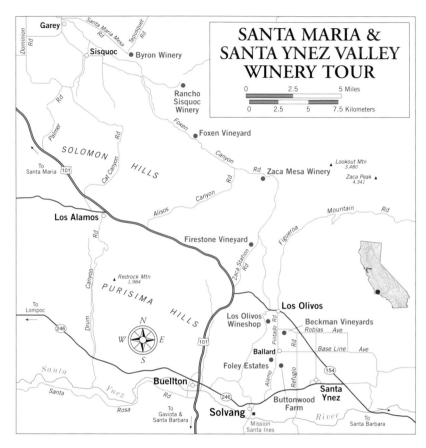

SANTA MARIA &
SANTA YNEZ VALLEY
WINERY TOUR

Garey
Santa Maria Mesa Rd
Tepusquet Rd
Dominion Rd
Sisquoc
Byron Winery
Rancho Sisquoc Winery
Foxen Canyon
Foxen Vineyard
Palmer Rd
SOLOMON HILLS
Cat Canyon Rd
To Santa Maria 101
Canyon
Rd Canyon
Zaca Mesa Winery
Lookout Mtn 3,480
Zaca Peak 4,341
Alisos
Canyon Rd
Los Alamos
Mountain Rd
Firestone Vineyard
Zaca Station Rd
Figueroa
Canyon Rd
PURISIMA HILLS
Redrock Mtn 1,984
To Lompoc
246
Drum
N W E S
101
Los Olivos Wineshop
Los Olivos
Pintado Rd
Beckman Vineyards
Roblas Ave
Base Line Ave
Ballard
Foley Estates
Alamo
Refugio
154
Santa Ynez
Santa
Ynez
Buellton
Rd
Buttonwood Farm
Santa Rosa
To Gaviota & Santa Barbara
Solvang
River
Mission Santa Ines
To Santa Barbara

0   2.5   5 Miles
0   2.5   5   7.5 Kilometers

■ The town of Solvang

Traveling north on US 101, a short drive on CA 246 takes you from Buellton to Solvang, a small town founded as a Danish colony early in the 20th century. Driving past half-timbered buildings, reminds me of the Old Country, and that makes me hungry—I always associate Europe with food, lots of it. I stop at Bit O'Denmark for a snack of lox and pickled herring, to fortify myself for the wine tasting to come. *473 Alisal Rd; 805-688-5426.*

Passing the old Mexican Mission of Santa Inés at the eastern end of town, turn left into Alamo Pintado Road, which brings you to the first wineries on this tour.

■ **Buttonwood Farm** *(805-688-3032)* and **Foley Estates** *(805-688-8554)* are known for the excellent merlot and sauvignon blanc they produce. **Beckman Vineyards,** formerly Houtz, *(805-688-8664)* also makes an excellent sauvignon blanc as well as wonderful chardonnay from local grapes.

BUTTONWOOD

SANTA YNEZ VALLEY

1996 Sauvignon Blanc

86% Sauvignon Blanc - 14% Semillon

But don't linger too long here, or you may not stay the course. There are only so many wineries you can visit in one day, and you really should concentrate on those in Foxen Canyon.

■ **Los Olivos Tasting Room and Wineshop**

Los Olivos is a Western crossroads village, and this first-rate tasting room comes as a bit of a surprise. It pours wines from local wineries too small to have tasting rooms of their own (a small tasting fee is charged). Expect to find hard-to-find bottlings here, from wineries not open to the public, like Au Bon Climat, Il Podere, Nichols, Qupe, and Vita Nova, at reasonable prices. *2905 Grand Ave; 805-688-7406.*

After a few sips (and purchases), head west from Los Olivos on CA 154 and turn right on Foxen Canyon Road. The setting and scenery make **Foxen Canyon** one of those glorious California valleys where meadowlarks

sing from fence posts, acorn woodpeckers flicker among the oaks, yellow-billed magpies squabble in the shrubbery, and quail unconcernedly saunter across the road. The combination of flowers and oaks, chaparral and dry soil, of the sun beating down on dry hillside grasses, and misty vapors rising from moist draws and vineyards, bestows a California air on the valley—a quality that appends itself to the wines as well. These tend to be big yet elegant, hearty yet complex, with many layers of flavor and pleasure.

■ **Firestone Vineyard**

Firestone Vineyard is the largest producer of the Santa Ynez Valley growing region, and known for excellent merlot, cabernet sauvignon, and, surprisingly (in this hot climate) riesling. *5017 Zaca Station Rd., Los Olivos; 805-688-3940.*

■ **Zaca Mesa Winery**

This winery is a few miles north of Firestone, on the west side of the road, where Foxen Canyon takes a sharp turn to the northwest.

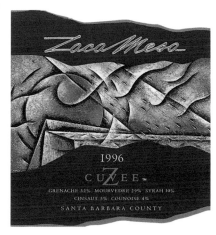

It's marked by a (working) windmill pumping water into a tank. The winery hides in a low-slung, wooden, ranch-style building shaded by oaks. Huge lawn chess pieces beckon in a courtyard. Wines worth tasting include chardonnay, pinot noir, and syrah. The best buy is a red wine called "Tapestry," a delightful blend of several varieties. A picnic area atop a knoll invites visitors to linger. *6905 Foxen Canyon Rd.; Los Olivos; 805-688-3310.*

The Santa Ynez Valley appellation ends just north of Zaca Mesa, and the vineyards and wineries to the east of Foxen Canyon Road are in the Santa Maria appellation. Back on the road, you'll make a happy discovery, if this is your lucky weekend.

■ **The Foxen Vineyard**

Not always open, but keep on the lookout for a sign on a small brown barn east of the highway. Be sure to taste the cabernet sauvignon, pinot noir, and chardonnay (I always buy a bottle of the reserve cabernet sauvignon, because it's so good). You can also taste these wines at the Los Olivos tasting room. *7200 Foxen Canyon Rd., Santa Maria; 805-937-4251.*

1996

FOXEN

ROTHBERG VINEYARD
MOURVEDRE
SANTA YNEZ VALLEY

ALCOHOL 13.4% BY VOLUME

■ **Rancho Sisquoc Winery**

It takes a bit of an effort to drive the narrow road to this small winery, but it's worth it.

A redwood frame church, the San Ramon Chapel built in 1875, stands on a slope above the entrance of the 2.5-mile-long driveway winding through woods and pastures to the winery. Rancho Sisquoc is still a working ranch, with the winery tucked away in an old barn. The wines, only sold at the winery, are delightful. They include merlot, chardonnay, and a very pleasing sylvaner. *6600 Foxen Canyon Rd., Santa Maria; 805-934-4332.*

Up the road, Foxen Canyon opens into the flood plain of the Santa Maria River with its vegetable and strawberry fields (look for vineyards on the bench-lands above the river). A side road (look for the sign) leads to the next winery.

■ **Byron Vineyard**

Winemaker Byron Kenneth Brown makes excellent chardonnays and pinot noirs at this winery owned by Robert Mondavi. A taste of the reserve pinot noir will tell you how good the wine made from this very fickle grape can get around here. *5230 Tepusquet Rd., Santa Maria; 805-937-7288.*

❖

From the Byron Vineyard, Santa Maria Mesa Road and Betteravia Road take you back to the US 101 freeway. (If you're traveling south on 101, leave the freeway at Betteravia, south of Santa Maria, and head east to Foxen Canyon Road, and reverse the route.)

■ POINT CONCEPTION

Point Conception, one of California's most important landmarks, is surrounded by private lands not open to the public. The only access is by boat across tumultuous seas. Or you may view the point from Amtrak's Coast Starlight passenger train, which runs along the coast here.

At Point Conception the West Coast bends sharply to the east, and the cold, south-bound California Current fights a warm current running north and west along the shores of the Southern California Bight. The meeting of these two ocean streams not only produces high waves but also dense fog, making this part of the coast very difficult to navigate. Looking for an answer to why this break in climate occurs here, at Point Conception, and not elsewhere on the coast, Marie De Santis, in her splendid book *California Currents,* interviews different scientists, but it is an old fisherman who gives her the answer that was immediate, assured, and to the point. Philip Vella has fished the California coast for 68 years, most of that time in northern waters. "Point Conception?" he said without a moment's hesitation. "God walks on the water below that point, and all the water above it He left to the devil."

So why do fishermen like Vella brave these devilish waters? Because they teem with fish. As the California Current is deflected away from the land by the rotation of the earth and by storm winds, the surface water is replaced by nutrient-rich waters from the deep. These nutrients in turn cause plankton to feed, breed, and expand in explosive "blooms" which in turn feed fish. It is these periodic upwellings and plankton blooms that make the California waters from Point Conception north to Cape Mendocino one of the great fishing areas of the world.

The cold waters of the northern current form a barrier to the marine life from warm southern seas as they slice across the warm southern current. Which is why divers and fishermen find few spiny lobsters north of Point Conception, and why abalones are much smaller north of the point. But halibut, shrimp, oysters, and Dungeness crabs thrive in the cooler northern waters.

■ LOMPOC

Pronounced "Lompoke," not "Lompock," as locals are quick to point out to you, this town takes its name from a Chumash word for "shell mounds." The city was founded in 1874 as an organized land colonization scheme on the lands of the old

CENTRAL COAST
RIVIERA

Ranchos Lompoc and Mission Vieja. The deeds of sale prohibited liquor on the land, and citizens were quick to take action against violators. When one imbiber's building was blown up, it was reported in the local paper as an act of God—an earthquake that had struck the transgressor's abode, but spared every other building in town. Flower seeds were long the mainstay of the local economy, along with winter vegetables, but today Lompoc is mainly a bedroom community for nearby Vandenberg Air Force Base.

■ MISSION LA PURISIMA

At the southern end of Lompoc, at 508 South F Street and Locust Avenue, a few weathered chunks of adobe wall and a historical plaque mark the site of Mission La Purisima, founded here in 1787. The first La Purisima, that is. The current Mission La Purisima, some four miles northeast of town, was built after the 1812 earthquake damaged the first mission, and a flood, triggered by the quake, destroyed the buildings. The new mission, which had crumbled almost as badly as its predecessor by the early 1900s, was fully and authentically restored by CCC workers

On September 8, 1923, a squadron of 11 U.S. destroyers steamed southward down the California coast. At Point Arguello (right) the lead ship ran aground in a thick fog. Before the captain could warn the others, six more destroyers followed the lead ship onto the rocks. The U.S. Navy lost more combat ships that day at Point Arguello than they did during the entire course of World War I. (Photo above courtesy of the National Archives)

during the 1930s. It is now the most complete of all the missions (and the largest historical restoration in the West), but administration by the California State Park System has led to neglect, and many of the buildings are suffering from premature deterioration. La Purisima Mission's sad claim to historic fame dates to the 1824 Chumash rebellion when disenchanted Chumash converts held the mission for a month before being overpowered by superior Mexican forces. Seven rebels were shot, but the four ringleaders were merely sentenced to hard labor. *The mission is located just off Highway 246 (you can't miss the signs), three miles northeast of Lompoc.*

■ JALAMA BEACH

A few miles east of Lompoc, winding, twisting Jalama Road curves southwest over hills, through draws, and down Jalama Creek to Jalama Beach, just 1.5 miles north of Point Conception. The sandy beach and 28-acre county park at the end of the road are very popular with surfers and fishermen. The park borders Vandenberg Air Force Base (one mile of beach access to the north allowed). Intrepid hikers head south from here along the beach or (trespass) on the railroad tracks to Point Conception.

■ OCEAN BEACH

Ocean Beach, west of Lompoc, is among the wildest on the coast, with some of the best shorebird watching. To reach it, drive west on CA 246 from Lompoc to a small parking area at the mouth of the Santa Ynez River, where an extensive marsh inside the river mouth, with nearly 400 acres of fresh and salt water, and a hard-packed sandy beach are backed by sand dunes and low hills.

The beach, a county park, is on the Vandenberg base, but open to the public for 1.5 miles north and 3.5 miles south of the beachhead. A trail along the river shore leads to the dunes and the long beach of hard-packed sand. Many consider Ocean Beach more of a "northern" beach because of its pristine sand, wind-blown dunes, and powerful surf. The water, outside the foamy waves, is often steely gray or cold green. Long, straight rows of breakers have a hypnotic effect as they crash onto the beach at regularly spaced intervals.

■ GUADALUPE–NIPOMO DUNES

North of the Santa Maria River, in southern San Luis Obispo County, you'll encounter vast and mysterious dunes. The 6,000 acres of these ancient dunes (some of them began to pile up 18,000 years ago), plus the vast expanse of the Nipomo

Dunes adjoining them to the north, are more sandy waste than you may care to explore in a lifetime, but they are also eminently fascinating. Despite their Sahara-like appearance, the dunes have lakes, marshes, and wetlands supporting a great number of birds and other animals. The lakes are younger than the dunes—they only date back some 16,000 years. Rare plants grow here, and the giant coreopsis, a shrub with golden sunflower blooms, grows huge here—the shrubs may be as much as eight feet tall. The yellow pond lily reaches the southern limit of its range here. The dunes may look white, golden, or blue to you in late winter and spring. Relax. You're not having visions. The wildflowers are in bloom. Grizzly bears once lived at the edge of the dunes; today the wildlife runs to smaller species, like kangaroo rats, which lead secret lives in the sands.

The dunes hold other secrets because Hollywood used them for years as a stand in for the Sahara Desert. Cecil B. DeMille shot *The Ten Commandments* in the dunes near Arroyo Grande and left the sets behind. The drifting sands soon hid them from view. Now and then someone launches an "archaeological" expedition to try and find them.

Nipomo Dunes is one of the few undeveloped coastal dune ecosystems in California. More than 180 species of birds inhabit this area and its surrounding wetlands.

During the Great Depression, a gaggle of artists, writers, and camp followers lived in a village of driftwood huts in the Callender Dunes west of Oceano. They called themselves the "Dunites" and published a literary journal called *Dune Forum.* All traces of the driftwood village have been swallowed by the sands.

Some 4,000 acres of the Pismo Dunes and a section of the beach are open to motor vehicles. Here the dunes are considered healthy enough to take that sort of abuse. All other sections are closed to cars and off-road vehicles.

🚗 The road leading to the southern part of the Nipomo Dunes at the mouth of the Santa Maria River was unmarked the last time I drove up CA 1, but it's easy to find. As you approach the small farming community of Guadalupe, head west on Main Street (which is the extension of Santa Maria's Main Street). The mouth of the river was once a county park but is now administered by the Nature Conservancy. There's a gate and a friendly guard, but no entrance fee. Watch for sand on the roadway and in the parking lot. This may be hard to navigate for rental cars, but the local beachcombers will happily pull or push you out of soft places.

❖

🚗 CA 1 passes through vegetable fields on its way north, bypassing the dunes. It touches the beach near the motorhome parking lots (that pass locally for campgrounds) of south Pismo Beach before rejoining US 101.

■ PISMO BEACH

This small, comfortable, down-to-earth beach town is a delight and still thoroughly unspoiled. The 1,250-foot-long fishing pier is an old-fashioned, laid-back place, where local kids cheer on surfer friends. It is nearly unchanged from when it was built back in 1881 to ship out local produce. Pomeroy and Hinds Avenues leading from CA 1 to the pier have fish 'n chips shops, cafes, surfboard and curio shops and other seaside diversions. Here is where farmers from the Central Valley come to vacation. The region's newspaper boxes carry Bakersfield and Fresno dailies. The pier is also a great place for watching surfers in action. It is lit at night.

Pismo State Beach north of here is flat and sandy until it is cut off by the cliffs of Shell Beach. A stairway at the end of Wadsworth Avenue (a few blocks north) leads to volleyball courts.

A peregrine falcon and a two-week-old chick nesting on Avila Beach, just north of Pismo Beach.

Pismo Beach was once famous for its succulent clams, which were overharvested so badly by farmers plowing the beach and feeding the clams to their hogs, that they almost became extinct. Of course, the locals don't blame the farmers for the clams' demise. A newspaper article prominently displayed on the pier places the blame right on the usual suspect, the sea otter.

North of Pismo Beach, the bay curves west. Shell Beach, the northern quarter of town, is an odd combination of tiny (formerly low-rent) cottages and new luxury lodgings.

US 101 heads north from Pismo Beach across a low divide and then follows San Luis Obispo Creek into San Luis Obispo. Just after the divide, Avila Road runs west to the San Luis Obispo Riviera.

■ SAN LUIS BAY

You can tell that this warm bay, sheltered from chill north winds by the San Luis Range (locally known as the "Irish Hills"), has a special climate, because castor beans grow wild by the roadsides—something you will encounter again in this region south of Gaviota Pass. San Luis Bay is one of the few unspoiled places on the California coast, despite an oil pier and some unsightly oil tanks atop a prominent hill (they have to ship the locally produced oil from somewhere!). That said, you can forget about the oil tanks, because, to tell the truth, you hardly notice them.

Cave Landing, a rocky headland, juts some 150 feet into the bay and forms a natural pier, where in the early 19th century Yankee skippers once loaded hides and tallow from Mission San Luis Obispo. The Chumash buried their dead in the shallow seaside caves; today the caves are popular with fishermen and trysting students from Cal Poly in nearby San Luis Obispo. One cave is open on both sides, forming a large arch that goes clear through the cliff. A natural terrace on its western side offers great views of Avila Beach, Point San Luis, and spectacular sunsets. Giant clumps of artichokes grow wild at the edge of the chaparral. Steep trails lead down to beaches on either side of the headland.

Avila Beach, about six miles north of Pismo Beach, is a small cozy fishing village popular with college students from Cal Poly in San Luis Obispo.

Port San Luis, in lee of Point San Luis to the west of Avila Beach, has a 1,320-foot-long fishing pier (lit at night). If you catch a really big one you can reel it in by feeding quarters to a coin-operated crane. I've enjoyed having a lunch of fresh fish and local microbrew at the Olde Port Inn at the end of the pier. The restaurant also has an excellent wine list of local bottlings. A couple of fish markets on the pier sell fish fresh off the boats. The view from the pier is spectacular. Port San Luis is a very scenic place, with scores of fishing boats anchored offshore beneath dark cliffs.

■ PECHO COAST TRAIL

The shores north of Point San Luis are still unspoiled (except for a nuclear power plant in Diablo Canyon, right smack on top of an earthquake fault), and were, until recently off limits to the public. The new 10-mile Pecho Coast Trail, which was supposed to go all the way to Montana del Oro State Park, is now open for 7.4 miles, by reservation *(805-541-8735).* It passes Port San Luis Lighthouse, a prefab 1894 wooden structure that is a clone of the Point Fermin lighthouse at San Pedro in Southern California, and continues on to Rattlesnake Canyon.

In the 19th century, when Port San Luis was known as Port Harford, its pier competed with the one at Avila Beach for business from San Luis Obispo farmers. A railroad connected the pier to the hinterland and steamships arrived at the wharf several times a week. The original wharf was destroyed by a tsunami in 1878. The People's Wharf in Avila Beach (built in 1868, destroyed by a storm in 1983, and since rebuilt) was the terminus of a rail line to San Luis Obispo until 1941, when rail workers pulled up the tracks behind the last train leaving for San Luis Obispo.

To reach the coast north of Point San Luis, drive back to US 101 and pick up CA 1 in San Luis Obispo.

CENTRAL COAST
RIVIERA

■ SAN LUIS OBISPO: HISTORY AND AMBIANCE

Writer Barbara Seymour is right when she says in her book, *Portrait of a Place: San Luis Obispo,* that "San Luis Obispo is not on the sea, but is historically linked to the sea." It's true, for Avila Beach and Port San Luis are as much part of the town as California Polytechnic State University, an institution of higher learning that has long exerted a positive influence on the former mission town.

San Luis Obispans are proud of their quiet, somewhat sleepy town. Bumper stickers advocate the SLO lifestyle, and downtown sees a lot more foot traffic than other West Coast communities.

❖

Father Junipero Serra.

San Luis Obispo was founded in 1772 as a mission by Father Junipero Serra, who had high hopes for the place. But the local Chumash, who had been friendly when the Portola Expedition passed through their valleys in 1769, and who had cheered on Spanish hunters in Los Osos Valley who killed grizzly bears to succor the starving missionaries and settlers at San Antonio and Monterey, turned sour when the padres tried to convert them to Christianity. They burned down several successive mission compounds by shooting flaming arrows into their thatch roofs, until Father Cavaller, the padre in residence, came up with the idea of molding clay roof tiles on wooden forms, firing them, and using them to cover the mission's roofs. The famed brick-red California mission tile was born.

The mission prospered when Yankee traders began (illegally) to row into Port San Luis to exchange hides for pots, pans, knives, needles, and other goods made in New England. It has served as a parish church since secularizations of the missions. The old adobe structure was encased in a wooden clapboard shell and disfigured with a New England–style spire until the original facade was restored in the 1930s. The church is unique among California missions because it incorporates the bell tower into the facade.

Cerro San Luis overlooks downtown San Luis Obispo from an altitude of 1,300 feet.
(Photo by Sean Arbabi)

■ VISITING SAN LUIS OBISPO

When I visit I always take a walk through the mission plaza, a tree-shaded park above the banks of San Luis Obispo Creek and linger over a cup of coffee at a creekside cafe. Later I'll visit the folksy historical museum (686 Monterey Street), with its good selection of local books, and stroll to the Ah Louis Store. Built of brick in 1874, it served as headquarters, post office, and social club for the Chinese workmen who dug the Southern Pacific railroad tunnels through the hard rock of the Cuesta Grade north of town. If it's a Thursday, I'll wander through the farmers market—the largest and perhaps most interesting market of its type in California—and go on to enjoy a splendid dinner at the Big Sky Cafe, a very friendly downtown restaurant on Broad Street (see page 372).

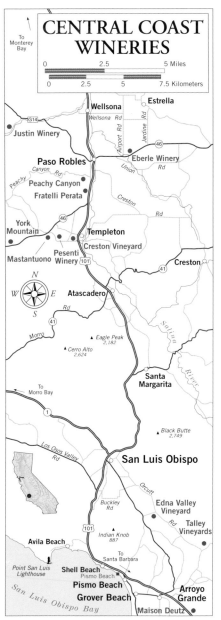

CENTRAL COAST
WINERIES

To
Monterey
Bay

0   2.5   5 Miles

0   2.5   5   7.5 Kilometers

Wellsona

Estrella

G14

Justin Winery

Paso Robles

Eberle Winery

Peachy Canyon

Fratelli Perata

York
Mountain

Templeton

Creston Vineyard

Pesenti
Mastantuono   Winery

Creston

Atascadero

Eagle Peak
2,182

Cerro Alto
2,624

Santa
Margarita

To
Morro Bay

Black Butte
2,749

Los Osos Valley
Rd

San Luis Obispo

Buckley
Rd

Edna Valley
Vineyard

Talley
Vineyards

Avila Beach

Indian Knob
887

To
Santa Barbara

Point San Luis
Lighthouse

Shell Beach

Pismo Beach

Pismo Beach

Grover Beach

Arroyo
Grande

San Luis Obispo Bay

Maison Deutz

In late winter and early spring the grass is green on the Cerro San Luis Obispo, a rocky hill (the core of an old volcano). A row of similar peaks—Bishop's Peak, Chumash Peak, Cerro Raumaldo, and Hollister Peak—marches northwest along the divide between the Chorro and the Los Osos Valleys like a row of giant, weathered dragon's teeth to the ocean at Morro Bay. Morro Rock is the furthest out of these volcanic plugs, all of which seem to have erupted along a common fault line.

❖

CA 1 heads west from San Luis Obispo through the Chorro Valley to the coast. Los Osos Road (at the southern end of town) traverses the Los Osos Valley and connects to CA 1 just south of Morro Bay via South Bay Boulevard. (See page 244 for Morro Bay.)

❖

Between San Luis Obispo and Arroyo Grande and farther north, in the region surrounding Paso Robles, are two distinct wine appellations worth exploring.

■ ARROYO GRANDE–EDNA VALLEY WINERY TOUR

The first winery on this tour sits on a slope just west of US 101 south of the town of Arroyo Grande. Access is from both the southbound and northbound lanes. Be careful when you cross the northbound lanes—traffic moves at freeway speeds.

■ Maison Deutz

The vineyards of the French-owned Maison Deutz surround the beautifully designed winery. They are planted on limestone soil and are cooled by the prevailing ocean breezes. Maison Deutz produces several excellent sparkling wines as well as excellent chardonnay and a superb pinot noir called Carpe Diem.

Take a glass of bubbly, walk outside and look west—you can sniff the salt air wafting in from the ocean, while sniffing and sipping glorious wine and bubbly. Afterwards, stop to look at the vineyards. You'll see grayish-white chunks of rock mixed into the dark loams and clays. That's limestone, which gives the grapes their special flavor. *453 Deutz Dr., Arroyo Grande; 805-481-1763.*

❖

Several other wineries lie east of Arroyo Grande within easy driving distance from US 101. Take CA 227, the backroad to San Luis Obispo, east from downtown and turn right toward Lopez Lake on Huasna Drive and stay to the left on Lopez Drive at a **Y** in the road. After passing Orcutt Road, look on the left for Talley Vineyards.

■ Talley Vineyards and
  Saucelito Canyon Vineyards

Be sure to taste the estate-grown chardonnay and pinot noir at the Talley Vineyards tasting room. Here, too, you may also taste the rich, complex zinfandels made from the 110-year-old vines of Saucelito Canyon Vineyards. *3031 Lopez Dr., Arroyo Grande; 805-489-0446.*

❖

Head back to the freeway on Lopez Drive or turn right onto Orcutt Road. Ignore Edna Ranch on the right side of the road. It's a fancy housing development pretending to be a winery. Continue north to Biddle Ranch Road.

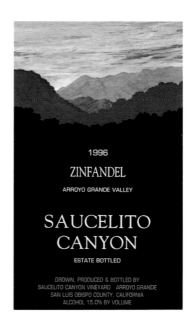

1996

ZINFANDEL

ARROYO GRANDE VALLEY

SAUCELITO
CANYON

ESTATE BOTTLED

GROWN, PRODUCED & BOTTLED BY
SAUCELITO CANYON VINEYARD   ARROYO GRANDE
SAN LUIS OBISPO COUNTY, CALIFORNIA
ALCOHOL 15.0% BY VOLUME

■ **Edna Valley Vineyard**

This winery is famous for its chardonnay, but it also produces excellent sauvignon blanc and a light pinot noir called "vin rouge" which is pleasant to drink and actually has more varietal character than the regular bottling. *2585 Biddle Ranch Rd., San Luis Obispo; 805-544-9594.*

❖

From Edna Valley Vineyard head west to Edna Valley Road. A right turn will take you to San Luis Obispo. A left turn and a right on Price Canyon Road takes you straight to downtown Pismo Beach.

EDNA VALLEY
VINEYARD

1996

Edna Valley

Chardonnay

PARAGON

Produced and bottled by
Edna Valley Vineyard
San Luis Obispo California USA
Alcohol 13.5% by volume

■ YORK MOUNTAIN–TEMPLETON WINERY TOUR

Highway 46, off Highway 1, heads east toward Paso Robles and along the way, takes you to several delightful wineries. You can also take this tour as a connecting drive between US 101 and the Coast Highway (CA 1).

1994
San Luis Obispo County
ZINFANDEL

YORK MOUNTAIN

PRODUCED AND BOTTLED BY
YORK MOUNTAIN WINERY, TEMPLETON, CALIFORNIA
ALCOHOL 13.5% BY VOLUME

■ **York Mountain**

Founded in 1882, this winery, high on the slopes of the eponymous 1658-foot peak, survived Prohibition only to go into decline in the 1970s. It has since earned its stripes with a beautifully spicy zinfandel, a rich merlot, and several sherry- and port-style dessert wines.

It's located on a pretty country lane north of the highway. *7505 York Mountain Rd., Templeton; 805-238-3925.*

■ **Mastantuono**
A few miles up the highway, just south of the junction with Vineyard Drive stands this Italian hunting chateau. Winemaker Pasquale Mastan makes a plucky zinfandel as well as a deeply complex reserve barbera, among other varieties, and a rich, well-rounded cabernet sauvignons. *2720 Oak View Rd., Templeton; 805-238-0676.*

■ **Pesenti Winery**
Farther up Vineyard Drive, on the north side of the road (watch those curves) you suddenly come upon this appealingly old-style Italian family winery with a broad spectrum of gutsy wines, including a very quaffable zinfandel. The winery was established in 1933 on vineyards planted in 1923. This is a fun, very relaxed place to visit. Come to think of it, so are the other wineries. As yet, San Luis Obispo County has none of the snobbism of Napa or Sonoma. *2900 Vineyard Dr., Templeton; 805-434-1030.*

■ **Creston Vineyard**
Just before Vineyard Drive crosses the US 101 freeway, you'll see the Creston Vineyard's tasting room on the left (north) side of the road (the vineyards are in the hills to the east). Be sure to taste the cabernet sauvignon and the blended reds. *Vineyard Dr. at US 101, Templeton; 805-434-1399.*

Other wines to look for while you're in the area are the sangiovese and merlot made by **Fratelli Perata,** the zinfandels from **Peachy** Canyon, the cabernet sauvignon from **Eberle Winery,** and the "Isosceles" Bordeaux grapes (cabernet sauvignon, cabernet franc, merlot) blend from **Justin Winery.**

■ MORRO BAY

Somehow a lot of folks who tell you how important Morro Bay is as a harbor, an estuary, a bird marsh, et al., often forget to mention how beautiful this bay is, with its wooded hills to the south and east, the sandy spit to the west, and monolithic Morro Rock to the north. Fortunately, there are many places where visitors can get close to all that beauty. If possible, bring (or rent) a kayak or canoe or other small boat. The bay is a birdwatcher's paradise.

No paved road leads onto the undeveloped three-mile-long sand and dune spit. The dunes reach heights of 85 feet. The surf on the ocean side is very rough and too dangerous for swimming. There is dirt-road access (four-wheel-drive vehicles only!) off Pecho Valley Road, but it's easier to get there by boat from the Morro Bay city waterfront. A water taxi makes regular trips from the marina on Embarcadero Road. Good clamming and birdwatching.

The city of Morro Bay has one of the most delightful bayfronts in coastal California, with access to piers and wharves in many places. Most Morro Bay streets running east-west end at the Embarcadero, which runs the length of the waterfront. A wooden boardwalk skirts the bay side of the Embarcadero past many of the restaurants and shops. City-owned T-Piers provide fishing access to the bay; parking is on the docks just off the piers, and both parking and piers are free. I have stayed in Morro Bay several times and found each new visit more relaxing than the last. The town and the waterfront are compact enough for walking, and I have walked all over—all the way out to the rock breakwater. I have browsed in shops and galleries along the Embarcadero, and I have visited the small, rather funky aquarium in the back of a gift shop. Several large tanks hold seals and sea lions that were injured or orphaned and cannot be returned to the sea (a sign says, "FEEDING ENCOURAGED"). Smaller tanks display local fish and invertebrates.

I have also enjoyed memorable meals with a view. At the Galley, I have enjoyed perfectly cooked local fish accompanied by San Luis Obispo County wine, while watching terns dive for their dinner outside my window. Rose's Landing Restaurant and Cocktail Lounge above the waterfront serves excellent and inexpensive fish 'n chips and martinis (see page 361).

There are a number of interesting things to do and sights to see in the area.

(see page 361)

Morro Bay is dominated by El Morro,
a 576-foot rock which is easily visible for miles around.

■ WHAT TO DO AND SEE IN MORRO BAY

■ El Morro

The city of Morro Bay is overshadowed by its monolithic 576-foot-high rock named El Morro, a Spanish nautical term meaning "bluff, rock, or hill serving as a landmark"—an apt description. The rock has indeed served as a landmark since the days when the Manila-Acapulco galleons sailed south to Mexico along the California shore. El Morro was even taller until rock quarrying operations, which lasted from 1891 to 1969, removed more than a million tons of rock for breakwaters and a causeway. The rock was not connected to the mainland until 1938. Today it is an ecological reserve protecting rare peregrine falcons. Climbing on the cliffs is prohibited, to protect the nesting resident falcon. And beware the rattlesnakes. According to locals in the know, the rock has more than its share of these venomous, long-fanged, and easily riled critters. There is, by the way, only one peregrine falcon nest on the rock: this predatory bird has a territory 10 miles in diameter.

■ Fishing

The docks bustle with fishing boats. Morro Bay and Avila Beach to the south account for more than half of all the commercial fish caught in the southern half of California. The "clam taxi" takes day trippers from Virg's Fish'n at 1215 Embarcadero on the waterfront across the bay to the three-mile-long sand spit protecting Morro Bay from the fury of the ocean. Charter vessels leave for full-day and half-day fishing trips; *805-772-1222*. These are particularly popular when the albacore are biting. Morro Bay

was once a major abalone processing center until overfishing led to the decline of the tasty snails. Of course, the blame is put on the sea otters.

■ The View

The view north of town is spoiled by three 450-foot high smokestacks of the Morro Bay Power Station. But you soon learn to block out the stacks and enjoy the scenery in spite of their bulky presence.

■ Embarcadero

The Embarcadero runs all the way from Morro Rock past the town's waterfront to Morro Bay State Park, south of town. The state park stretches across the marshes at the mouths of Chorro and Los Osos Creeks inland to the slopes of Black Hill and Hollister Peak. The Morro Bay Natural History Museum has exhibits focusing on the bay's ecology; *805-772-2694*.

■ Montana Del Oro State Park

Located south of Morro Bay, this state park has a wild seashore with sea stacks, caves, and arches. Inland areas are covered with wildflowers in spring. The park takes its name from 1,347-foot-high Valencia Peak which is painted golden in spring and early summer by yellow mustard and orange poppies.

■ Los Osos State Reserve

This pristine reserve, located south of Los Osos Valley Road, has some of the most beautiful live oaks on the California coast.

■ CAYUCOS TOWN AND BEACH

North of Morro Bay the Coast Highway passes sandy **Morro Strand State Beach South** (until recently known as Atascadero State Beach) and **Morro Strand Beach.** You might want to pull off the highway at **Cayucos Beach** for some birdwatching. Willets, black and ruddy turnstones, semipalmated plovers, and others hang out here even in summer, when their more enterprising brethren are north in the arctic raising broods. Access is from parking lots (follow signs) and from trails and steps at street ends.

Cayucos itself is a delightful small town, so popular with vacationers that its lodging rooms are booked all summer long. You'll understand why, if you stroll along Ocean Avenue and walk out onto the narrow, rustic wooden pier.

Point Estero, west of Cayucos, marks the northern end of Chumash territory and the beginning of the Salinan territories. When the Portola Expedition passed through here in 1769, Chumash canoes lined the beach at Cayucos. Cayucos got its pier in 1875. It was a regular stop for the Pacific Steamship Company ships and was used to ship out local dairy products. Later abalones were dried here, for export to San Francisco and Japan. At Estero Bay, Chinese gathered sea lettuce and dried it for export until China closed its ports following World War II.

Beyond Cayucos, CA 1 runs inland, past **Harmony,** a hamlet with a couple of restaurants, galleries, a pottery, and a winery.

■ CAMBRIA

One of the most pleasant, friendliest towns on the central coast is tucked away off the highway in a pretty valley. Cambria had its beginnings in 1862, when cinnabar ore, from which quicksilver (mercury) is extracted, was found in the Santa Lucia Mountains to the east. Copper, quicksilver, dairy products, and cattle hides produced in the area were loaded onto schooners at San Simeon Bay, until Cambria got a pier in 1874. The coastal shipping trade ended in 1894 when a rail line from San Luis Obispo reached Cambria. Yet the village remained relatively isolated until 1937, when the Coast Highway opened between Carmel and Cambria. The pines on the knolls to the west are one of only four native stands of Monterey Pines in the world (the others are in Monterey, Santa Cruz, and San Mateo Counties near Point Año Nuevo, and in Baja California).

West Village on the seaward side of CA 1 is the newer residential part. In the 19th century, few people lived here, because this was the port district. Besides, there was a rather smelly whaling station as well.

Shamel County Park, west of CA 1 on Windsor Road, has trails leading to tidepools and surf fishing spots, plus a picnic area and swimming pool.

Moonstone Beach, at the northern end of Cambria, is named for the milky white agates that can be found in the sand. It marks the southern boundary of the California Sea Otter Game Refuge, which extends from here north to the Carmel River in Monterey County. From Moonstone Beach the Coast Highway winds north above the shore to San Simeon.

🚙 NOTE FOR DRIVERS CONTINUING NORTH:

The preceding chapter, Golden Gate to San Simeon, describes sites along the coast to San Francisco, travelling north to south. Thus its description of Hearst Castle begins at the end of that chapter on page 204. We hope drivers continuing north won't find it too onerous a task to switch directions as they read this chapter. Our reason for having done this? The majority of travelers to that area begin their trip by driving south from San Francisco.

The idyllic town of Cambria is nestled in a lush valley among these hills along the central coast. (Opposite) Monterey pines.

CENTRAL COAST RIVIERA

L.A. METRO

& ORANGE COUNTY

■ HIGHLIGHTS

Malibu
Santa Monica
Venice
Palos Verdes
Santa Catalina Island
Newport Beach
Laguna Beach

■ TRAVEL OVERVIEW

Eureka

Mendocino

San Francisco

Direction of travel in this chapter is north to south

L.A. METRO & ORANGE COUNTY

San Diego

The Santa Monica Mountains drop sharply into the ocean at Malibu in northwestern Los Angeles. Because they run east-west (instead of north-south), the ocean shore also runs laterally. Which means that the beaches face south, protecting the waters from cold northerly currents and allowing them to soak up a maximum of sunshine.

Where the mountains meet the sea, the coastline is broken by rocky headlands and sandy pocket beaches. A wide crescent of sand sweeps around the shores of Santa Monica Bay to the Palos Verdes Peninsula. These beaches are backed by a wide coastal plain packed with houses, industrial parks, and shopping malls. South of Venice, power plants and refineries tower over the shore in several places.

The 15-mile-long shoreline of the Palos Verdes Peninsula has spectacular views of the ocean, small coves, and splendid tidepools. South of the Los Angeles–Long Beach superport lies Orange County, the "SoCal" of the popular imagination. Filled with fashionably casual people in excellent physical condition who are wearing Italian sunglasses, its beaches are awash with surfers and sunbathers exuding a golden immortality.

■ TRAVEL BASICS

Driving

Los Angeles is known as a chaotic place, an anti-city, where even a network of freeways fails to create order. A majority of L.A. and Orange County's major attractions—museums, celebrity cemeteries, temples, theaters, movie studios, shopping malls, Rodeo Drive, Universal City, and Disneyland—are strewn all over the place, like meatballs on a plate of freeway spaghetti. Even worse, they are separated by miles of congested roads. The coastal "attractions," on the other hand, are lined up, like beads on a string.

Yet, practically speaking, no one wants to drive along the coast between Malibu and San Clemente. It's too slow, too crowded, and in a sense too depressing, what with urban sprawl and ubiquitous oil derricks. Better to pick a few of the places described here and go enjoy them, but don't try to do too much.

Coast Road Names: CA 1 starts out as the Pacific Coast Highway in Malibu, changes its name to Palisades Beach Road in Santa Monica, before heading away from the coast at Colorado Avenue (whose end is the Santa Monica Pier) and merging with I-10, the Santa Monica Freeway for a few blocks. When it leaves the freeway to head south, it becomes Lincoln Boulevard, a name it keeps until it takes a turn around LAX airport and becomes Sepulveda Boulevard. It keeps that name through El Segundo and Manhattan Beach until it crosses Artesia Boulevard (CA 91) and resumes its proper name of Pacific Coast Highway, popularly referred to as PCH.

Climate

Dry and warm year-round. The rare winter rainfall only amounts to a total of 12 inches per season, usually falling in January or February. Fog is common along the beaches between Santa Monica and Palos Verdes during the summer, but usually burns off by midday. Summer temperatures average between 75 and 85 degrees (except when the warm Santa Ana winds blow). **Water Temperature:** Averages 65 to 75 degrees year-round.

Food and Lodging

Excellent restaurants can be found in the L.A. area, and all major hotel and motel chains are well represented. (For **lodging and restaurant listings** see pages 339–390.)

■ EARLY MORNING LIGHT

Early in the morning, as the sun cleared the eastern horizon, I was ready. Brush poised, water color paper moistened, paints squeezed from their tubes, I waited for the light. I tried to capture the rainbow-hued pastel colors the morning sun bestows on the coastal ridges of the Santa Monica Mountains, dissolving the outlines of land and sea, sky and earth, and merging them into each other for a few evanescent moments.

I had tried to catch the images on film, with no success. Now, high on a dry ridge above Latigo Canyon, I struggled with paint and reality. But success remained elusive. Not nature, but my vision was at fault. My eye could see, but not grasp the fleeting changes as ridges and mountains became translucent and bled into each other, and the bulk of a distant peak shone through a nearby range. Hills

A backpacker enjoys the "transcendental light" of a coastal mountain sunset.
(Photo by Sean Arbabi)

rose to float away. Then, in an instant, it all changed. The land resumed its solid shapes and earth-drab colors; the ridges once again rose sharply against the pale morning sky.

I suspect this optical illusion of transcendental light is an interplay of the sun's rays as they are filtered through an amalgam of the dry land air and moist ocean air (with perhaps a touch of smog from the San Fernando Valley to the east) that dominates the climate of these mountains. This illusion of light does not happen when fierce Santa Ana winds sear the slopes with desiccating desert air, or when fog drifts inland, up the canyons from the beach.

Fog sustains life on this coast of little rain. Its minute water particles cling to the clumps of grass, to the branchlets of sage and wild lilac, and to the leathery leaves of oaks. The film of water flows downwards, forming drops which fall to the ground and moisten the soil, much like rain, but slower, more patiently.

As the sun warms rocks and bluffs, hawks rise on the updrafts to scan the chaparral for prey. Kangaroo rats and mice live here, rabbits and deer, sparrows, jays, and quail. The hawks share the top of the food pyramid with coyotes, bobcats, and cougars. Casual visitors rarely see these but, vultures, like the hawks, are easy to spot as they glide on the wind, patiently drawing circles in the air, waiting for a meal.

Vultures and hawks also patrol the shore and coastal bluffs, but when the fog drifts in from the sea and thickens over the land, they float inland, toward the sun, just like human sun worshippers who abandon the beaches to the few who stay to enjoy the long, empty strand with the gulls, terns, sanderlings, and snowy plovers.

At night, owls hoot in the live oak and sycamore woods; frogs chirping in the draws bear proof that there's water in the deep folds of these dry hills.

■ SANTA MONICA MOUNTAINS

In the heart of the Santa Monica Mountains and along their ocean front are preserved some 150,000 largely undeveloped acres of mountains, seashore, grassy glens, with the southernmost stands of valley oak, rocky hillsides where mountain lions lurk, and tall cliffs where golden eagles nest. What these mountains lack in altitude—the highest point, Sandstone Peak, is only 3,111 feet above sea level—they make up for in ruggedness. The hills are deeply folded and cut. Malibu Canyon, a spectacular gorge 1,400 to 1,800 feet deep, bisects the mountain range. There are a variety of parks within the system, many offering horse, bicycle, and hiking trails.

———— •◆• ————

■ **Sycamore Canyon and Cove**
Lying on either side of PCH (the Coast Highway), both Sycamore Cove and Canyon are part of the much larger Point Mugu State Park. The cove provides access to a pocket beach where campers and day visitors swim, fish, and birdwatch. Sycamore Canyon is a riparian woodland with a trail that leads into Point Mugu. *The cove is west of the highway; Sycamore Canyon is across the the highway in Ventura County. 805-488-5223.*

■ **Malibu Creek State Park**
The park's 5,000 acres support portions of Malibu Creek, streams, Century Lake, and miles of hiking and horse trails. There's also a campground and picnic area. Twentieth Century Fox Studios once owned part of the park and used the area to film the scenes for *Butch Cassidy and the Sundance Kid, Dukes of Hazzard,* and *M*A*S*H,* among others. *Take Malibu Canyon Rd., six miles north from PCH; 818-880-0367.*

■ **Topanga State Park**
Thirty-five miles of trails (hiking, bicycling, and horseback riding) wind through canyons and along ridges in this 9,000-

acre park. The popular Eagle Rock/ Eagle Spring trail from Eagle Junction affords panoramic views of the ocean and the San Fernando Valley. There are both hike-in and equestrian camp sites. *20825 Entrada Rd., off Topanga Canyon Blvd; 310-455-2465.*

■ **Will Rogers State Historic Park**
Former home to humorist and silver screen star Will Rogers (the Cowboy Philosopher). Polo matches are played every Sunday to honor Rogers. Tours of the house. Facilities include an interpretive nature center and exhibits on local flora and fauna. The lawn is a good picnic spot. Hiking, horseback riding. *16000 block of PCH, Pacific Palisades; 310-454-8212.*

■ **Temescal Gateway Park**
The most popular hike here is the waterfall, but as with all the waterfalls in these mountains, don't expect a violent gush of water. Most times of the year, you'll be lucky to find any water at all. The park, spread out across both sides of Temescal Canyon Road, has a playground, picnic tables, and hiking trails with ocean views. Free roadside parking. *Temescal Canyon Rd. and Sunset Blvd., Pacific Palisades; 310-454-1395.*

■ ALONG THE SHORE

If the mountains provide a welcome respite from the hurried life of the city, the beaches are the centers of action. One reason the beaches along the Malibu shore west of Santa Monica Bay are so popular is because they face south, and are thus exposed to less fog and more sun than nearby urban beaches. Which is also why they are crammed with houses and flower gardens—and why the public strand is often jammed even in mid-week. Malibu has long been the place for stars and starlets, the well-to-do and the ostentatious, as you can easily tell by looking at some of the homes. Practically the entire entertainment industry owns real estate on Broad Beach (six miles north of Paradise Cove) including Goldie Hawn, Frank Sinatra, Neil Simon, Robert Redford, Michael Ovitz, Sylvester Stallone, Eddie van Halen and Valerie Bertenelli, Mel Gibson, Emilio Estevez, and Ted Danson. Steven Spielberg owns a couple of houses on the beach.

The shore has many public beaches—a few of them between the sea and exclusive, gated housing compounds. Anyone listening to the surf will have to agree that Malibu is aptly named: the Chumash Indians called this place *humaliwo,* "the surf sounds loudly."

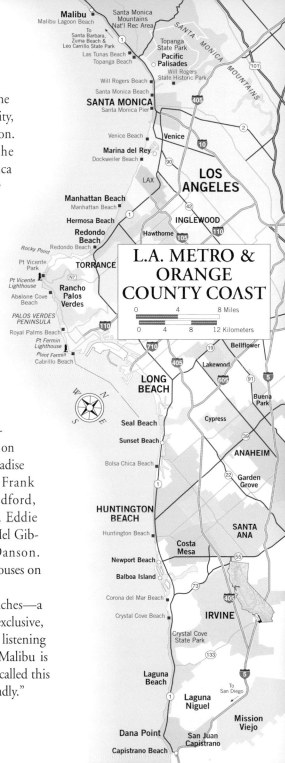

■ LEO CARRILLO STATE PARK

Just south of the Los Angeles County line, this park is an oasis of sandy beaches, rocky shores, meadows, and streamside woods—one of the most magic places on this coast. It is large enough (2,190 acres) to allow urban refugees to escape from the crowds, yet compact enough to make a hike from campsite to beach a pleasing walk. The rocky promontory of Sequit Point has shallow sea caves and tidepools, the creek is lined with shade-giving trees, and the hillsides are covered with fragrant chaparral. Coveys of California quail visit campsites at dusk, before they fly into nearby shrubs to roost. At night, the canyon is filled with the chirping of frogs and the refreshing aromas of coastal sage and yerba santa.

The tidepools at Leo Carrillo are arguably the best in Southern California—look for sea hares, starfish, and fronded sea palms. The rangers are quite helpful.

LEO, "PANCHO," AND THE NONPLUSSED ANGELENOS

Few people seem to know that Leo Carrillo, after whom the park is named, was not only the actor who played Pancho in the *Cisco Kid,* but also a member of one of California's most prominent pioneer families, who traced his lineage back to Raymundo Carrillo, a sergeant who helped found the Presidio of Santa Barbara in 1782. I heard much of the family history in the mid-1960s from Theo, one of Leo's brothers who owned orange orchards in the Santa Ana Canyon and oil wells in the hills. With old-fashioned California generosity, Theo once made me a special-occasion gift of an electric orange squeezer (one of the first ones made), saying that the juicer came with as many oranges from his orchards as I needed to keep me in juice. The orange groves were replaced long ago by shopping malls and tract homes, but the juicer still works.

It seemed like a fitting tribute to Leo's memory that a movie crew was shooting at the beach. It was a low-key affair, with the surfers and swimmers hardly taking any notice of the actors and technicians. Angelenos take everyone, even their stars, in stride. That was quite a contrast from Washington State where Kevin Costner shot some movie scenes the week before, and the state parks department shut down and blocked off one entire section of Deception Pass State Park (the most popular park in the state). In Southern California, it would be decidedly uncool to stare at a star or ask for an autograph.

I mentioned this a few days later, over lunch, to beach resident Bill Burden, who agreed with my observation but said that some shows are more popular than others. The shooting of a *Baywatch* segment at Will Rogers State Beach attracts so many spectators, he said, that vendors put up bleachers and sell refreshments.

L.A. METRO

🚐 Driving the Area

From Leo Carrillo State Park east to Point Dume, the view of the ocean from the road is relatively unobscured, but houses crowd the shores and block the view entirely from Point Dume to Topanga. Yet the beaches are still there in their expansive glory and more accessible to the public than ever. For points of access, look for signs by the side of the road.

■ MALIBU

What *is* Malibu? There is no downtown and no obvious center of town here. Rather, Malibu is that most typical of Southern California towns, an incorporated city that takes in various housing developments in the Santa Monica Mountains and along the 27-mile stretch of shore from the southern end of the Ventura County line south to Pacific Palisades. There are few commercial ventures along the Coast Highway—no shopping malls and seemingly no industry.

There is a Malibu shopping area of course, but I only learned this recently after I stopped by the market at the intersection of the Coast Highway and Trancas Canyon looking for picnic supplies. After squeezing my nondescript car between a BMW and a Porsche, I went inside and found the selection of foods not at all what I had expected to see in affluent Malibu. I began complaining about this to a woman who was waiting in the check-out line with me, telling her that in my opinion the selection of breads was minimal, and the seafood and produce were not nearly fresh enough to meet my standards. My fellow shopper explained that this market is a neighborhood market, one of the few remnants of the "old Malibu," where ranchers and ranchhands outnumbered the movie moguls and personal assistants. These days Trancas Market's customers are surfers and sunbathers who walk up from Zuma to buy chips and drinks.

If I wanted fresh breads and good produce, she suggested I try the Hughes Family Market (at Webb Way and PCH) where she had once stood in line with Olivia Newton John. Hughes Market, apparently, has a turbo cooler which can chill a liter of 7-Up in 30 seconds, with settings for four temperatures. Or, if I wanted to check out the local scene, she thought I might want to try the Malibu Country Mart, east of PCH on Cross Creek Road, with its boutiques, cafes, and restaurants, including Bambu—a sushi, chili fries, "movie-star hot spot."

L.A. METRO

The beach community of Malibu embraces one of the most famous stretches of coastline in California.

■ MALIBU BEACHES

Public access points to Malibu beaches can be difficult to spot, especially in the residential areas; look for the brown signs.

■ El Pescador, Las Piedras, and El Matador

These narrow, sandy beaches are often quite deserted when other beaches are packed to capacity. These are ideal places for an oceanside picnic. El Matador, with its natural rock arches, is the prettiest. Body surfing tends to be poor here because of rip tide. Each has 20 to 40 parking spots and rough trails or stairways down to the ocean. *32000 PCH and north.*

■ Zuma State Beach.

If the surf is up, even if it's a Monday, the parking lots at wide, sandy Zuma—the largest beach on the Malibu shore—will most likely be full. More than two miles long, Zuma is one of the finest white-sand beaches in California. The crowd largely consists of teenagers and bodybuilders. Teens commune especially between towers 6 and 7 at Zuma. This broad, flat beach has volleyball, a fast-food stand, and waves strong enough for bodysurfing. *30000 PCH.*

L.A. METRO

■ **Point Dume State Beach**

A steep set of stairs leads down sandstone cliffs to Point Dume's sandy beach. Rocky tidepools have giant green sea anemones and other intertidal animals. Point Dume is fairly difficult to reach, but it's worth the effort. You have to hike to the point up from the beach, over a stairway from Westward Beach Road, and then take a trail to the Point Dume Whale Watch. Take up surveillance from one of the benches here, and keep an eye out for the California gray whales during their migration from November to May. While there is pedestrian access to the point from the housing development atop the bluff, there is no parking. Curiously, all of the residential roads are posted: NO PARKING. FIRE LANE. Offshore kelp beds teem with fish and support many seabirds, like the brown pelicans roosting on offshore rocks.

Madonna and Sean Penn's wedding took place at a friend's estate on Point Dume, beneath helicopters filled with photographers. Barbara Streisand owns a compound of three houses on Point Dume. *South end of Westward Ave.*

■ **Westward Beach**

Technically part of Zuma and part of Point Dume County Beach, this pleasant beach is a good place for surfing, boogie boarding, and swimming, and is often less crowded than its better known neighbors. (It's also referred to by locals as "Free Zuma" because there's street parking on Windward Beach Road off PCH.) One of the best coastal hikes in Malibu (especially during low tide) begins here. The two-mile trail leads to Point Dume's whale-watching spot, a number of tidepools teeming with marine life, and finally to Paradise Cove. Near the parking lot is the spot where Charlton Heston fled from the apes in *Planet of the Apes*. *West of Point Dume off Westward Ave.*

■ **Malibu Lagoon State Beach**

This beach is known for serious surfers who come here for the perfectly shaped waves. Longboarding is popular and some surfers use the antique wood boards. Connected **Surfrider Beach** was popularized by surfing movies in the 1950s and 1960s (i.e. *Gidget*) and has needed no advertising since. I do sometimes wonder if surfing would have become as popular a sport as it is if it had not attracted the attention of film directors and song writers. Once it was glorified in the movies, it just had to catch on—especially since it was practiced on warm, scenic beaches. *Pacific Coast Highway and Cross Creek Rd.*

■ **Malibu Lagoon**

This lagoon was the southernmost village of the Chumash, who fished here and gathered mollusks. More than 200 species of birds have been observed on or near the lagoon, including elegant terns, belted kingfishers, and American goldfinches.

L.A. METRO

fornia beach in countless movies (including three more of Frankie and Annette's beach parties), rock videos, and television shows. There's ample but expensive parking at this privately owned beach. The approach by foot is down a big hill. *28128 PCH.*

■ **Crowded Surfing Beaches**
From Malibu Canyon west to Santa Monica, the beaches are crowded even on weekdays. The parking strips at **Las Tunas State Beach** and **Topanga State Beach** are usually full, and the waves are crowded with surfers floating just outside the surf line like sea lions waiting for a run of smelt. Surfers are the most amphibious of Americans. In their wet suits, which look like the skin of amphibians, they appear to be spending as much time in the water as out. At Malibu, where the water is quite warm in summer, many wear no wet suits at all, or merely short body suits.

■ **Paradise Cove**
Most of the time this is a quiet cove, ideal for swimming and sunbathing, except for the days when movie crews take over. Ever since 1963 when movie audiences went to Frankie Avalon and Annette Funicello's first *Beach Party,* Paradise Cove has appeared as the quintessential Southern Cali-

■ MUSEUMS OF INTEREST

The Malibu Lagoon Museum occupies an Andalusian-style beach house built in 1929 for Merrit Huntley Adamson and Rhoda Rindge Adamson, daughter of Frederick Hastings Rindge and May Knight Rindge, last owners of the Rancho Malibu land grant (that was awarded to Jose Tapia in 1805 and bought by the Rindges in 1887). The Rindges tried to run their ranch as a private empire, blocking a public highway across their land until they exhausted their fortune in lawsuits. The final defeat came in 1929, when the Pacific Coast Highway opened. The mansion is adorned with decorative tiles made by Malibu Potteries, a highly acclaimed local studio which produced ceramics from 1926 to 1932. *23200 Pacific Coast Highway; 310-457-8143 or 818-706-1310.*

The reconstruction of a Pompeian villa which served as the **J. Paul Getty Museum** until 1997 is hidden away just north of the Pacific Coast Highway, between Coastline Drive and Sunset Boulevard. The museum was closed in anticipation of the new and larger museum and arts complex which opened in the Santa Monica Mountains in December 1997. The villa is scheduled to reopen in 2001 as a center for the study of Roman culture.

You can't miss the **new Getty Museum** if you take Interstate 405 through the mountains at Sepulveda Pass. Perched in the hills just off the freeway, high above Bel Air and Brentwood, this group of glass and concrete buildings dominates the skyline. The Getty is the world's richest museum, with an incredible collection of art, including such masterpieces as Andrea Mantegna's 1495 *Adoration of the Magi*, and Rembrandt's first (1632) landscape, *The Abduction of Europa.*

If you plan to arrive by car you need to make parking reservations well ahead of time. The museum encourages visitors to arrive by public transportation and will give directions on how to take a bus from West Los Angeles. Even so, you can't walk right up to the museum but have to take a tram up the hill. Admission is free but parking is $5 a day. Is it worth the effort? You bet. *Reservations, 310-440-7300.*

The Getty Museum houses one of the world's finest collections of classical art, including this Bathing Venus urn, ca. 1559. (Courtesy of J. Paul Getty Museum)

THE LIFEGUARD

He lived in Malibu, the place by the sea which the Indians called the Humped Mountain, and which in French, if you sang it, sounded like Evil Owl—*Mal Hibou*, Malibu.

When he was a young man he became a lifeguard at Will Rogers' beach. He sat on a chair twelve feet high and studied the moods of the sea. He had no need of weather bureaus. He knew by every undulation, every contortion, every flourish and flounce of the waves, the sea's exact mood and whether it would be treacherous for the swimmers, or tender and mocking. He knew the omens of the clouds, read the future in their colors and density. He knew the topography of the sand covered by the sea as if he had mapped its depths. From where he sat the cries of the gulls, of children and bathers all fused together and made a sound he liked, *musique concréte*. He had never been concerned with words.

He knew the entire coast from Will Rogers' beach to where Malibu became wild and solitary.

—Anaïs Nin, *Collages*, 1964

■ PACIFIC PALISADES

Above the Coast Highway, on the edge of some very unstable bluffs, which seem to erode further with every rainstorm, perch the expensive homes of Pacific Palisades, an exclusive community founded as a Methodist retreat. From the 1920s to the 1940s, writers, artists, actors, and architects made it the art center of Los Angeles.

Will Rogers State Beach, a three-mile-long sandy beach popular for swimming, diving, surfing, and body surfing, takes up much of Pacific Palisades' oceanfront. Fishermen cast for surfperch, halibut, and bonito; gulls, sanderlings, willets, and other shorebirds hang out along the littoral edge. *16000 Block of Pacific Coast Highway.*

South Bay Bicycle Trail, a scenic and immensely popular 22-mile coastal route runs from Will Rogers State Park to Torrance County Beach. Though this is technically a bicycles-only path, weekends bring about constant battles between in-line skaters and bicyclists.

🚐 To reach Pacific Palisades from downtown L.A. or Westwood, take Sunset Boulevard west to its end at the Pacific Coast Highway.

L.A. METRO

■ SANTA MONICA

Santa Monica's oceanfront is one vast beach, backed by low bluffs and tall palm trees, condominiums, and hotels. Santa Monica is more than surf and sand and sun, more than palm trees swaying in the ocean breeze. It has wide boulevards, sidewalk cafes, great restaurants and shops, and beautiful homes with large gardens and red-tiled roofs. It also has a large population of drifters and homeless people, and busloads of tourists crowding the Promenade, Boardwalk, and Pier.

It was named by Father Juan Crespi of the Gaspar de Portola Expedition of 1769, which camped at a spring hereabouts. For some unfathomable reason, the spring reminded Crespi of St. Monica's tears shed for her heretic son St. Augustine. In 1828, the extensive local grasslands were granted to Francisco Sepulveda, a former alcalde of the Pueblo de los Angeles.

In the 1880s, railroads linked Los Angeles to the east coast and the city's population skyrocketed. Beach resorts and private clubs began to spring up all over Santa Monica. William Randolph Hearst threw extravagant Hollywood bashes at

Pacific Coast Highway in Santa Monica, ca. 1907.

L.A. METRO

Mr. Hearst's Beach House

Newspaper magnate William Randolph Hearst is known for his castle, San Simeon, but he also built himself a beach house in Santa Monica—it had 100 bedrooms and 55 bathrooms. The 37 fireplace mantels were from English estates, and the paintings on the walls were by Rembrandt, Hals, Reynolds, and Rubens.

*T*he beach house did not have the pretense of a museum or a castle, but was a sunny, light, informal place devoted to endless fun . . . and it quickly became the epicenter of the movie colony's social activities. On weekends there were always at least fifty or sixty visitors about. . . . Guests who liked to swim had their choice of the ocean a few feet away or a beautiful hundred-foot pool with a Venetian marble bridge spanning the center of it.

[Mr. Hearst] devised some of the most ingenious events the town had ever seen.

There was the kid party, where the handsome Clark Gable came dressed as a Boy Scout and Norma Shearer and Joan Crawford were frilly little Shirley Temples. Another was the sumptuous Early American party with Mr. Hearst appearing as James Madison, another firm believer in the Constitution and gracious living, and his five sons all outfitted as sailors of our young Republic. In keeping with the theme, Norma Shearer came as Marie Antoinette, representing our French ally during the Revolution. But the *pièce de résistance* was the five-tiered cake fashioned like a replica of Independence Hall.

—Ken Murray,
The Golden Days of San Simeon, 1971

Hearst (center) hosts a costume ball at his Santa Monica beach house. To his left are Douglas Fairbanks, Sr. and Mary Pickford, and to his right, Charlie Chaplin and Theda Bara.

his seaside mansion, and Santa Monica Pier's grand ballroom, once the largest in the world, welcomed 5,000 nightly. In the 1920s and 1930s, illegal gambling ships were anchored offshore. and Raymond Chandler portrayed it as sleazy "Bay City" in *Farewell, My Lovely.* After Cary Grant and Mary Pickford bought land here, it became known as "The Gold Coast."

Santa Monica's beach is still one of the most popular in Southern California, not only with people, but with movie and television producers. David Hasselhoff's lifeguard station on *Baywatch* is at 16000 Pacific Coast Highway

Stairway *(at Santa Monica's Palisades Park) by James Doolin, 1991–1992. (Koplin Gallery, Santa Monica)*

and the beach club on *Beverly Hills 90210* is at 415 Palisades Beach Road (PCH). A short list of recent movies using Santa Monica backdrops include *Speed, The Truth about Cats and Dogs, White Men Can't Jump, Heat,* and *Forget Paris.* Movie stars even own some of the restaurants here and in adjacent Venice, including 72 Market Street (Dudley Moore and Liza Minnelli) and Schatzi on Main (Arnold Schwarzenegger).

Today, the price of Santa Monica real estate is among the highest in L.A. County. Along Ocean Boulevard there are a number of large hotels, and upscale apartment buildings overlooking the ocean, and the streets are so wide it doesn't seem as crammed as most popular beachfronts. At the same time, many of the town's apartments are surprisingly down at the heels. The quality of the food in the area is quite high, and there is some interesting (if not widely praised) architecture, including a few buildings by Frank Gehry—the most outrageous being the much-magnified pair of binoculars which houses the Chiat-Day advertising agency.

L.A. METRO

■ WHAT TO DO AND SEE IN SANTA MONICA

■ Santa Monica Pier

Santa Monica's original Pleasure Pier, the brainchild of Coney Island showman Charles Looff, opened in 1917. It has a hand-carved carousel; a variety of amusement park rides, including a giant Ferris wheel with a dizzying view of the Pacific; game booths; and arcades.

Free summer concerts (the Twilight Series) are held on the pier every Thursday evening. UCLA's Ocean Discovery Museum is located *under* the pier.

Walking the pier at night is still one of the more romantic ways to enjoy the city, especially now with the safe-guarding presence of the Jetsons-style police station near the carousel. At anytime of day you'll be sharing the pier with families, fishermen, and street musicians. The Mexican restaurant, Mariasol, at the end of the pier has the best outdoor deck in the city, and if you're lucky you might find a good chili dog at one of the food stands.

There are ordinary chili dogs in this world and glorious ones. A good chili dog needs to be all-beef, preferably kosher, and about a foot long. It needs to be grilled, not microwaved, and served on a hot, fresh bun. It needs to be topped with homemade chili (with or without beans) and a few pickled chilies (preferably chipotles). Such a chili dog is ambrosia for the gods.

Santa Monica Pier.

L.A. METRO

■ **Santa Monica State Beach**

A three-mile beach that extends south from Will Rogers State Beach is not only one of the most popular beaches in the L.A. area, but also one of the few where the melting pot truly works, since members of all races mingle here and get along splendidly.

■ **Shopping**

The European-style, pedestrians-only **Third Street Promenade,** mobbed on weekends, is the liveliest shopping district in Santa Monica. You'll find upscale restaurants side by side with ethnic fast-food outlets, the best of which is Benita's Fries where Belgian-style French fries are the only item on the menu (aside from dozens of dipping sauces); three multiplex movie theaters; unusual shops like Dom with its seemingly infinite assortment of kitschy housewares; and three exceptional bookstores (Midnight Special, Arcana, and Hennesey and Ingalls). At the the southern end of the Promenade is the enormous, pastel, and angular Santa Monica Place shopping mall, designed by architect Frank Gehry. (The Promenade is on Third Street, between Wilshire Blvd. and Broadway.) Toney **Montana Avenue** and eclectic **Main Street** are both lined with trendy restaurants, furniture stores, sidewalk cafes, and boutiques.

■ **Farmers Market**

There are farmers markets every day of the week in Los Angeles but the largest is in Santa Monica, two mornings a week at the

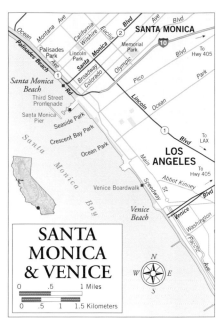

SANTA MONICA & VENICE

Third Street Promenade and Arizona Avenue. Flowers, fruits, vegetables, and herbs are sold every Wednesday from 9:30 A.M. to 3:30 P.M. and on Saturday from 8:30 A.M. to 1:00 P.M. Don't miss the fantastic tamale stand with gourmet varieties like spinach and leek, sun dried tomato, and barbecued chicken with habañero salsa.

■ **Palisades Park**

Set on a cliff overlooking Santa Monica Beach, this palm-lined park is a good place for running, walking, and watching the sunset. Pedestrian bridges and stairways lead from the park down to the beach. The park runs parallel to Ocean Ave., between Colorado Ave. and Adelaide Dr.

L.A. METRO

■ VENICE

If Southern California is the epicenter of the nation's wackiness, Venice is the very heart of that epicenter. When I last approached **Venice Boardwalk,** I was greeted by a "pink man." Dressed in pink Spandex, he fluttered his pink cape at me. He was friendly without trying to sell me anything. He pointed to the top of some palm trees where, high above the beach, a tightrope walker in formal dress casually strutted, waving a black parasol.

Scantily clad skaters, some wearing little more than a G-string, scooted by, zigzagging around the bicycle riders who cruised past the palm readers, the crystal sellers, and T-shirt vendors at a slightly slower pace. All about swirled the aromas of tacos, chilies, and cilantro. It's not suprising to me that Venice is very popular with tourists from Europe and Asia who come here to learn what Americans are really like. *The Boardwalk runs parallel to Venice Beach, between Navy Street and Washington Boulevard.*

Muscle Beach, actually part of the boardwalk, is a local institution where both men and women show off their bodies. It was originally named for the mussels attached to the pilings of the Santa Monica Pier. During the Great Depression, mussel became muscle, when WPA workers started an exercise program for local kids. Today, the name has traveled south to Venice Beach. *20th Street and Ocean Front Walk.*

Venice Beach is a wide, sandy, surprisingly uncrowded, palm-tree-lined beach between the hypo-lively Venice Boardwalk and the ocean. Many of the folks coming to experience the Boardwalk never actually walk out onto the beach. *Extends from Marine Street to Spinnaker Street.*

Venice Boardwalk.

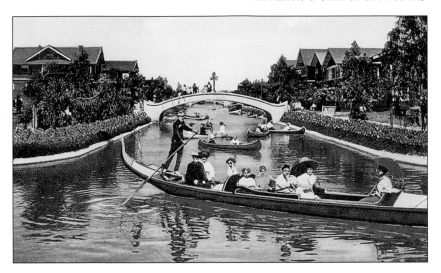

In the early 1900s Venice developed as a beach resort
fashioned after its Italian namesake, complete with canals and gondolas.

Venice eccentricity goes back a long time, to 1904, when a tobacco magnate named Abbot Kinney bought 160 acres of coastal salt marsh south of Santa Monica and set out to create a new cultural center for the nation by carving canals and a central lagoon from the briny fens and naming the place "Venice." He built an arcaded hotel, the St. Mark, spanned the canals with Venetian-style bridges, and began to attract crowds with appearances by such notables as author Helen Hunt Jackson, actress Sarah Bernhardt, and the Chicago Symphony. But a roller coaster, the bath houses, and casinos he had also provided attracted more visitors than the sedate star acts at the auditorium.

When oil was discovered in Venice in 1929, spilled crude polluted the canals, and all but four were paved over. House prices and rents plummeted as Venice became a slightly seedy but comfortable neighborhood. In the 1950s, beatniks moved in, followed in the 1960s by hippies. These were followed by poets, writers, and artists and by others seeking "alternative" lifestyles. And then the inevitable happened. As in Carmel, Laguna Beach, and Mendocino, the artists attracted everyone else and before long gentrification of the canal neighborhoods was well on its way. Today, Venice is an eclectic amalgam of all of the above, with an occasional fight among street gangs thrown in.

To see Venice's few surviving canals, take a stroll along Dell Avenue which runs south from Venice Boulevard.

■ MARINA DEL REY AND PLAYA DEL RAY

If you spend a lot of time around boats, Marina del Ray will look like a place you've seen before, on both coasts. This small craft harbor—the largest in the world—appears a bit generic in its layout and architecture, but it does have its attractions. It's a good, relatively safe place for families—kids often walk along the fisherman's village pier by themselves. Burton Chase Park is a pleasant park with a panoramic view of the main channel, picnic tables, a fishing pier, and visitor docks. Walking along the path bordering the marina you may recognize it from the many *Charlie's Angels* episodes filmed here. It's long been known for its swinging singles scene, '70s style. During the holidays, all the boats are lit up with colored lights; most marinas have boat parades. The popular Cheesecake Factory restaurant has a large patio on Mothers' Beach.

At Playa del Rey, south of the harbor jetty, Del Rey Lagoon, a 13-acre remnant of the once vast Ballona Lagoon wetlands, is surrounded by a grassy park with picnic tables.

■ MANHATTAN BEACH AND HERMOSA BEACH ·

Manhattan Beach and its neighbor, Hermosa, are special places. Catering mostly to residents, they have escaped the tourist rush and have maintained a pleasant (dare we say "wholesome") small-town atmosphere. You'll notice the change of mood as soon as you cross the Manhattan Beach city line. The streets are clean, houses and yards are taken well taken care off, and flowers bloom in gardens and window boxes.

I discuss the local scene over lunch at Pierre's Cafe on Manhattan Beach Boulevard with Westside resident Shari Dunn and Hermosa Beach resident Bill Burden.

Burden climbs out on a limb by calling Manhattan and Hermosa Beaches "the only real beach towns in California." But he admits that centralization of resources (i.e. outlet malls) is affecting the beach towns as much as other small towns throughout the country. The towns have changed in recent years, he says; the hardware stores are gone, and some of the markets, and you now have to drive all the way to Sepulveda Boulevard (about 14 city blocks) to do your shopping.

Manhattan and Hermosa Beaches have distinct personalities: Manhattan is a yuppie family town and Hermosa is a slightly wilder, singles' town. The two are connected by The Strand, a concrete walking/biking path which is much less hectic

Heading for the beach.

than the Venice Boardwalk. Dunn says that the towns are very popular with young people, waitresses, bartenders, flight attendants, and pilots who play volleyball during the day. Burden adds that some folks living near the beach put up their own volleyball poles and guard them jealously against intruders. That way they always have a place to play.

Teenagers arrive by bus. Some have bicycles outfitted with a surfboard carrier in the back, which makes the bike, with the board loaded, look like some weird terrestrial land sailing craft.

Many of the pier fishermen, who are mostly Hispanic or Asian, also come by bus. They catch halibut, mackerel, opaleye, several species of surfperch. The surfers are mostly locals. Anyone lying in the sun, slowly baking on the sand, is probably an out-of-towner, for, claims Peter Theroux in his book *Translating L.A.,* the citizenry resorts to "sun block, sun hats, . . . and parasols." Cafes, restaurants, a brew pub, and bookstores are on or near Pier Avenue.

L.A. METRO

■ REDONDO BEACH

When I spent a night in a Redondo Beach motel near the marina, I was puzzled to notice that most of the other guests were mothers with small children, but then I remembered that my wife, a native Southern Californian, had told me about the summers she and her mother stayed near the beach. Her father, who did not much care for beaches, visited on weekends.

Redondo Beach attracts day-tripping families from the hinterland as well, because large parking garages near the pier and beach allow for easy access. As I walked from my motel to the Redondo Beach Pier, I saw more families, of all races—more diversity than I had seen in any other beach community.

Most of the old pier burned down a few years ago, and I was at first put off by the modernistic concrete and steel structure that replaced it. But no one else seems to mind. This is by far the most popular pier I have visited. The city council is considering renaming it "The Pier at Redondo Beach." The new pier, which arcs out to sea, is thronged with families out for a stroll, joggers, walkers, and fishermen. It's as close to a maritime theme park as a California pier gets, with its nautical shops and restaurants. The attached 300-foot-long Monstad Pier is one of the best fishing spots in Southern California, and therefore very crowded. At the foot of both piers stands a small bronze bust of George Freeth, who introduced surfing to California at Redondo Beach in 1907.

If you walk along the pier and the boat basin, some of the "gulls" you will see perched on the party boats aren't gulls at all, but black-crowned night herons— gray and black adults and brown-streaked juveniles. I've seen a young heron here practicing his hunting technique by stalking and pouncing on the bright stainless steel bolts holding the flying bridge to the cabin roof. When the heron got too close to a sea gull (they're about the same size, though the heron's neck and legs are longer and its feet are not webbed), the gull chased the heron off, its tail tweaked by another heron. *A parking garage behind the pier at the end of Torrance Boulevard allows easy access for a fee.*

❖

If as you drive along the Esplanade, a strange bird soars up from below, it will probably turn out to be a remote-controlled sailplane whose "pilot" flies it in perfect harmony with the gulls soaring on the updrafts.

The beach is sandy and wide, and very popular with families who come here to

BIKINI SHOPPING IS SERIOUS BUSINESS

by Jill Bell

In and around the beach communities of Southern California, summer is a warm blend of soaking in the sunshine, frolicking in ocean waves, and diving into backyard swimming pools. As a young girl growing up in Santa Monica, I spent most days during summer vacation wearing a bathing suit. For my girlfriends and me, the rituals of summertime were always preceded by an afternoon of swimsuit shopping.

As summers passed by, the years of my life were marked by swimsuits in a variety of styles, shapes, and colors. One of my favorites was a diver's-style one piece suit, bright red with one large strap up the back. My best friend had an identical suit that year, and we ran around the beach with the confidence of young girls who have deliberately chosen to dress exactly alike.

The next summer, I noticed that my friends were wearing a new style of bathing suit: the triangle top bikini. When we went shopping, I selected a few bikinis and marched into the dressing room. I fumbled with the string ties and turned to look in the mirror: a stranger stared back at me. My bones seemed to stick out all over the place, and no matter what style or size bikini I tried on, some part of it didn't fit right. Compared to the all-purpose, made-for-fun, one-piece swimsuits I had always worn, the bikini was complicated and embarrassing. When the store clerk sauntered into the dressing room and said, "Can I help you?" I wondered, "How can *she* help!" Would my summer now be ruined? How was I supposed to body surf in a swimsuit that was loose and tight in all the wrong places? All of my friends wore bikinis that year, but I just couldn't.

The summer before my senior year in high school, I went to South America as an exchange student and bypassed the bathing suit ordeal. When I returned, I became too busy with college applications to think much about the joys of summer. When I went shopping for a swimsuit that spring, I found myself face to face with another stranger in the dressing room. Many of the new styles of bikinis seemed to have been designed just for me. I purchased several and hit the beaches, ready to enjoy all the rituals of another California summer.

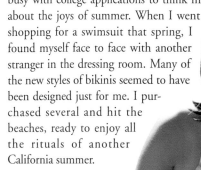

(Photo by Susan Scheding)

A lone surfer finds perfect solitude in the ocean's evening glass-off.

chase frisbees, play volleyball, or swim (though there have been some complaints about pollution, especially after storm run-off enters the ocean).

■ PALOS VERDES PENINSULA

A former oceanic island, this peninsula is connected to the land on its eastern slopes by alluvial outwash from the L.A. River. The peninsula has 13 distinct marine terraces, which rise in succession from sea level to 1,200 feet. Its highest point is San Pedro Hill, at 1,480 feet.

Before the Spanish settled on this coast, Gabrielino Indians camped in the coves, fished from the headlands, and pursued sea mammals in sturdy canoes (thought to have been of Chumash design). After colonization, Palos Verdes became a rancho in the vast Sepulveda holdings. Residential communities were first laid out in the 1920s, and today several cities share the peninsula. (Watch for traffic cops of all jurisdictions hiding behind bushes and ever ready to pounce on speeders). It's very green here, rolling hills, not overdeveloped. The people of Palos Verdes are (for the most part) wealthy. Many have estates and stables, and they tend to be conservative politically, and in the way they dress.

L.A. METRO

■ PALOS VERDES PENINSULA BEACHES AND PARKS

■ Malaga Cove

Also called "Rat Beach" (for Right After Torrance), this cove has the only sandy beach on the peninsula and is popular with swimmers, surfers, and divers. Nearby is a popular surf spot called "Haggerty's" (by trail from Paseo del Mar or along the shore form Torrance County Beach).

■ Lunada Bay

Local surfers have been known to throw rocks at non-locals who try to surf this favorite spot, but sunbathers aren't usually in much danger. Lunada Bay, and several other small coves are protected in the **Palos Verdes Shoreline Preserve,** which takes in the entire 4.5-mile oceanfront of that city. Dirt paths lead from the unimproved blufftops down to secluded beaches. There is ample street parking.

■ Point Vicente Park

North of the 1926 lighthouse, this park has blufftop trails, picnic tables, viewing platforms, and an interpretive center. The lighthouse is not open to the public. South of the point, a steep trail leads from a blufftop parking lot to the rocky beach of the **Point Vicente Fishing Access,** which is popular with divers and fishermen.

■ Abalone Cove Beach

There's a blufftop (fee) parking lot here with a steep dirt path to the shore of Abalone Cove with tidepools and rocky beaches beneath 180-foot-high cliffs. On the blufftops you can see (but don't touch!) prickly pear and coast cholla cacti. Smugglers Cove to the east was popular with rum runners during Prohibition. Nearby Wayfarer's Chapel, designed by Lloyd Wright, a son of Frank Lloyd Wright, in 1946, perches precariously next to a major landslide. The slide has destroyed homes and is still active, moving slowly, a few inches a year, on slippery rocks greased by an increased supply of ground water. Because of the slide the much-repaired road at Portuguese Bend resembles a roller coaster.

———— ◆ ————

■ LOS ANGELES AREA PORTS

The Port of Los Angeles started as a shallow, muddy bay, not deep enough to float a schooner. Its dramatic transformation started with dredging in 1870s. Today it is, with the Port of Long Beach, one of the largest artificial harbor complexes in the world, and perhaps the ugliest as well. Since there is little public access by land, its 28 miles of shoreline, eight shipyards, and several marinas are best viewed from one of the many harbor tour boats. See the following page for details on area beaches, museums, and other interesting sights, including the *Queen Mary.*

L.A. METRO

■ WHAT TO DO AND SEE IN SAN PEDRO AND LONG BEACH

■ **Royal Palms State Beach**

Mother Nature took a bite out of the works of man when a storm washed the Royal Palms Hotel into the sea about 75 years ago. The garden terraces with their majestic palms remained. The tidepool-studded rocky shoreline is reached by a dirt path down steep steps. The park is very popular with surfers and divers. White's Point Beach is to the immediate east. It is also reached by a steep trail and by a steep, paved road off Weymouth Avenue.

■ **Point Fermin Park**

Point Fermin Park has a prefabricated wooden 1874 lighthouse and several huge Moreton Bay figs (a.k.a. rubber trees). Two steep but well-maintained trails drop down to the beach; one from Barbara Street, the other from Meyler or Roxbury Streets.

■ **Angels Gate Park**

This former upper reservation of Fort McArthur, where big railroad guns were once kept for shelling any enemy ships foolish enough to attack Los Angeles Harbor, overlooks Point Fermin.

■ **Cabrillo Beach**

A superb beach to explore during low tide and when the grunion are running (at night after the full or new moons between March and August).

■ **Harbor Tours**

Spirit Cruises. *Berth 77, San Pedro; 310-548-8080.*

■ **Cabrillo Marine Museum**

A new museum with fine aquariums. *3720 Stephen M. White Dr.; 310-548-7562.*

■ **Los Angeles Maritime Museum**

A museum dedicated to ship models, including one of the *Titanic.* Also houses U.S. Navy memorabilia. *Foot of Sixth St. at Sampson Way, Berth 84; 310-548-7618.*

■ **Ports O'Call Village**

North of the fishing-boat docks, between berths 75-78, is one of the very few "fisherman's villages" that works, perhaps because there has been a recent influx of Asian seafood merchants who sell fish and shellfish both fresh and cooked. The spacious outdoor dining patios are great places for watching the ships go by, while munching fresh seafood and sipping cold beer.

■ *Queen Mary*

This was the world's largest passenger liner and has an accompanying village of "English" shops. *1126 Queen's Hwy., Long Beach (end of Hwy. 710); 562-435-3511.*

■ **Beaches and Residential Areas**

Belmont and Naples (a Venice-style island settlement) on the southeastern end of town have kept their charm and remain surprisingly unchanged. The Peninsula residential area has the ocean on one side and Alamitos Bay on the other. The uncrowded bayside beaches overlook Naples Island; from here you can kayak (rentals available), windsurf, or take a gondola ride.

The Queen Mary, *berthed in Long Beach Harbor. (Photo by Mark Wexler).*

■ SANTA CATALINA ISLAND

Catalina, as Southern Californians call the island for short, is sufficiently exotic to excite the imagination, yet comfortably close to home, only 19 miles offshore from Long Beach (26 miles from Newport). Visitors come here to enjoy the laid-back resort town of Avalon, to swim, beachcomb, hike, bike, go fishing, or take one of several bus or boat tours exploring the island.

❖

The third largest of California's Channel Island's is, like the others, part of a submerged, steep-sided mountain range that may or may not have once been connected to the mainland (geologists disagree on this point). While the island's climate is mild (and frost-free), fog and wind can chill things down considerably. The island's

Catalina *by Alson Skinner Clark, 1920. (Courtesy of Westphal Publishing, Irvine, CA)*

⛴ GETTING TO CATALINA

- **Catalina Cruises** leave daily from Long Beach to Avalon; seasonal service to Two Harbors. *Long Beach Terminal, 320 Golden Shores Blvd., Long Beach; 562-436-5006.*
- **Catalina Express Commuter** leaves from San Pedro and Long Beach to Avalon and Two Harbors. *310-519-1212 or 310-510-1212.*
- **Catalina Flyer** A fast catamaran from the Balboa Pavilion in Newport Beach to Avalon. Leaves the Balboa Pavilion daily at 9:00 A.M. and leaves Avalon at 4:30 P.M. Reservations required. *949-673-5245.*

🚗 ABOUT CARS

Visitors may not bring their cars onto the island; you get around on foot, by public transportation, or in a rental golf cart. Bicycles are allowed in the backcountry by permit only.

---

flora differs somewhat from that of the mainland, containing species that vanished from the continent thousands (even millions) of years ago. The most notable of these is the Catalina Ironwood, a broad-leafed evergreen with shaggy reddish bark. It has simple, lanceolate leaves and grows only on Santa Catalina Island (ironwoods growing on other Channel Islands have feathery leaves).

Catalina was about as densely settled as it is now (about 3,000 permanent residents) in prehistoric times, but the center of population was in the northwest on the Isthmus, now occupied by the village of Two Harbors. The Gabrielino Indians who lived here were much like the Chumash to the north, with whom they kept up a lively trade in soapstone vessels, tools, and canoes.

Avalon (year-round population about 2,500) is the island's metropolis. Spread over the slopes of a semi-circular bay, it looks Mediterranean, with its white houses, palm trees, steep cliffs, and blue waters, and scores of pleasure boats. Avalon also has numerous hotels, restaurants, shops, fishing tackle and charter services, boat rentals, a supermarket, a hardware store, other amenities of mainland civilization, and the famous "**casino**," a squat, white, red-roofed Moorish-style tower at the northern point of the harbor.

■ WHAT TO DO AND SEE IN CATALINA

For more information on the following tours, activities, and sights on Catalina contact the Catalina Island Visitors Bureau on Green Pleasure Pier; 310-510-1520.

———— • ◆ • ————

■ **Avalon Casino**

Don't let the term "casino" fool you. This is not a gambling hall but an entertainment complex. The word "casino," as its name (a small "casa") indicates, was first used for Italian garden houses and pavilions and can still be found used in this fashion in some garden books; later the name was applied to pavilions where musicians performed for the owners of the garden; still later dance floors were added. It is in this sense that "casino" is used here. Today, the casino houses a movie theater, and a museum with a collection of Indian artifacts. A beautiful promenade runs along the waterfront from Avalon to the casino.

■ **Wrigley Memorial Botanical Garden**

At the head of Avalon Canyon is a famous collection of native island plants, cacti, and succulents. It can be reached by a gently sloping, 1.7-mile road from Avalon (or by shuttle tram).

■ **Other Avalon Attractions**

Holly Hill house, an elaborate mansion built by a bachelor for a bride who never came; the Wrigley's former cottage; and the adobe where writer Zane Grey spent his last days (both of them now B&Bs). The Wrigley (chewing gum) family once owned much of the island.

■ **Island bus and boat service**

Daily scheduled bus and boat service leaves Avalon for Two Harbors, the village on the isthmus, which is Catalina's other settlement. Two Harbors is very popular with boaters (because of the sheltered anchorage) and has a general store, a snack bar, restaurant, and a couple of lodging places. *For local tours, consult the Two Harbors Visitors and Information Office at 310-510-2800.*

■ **Scuba Diving and Snorkeling**

Catalina's Underwater Park has a spectacular kelp forest, and swimming around the wrecked ships are bat rays, octopuses, garibaldi, and halibut. The Lover's Cove Marine Preserve is a prime snorkeling-only spot.

■ **Hiking and Biking**

Roads and trails lead to within a mile of the western tip of the island. Trails vary in quality: from goat tracks to foot paths to jeep and fire roads. You'll need both hiking and biking permits if you leave Avalon; no charge. *Pick up permits at Two Harbors Visitors Center, Airport-in-the-Sky, or the Conservancy office in Avalon at 125 Claressa St.; 310-510-0688.*

■ **Drinking water and hot weather**

None of the water found in island streams is potable. While drinkable water is available at improved campgrounds, always carry enough to tide you over. The island can get quite warm, especially inland, away from the sea. Because the weather can vary as much as 30 degrees between the coast and the inland valleys, wear layers of clothing and be ready to peel as necessary.

■ **Tours on the Island**

The Santa Catalina Island Company's Discovery Tours provides several ways for visitors on a limited schedule to see the island. *Visitor's Information Center, 800-428-2566.*

Avalon Scenic Tour and Casino Tour. A 50-minute excursion, including a history tour and a visit to the casino.

Skyline Drive. Takes visitors to island mountains, where you'll see ironwood trees, and through deep canyons to hidden coves. En route, you'll encounter bison (left over from the making of a Western movie), and perhaps deer and wild boar. Two hours.

Inland Tour. A guided tour takes visitors further into the mountains and to the Wrigley's Rancho Escondido, a breeding ranch for Arabian horses. Half-day.

Boat Tours. You can also take a tour in a glass-bottom boat or semi-submersible to get a close-up look at the kelp beds and the creatures inhabiting them—without having to don scuba gear. Or you can take a nighttime flying fish trip. The flying fish visiting Santa Catalina's offshore waters are quite large and can easily be seen in the boat's searchlights as they take off from the water (and splash back after their "wings" dry out).

Soapstone Quarry Tour. View the remains of bowls and ollas that were made long ago by the island's original inhabitants, the Gabrielino Indians. *Two Harbors Visitor Center; 310-510-2800.*

A summer day in Avalon in the late 1890s. The rock in the background of this photograph is where Avalon's "casino" was built 30 years later. (Santa Catalina Island Company)

■ ORANGE COUNTY OVERVIEW

Orange County is an enigma; it can be both beautiful and unattractive, an amalgam of the Beauty and the Beast. Thirty years ago there were still more orange groves here than housing tracts or freeways. On winter nights the orange blossoms would open and their dense, tropical scent would permeate the air. Today, one of those orange groves is part of a freeway—ironically named the "Orange" Freeway.

Northern Orange County is part of the flat Los Angeles basin; southern Orange County is hilly or mountainous. In the north, the shores are primarily sandy beaches or coastal lagoons and marshes; to the south they are dominated by rocky cliffs with sandy pocket beaches.

Much of northern Orange County (and most of the coastal plains and terraces) has been swallowed by urban sprawl, but there are still open, wild spaces as well, mostly in the San Joaquin Hills and Santa Ana Mountains. The dense chaparral and big-cone Douglas-fir forest surrounding Santiago Park (Old Saddleback) are as wild as any western mountain landscape. The reason so much wilderness has survived is because much of the mountainous back country is U.S. Forest Service land.

Orange County has all of the amenities you would expect from a 20th-century American suburban community and several of the beaches are spectacular.

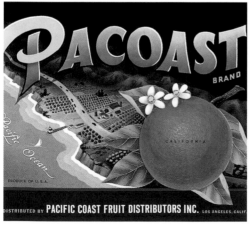

An orange crate label from the glory days when orange were grown thoughout Orange County.

■ TRAVELING AND ACCESS TO ORANGE COUNTY BEACHES

🚗 Orange County can be reached via I-5 from Los Angeles and San Diego, and via CA 1 (PCH) along the coast, and via the Riverside Freeway (Highway 91) from I-15 and Riverside. Many north-south, and several east-west roads end at the beach; but the coast is reached most easily by Beach Blvd/Highway 39; the Costa Mesa Freeway/ Highway 55; and Laguna Canyon Road/Highway 133.

Because so many Orange County beaches hide behind fences, and because too many people live here on too little land, trips to the Orange Coast should be planned with

care. A driving trip along this coast might be disappointing and frustrating. Try to avoid driving during the morning or evening rush hours, and be prepared for delays on any warm weekend day.

Beginning at the southern end of Sunset Beach, many state beaches, county beaches, private beaches, the uplands and the residential neighborhoods are fenced in and can be entered only through gates, by paying a fee, or by using a key card. Even the beaches at Bolsa Chica and Huntington Beach, which were wide open not so long ago, are now fenced in. There's a welcome break in the chain links at Newport Beach, but the fences sprout again at Corona del Mar, skip Laguna Beach, and appear now and again south to San Clemente. In northern San Diego County they are replaced by the fences of the Camp Pendleton Marine Corps Base.

Access to long, sandy beaches north of Newport Beach is usually easy at most times. But try to arrive early on warm and sunny summer weekends, for the parking lots may fill early. All of these beaches are great for loafing, swimming, or floating just outside the surf line. I know, because I've tried them all—many times.

South of Newport the going gets more iffy. An updated copy of the *California Coastal Access Guide* becomes essential to tell you which access points are open and which are not, and how to get there.

ORANGE COUNTY

■ BEACHES NORTH OF NEWPORT

■ Seal Beach

Seal Beach was founded in the early 1900s, as a resort. But, like many of these beach communities, it didn't take off until oil was discovered there. Today, there are no relics of the oil boom. The mile-long beach is lined with colorful cottages. Palms bend to the seawind, and you can walk out onto the pier, a favorite local fishing spot. *Turn off the Coast Highway onto Main St., go west to Ocean Ave. The beach can be reached from Ocean Ave. between First Street and Dolphin Ave.*

■ Sunset Beach

A sandy beach reached from street ends from 2nd Street to 26th Street. A grassy linear park with a bike path and on-street parking runs one block to the east.

■ Bolsa Chica

In the 1950s and early 1960s this six-mile-long sandy beach was known as "Tin Can Beach" for good reason. Now, like other Orange County beaches, Bolsa Chica has been spiffed up, with fee parking lots, picnic areas, fire rings, and food concessions. The beach may not be usable at high tide because the surf runs right up to the edge of the low bluff. *Easy access off Coast Hwy.*

■ Huntington City Beach

This broad, sandy beach west of the Pacific Coast Highway, between Main Street and Beach Boulevard is again the site of international surfing competitions. (They were cancelled after a massive riot during a professional surf championship in 1986.) Pay parking lots; food concessions, etc.

■ Huntington State Beach

This wide, two-mile-long beach with volleyball courts, bike paths, showers, and food stands is popular with families of all ethnic backgrounds. Entrance fee. *Stretches along Pacific Coast Hwy. from Beach Blvd. to the Santa Ana River.*

■ International Surfing Museum

This shrine to the history of surfing has a permanent exhibit on Duke Kahanamoku (1890–1968), the father of modern surfing, who frequented the break just south of the pier. The display includes some of his boards, photos of him in action, and the hood of his Lincoln convertible with its surfer hood ornament. The exhibit also includes the groovy tunes of surf music. *411 Olive Ave., two blocks up from the Huntington Beach pier; 714-960-3483.*

Hood ornament on display at the International Surfing Museum.

■ NEWPORT BEACH

The unique topography of this beach city is determined by the way the city spreads along the shores of Newport Bay (the old Santa Ana River estuary), a wide inlet that's the drowned mouth of the river. Part of the city covers the Balboa Peninsula, a several-miles-long sandy spit formed in 1825 by a huge Santa Ana River flood. The river has since been diverted and enters the ocean to the north of town. Several artificial islands in the bay serve as exclusive and very expensive residential neighborhoods (where you can rent houses in the summer months).

The town of Newport Beach is famous for its wealth and for its vast yacht harbor with more than 10,000 boats. The annual Christmas Boat Parade of Lights is the town's most important event—it's wonderful to watch: kind of like the Rose Parade at night with a Christmas theme.

Newport Beach—*the beach*—is a delight. There are no fences in sight—you can walk onto the beach from the ends of peninsular streets, and I have found free all-day parking only two blocks from the pier. My old rule has long proved its value: if you're looking for free parking, follow a surfer.

Newport Beach has been a fashionable resort since before 1908 when this photo was taken. (California Historical Society, Los Angeles)

Newport Aquatic Center on Newport Bay offers lessons in canoeing, kayaking, and Olympic rowing. *1 Whitecliffs Drive. From* PCH *head north on Dover Drive and turn right on Whitecliffs Drive; 949-646-7725.*

❖

🚗 You reach the **Balboa Peninsula** by taking the well-marked Balboa turnoff from the Coast Highway. The seaward side of Main Street ends at Balboa Pier, which is so popular with local fishermen that some have formed "clubs." The beach (as opposed to the town) of Newport Beach faces the ocean at the west end of the peninsula.

Along the road to the pier you'll notice the Victorian **Balboa Pavilion** at 400 Main Street. Facing Newport Bay, it is a California classic that served as a dance hall well into 1940s, was restored in 1962, and is now the terminus for the *Catalina Flyer,* a fast catamaran that leaves from here daily for Catalina Island *(see page 279).*

The **"Wedge"** at the end of the peninsula is a famous place for body surfing. The break can be punishing and the currents swift, making it unsafe for all but the strongest swimmers. When the waves are up, they often reach over 15 feet. Watching experienced body surfers skip along the waves makes for a great morning of free entertainment.

■ NEWPORT BEACH PIER

You have to arrive early at the foot of the Newport Beach pier where the dory fleet lands if you want to have the pick of the freshest fish and shellfish. On my last visit, I was slowed down by one of those ubiquitous Orange County traffic jams, and by the time I made it there several dories had already returned, and the sales counters were covered with fish. Because I'd heard rumors that some of the dorymen might be buying their fish from larger boats instead of catching them themselves, I took a close look at these fish. The rumors were malicious. These fish were *fresh,* and in no time at all, the catch was sold.

Soon, more dories came in, racing through the surf to run the boats up on the beach as high as possible. I watched as one dory went out again. The doryman nonchalantly edged it up to the surf, began to push harder as the boat began to float, waited for a lull between the breakers then, after a final shove, he jumped in and started the outboard motor. By the time the next breaker hit the beach he was ready. The dory almost stood straight up on its tail as it hit a large breaker. Then, with a big splash, it was safely outside the surf.

Fishermen face the sunset on a warm Southern California evening.

■ BALBOA ISLAND

A tiny car ferry runs from the pavilion to Balboa Island, a small, quaint island paradise in Newport Bay which is circled by a boardwalk and tiny waterfront houses, boat slips, and small sandy beaches. Marine Avenue, which crosses the island, has small shops, food stores, and cafes. You can return to the mainland via Marine Avenue which connects directly to Highway 1.

■ CORONA DEL MAR

Corona del Mar is a southern extension of the city of Newport Beach. Along the highway it looks like a miles-long stripmall, but its backstreets are filled with small, quaint houses. The coves below have lovely, small, sandy beaches.

■ China Cove Beach

A pair of small sandy coves on the east side of the harbor, near the channel. *Pedestrian access is by stairs from Ocean Blvd.*

■ Rocky Point

A small sandy cove at the east side of the harbor channel, with many small caves (formerly called "Pirates Cove"). Access from Ocean Blvd. or by path from China Cove Beach or over the rocks from Corona del Mar Beach to the east.

■ Corona del Mar Beach

This very popular, sandy beach just east of the Newport Harbor entrance has picnic tables, volleyball nets, and other amenities. The harbor jetty breaks are popular with surfers. There's a pay parking lot at the beach; metered parking on the bluff above.

■ Little Corona City Beach

A gem of a beach tucked away in a sandy cove with rocky reefs and tidepools. To reach it follow the walkway from Poppy Ave.

Crystal Cove State Park *by Jack Wilkinson Smith. (Joan Irvine Smith Fine Arts, Irvine)*

■ CRYSTAL COVE STATE PARK

If you're driving the Coast Highway, you'll breathe a sigh of relief when you leave the coastal housing and shopping developments behind and drive through the wide open spaces of Crystal Cove. This oasis is truly a blessing, with its three-odd miles of sandy coves and beaches, its grassy terraces and wooded canyons, and 18 miles of hiking trails. Marvelous tidepools here; nothing like poking among them at sunset when the water is bright with color.

■ LAGUNA BEACH AREA

Laguna Beach has preserved the timeless charm of its cliffs, trees, and buildings, accented by cascades of flowers. The town is as delightful as ever, especially at those magic spots where a gap in the cliffs reveals a sandy beach. (Prepare for traffic jams on your way into town; parking can be a problem.)

Lifeguard tower at Laguna Beach.

L.A. METRO &
ORANGE COUNTY

The junction of Broadway and PCH, known as the "village," is the heart of Laguna Beach. It is here, at **Main Beach,** where Laguna Canyon meets the ocean. At times it seems that all of the town's life takes place on the boardwalk running along the strand. You'll find the usual volleyballers here, kids on skateboards, surfers, divers, young boys strutting like Adonis and girls who look as fresh as if they had just stepped newly formed from the sea foam. But this is also a beach where families stroll on the boardwalk, or spread blankets beneath the bluff for *al fresco* meals, and where old folks come to soak up the sun as well as a bit of the youthful energy of this village beach. Laguna has long been the home to one of the biggest volleyball competitions on the coast. Main Beach has three courts with nets, one with a net strung between two palm trees. It's also home to one of the most competitive (and definitely the most scenic) pickup basketball courts anywhere. Top-notch athletes, including college players from UCLA and ex-professionals, do battle against a backdrop of the blue Pacific and swaying palm trees.

The broad sweep of Laguna Beach.

Junior lifeguards are put through their paces prior to a tough day on Laguna Beach's Main Beach.

Because artists have always lived here—especially when Laguna Beach was considered to be way out in the boonies and rents were more affordable—this has always been a town filled with crafts shops and galleries bordering the Pacific Coast Highway and lining Forest Avenue. Today's exhibits include plenty of pastel seascapes and unhappy clowns, but there's serious art as well. The summer-long Pagent of the Masters and Sawdust Festival offer a diverse and in-depth look at the art scene.

For years, anyone who drove through town looked for the Laguna Greeter, a white-haired, white-bearded old man who always stood on the ocean side of the highway, smiling and waving at passing motorists. (There are now two statues of him, one outside Greeter's Restaurant and one in front of the Pottery Shack. Since 1981 there's been a new greeter, Mr. Number One Archer.)

Near Laguna lies a string of fine beaches.

ORANGE COUNTY

His Friends, the Seals

*O*ne night he walked on to the end of a natural rock jetty and came upon a shoal of seals. They swam, dived, clowned, but always crawled back to the rocks to have their young ones there. They kissed, barked, leaped, danced on their partly fused hind limbs. Their black eyes were like mirrors reflecting sea and sky, but the ogival shape of their eyelids gave them an air of compassion, almost as if they would weep with sympathy. Their tails were of little use except for swimming but they liked to shake their webbed flipper-like limbs as if they were about to fly. Their fur shone like onyx, with dark blue shadows under the fins.

They greeted the man with cries of joy. By this time he was an old man. The sea had wrinkled his face so intricately, it was a surprise when his smile scattered the lines to shine through, like a beautiful glossy fish darting out of a fishing net.

The old man fed the seals, he settled near them in a cave, cooked his dinner, and rolled over and fell asleep with a new feeling of companionship.

—Anaïs Nin, Collages, *1964*

■ Laguna Beaches

■ Crescent Bay Point Park

A lawn and paved walkway off the Coast Highway with views of Laguna Beach and of the Seal Rocks, where sea lions haul out. *Turn off CA 1 onto Crescent Bay Drive toward the ocean.*

■ Pocket Beaches

A good number hide in small coves accessible by well-marked walkways or stairs. Look for them off Cliff Drive and on street ends south of Main Beach. The beaches at the end of Oak Street, Brooks Street, and Thalia are particularly appealing.

■ Heisler Park

A pretty, grassy park on the bluff above Picnic Beach and Rock Pile Beach. There's a paved walkway south to Main Beach.

■ Aliso Creek

Dominated by a short, uniquely designed pier, this beach has an appealing stretch of fine white sand and inviting blue waters. The currents can be powerful, and the shorebreak makes it a popular place for skim-boarding. The parking lot is almost on the sand, making for easy access.

■ Salt Creek Beach Park

Just south of Laguna, this long, sandy, beautiful beach is popular with surfers, swimmers, and sun hounds. Head north along the sand toward Monarch Bay to escape the crowds. Easy access off the highway. Large metered parking lot, grassy area, basketball courts.

Orange County

■ DANA POINT

The natural beauty of this cove has been destroyed by its breakwater and marina, and the last piece of natural beach on the west end of the cove is now hidden beneath the sprawling buildings of (ironically) the Orange County Marine Institute. Exhibits inside the building celebrate what used to be here. Big placards sport renderings of an even bigger institute planned for the cove, and solicit donations. Fragile clifftops are crowned by oversized edifices that look as though they had been assembled from a mail order catalog of generic California beach houses.

On the waterfront sea wall, you'll find a replica of the brig *Pilgrim,* in which author Richard Henry Dana sailed to these shores in the 1830s. Dana, who called this cove "the only romantic place on the California coast," would be appalled if he could come back and see the change.

A paved walkway runs along the shore of the boat basins. Most of the restaurants overlooking the boat basin are so generic they might as well be in a mall. But one place, Jon's Fishmarket, has class and excellent fish 'n chips and seafood chowders. The outdoor dining area is always packed with happy diners. Why, I wonder, could Dana Point Harbor not have become another Newport Beach instead of merely turning itself into another generic marina?

Cliffside homes are perched precariously over the ocean along this stretch of the coast.

On my last visit I stopped at the bait and food shop at the foot of the new fishing pier. For old time's sake, I ordered a chili dog. The back wall of the shop was decorated with large black and white photos of Dana Point as it looked before the marina was built. I told the old woman fixing my chili dog that I used to come here a lot back then and loved it.

"Everybody loved it back then," she replied sadly.

At **Ken Sampson Overlook** you can see the ocean and harbor from a gazebo built on the very spot where author Richard Henry Dana and his fellow sailors threw "California bank notes" (dried cattle skins) off the bluff to be loaded onto the brig *Pilgrim* anchored in the cove below. *(South end of Amber Lantern and Violet Lantern Streets.)*

Heritage Park (at the foot of Golden Lantern Street and El Camino Capistrano) has a grassy blufftop overlook with benches and wheelchair-accessible paths overlooking Dana Point Harbor. A stairway leads down to the harbor.

Doheny State Beach, just south of the harbor, has something for everyone. There is a campground with 120 sites, a great beginners surf spot, a bike path, visitors center, divers park, and more. Before the jetty went in for the harbor, Doheny was a famous surf spot known as "Killer Dana" to the locals, and it was mentioned in the Beach Boys' ode, "Surfin' USA."

■ MISSION SAN JUAN CAPISTRANO

The cove at Dana Point was once part of the vast landholdings of Mission San Juan Capistrano, whose partially reconstructed ruins stand several miles inland, in the small town of San Juan Capistrano.

San Juan (19th-century visitors referred to the place as "San Juan," not "Capistrano") once had the largest stone church of any of the missions, but it collapsed during an early 19th-century earthquake, killing several worshippers, and was never rebuilt. The original mission chapel is still intact, and it is the only church still standing at any of the missions where Father Junipero Serra celebrated mass.

The mission grounds are beautifully landscaped and offset by fawn-colored arches and a low, multi-bell campanile, considered to be the most romantic of any California mission. The reconstructed sections of the mission's work areas will give you a good idea of how the missionaries and Indians prepared food, made wine, and performed their daily tasks of maintenance.

This mission is quite definitely worth a short detour from the coast (follow I-5 and look for signs directing you to San Juan Capistrano and its mission). The Ortega Highway, CA 74, runs east from San Juan Capistrano through the very rugged Ortega Mountains. It eventually drops down the sharp

Capistrano Mission *by Elmer Wachtel, 1900.*
(Courtesy of Fleischer Museum, Scottsdale)

escarpment of the Coast Range to Lake Elsinore in a series of hairpin turns. There's a great view of the lake and the interior valleys from the top of the cliff. Far in the distance to the southeast, you can just make out the hills of the Temecula wine district.

■ SAN CLEMENTE

Much of this town sits atop cliffs, but at the main beach and municipal pier the cliffs open like the tiers of an amphitheater, allowing for easy access to the shore. With the sun lighting up the flowers and the sea, and with throngs of smiling people walking to the beach, San Clemente can lay claim to being one of the most delightful places on the Orange County coast. It's also a funky seaside village—a cultural hodgepodge where Marines in fatigues, barefoot and shirtless surfers, Latin American immigrants, and *nouveau riche* meld together among one-room bungalows and multimillion-dollar mansions.

The last time I walked the streets of this quaint, active town, passing surf shops, thrift stores, sushi bars, authentic Mexican markets/restaurants, and throngs of healthy, laid-back locals, I ended up at the Fisherman's Restaurant and Bar at the foot of the San Clemente pier, a long-time favorite for tourists and locals alike. Over a wonderfully fresh cut of yellowtail, I stared out at the sea and tried to envision President Richard Nixon sneaking out of his nearby "western White House" back in the late 1970s, to sit at the bar with the tanned crowd dressed in flip-flops and tank tops, enjoying an afternoon beer or two. But I failed to conjure up the image.

ORANGE COUNTY

SAN DIEGO COAST

■ HIGHLIGHTS

Del Mar
La Jolla
City of San Diego
Coronado
Cabrillo National Monument
Mission Beach
Ocean Beach
Crossing the Border

■ TRAVEL OVERVIEW

North of the city of San Diego, small sea-side towns are strung all along the coast, interrupted now and then by a lagoon. You'll understand why people flock to these beaches when you touch the water and feel how warm it is. There's also a special quality to the light that makes you want to linger on the sand, looking outward to the blue swath of the Pacific.

The city of San Diego is central to this area and spreads from the northern, hilly shores of San Diego Bay west to the ocean and east up the valley carved by the San Diego River.

San Diego manages to be both a generic U.S. city, and one with a distinct personality. If its downtown architecture is much like that in the rest of the U.S.—highrises, malls, and all that, the scene is heavily leavened by the restored Victorians in the Gaslamp Quarter and more commonly, by the neo-Mediterranean architecture: arched entrances, white walls, and red tile roofs. This feels appropriate, not only because it's set in a Mediterranean climate, but also because the area was a Spanish colonial outpost between 1769 and 1820 and, for another 28 years, part of an independent Mexico. Late 20th-century Mexican influences, brought north by immigrants, have turned some quarters, like Old Town, into vibrant centers of Mexican culture. Drive just a few miles south of San Diego and you will be in Mexico.

■ TRAVEL BASICS

Getting There
Between Oceanside and La Jolla, old US 101 is a four-lane highway whose narrow lanes wind along bluffs. It opens to a boulevard between Pacific Beach and Point Loma. From Coronado, a four-lane highway runs south along Silver Strand Beach to Imperial Beach and the U.S. border with Mexico. **Rental car companies** warn about driving in San Diego because of the high rate of auto-theft. Few such companies allow their cars across the Mexican border, but there are a few exceptions; see page 338.

Climate
This stretch of coastline boasts the most equable climate in the United States. Temperatures hardly vary from the 70s in the summer and the 60s in the winter. Annual rainfall is less than 10 inches, usually falling in a handful of winter storms, or the odd summer monsoon thunderstorm when moisture from the southwest makes its way as far west as San Diego—a rare event and unique to this part of the California coastline. **Water Temperature:** upper 50s and 60s year-round, occasionally low 70s.

Food and Lodging
You'll find good, fresh food in San Diego County and a great deal of excellent Mexican cuisine. Strawberries ripen to perfection in the coastal valleys, and apples in the nearby mountains, as do avocados (which you can buy ripe from farmers markets), cherimoyas, lemons, limes (which taste better here than almost anywhere else), macadamia nuts (grown to perfection in the foothills east of San Luis Rey), and tree-ripened oranges and pine nuts (collected from piñons growing on the desert side of the mountains). There's even a limited supply of local wine.

The ocean produces great variety of fish and shellfish, including some warm-water fish like yellowtail, bream, tuna, marlin, and swordfish. The spiny lobsters from near-shore water are particularly fine (especially if you can enjoy them grilled and swathed in olive oil, garlic, and chili sauce).

As for lodging, there are many fine hotels and resorts in this area as well as inexpensive beach motels. (For **lodging and restaurant listings,** see pages 339–390.)

■ ABOUT NORTH COUNTY

If you like broad, wide-open, sandy beaches pummeled by a roaring surf and quiet, protected coves, flocks of shorebirds, and friendly people, San Diego's North County is the place you've been looking for. The beaches here are wider and less crowded than those of San Diego to the south and Orange County to the north. The water is temperate enough for swimming, the waves shaped right for surfing, and the sand is soft and warm underfoot.

Shorebirds are plentiful because many of the best beaches form sand barriers across the mouths of creek or river lagoons. Since this gives sanderlings, willets, dunlins, dowitchers, and other sandpipers a chance to double dip, they hang out in great flocks. The local folk are friendly because their beaches have not yet been overrun by city crowds. Even the local surfers are friendlier than they are elsewhere and won't throw rocks at visiting "kooks." Besides, a lot of people have settled here because they wanted to get away from the city and enjoy an "alternate" lifestyle. Which is why you'll find many coffeehouses and vegetarian restaurants. One friend, who knows the area well, described it as a place where "vegetarians run rampant; it feels more like Santa Cruz than La Jolla."

North County doesn't make everyone happy. Despite several new resorts, its small towns don't have the glamour of La Jolla or Carmel. But there is a lot of charm: " you just need to slow down to enjoy it."

The best way to visit North County is on Old US 101, the road of many names. Never mind the names. You can't get lost, since this is the only broad boulevard running north-south near the beach.

■ CAMP PENDLETON AREA

Just south of San Clemente, along the San Diego Freeway (I-5), the rare, inviting sight of undeveloped coastal land comes into view, punctuated by the two giant orbs of the San Onofre nuclear power plant. While the hulking reactors inspire a bit of fear, the long, sandy beaches of **San Onofre State Beach** offer great swimming, surfing, exploring, or just plain relaxing. The state park also allows for access to the **San Mateo Creek marsh** (just south of the Orange County line). Both the power station and the beach are on land leased by the state from the Marine Corps.

Camp Pendleton pre-empts the coast for 18 miles, about a quarter of the San Diego County coastline. Yet, curiously, it does not show up on many of the tourist maps handed out by local promoters—which often show but a tiny gap between Oceanside and San Clemente. The landscape looks much as it did more than a hundred years ago. It remained unspoiled because it was preserved as Rancho Santa Margarita y Las Flores, one of the last and largest of California's original land grant ranchos, which was founded in 1823 as an overnight way station of Mission San Luis Rey on El Camino Real. During World War II, the U.S. Marine Corps took over the ranch as a training center and as a place for staging maneuvers, and scores of tanks can still be seen churning up dust storms. **Las Flores Marsh and Santa Margarita Marsh** have been preserved as wildlife refuges and the Marines have also introduced (non-native) bison.

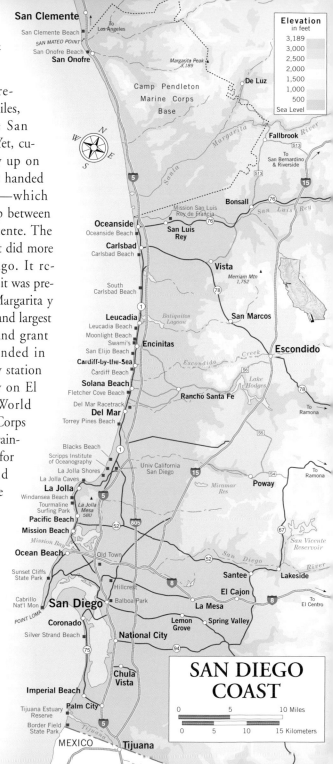

Elevation
in feet
3,189
3,000
2,500
2,000
1,500
1,000
500
Sea Level

SAN DIEGO
COAST

0   5   10 Miles

0   5   10   15 Kilometers

■ OCEANSIDE AND SAN LUIS REY

The San Luis Rey River, which rises near Mount Palomar, debouches into the ocean just south of **Oceanside Harbor,** a rather drab and dull small-boat port with the usual facilities. **Harbor Beach** is the port's only highlight. **Oceanside City Beach** runs along the town's ocean front and is partially accessible by the Strand, a paved road that has a habit of dead-ending at pay parking lots. But there's plenty of on-street parking as well. A few blocks from the beach it's free. Steps lead down to the Strand from **Linear Park,** a landscaped concrete walkway along the blufftop with benches and view platforms.

This uncrowded beach, overtowered by tall palm trees swaying in the sea wind, is about as close to the "ideal" Southern California beach as you can get nowadays. At Oceanside, the color of the water changes, taking on a turquoise sub-tropical hue, and you see more swimmers in the water than you do to the north. Palm trees look healthier than they do up the coast, and tender tropical and sub-tropical shrubs and flowers—who hide their pretty heads behind tall garden walls from Santa Barbara to San Clemente—proudly expose their bright faces to the sea breeze.

People thrive here too, as you can tell by all the smiling faces that greet you on a walk to the end of the 1,900-foot Oceanside Pier. And if the hike along the pier makes you hungry, you can satisfy your appetite with turkey pot pie, hearty chili, or a fresh-baked apple pie ar Ruby's Diner, a retro-50s restaurant at the tip of the pier.

*A Mexican fanpalm overlooks
Swami's beach in Encinitas.*

■ CARLSBAD

Carlsbad got its name from a mineral spring whose waters were supposed to have the same qualities as the famed Carlsbad spring in the Czech Republic. Carlsbad has managed to keep its village charm while attracting visitors with its beaches, restaurants, and excellent lodging facilities (see page 344 for listings).

■ Carlsbad oceanfront

The Carlsbad oceanfront is divided between **Carlsbad State Beach,** a sandy and rocky beach with overlooks on the blufftops, and **Carlsbad City Beach** to the north (accessible by stairs at the north end of Ocean Street, and at several cul-de-sacs).

■ South Carlsbad State Beach

This beach extends north for four miles from Batiquitos Lagoon, an important resting place for migratory fowl. Birdwatchers may watch the birds from trails along the eastern and western shorelines. The state beach has campsites along the bluffs, hot showers, a laundromat, and a grocery and bait store. The Encina Fishing Area on the Coast Highway is very popular with fishermen because the fish of Agua Hedionda Lagoon are known to bite eagerly. Much of the small town of Carlsbad sits atop bluffs between Agua Hedionda Lagoon and Buena Vista Lagoon.

■ Buena Vista Lagoon

The lagoon, which separates Carlsbad from Oceanside, is one of the best birdwatching places on the south coast. At **Maxton Brown Park** on the Carlsbad shore, a paved path leads to an overlook with benches and picnic tables. To the east, a duck feeding area on Jefferson Street, south of CA 78, has a paved parking lot and benches. The **Buena Vista Audubon Nature Center** in Oceanside has nature exhibits and a short trail along the shoreline; *2202 Coast Highway; 760-439-2473.*

■ ENCINITAS AND CARDIFF-BY-THE-SEA

Encinitas is a sleepy seaside town with small but quaint main streets, flowering gardens, and some good vegetarian restaurants. **Quail Botanical Gardens,** just off Encinitas Boulevard (one block east of Interstate 5), is worth a visit to see its ancient cycads, palms, flowering trees, and the largest collection of bamboo in the United States. *760-436-3036.*

Fuchsia-flowered gooseberry.

The town of **Leucadia,** which is actually a part of the city of Encinitas, grows and sells more flowers (especially poinsettias) than any other town in the U.S. and in the early spring the hills north of Palomar Airport Road are a blanket of brightly colored blossoms.

Nearby **Cardiff-by-the-Sea** is a small, laid-back coastal community. If you're looking for a place to stock up on picnic provisions before heading to one of the area's fine beaches, try the Seaside Market or pick up a smoothie and veggie burger at Ki's, both on CA Highway 1. Or you can hang out at Miracles Cafe at 1453 San Elijo Avenue, a coffeehouse that gives you a good sense of what North County is all about. For instance, a local recently told me that Rob Machado (one of the most famous surfers competing today) lives nearby and if he's at Miracles, or simply walking by, the same day you're there, good luck getting any of the normally friendly staff to pay attention to you. There's also a famous bar, right on the beach, the Kraken at 2531 S. Highway 101.

■ **Moonlight City Beach**
Especially popular with the pre-teen boogie board set and families, Moonlight Beach has volleyball and tennis courts, a snack bar, and picnic tables. At Neptune Avenue, a long, partly stone stairway leads down to narrow, cobbled Stone Steps Beach. To reach narrow, sandy **Encinitas Beach** you have to walk north below the bluffs from Stone Steps, or south from Beacon's Beach (formerly known as Leucadia State Beach).

■ **Swami's** *(see photo page 300)*
The golden cupolas, lush gardens, and meditation area of the mosque-like **Self-Realization Fellowship Hermitage** sprawl conspicuously on the ocean side of the highway. The grounds are open to the public, but don't worry, no one will try to convert you. The exotic property inspired locals to name the beach below "Swami's," a narrow strip of sand popular with both surfers and surf fishermen. *Stairs at 216 K St.*

■ **San Elijo State Beach**

San Elijo is the southernmost state beach with full camping facilities. Park headquarters have a tidepool display and a native plant garden. Even though the beach is mostly cobble rather than sand, it is popular with swimmers, surfers, divers, and fishermen. San Elijo Lagoon is very marshy and particularly rich in birds.

■ **Cardiff State Beach**

A stretch of warm sand between the ocean and San Elijo Lagoon segregates surfers (southern half) and swimmers (northern half). The southern part of the park also has tidepools. If the surf isn't cooperating, you can always look at marine critters or watch the birds in the lagoon do their thing.

■ SOLANA BEACH

Solana Beach seems modest compared to its more glamorous neighbor Del Mar, but it has a rather funky, post-modernist city hall that looks like a colorful, overblown clock radio, and a couple of good beaches: Fletcher Cove Park with basketball and shuffleboard courts for those not limber enough to surf or play volleyball; Seascape Shores with volleyball courts in the sand and good surfing offshore (reached via stairways near the 500 and 700 blocks of Sierra Avenue); and Tide Beach, another good surfing and swimming spot, with some great tidepools where you can spend hours observing the near-shore life. But Solana Beach's greatest local fame stems from a seemingly humble quonset hut converted into a music club. The Belly Up Tavern draws big-name blues and rock stars; located at 143 S. Cedros Avenue.

■ DEL MAR

You haven't experienced true relaxation until you get to Del Mar. Even though the horse racing season is in full swing by mid-July, you wouldn't know it, if you hadn't read about it. The beach marches to a different drummer. There isn't even a traffic crush, because the race track is easily accessible from I-5 to the east. But the beach parking lots are full, and bobbing out in the water beyond the breaking surf, surfers are lined up waiting for the next perfect set.

Del Mar has a number of excellent beaches: wide and sandy City Beach where surfers and grunions run in season; and Del Mar Bluffs City Park at the mouth of the San Dieguito River.

Del Mar City Beach.

Well-heeled Del Mar Plaza has a number of ritzy shops and galleries, and best of all a glorious sundeck where colorful wooden chairs invite shoppers to relax with a Pellegrino and look out over Camino del Mar, the picturesque train station, grassy Del Mar Park, and of course, the sparkling ocean.

■ TORREY PINES

Torrey Pines is a place *and* a type of pine tree—a unique yellow pine with five long needles (eight to 13") instead of the more common two or three. In coastal gullies, they slowly grow from 20 to 60 feet tall, and take on spectacular shapes because branches broken off by the wind die back to the main trunk. Living branches stretch away from the ocean, as though they were trying to flee the sea wind. Oddly enough, even though this pine has such a limited natural habitat, it thrives in cultivation, rapidly grows to a height of 40 to 60 feet or even taller and, (unlike another rare conifer, the Monterey cypress), thrives away from the coast, even in such arid regions as the high desert. With ample water, it turns bushy and mean.

Torrey Pines State Beach is the best place to appreciate these pines. (Park your car at the bottom of the long descent to the beach made by the Coast Highway and hike in.) That can be quite an adventure, because the pines grow on the slopes of deep ravines eroded from the cliffs, but it's a very scenic hike. Looking up at the pines looming high above you will impress you for life. If you're not into pines, the wide, sandy beach beneath the colorful sandstone cliffs is great for swimming, surfing, and clamming. As you dig for cockles and pismo clams, keep in mind that the largest pismo clam ever found weighed more than four pounds. That boulder your shovel hit may actually be a giant clam.

Torrey Pines City Park not only has trails to famous Black's Beach, but a glider port as well for hang gliders. While parking restrictions may make access to Black's and the city park difficult at times, access to Torrey Pines State Reserve is restricted by rangers who want to minimize the impact of visitors on one of the two places where the world's rarest pine is protected from firewood cutters and real estate developers (the other is on Santa Rosa Island, off Santa Barbara). The park is a bit scruffy as Southern California wildlands are wont to be, but has some great views of ocean- and wind-sculpted pines from the eroding sandstone bluffs. A visitors center in an old lodge has interpretive displays that tell you about these rare trees.

Las Penasquitos Lagoon east of Torrey Pines State Beach is one of Southern California's few undisturbed salt marshes and has the birds to prove it. Look for least terns and snowy plovers near the edge of the sand (don't step on their eggs or young), and for light-footed clapper rails in the dense tangle of reeds. Wintering ducks and shorebirds make this a bird watcher's delight in fall, winter, and spring.

If you couldn't get into the **Torrey Pines State Reserve,** because too many people arrived before you, head for the Torrey Pines State Reserve Extension north of the lagoon. Park your car on a dead end street off Del Mar Heights Road, ignore the subdivisions, and head for the woods. Numerous trails through the reserve open up to great views of the lagoon, the ocean, and the main reserve. And, of course, Torrey pines.

■ BLACK'S BEACH

To reach one of the world's greatest surfing beaches (and most infamous nude beaches), Black's, most people hike down a steep road starting at the end of Blackgold Road (only residents are permitted to drive down the road). The path is

owned by the University of California and the landowner reserves the right to revoke its use. (If the Marines at Camp Pendleton can't keep out surfers, how will UC do it?) There are a few, rougher alternatives to the road (see below) but Black's relatively limited access has kept this wide, white-sand beachscape unspoiled.

Serious surfers prefer to trek down to the beach via the Goat Trail, a steep, rugged scramble down scrubby cliffs reached from a blufftop overlook at the end of La Jolla Shores Lane. Maneuvering down the Goat Trail, surfboard in one hand, wet suit in the other, this is either a test of grace and balance or a show of bravado.

Because Black's is across the street from the UC San Diego campus, it's extremely popular with students during the day and for beach parties at night. *Street parking is available but limited on La Jolla Farms Road and Blackgold Road. There's also free parking at the glider port on Torrey Pines Scenic Drive.*

■ SCRIPPS INSTITUTE OF OCEANOGRAPHY

The UC San Diego campus started out in 1912 at the Scripps Institution. In 1964, when some 1,200 acres of a former U.S. Marine training base atop a eucalyptus-covered plateau became available, the university expanded into a major campus. When you consider how much high-powered mental energy radiates from Scripps, the University, and the nearby Salk Institute for Biological Studies, you're almost glad that this neighborhood has its share of surfers and sunbathers. But if you make their acquaintance you usually discover they're from Scripps, Salk Institute, and UCSD.

Scripps Institute of Oceanography is one of the world's truly great scientific institutions. Founded in the boathouse of the Hotel del Coronado in 1903, Scripps moved to its present site in the early 1900s and has developed into a preeminent center for earth-sciences research. The institute studies geology, geophysics, climatology, oceanography, and biology, and has a fleet of four ships in seas around the world.

There are surfboards in most, if not all, of the cliffside labs at Scripps. Dave Fields, a PHD candidate from Scripps, admits that many of the students and

(preceding pages) Black's Beach, across the street from the UC San Diego campus, is a famous nudist and surfing beach.

The thousand foot Scripps Pier, built by one of the world's foremost institutions of oceanography, is just south of Scripps Beach and tidepools. The institution's research ships, which study the ocean floor, moor here and are occasionally open to the public.

teachers surf between classes. (Sandbars on either side of Scripps Pier turn out reliable peaks year-round.)

The beach and tidepools are part of a series of underwater reserves stretching from the southern city limits of Del Mar, south to Goldfish Point in La Jolla. If you want to learn more about the shore and the ocean, be sure to visit the associated **Stephen Birch Aquarium,** perched on a cliff above La Jolla Sands. This dazzling place has a number of interactive, hands-on exhibits and is a wonderful place to take children. There's even a "Dive after Five" event where for $20 guests stand outside near the kelp tank, munching on tacos, drinking cocktails, watching the sunset and, via microphones, chat with divers feeding fish in the tank. The aquarium also arranges two- and three-hour whale-watching cruises. *2300 Expedition Way (from I-5, exit on La Jolla Village Drive; turn west on Expedition Way); 619-534-3474.*

SAN DIEGO COAST

SALUBRIOUS AIR, *THERE*

*T*he charm of Southern California is largely to be found in the air and the light. Light and air are really one element: indivisible, mutually interacting, thoroughly interpenetrated. Without the ocean breezes, the sunlight would be intolerable; without the sunlight and imported water, virtually nothing would grow in the region.

The geographers say that the quality of Southern California's climate is pure Mediterranean—the only specimen of Mediterranean climate in the United States. But such words as "Mediterranean" and "subtropical" are most misleading when applied to Southern California. Unlike the Mediterranean coast, Southern California has no sultry summer air, no mosquito-ridden malarial marshes, no mistral winds. A freak of nature—a cool and semimoist desert—Southern California is climatically insulated, shut off from the rest of the continent. As Helen Hunt Jackson once said, and it is the best description of the region yet coined, "It is a sort of an island on the land."

—Carey McWilliams, *Southern California Country,* 1946

. . . UNTIL THE SANTA ANA WINDS STRIKE

*A*bout 1 o'clock p.m. (on June 17, 1850) . . . a blast of hot air from the northeast swept suddenly over the town, and struck the inhabitants with terror. It was quickly followed by others. At two o'clock the thermometer exposed to the air rose to 113°, and continued at or near that point for nearly three hours, while the burning wind raised dense clouds of impalpable dust. No human being could withstand the heat. All betook themselves to their dwellings. . . . Calves, rabbits, birds, etc., were killed, trees were blighted, fruit was blasted and fell to the ground, burned only on one side; the gardens were ruined. At five o'clock the thermometer fell to 122° [sic], and at seven it stood at 77°.

—*As recalled by Walter Lindley, M.D., and Joseph Widney, M. D. in 1888*

■ LA JOLLA

San Diego's coastal communities were described by historian Kevin Starr as "a seaside celebration of sun and sky, an urban area for the Mediterranean encounter of line, color, warmth, and spaciousness." Nowhere is this more true than in La Jolla, with its very Mediterranean coast; narrow winding streets, with houses edging right up to edge of cliffs; fragrant flowers everywhere; sandy beaches below rocky precipices; sea caves; and ocean waters pleasantly warm for swimming. Here, more than anywhere else, beach neighborhoods are part of the shore; the houses and gardens are fully integrated with the sea and sand and surf and rock. No one seems quite sure how La Jolla got its name or who named the place. "Jolla" is supposedly a corruption of either Spanish *joya* ("jewel") or *hoya* ("hollow,") depending on which writer you believe. Coincidentally, both explanations fit.

From a visitor's viewpoint, La Jolla is an embarrassment of riches. After a couple of days, you feel like you'll need at least a year or two to begin exploring, and much more time to experience it all. The beaches are small but special sandy pockets tucked into rocky coves. Some are sandy the year-round, on others, winter storms wash away and expose the underlying boulders, until the gentle currents of summer restore the sand.

Downtown La Jolla is a very compact place and you might consider parking your car and walking. Locals say that "the true test of positive thinking is finding a parking place at the cove in summer." But it's really much easier to discover all the special little beaches if you walk rather than drive.

La Jolla is a shopper's mecca (perhaps because it began life as a beach town where wealthy Easterners settled), and La Jolla folks have distinct style: even a mail carrier looks like her short skirt and airy blouse are tailor-made. The **main shopping areas** are Prospect Street and Girard Avenue. Shopping in La Jolla is not as intimidating as it used to be. A few resale designer stores have crept in next to the snooty Armanis and Ralph Laurens. The dress code in La Jolla is decidedly different than in all other parts of San Diego. Expensive Casual here—Cole-Haan sandals rather than drugstore flip-flops, for one. If you don't already have this type of wardrobe there are plenty of shops that reinforce the style.

If you get worn out from all that shopping, stop at the Whaling Bar in the beautiful La Valencia Hotel on Prospect for a cooling martini, and reflect on the fact that such movie greats as Greta Garbo, Mary Pickford, and Douglas Fairbanks were here before you. The patio affords spectacular views. There are also several pleasant cafes nearby, including Girard Gourmet at 7837 Girard Avenue.

San Diego Museum of Contemporary Art on Prospect Avenue is starkly elegant with enormous windows facing the ocean. Modern art and the very cutting edge of what's in right now—painting, sculptures, prints, drawings, videos, installations, designs are on display. *700 Prospect Street; 619-454-3541.* A few miles away on the on the UCSD campus is the highly regarded **La Jolla Playhouse,** founded in 1947 by Gregory Peck and Dorothy McGuire. *2910 La Jolla Village Drive; 619-550-1010.*

■ LA JOLLA BEACHES AND BEACH WALKS

■ La Jolla Shores Beach–Kellog Park
A mile and a half north of downtown La Jolla is La Jolla Shores where grassy lawns, palm trees, and picnic tables front a wide, sandy beach. Launch a kayak, swim, or dive. Native American artifacts have been uncovered by divers at the north end of the park but remember: no touching. If you find anything interesting, be sure to call a ranger's attention to it. For a sandwich to take to the beach, try the marvelous **Cheese Shop** on nearby Avenida de la Playa.

■ La Jolla Cliffs
Seaside cliffs carved into shelves and ledges where gulls, cormorants, brown pelicans,

Pelicans watch over La Jolla Cove.

The Windansea Surf Club furnishes the beach shack with new palm leaves when needed.

and other seabirds roost, extend along the shore for several miles south of downtown. A grassy clifftop picnic area at **Ellen Scripps Park** is very popular on summer weekends. A path and stairs lead down to **Boomer Beach,** a world-famous spot for bodysurfing (experienced surfers only!).

■ La Jolla Cove

The small beach at the cove has been popular with locals and visitors since 1960. It looks more pristine now than ever. At one time, there was a heated saltwater pool here, at another, the main attraction was a diver who doused himself with oil and set himself aflame before plunging into the sea.

The cove's clear waters and abundant sea life (protected as an underwater reserve) attract a number of divers and snorkelers.

Locals swim out to the buoy floating 100 yards from the beach.

■ La Jolla's caves

The sea has carved the rocks into caves beginning east of the cove, near Goldfish Point. Once accessible only by boat, one of the seven caves can now be entered through a tunnel (artificial) via the La Jolla Cave and Shell Shop; *1325 Coast Blvd.*

■ The Coast Walk

This dirt path along the bluffs provides a panoramic view of ocean, beach, and caves. Unfortunately, the trail has been severely damaged by storms and erosion, making portions of it decidedly unsafe. *Found on Torrey Pines Rd. just east of Prospect St. or on a path adjacent to 1325 Coast Blvd.*

■ WINDANSEA BEACH

Located below Neptune Place, this is a surfer's mecca. A large rock 500 feet off-shore helps kick up the large surf, which dramatically adds to the already spectacular scenery. The beach supposedly was the setting for the surfer subculture mocked by Tom Wolfe in his "non-fiction" book *The Pump House Gang*. In the 1950s, beat poets like Allen Ginsberg and Lawrence Ferlinghetti read their poems at the Pour House, a popular, but now defunct restaurant a few blocks up the hill on La Jolla Boulevard. Windansea surfers have a reputation of being extremely territorial and rude to newcomers. Photographers (and people who want their photos taken) love Windansea. Commonly seen here are large families having a group portrait taken, fashion shoots, and high school volleyball teams posing for the yearbook. And just as vacationing Arizonans are always found at Mission Beach, Brazilian tourists are a fixture at Windansea during the summer—they're easy to spy, just look for thong bathing suits.

Walking north across the sea-carved boulders of Windansea will lead you to **Marine Street Beach,** a pleasant swimming and sunbathing beach with fine white sand and warm water. **Horseshoe Reef,** a bit farther north of Marine Street, is popular with surfers.

■ HERMOSA TERRACE PARK

The last time I visited Hermosa Terrace Park on Winamar Avenue (off Camino de la Costa), it was a very hot summer afternoon and a wedding was in progress. Unlike local party goers, who like to dress up in tuxedo tops and cut-off jeans, the members of this party were dressed to the hilt—white gown for the bride and tails for the groom. They must have been sweltering, especially since they had their backs turned to the view, and the sea breeze, as they faced the minister. My first question was if they would all jump into the ocean afterwards to cool off. But really: Where did they find parking for all those guests? Parking is always a problem. Not just in La Jolla but in other coastal towns as well.

Windansea Beach is one of the most popular surfing beaches in Southern California.

La Jolla's Pump House

Text and photos by Adam Ballachey

Tom Wolfe put La Jolla on the literary map with his biting 1968 essay, "The Pump House Gang." Undoubtedly his satire wasn't much appreciated by the town's literate and prosperous citizens. Who wants to be cast as a sun worshiping, Dionysian provincial, even if it means literary immortality? And especially by a pasty little East Coast writer in a robin's egg blue suit and black and white wing tips. But in fact those Wolfe described probably remained unaware of his book and indifferent to his opinion.

❖

The tattooed surfer, pictured below, is the sort of person Tom Wolfe would have thought worthy of his prose. Nathan Jernigan grew up in La Jolla, blocks from Windansea, and he's lived as far away as Santa Barbara. He works a little here and there, and lives for the ocean.

Wolfe wrote of the people who followed this lifestyle, ". . . they have this life all of their own; it's like a glass-bottom boat, and it floats over the 'real' world, or the square world or whatever one wants to call it. They are not exactly off in a world of their own, they are and they aren't. What it is, they float right through the real world but it can't touch them."

Nate's back: "It's not the critic who counts , . . . " a Teddy Roosevelt quote.

"The surfers around the Pump House use that word, mysterioso, quite a lot. It refers to the mystery of the Oh Mighty Hulking Pacific Ocean and everything. Sometimes a guy will stare at the ocean and say, 'Mysterioso.'" —Tom Wolfe

Nathan Jernigan is 25, the age Wolfe describes as "the horror dividing line," between youth and adulthood. Describing the beach where Nate and his friends surf, Wolfe wrote: "This beach is verbotten for people practically 50 years old. This is a segregated beach. They can look down on Windansea beach and see nothing but lean tan kids. . . ."

Nate's customized '65 Dodge pick-up.

■ BIRD ROCK

One of La Jolla's southernmost beaches, Bird Rock supposedly got its name not from the large guano-covered offshore rock where cormorants and pelicans like to hang out, but from a Mr. Bird, who first developed this area in 1907. The Bird Rock Inn, built from local beach stone, once stood at the foot of Bird Rock Avenue. Charles Lindbergh enjoyed dinner here before he flew the *Spirit of St. Louis* from North Island to New York and Paris. A stairway at Bird Rock Avenue provides access to the beach below with its fascinating tide pools.

■ ARRIVING IN SAN DIEGO

San Diego has always brought out the superlatives in visiting writers. Henry James was bowled over by a surfeit of "nature and climate, fruit and flowers," and warbled that "The days have been mostly here of heavenly beauty, and the flowers, the wild flowers just now in particular, which fairly rage, with radiance, over the land, are worthy of some purer planet than this. I live on oranges and olives, fresh from the tree and I lie awake at night to listen, on purpose, to the languid list of the Pacific which my windows overhang." (A tough man, that Henry James: eating olives fresh from the tree and not puckering up.)

Kevin Starr, in *Americans and the California Dream, 1850-1915,* called San Diego, the "fulfillment of the dream of California as a Mediterranean littoral."

While the Spanish-style buildings of Balboa Park, San Diego's palm-lined boulevards, and mission-style homes have been described as "nostalgia for an imagined past," it is a nostalgia that works, making San Diego uncommonly attractive. Since the city borders a protected bay, it also has a long and interesting waterfront. There's enough to see here to take up an entire vacation. Highlights include the Commercial Basin with its fleet of tuna clippers; Shelter Island created from dredge material; La Playa, the beach where Yankee ship captains cleaned and dried the hides they acquired from California missions and ranchos; Spanish Landing Park, where the galleons supplying the presidio and mission moored; the Embarcadero with its walking trail; the Maritime Museum with the old windjammer *Star of India,* and a former San Francisco Bay ferry *Berkeley.*

Across the bay lies the U.S. Naval Station on North Island, at the tip of the Coronado Peninsula, where naval aviation was invented in 1911 and where

Charles Lindbergh took off in 1927 on the first leg of his flight to fame. Just below the base, the resort town of Coronado hugs the shore.

The Mexican border is half an hour south of San Diego, and its presence makes itself felt everywhere. Just turn on your car radio and you'll be surprised how many stations are Spanish and play Mexican music. Flip the channels in your San Diego hotel room, and you'll discover several Spanish-language TV stations. As you drive through San Diego's neighborhoods, look around, and you'll find many restaurants serving Mexican food and, primarily in the suburbs, shop signs entirely in Spanish. South of the border it's the other way around—you'll find many shop signs in English.

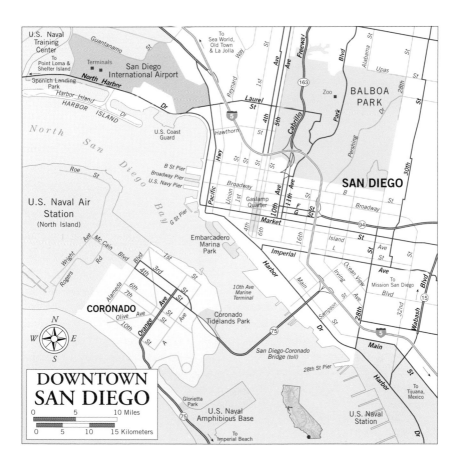

Balboa Park.

■ WHAT TO DO AND SEE IN SAN DIEGO

■ Balboa Park

This 1,400-acre park is one of the great urban parks of the West. It contains the San Diego Zoo and has more attractions than you can possibly enjoy in just one visit. **El Prado** has beautiful gardens and 10 museums, including the **Natural History Museum** *(619-232-3821),* the **San Diego Model Railroad Museum** *(619-696-0199),* the **Museum of Photographic Arts** *(619-238-7559),* the **Museum of San Diego History** *(619-232-6203),* and the **San Diego Museum of Art** *(619-232-7931).* There's also a Moreton Bay fig tree (rubber tree), 40 feet tall, with a limb spread of more than 100 feet. A replica of Shake-speare's **Old Globe Theatre** is part of a three-theater complex *(619-239-2255).* Many of the Spanish-Mediterranean–style buildings were erected for the 1915 Panama-California Exposition. *Off I-5 at Park Blvd., or by Hwy. 163, which cuts through the park.*

■ Balboa Park [San Diego] Zoo

This world-famous zoo, with a beautiful setting amongst hills, shrubs, and trees, has more than 4,000 exotic animals (926 species) living in as natural a habitat as possible (there's a notable absence of wire cages). *Balboa Park, east of downtown, off Hwy. 163; 619-234-3153.*

The affiliated 2,200-acre **Wild Animal Park** has even more wild animals living in a wild habitat. *15500 San Pasqual Rd., Escondido; 760-747-8702.*

■ **Old Town**

San Diego was founded here in 1769, on a slope above its bay, by a Spanish expeditionary force. Buildings dating from 1821 to 1872 survive and have been beautifully preserved in a state historic park. The place looks and feels authentic, down to the unpaved dusty streets and plaza. Highlights include the 1820s **Casa Estudillo** and **Casa Bandini** (which is home to a restaurant); the **Casa Carrillo,** the first house built outside the presidio, which once occupied this site, the **Casa de Machado y Steward,** the **Light-Greeman House** (1840s; originally a saloon operated by a liberated slave and his friend, who were among San Diego's first black settlers), the 1865 **Mason Street School,** and the original home of the *San Diego Union* newspaper (1868).

There's ample free parking off Pacific Highway west of the railroad tracks (reached by a pedestrian underpass). *Old Town State Park Headquarters, Old Town Plaza; 619-220-5422.*

■ **Sea World**

Set on 150 acres on the southern shores of Mission Bay, this aquarium-cum-amusement park packs in a lot of sea life, ranging in size from sea stars to orcas. There are daily shows, plus nighttime shows in summer, followed by fireworks. *On Mission Dr., off I-5 or I-8; 619-226-3901.*

One of the best shows (and jobs) at Sea World.

San Diego waterfront. (Photo by Sean Arbabi)

■ **Bay and Waterfront**

San Diego's downtown borders an interesting waterfront, overlooked by many of the city's better hotels. The "West End" has restaurants and galleries. Amtrak stops at the historic, Spanish-style Santa Fe Railroad Station. **The San Diego Museum of Contemporary Art** is in the American Plaza; *619-234-1001*. There's also a "Centre City" stop of the **San Diego (Tijuana) Trolley**. Along the Embarcadero, the **B Street Pier** is an international cruise ship terminal; *619-686-6388*.

On some weekends, **Navy ships** tying up at the Broadway Pier are open for visitors. If you've never clambered all over an aircraft carrier, this may be your chance.

The highlight of the **Maritime Museum** just north of the Broadway Pier is the barque *Star of India* which holds workshops in which ordinary folks can learn how to raise sails on an old-fashioned windjammer; *1306 North Harbor Dr.; 619-234-9153*.

■ **Shelter Island**

A man-made island with yacht clubs, restaurants, the **Commercial Basin** with its fleet of tuna clippers, and San Diego's oldest and most respected charter boat outfits. *H&M Landing, off Scott St.; 619-222-1144.*

■ **Cabrillo National Monument**

The 1854 lighthouse at the tip of Point Loma has an interpretive center with a great bookstore, views from lookout points above the cliffs, nature walks, and tidepools. *At the southern end of Catalina Blvd., reached from downtown and I-5 via Rosecrans and Canon Sts. and Catalina Blvd.; 619-557-5450.* (Also see pages 329-332.)

■ **Spanish Landing**

Spanish ships *San Antonio* and *San Carlos* anchored here in May of 1769 and established a camp, where they greeted the overland party led by Portola (which included Father Junipero Serra). From here began the exploration of California. Later ships supplying the presidio and mission moored here. *Spanish Landing Park on N. Harbor Dr., west of Lindbergh Field.*

■ **Mission San Diego**

The first mission in California was founded on July 16, 1769 near the presidio in what is now Presidio Park in Old Town (San Diego Viejo). Five years later, the mission was moved upriver, away from the baneful interference of presidio soldiers who preyed upon the Indians the padres were trying to convert. The mother mission of Alta California, San Diego's buildings were completed in 1813 only to fall into ruin as an independent Mexico withdrew its support from missions. It was rebuilt between 1915 and 1931. *Take I-8 east from I 5; go north on I-15 to Friars Rd. and take the exit going east. At the bottom of the hill turn left onto San Diego Mission Blvd. The mission is two blocks east, on the left side of the street; 619-281-8449.*

■ **Gaslamp Quarter**

This 16-block downtown district, centered at Fifth and Market, has so many old buildings it has been designated a National Historic District. Beautifully reconstructed buildings now house restaurants, nightclubs, galleries, and shops. *Fifth and Market; pay parking lots.*

■ **Hillcrest**

This uptown neighborhood is San Diego's gay district (one local radio station called it the "Castro District of San Diego"). It is known for its tree-shaded streets, chic restaurants, bars, and shops. Many turn-of-the-19th-century homes have been lovingly restored. *Centered on University Ave. near Fifth and Sixth.*

Mission San Diego was founded in 1769.

■ GETTING TO SAN DIEGO'S BEACHES

It's the first hot Saturday of summer and the San Diego beaches and all of the roads leading to them are packed with cars. Beach parking lots have been full since 9:00 A.M., and San Diegans eager to cool off in the surf circle the beach blocks, hoping for an elusive parking space. Mixed in with the locals are many cars with out-of-state license plates, mostly from Arizona (where the day's temperature is 104 degrees, with thunderstorms). Despite the 80-degree heat and the traffic, drivers don't loose their tempers. As car air conditioners overheat, they roll down the windows to let in the ocean breeze. It's part of the local lifestyle to be laid back, to take life and its competitions with a grain of sea salt (even for Angelenos who have driven south to escape the frenzy of their megalopolis). A billboard along the Coast Highway, announcing the start of the horse racing season at nearby Del Mar race track, happily proclaims "May the horse with the coolest name win."

I had been forewarned about the gridlock by a friend: "At this time of year," he said, "you have to hit the road at 4:00 A.M. to avoid traffic jams."

It wasn't quite that bad. Traffic moved, albeit slowly. And who was in a hurry anyway? If you got tired of circling the same block over and over again, you could always drive south to the less crowded shores of Coronado, Silver Strand, and Imperial Beach.

■ PACIFIC BEACH

A boardwalk runs from Mission Beach north to **Pacific Beach** ("PB"), which is known, despite its somewhat sedate image, as the "party town" of San Diego County. Most of these parties do not happen on the beach, however, but in beach-side (or near-beach) apartments and condos, or in the bars and music clubs strung along Garnet Avenue. Crystal Pier, at the foot of Garnet Avenue, is a combination fishing and pedestrian pier and hotel, and there's a good farmers market here on the weekends. Though it is known for being the only place on the coast with lodgings over the ocean (which were recently upgraded), the rooms are actually above the sandy beach (unless the tide is very high). You can't miss Crystal Pier. Its entrance is marked by a huge arch. Mission Boulevard is also one of the best places in Southern California to shop for bathing suits.

Pacific Beach Park has a grassy picnic area, street end access to the beach, as well as separate paved pedestrian and bicycle pathways. At Palisades Park to the north, paths lead from a grassy picnic area down to the wide sandy beach. The waves

Tourmaline Surfing Park is a favorite beach for beginners.

breaking onto the rocky shores of **Tourmaline Surfing Park,** below False Point, are popular with surfers (especially beginners and longboarders) and kayakers. To sign up for a surfing lesson contact the Mission Bay Aquatic Center (see page 326). There are many more splendid little beaches, most of them accessible via the dead ends of roads, between Pacific Beach and La Jolla. (See page 311 for more on La Jolla).

■ MISSION BAY

Mission Bay, to the immediate east of Mission Beach, is the world's largest civic aquatic park, and borders the eastern shore of the Mission Beach peninsula. This bay is Southern California's most popular water playground. It's one of those places that tries to have something for everybody: Mission Bay Park encompasses the entire shoreline of the bay. *(Call the Mission Bay Visitor Center; 619-276-8200, for information).* People come here to sun on protected sandy beaches, to waterski, to snorkel, to swim, sail, paddle, or dine. **Sea World,** a 135-acre aquarium and theme park, is very popular (despite rather steep admission fees). It has performing sea mammals but lacks the immediacy and excitement of the Monterey Bay Aquarium on the central California coast.

A few years ago, Mission Bay was the center of activities for the America's Cup races. But no one much wants to talk about it, perhaps because the American boat lost the cup to New Zealand.

The Mission Bay Aquatic Center rents Hobie cats, windsurfers, and sailboats and offers classes in sailing, surfing, windsurfing, waterskiing, and diving. *Santa Clara Point, east off Mission Boulevard in Pacific Beach; 619-488-1036.*

■ MISSION BEACH

Popular Mission Beach, west of Mission Bay (and Sea World), is very accessible—it's right at the end of the I-8 freeway, and is divided into an eastern and western half by Mission Boulevard and into northern and southern sections by an amusement park called Belmont Park.

Mission (as it's locally called) is filled with old-fashioned beach ambiance: children chasing each other through the sand, sailors on leave eyeing the girls, the yells and screams of people riding the roller coaster, arcades thronged with junior high kids, and skateboarders weaving in and out of the crowd. **Belmont Park** has a number of restaurants; a carousel; the Giant Dipper, a recently restored 65-year-old roller coaster; and the Plunge, a vast indoor saltwater swimming pool.

Shops line the paved boardwalk running south along the beach. On a warm, sunny day this can be a very active place, with joggers, bikers, skaters, and attention seekers—a bit like Venice Beach south, but imbued with that unique San Diego live-and-let-live mellowness. Watching the sometimes overt sexual antics of the local pleasure seekers makes you understand why San Diego is the adult video capital of the nation. No. Not rentals. They're *produced* in San Diego.

■ OCEAN BEACH

Ocean Beach to the south is separated from Mission Beach by the mouth of the San Diego River. Just east of here, I-5, the major north-south highway, and I-8, a major east-west route, cross. I-8 runs west from the interior valleys almost to the beach, funnelling folks from Mission Valley and the San Diego State University campus (as well as from the Imperial Valley and Arizona).

Ocean Beach got its start in the early 1900s, as a cluster of weekend beach cabins. In the 1920s and 1930s, when San Diego began expanding toward the beach, many of these cottages were converted into year-round homes. Because they were small, they provided inexpensive housing near the beach and were popular with surfers and beach bums during the 1950s and 1960s.

Even on a sunny, hot summer's day not everyone is here to swim and sunbathe. Fishermen stand shoulder by shoulder on the Ocean Beach fishing pier, hoping to catch a mess of yellowtail, bonito, corbina, or surf perch for the backyard barbecue. This pier is, at 2,100 feet long, the longest public pier on the West Coast. Other visitors just walk onto the pier to catch a whiff of the cooling ocean breeze, or they stroll along the palm-shaded boulevards, or browse in the eclectic antique shops of Newport Avenue, a block north of the pier (no parking meters!). Or they while away the afternoon at the O.B. Pier Cafe, a funky coffeehouse on the pier, or the Sunshine Company Saloon (5028 Newport Avenue), or revitalize their systems with a burger from Hodad's (5010 Sunset Avenue). A sign reflects the local spirit: "No shirt, no shoes, no problem."

Some of the nearby beach towns have gone "upscale" only in recent years, as waterfront property anywhere in the West has skyrocketed in value. Ocean Beach is a good example, but it has kept its populist atmosphere and is still funky—and very popular. Ocean Beach has a definite hippie/reggae flip flops–only feel (blended with a dose of second-hand/antique-shop atmosphere) that's unique to this part of town. It looks and feels more like something out of Portland, Oregon, than Southern California (if you take away the palm trees). Locals hang out at a great bar called Pacific Shores on Newport Avenue. Winston's Beach Club just off Newport Avenue on Bacon Street books reggae and local bands nightly.

There are more interesting restaurants in Ocean Beach than you can possibly sample in one visit. Nati's, the most popular breakfast place is, fittingly, on Bacon Street. In contrast to the shimmering newness of most San Diego neighborhoods, Newport Avenue is a throwback to the era of small towns and Main Streets—an old-fashioned movie theater, diners, family-run businesses, faded signs and storefronts.

Every Wednesday from 4:00–7:00 P.M. (till 8:00 P.M. in spring and summer) a farmers market is held in the 4900 block of Newport Avenue. This is a great place for checking out the tasty and uncommon produce of San Diego's backcountry, from apples and cherimoyas to macadamia nuts and piñon pine nuts.

Ocean Beach Park, north of the pier, has a sandy beach interspersed with rocky outcroppings and tidepools. It is a prime surfing beach where the famed Hawaiian surfer Duke Kahanamoku gave surfing exhibitions back in 1916. Expect the hardcore surfers to yell at the mere swimmers (the "speed bumps,") to get out of the way, but it's all good-natured fun. Even if surfing and volleyball seem at times more a vocation than a vacation.

If the surf looks right, rent a surfboard at the South Coast Surf Shop and give it a try. Surfing is much easier than it looks (though I've often heard otherwise) but only if the waves are low. Beginners should not attempt waves that are more than knee high. Doug Werner, in his excellent book, *Surfer's Start-up: A Beginner's Guide To Surfing,* has some very good advice for novice surfers. It's a good book to read *before* you head for a surf shop and beach.

Dog Beach, at the north end of the park, is the only beach in the city of San Diego where dogs are allowed to run free during the day. (Coronado and Del Mar also have designated dog beaches.)

Ocean Beach City Park, south of the pier, has a rocky shore with pocket beaches and tidepools accessible by stairs from Santa Cruz, Bermuda, Orchard, and Narragansett Avenues.

■ SUNSET CLIFFS PARK

Sunset Cliffs Park, along Sunset Cliffs Boulevard, is about as wild as a city park can get. Rough trails lead down rather unstable cliffs to secluded sand or cobble pocket beaches. Many of these trails start at a parking area at the end of Cornish Drive. Beware: both the cliffs and trails are heavily eroded and can be quite dangerous. Chances are you'll decide the spectacular scenery is worth the risk.

Sunset Cliffs is considered one of the three or four best surfing beaches in San Diego, though the water is cooler here than in La Jolla and points north. The surf in winter is especially good. Large, flat rocks, strewn over a narrow strip of sand, extend far out into the water. The kelp beds offshore are responsible for the distinctive smell of seaweed onshore. There are fine tidepools here and great diving (for more experienced divers).

■ POINT LOMA

On a clear day, the view from Point Loma is spectacular. You can look all the way south to Tijuana, Mexico, and may even discern the Coronado Islands a few miles offshore, just south of the border. You can look east to San Diego, with its bayside waterfront, and you can see two airfields from Point Loma: the Naval Air Station on North Island, at the head of the Coronado Peninsula, and Lindbergh Field near the bayshore. Eighty-one acres of the Point Loma Peninsula are set aside as the **Cabrillo National Monument.** (Also see page 322.)

🚗 From Sunset Cliffs Boulevard, a left (east) turn on Hill, and right (south) turn on Catalina will take you to Point Loma, and to the national monument. Curiously, no direct arterial route leads to this monument, one of the most popular in the nation. Please note that Point Loma Boulevard does *not* take you directly to Point Loma. It takes you to Ocean Beach. However, a left on Nimitz and a right on Catalina will take you all the way to the Point Loma Lighthouse.

Lover's Leap at Point Loma, 1905. (California Historical Society, Los Angeles)

En route to the monument, you'll pass through **Fort Rosecrans National Cemetery** with its somber grave markers. You can't miss the lighthouse and **Cabrillo National Monument.** They're at the very end of the road. The **Whale Overlook** is a great place to observe California gray whales as they pass by on their way from the Bering Sea to Baja.

The monument (where you must park and from which you walk to Point Loma) charges a parking and admission fee, and closes at sunset in summer and 5:15 P.M. the rest of the year. The **Old Point Loma Lighthouse** was built in 1854 with sandstone and bricks shipped south from Monterey. From its perch on the rocky spine of the peninsula, 462 feet above the ocean, you have a clear view, because the native vegetation of the point, coastal scrub, does not grow very tall. This lighthouse has been out of commission (and a major visitor attraction) since 1891, when the Point Loma Lighthouse further down the slope replaced it, because fog often obscured the beam of the higher light.

Below the lighthouse is a **visitors center** with an excellent bookstore. The 1.5-mile **Bayside Trail,** which runs through the scrub along the eastern slope of the point, passes abandoned World War II gun emplacements and is a great place for watching local sea birds, as well as hawks, herons, and pelicans. The **Point Loma Ecological Reserve,** on the southwest shore of the monument, has great tidepools with sea snails, sea stars, green sea anemones, giant keyhole limpets and, in deeper water, abalone and spiny lobsters. If you're lucky, you'll come across a sea hare, a shockingly large marine slug that may grow to a length of 15 inches.

Near-shore waters support one of the largest kelp beds in California. Vast as they are, these kelp beds were almost destroyed between 1947 and the 1960s by herds of voracious sea urchins. Urchin populations had once fallen and risen with the supply of kelp but the urchins, scientists learned, were subsisting on sewage effluents, giving the kelp no chance to regenerate between attacks. All sorts of measures were tried to cut back on the urchin population. But when divers learned that Asian gourmets paid high prices for sea urchins, the spiny creature was in trouble. Within a few years its status went from oversupply to overharvested. The kelp took advantage of the respite, and vast kelp beds once again sway in offshore waters.

(preceding pages) Point Loma Lighthouse.

■ CORONADO PENINSULA

Geologically speaking, the Coronado Peninsula is part of Mexico, since it was formed by sand carried to sea by the Tijuana River and washed north by ocean currents. Originally, the tip of the peninsula consisted of two sandy islands connected by marshes which, like many of the San Diego Bay marshes, have long been filled in.

Even though Coronado is connected to San Diego Bay by a narrow sand spit that runs south to Imperial Beach, it is for all practical purposes an island and acts like one. The northern tip (technically known as "North Island") has a naval air station, the southern part has fancy resorts, restaurants, and splendid beaches.

🚐 CA 75 crosses San Diego Bay from I-5 near downtown San Diego to Coronado, runs south over the spit to Imperial Beach, and turns back to I-5, allowing for a leisurely loop trip. You can reach the Coronado Peninsula via the 2.3-mile Coronado–San Diego Bay Bridge. Or you can take the passenger-bicycle ferry which departs from the foot of the Broadway Pier in San Diego every hour on the hour, and leaves Coronado on the half-hour; *619-234-4111;* fee parking at the Broadway Pier.

———— •◆• ————

■ WHAT TO DO AND SEE IN CORONADO

■ Hotel del Coronado
A vast, turreted Victorian complex built of wood, Hotel del Coronado dominates the Coronado oceanfront. You can't miss it. It's the place that looks like a big, white wedding cake. While the hotel has maintained its standards of excellence and is still as popular now with visitors as it was back in 1888, when it first opened, friends who spend a lot of time in Coronado prefer to stay at the Meridien and visit the Coronado for drinks and atmosphere.

■ Town of Coronado
This is a pleasant, albeit pricey, beach town with the usual shops and restaurants, and several excellent beaches.

■ Coronado Beaches
City Beach, which runs north from the hotel to the naval air station, is one and Coronado Shores Beach which runs south to Silver Strand State Beach, is another. These beaches are very popular. For one thing, the water here may reach 70 degrees by late summer, for another, the sand holds

pismo clams (which are eagerly sought after by local as well as visiting clam diggers).

■ **North Beach** can be a good place for summer surf since it's the only south-facing beach. There's also great body surfing here and it's rarely crowded. Navy Seals train on Coronado, just north of Silver Strand State

Beach. Head for the RRR's Market to stock up on picnic supplies.

■ **Coronado Beach Historical Museum** The museum provides background information and sells an excellent self-guided tour booklet; *1126 Loma Ave., 619-435-7242.*

Beach attire at the Hotel del Coronado today (above) and in the 1880s (opposite).

■ SILVER STRAND STATE BEACH

The long and narrow sandy spit that runs from Coronado south to Imperial Beach has access to both the ocean beach and the bay. That's because the spit is as narrow as half a city block in places. A pedestrian tunnel under the highway connects both sides of the park. The beach is popular for swimming, clamming, catching grunion, surf fishing, and combing the high tide line for shells. There are a multitude of shells here, including some exotic ones not found further north. The bay

side has a calm water swimming area. A residential area at the southern end of Silver Strand, and the bay side of the spit, is cut into many channels and peninsulas and has as many boats and docks as cars and garages.

The northernmost part of the flat, 10-mile-long Silver Strand belongs to the Navy, the southernmost to the residential community. Trailers/motor homes are on the ocean side of the park and they can be virtually wall-to-wall.

■ IMPERIAL BEACH

Imperial Beach, which likes to call itself an all-American city, was founded by promoters who wanted to attract vacationing farmers from California's Imperial Valley. Today, it is a very pleasant and "relatively" low-cost beach town with a splendid sandy strand (which was widened a few years back by dredge spoils from San Diego Bay). The beach is popular with surfers and swimmers but not always safe, because of dangerous currents and riptides. Another danger is less visible: effluent from the Tijuana River to the south—"a green ribbon of sludge," as a writer for a San Diego newspaper described it "which is carried north by ocean currents."

But the Tijuana sewage which offends us doesn't deter birds and other wildlife, making the **Tijuana River National Estuarine Reserve** south of Imperial Beach uncommonly rich in species. A sewage treatment plant is being planned for the U.S. side of the border. In the meantime, an odoriferous cloud continues to hang above the estuary. Who knows for how long the remedies, in the form of treatment plants, will always be just one step behind the flush of the growing population? But the birds (and the phytoplankton, algae, insects, crustaceans, fish, et al.) who live in the marsh are thriving.

One quarter of California's endangered lightfooted clapper rail population hangs out in the marsh's tules, harriers are common, and black skimmers, reddish egrets, and peregrine falcons are encountered occasionally. There is an excellent visitors center whose rangers give guided tours of the marsh. True, a faint whiff of sewage hangs over the marsh, but you'll hardly notice after you've spotted your first skimmer. *301 Caspian Way; 619-575-3613.*

Walking along the estuary's trails you can see Tijuana's Bullring-by-the-Sea at the foot of the Tijuana Mountains. The bullring (open May through September) is just outside of town in Playas de Tijuana. Drive or take a cab from the border and buy tickets at the bullring or book a tour with Five Star Tours; *(619) 232-5049.*

"America really begins at Imperial Beach," one writer stated, because Border Field State Park to the south is often a no-man's land abutting the Mexican border fence, where *La Migra* rounds up illegal Mexican immigrants. Curiously, Border Field is the only beach south of San Luis Obispo County where horseback riding is legal. Go by all means, if you feel an urge to visit the southwesternmost point in the continental United States.

■ VISITING MEXICO

Tijuana (pop. 800,000) is a border town with all the good and bad that that implies. It can be a civilized frontier, or it can be very raw—as it is in the shanty towns sprawling over suburban hills. Tijuana has grown too fast and it's a mess, but even the barrios have their charm. Don't be surprised if you see an automobile parked in the dusty unpaved street outside a shack nailed together from packing crates, and see a TV antenna sticking up from the roof. Mexicans are great architectural inventors, and their haphazard creations tend to have a roguish charm and panache. Colors are usually primary and intense—red, white, blue, green, yellow—with an occasional purple and orange.

There's work in Tijuana, and immigrants flock here from all parts of Mexico to toil in the sweatshops or *maquilladoras* set up by U.S. and Asian multi-nationals to take advantage of low wages and the North American Free Trade Agreement.

There are some wonderful restaurants in Tijuana *(see* "LODGING & RESTAURANTS," *page 378)* and even some great taco and snack stands, but to try the latter it's best to ask the advice of a local or a trusted friend. Food aromas wafting through the suburbs have uncommon nuances, beyond the commonly encountered fragrances of fresh-ground masa, hot lard, and roasted chili.

Shops near the border and along major downtown streets cater mainly to visitors. You can pay with U.S. dollars for all purchases, but you'll pay more. Unfortunately, many shops near the border have turned into outlet malls in recent years which sell the same merchandise you'll find at U.S. outlets but for less money. (If you stay outside the U.S. for more than 24 hours, you can brings back $400 worth of goods duty-free.) But you can also find shops, especially in the downtown area, where you can buy Mexican things: Taxco silver, regional pottery, papier mâché animals and fruits, and other folk art.

Highway 1, a toll road, will take you south to Ensenada with its beaches and beachfront restaurants, hotels, and condos, and to the rest of Baja California; Highway 2 takes you east to Tecate and the rugged Sierra San Pedro Martir, and to Mexicali and the rest of Mexico. If you have the time, you should take at least a short drive into the mountains. The landscape here looks the way Southern California did before urban sprawl infested the region.

GETTING TO TIJUANA

Sixteen miles south of San Diego, I-5 ends at the Mexican border, just north of Tijuana. The border crossing is open 24 hours a day. For a short visit, a passport is not necessary, but we recommend that you bring one.

If you're taking your car across be sure to buy supplemental insurance. Your U.S. insurance is not valid south of the border (and Mexico has a nasty habit of throwing the victims of traffic accidents into jail—unless they can prove fiscal responsibility—until proven innocent).

You don't have to take your car: take the last U.S. exit (the one that reads "Last U.S. Exit Parking" and park your car. You can walk to Tijuana, or you can take a taxi (always be sure to negotiate the price before getting into a cab), or you can take the bright red Mexicoach Shuttle from the border station into Tijuana (it leaves every 30 minutes from 9:00 A.M. to 9:00 P.M. and the cost is $1.)

RENTING CARS

Renting a car in the San Diego area can be a bit trickier than elsewhere: Rental car companies warn about driving in San Diego because of the high rate of automobile thefts. Supposedly that's because of the proximity of the Mexican border. Few U.S. rental companies allow their cars across the border. Two exceptions are Bob Baker Car and Truck Rental, *730 Camino del Rio, Mission Valley Auto Circle, 619-297-3106;* and Fuller Ford Auto Leasing and Rental, *560 Auto Park Drive, Chula Vista, 619-656-3370.*

L O D G I N G &
R E S T A U R A N T S

🛏 *Lodging Rates:*
per night, one room, double occupancy
$ = under $80; $$ = $80–130; $$$ = $130–200; $$$$ = over $200

✕ *Restaurant Prices:*
average dinner entree
$ = under $10; $$ = $10–17; $$$ = $17–25; $$$$ = over $25

Albion

🛏 **Albion River Inn.** 3790 CA 1; 707-937-1919 or 800-479-7944 $$$
One of the finest inns on the northern California coast. Ocean views from New England-style clifftop cottages, which boast fireplaces and decks. Guests enjoy the spas and gardens; full breakfast *(see below)*.

✕ **Albion River Inn.** *See above.* $$
Guests love this place; there's limited room for non-guests. Full breakfast and dinner are served in the restaurant-bar. Straightforward but very nicely done food: grilled meat, fish, and poultry; tasty pastas, and fresh vegetable dishes.

Aptos

✕ **Cafe Sparrow.** 8042 Soquel Dr.; 831-688-6238 $$
Continental cookery at its best in a restaurant that was almost wiped out by the 1989 Loma Prieta earthquake.

Arcata

🛏 **Hotel Arcata.** 708 Ninth St.; 707-826-0217 $
A 1915 downtown hotel that was once the town plaza's showcase, then fell on hard times, has recently been restored. The place feels comfortably old; were it not for the sushi restaurant in-house *(see below),* you might feel you'd stepped back in time.

🛏 **Lady Ann.** 902 14th St.; 707-822-2797 $$
Arcata's foremost B&B is just a few blocks from the plaza in a quiet, residential neighborhood.

✕ **Abruzzi.** 791 Eighth St. (Arcata Plaza); 707-826-2345 $$
Delectable, garlicky Italian food, prepared with gusto, arranged beautifully, and served with a smile.

✕ **Humboldt Brewing Company.** 856 Tenth St.; 707-826-BREW $
Good local microbrews.

OREGON

Malibu
Santa Monica
Venice
Marina del Rey
El Segundo
Manhattan Beach
Hermosa Beach
Redondo Beach
Long Beach
Seal Beach
Sunset Beach
Newport Beach
Laguna Beach
Capistrano Beach
Dana Point
San Clemente
Oceanside
Carlsbad
Encinitas
Cardiff
Solana Beach
Del Mar
La Jolla
San Diego

Crescent City
Klamath

Trinidad
Samoa
Arcata
Eureka
Petrolia
Ferndale

REDWOOD COAST
Page 137

Shelter Cove

Fort Bragg
Little River
Mendocino
Albion
Elk
Philo
Point Arena
Boonville
Gualala
Guerneville
Healdsburg
Timber Cove
Graton
Jenner
Bodega Bay
Valley Ford
Inverness
Marshall
Point Reyes Station

SONOMA & MENDOCINO
Page 101

LOS ANGELES, SAN DIEGO AREA

MARIN COAST
Page 72

SAN FRANCISCO BAY
Page 62

San Francisco

San Gregorio Beach
Pescadero
Davenport
Santa Cruz
Aptos
Capitola
Pacific Grove
Moss Landing
Monterey
Carmel

GOLDEN GATE TO SAN SIMEON
Page 167

Big Sur

SAN FRANCISCO AREA

Larkspur
Olema
Bolinas
San Rafael
Stinson Beach
Tiburon
Muir Beach
Sausalito
Berkeley
San Francisco
Oakland

Moss Beach
Half Moon Bay

Cambria
Cayucos
Morro Bay
San Luis Obispo
Avila Beach
Pismo Beach

CENTRAL COAST
Page 209

Solvang
Santa Barbara
Goleta
Montecito
Ventura
Malibu
Los Angeles

LOS ANGELES & ORANGE COUNTY
Page 255

SANTA CATALINA ISLAND

San Clemente
Oceanside
La Jolla
San Diego
Imperial Beach
Tijuana

SAN DIEGO COAST
Page 299

MEXICO

COASTAL CALIFORNIA
LODGING & RESTAURANTS

TOWNS WITH LISTINGS IN THIS BOOK

✗ **Tomo.** Hotel Arcata, 708 Ninth St.; 707-822-1414 $$
You might not expect it, but the 1915 hotel is home to a great sushi restaurant. A bit pricey, but the food's fresh and skillfully prepared and the staff is friendly, if in no more of a hurry than the rest of Arcata.

Avila Beach

⌂ **San Luis Bay Inn.** 3254 Avila Beach Rd.; 805-595-2333 or 800-438-6493
Laid-back time-share resort near sandy beaches.

✗ **Olde Port Inn.** Port San Luis Pier 3; 805-595-2515 $$$
The best fresh fish around, excellent local wine list. Beautiful views of fishing boats bobbing in the lee of the rocky headlands.

Berkeley

✗ **Cafe Rouge.** 1782 Fourth St.; 510-525-1440 $$-$$$
Fantastic Southern French/Northern Italian-influenced cuisine is served in this spacious, lively restaurant. Meat's the specialty here—there's a charcuterie in the back—but stop at the zinc bar first for oysters and a cocktail. Great art and a chic and modern yet comfortable decor.

✗ **Chez Panisse.** 1517 Shattuck Ave.; 510-548-5525 Downstairs: $$$$ Cafe: $$
Chef Alice Waters and the kitchen staff at this renovated Craftsman-style home are California cuisine legends. Downstairs, they do a pre-set, prix-fixe dinner; call ahead to find out what's being served on which night, and to reserve a space. Expect seemingly simple yet exquisite preparations of the freshest produce, meat, fish, poultry. Upstairs, more casual fare—salads, risottos, pizzas—is served.

Big Sur

⌂ **Big Sur River Inn.** CA 1, 3 miles north of Pfeiffer–Big Sur State Park; 831-667-2700 $$$
A motel with restaurant right on the Big Sur River (but miles from the next beach). The complex includes a gas station, grocery store, and gift shop.

⌂ **Deetjen's Big Sur Inn.** CA 1, 5 miles south of Pfeiffer–Big Sur State Park; 831-667-2377 $$$
The cabins and main building of this small, old inn are tucked into a damp redwood canyon. The rooms are truly rustic: drafts can come through the redwood-plank walls, but heaters and comforters will keep you warm. A good restaurant is located in the main building (see below).

⌂ **Post Ranch Inn.** CA 1; 831-667-2200 or 800-527-2200 $$$$
Guests are driven up 1,200 feet above the ocean to the redwood guesthouses at this secluded resort. Views from the elaborately equipped rooms—spa tubs, stereos, decks, but no TVs—are of ocean or mountain, inspiring you to wander the grounds or hike on nearby trails.

⌂ **Ventana Country Inn Resort** CA 1, 2.5 miles south of Pfeiffer–Big Sur State Park; 831-667-2331 $$$$
An upscale, modern, weathered-cedar

resort that appears to have something for everyone (as long as visitors have the big bucks to pay for it all). The Swedish-style rooms have lots of glass so that guests can have views of the ocean, 1,200 feet below. The restaurant here is excellent *(see below)*.

✗ **Deetjen's Big Sur Inn Restaurant.** *See above;* 831-667-2377 $$

The delectable menu is based on local ingredients and might best be described as California cuisine with a touch of European finesse—most evident in the sauces.

✗ **Nepenthe.** CA 1, 4 miles south of Pfeiffer–Big Sur State Park; 831-667-2345 $$

A relaxing place with great food and super service. Henry Miller and Jack Kerouac, among others, ate here. The view down the coast alone is worth a visit. The Ambrosia Burgers are famous, but the fish sandwiches are even better. Crowded in summer, Nepenthe is more enjoyable in the off-season. Downstairs, **Cafe Kevah** (831-667-2331), has less expensive food and an oceanview deck, but it's closed in the off-season.

✗ **Ventana Country Inn Resort.** *See above;* 831-667-2331 $$$$

The California cuisine served in this beautiful and woodsy two-tiered restaurant leans toward Mediterranean-style vegetables—artichokes, zucchini, peppers—and showcases regional cheeses and seafood from the Monterey coast.

Bodega Bay

⛫ **Inn at the Tides.** 800 CA 1; 707-875-2751 or 800-541-7788 $$$

Wood-shingled cottages high on a hillside overlooking the bay Bodega Head, and the ocean, surrounded by meadows where California quail call in the evening. Romantic place for watching sunsets.

Bolinas

✗ **Bolinas Bay Bakery and Cafe.** 20 Wharf Rd.; 415-868-0211 $

The bread, pastries, and pies sold in the bakery are made from organic ingredients. The cafe offers soups, salads, and sandwiches; they close around 6 P.M.

✗ **Smiley's Schooner Saloon.** 41 Wharf Rd.; 415-868-1311 $

This historic saloon dates back to lumber schooner days.

Boonville

⛫ **Boonville Hotel.** CA 128 in the center of town; 707-895-2210 $$

A few rooms above the restaurant comprise the hotel here. *See below.*

✗ **Boonville Hotel.** *See above;* 707-895-2210 $$

This small dining room has blossomed into a cozy spot where local winemakers hang out. The decor is simple but tasteful; likewise the food's excellent, never overworked.

✗ **Buckhorn Saloon.** 14081 CA 128; 707-895-2337 $

Upstairs from the **Anderson Valley Brewing Company,** the Buckhorn offers a more casual option than the Boonville Restaurant across the street. Locals and visitors alike come here for a tasty pint and a plate of nicely prepared pub food—fish 'n chips, hamburgers. In fair weather visit the large redwood deck.

Cambria

▦ **Cambria Sea Otter Inn.** 6656 Moonstone Beach Dr.; 805-927-5888 $$
A comfortable inn with gas fireplaces in all rooms.

✕ **Ian's.** 2150 Center St.; 805-927-8649 $$
A modern, clean-lines dining room is the setting for eclectic California cuisine, from a duck quesadilla with pumpkin seeds and raisins to a classic California dish of asparagus on baby greens with chèvre and pignolis.

✕ **Sow's Ear.** 2248 Main St.; 805-927-4865 $-$$
Regional American cuisine is given a Central Coast lift with fresh local shellfish, produce, and cheeses. Chicken-and-dumplings are divine; more upmarket are dishes like salmon in parchment.

Capistrano Beach

✕ **Olamendi's Mexican Cuisine.** 34660 PCH; 949-661-1005 $$
Very popular place with great burritos.

Capitola

▦ **Capitola Venetian Hotel.** 1500 Wharf Rd.; 831-476-6471 $$
A funky old hotel that has weathered storms well since it was built in 1920, along with the adjacent condominium complex—the first of its kind in the state.

▦ **The Inn at Depot Hill.** 250 Monterey Ave.; 831-462-3376 $$$
This former railroad station is today a lavish inn. Each room is themed: the Railroad Baron room is done up like a luxurious railroad car. All rooms have fireplaces; many have hot tubs. Excellent breakfasts.

✕ **Gayle's Bakery and Rosticceria.** 504 Bay Ave.; 831-462-1200 $
You'll have to wait in line at this extremely popular place for sandwiches, salads, pastas, and stews. But it's worth it.

✕ **Pizza My Heart.** 209A Esplanade; 831-475-5714 $
Tasty pizzas, quick and cheap.

Cardiff

✕ **Beach House.** 2530 S. US 101; 760-753-1321 $$$
A rather posh seafood restaurant close to the beach, with valet parking (of all things). But the seafood is fresh and well-prepared; the views are great. Lunch and dinner.

✕ **Las Olas.** 2655 S. US 101; 760-942-1860 $
An inexpensive local favorite, this Mexican restaurant across the highway from the beach has served consistently good food for years. Lunch and dinner.

✕ **Miracles.** 1953 San Elijo Ave.; 760-943-7924 $
Wonderful coffeehouse; a good place to get a sense of North County. Breakfast, sandwiches, and salads.

Carlsbad

⊡ **Carlsbad Beach Terrace Inn.** 2775 Ocean St.; 760-729-5951 $$$
A popular motel across the highway from the beach. Some rooms have a beach view.

⊡ **Carlsbad Inn Beach Resort.** 3075 Carlsbad Blvd.; 760-434-7020 $$$
Old World–style hotel set on a wide landscaped lawn in the center of town. A bit of Europe in sunny Southern California.

⊡ **Four Seasons Aviara.** 7100 Four Seasons Point; 760-931-6672 $$$$
Set on 30 acres of coastline, this new Four Seasons resort offers 6 tennis courts, a golf course, and over 300 rooms.

✕ **Harbor Fish South.** 3779 Carlsbad Ave.; 760-729-4161 $
An outdoor patio with lots of atmosphere. Fried fish and shellfish; hamburgers.

✕ **Nieman's.** 2978 Carlsbad Blvd.; 760-729-4131 $$$
In the oldest Victorian structure in town. This place is rather formal: proper attire is required. **Niemans' Seagrill** is less formal.

✕ **Pelly's Fish Market.** 7110 Avenida Encinas; 760-431-8454 $
Great seafood chowder and grilled fish.

Carmel

⊡ **Carmel Garden Court Inn.** Torres and Fourth Sts.; 831-624-4935
Surrounded by riotously colorful gardens and flowering bushes, this B&B offers five patio minisuites in the garden, as well as rooms in the main house, where champagne breakfast is served. Fireplaces in all rooms.

⊡ **Carmel Highlands.** CA 1, 4 miles south of Carmel; 831-624-3801 or 800-538-9525 $$$$
This classic coastal inn was built in 1916 (long before the highway to the south was built) and renovated recently. It's very popular with honeymooners: 1,000 weddings are performed here each year.

⊡ **Cypress Inn.** Lincoln and Seventh Sts.; 831-624-3871 $$$
A Carmel landmark for decades and partly owned by Doris Day, this Moorish–style inn boasts a spacious lobby, large marble bathrooms, and 34 cozy guest rooms.

⊡ **Sandpiper Inn.** 2408 Bayview Ave.; 831-624-6433 $$-$$$
A block from the beach, this 1920s Prairie-style inn boasts large, airy rooms with skylights, fireplaces, and sea views. The gardens are filled with rhododendrons and azaleas.

✕ **Casanova.** Fifth Ave., bet. Mission and San Carlos Sts.; 831-625-0501 $$$
This romantic, family-run restaurant offers Italian and continental classics including rich pastas, grilled salmon, rack of lamb, and veal Provençal.

✕ **Crème Carmel.** San Carlos St. and Seventh Ave.; 831-624-0444 $$$
Innovative California-French cuisine is the focus at this small, attractive restaurant. Roast duck might be served with a ginger tamarind glaze or with a classic peppercorn Madeira sauce. Tucked behind a courtyard, the tone at this hidden spot is relaxed.

✗ **Hog's Breath Inn.** San Carlos St., bet. Fifth and Sixth Aves.; 831-625-1044 $$
This restaurant-saloon is owned by former Carmel mayor/actor/director Clint Eastwood. Basic fare: order a Dirty Harry Burger (hmm) and Clint's own Pale Rider Ale.

✗ **Pacific's Edge.** At the Carmel Highlands Inn, *see above*; 831-624-3801 $$$
If this resort dining room didn't have such spectacular ocean views, the award-winning menu would draw crowds anyway. Central Coast ingredients star: Monterey Bay smoked salmon with Carmel Valley greens and sweet corn fritters.

Catalina

⌂ **Inn on Mount Ada.** Avalon; 310-510-2030 $$$$
This intimate, lavish hotel occupies the old Wrigley mansion. The 6 guest rooms have ocean views; all meals are included.

✗ **Avalon Seafood.** On the pier; 310-510-0197 $
Don't miss fish 'n chips at this quaint spot. You can buy bait here, too.

✗ **Cafe Prego.** 603 Crescent Ave.; 310-510-1218 $$
In the evening, feast on sumptuous pastas and Italian seafood dishes by candlelight, or come here for a satisfying Sunday brunch.

Cayucos

⌂ **Cayucos Beachwalker Inn.** 501 S. Ocean Ave.; 805-995-2133 $$

A plain motel within walking distance of the beach. Just try to get in during the height of the summer beach season. The beach, of course, is spectacular.

✗ **Sea Shanty.** 296 S. Ocean Ave.; 805-995-3272 $
A small restaurant serving fresh fish.

Crescent City

⌂ **Crescent Beach Motel.** 1455 US 101, 2 miles south of town; 707-464-5436 $
Crescent City has no fancy hotels, B&B's, or restaurants. This oceanview motel is your best option, as is the Beachcomber restaurant next door (707-464-2205, $$). Make reservations! In summer, Crescent City motels fill up fast.

Dana Point

⌂ **Best Western Marina Inn.** 24800 Dana Point Harbor Dr.; 949-496-1203 $$
Moderately priced lodging on the harbor.

⌂ **Ritz-Carlton Laguna Niguel.** 1 Ritz-Carlton Dr.; 949-240-2000 $$$$
A Mediterranean-style resort set into cliffs 150 feet above the water. Service is very attentive (it *is* a Ritz); rooms are deluxe, but comfortable and not over-the-top. Some consider it the best hotel in the country.

✗ **Jon's Fish Market.** 34665 Golden Lantern St.; 949-496-2807 $
This moderately priced seafood market and eatery is the most popular place in the harbor. Outdoor dining near the boat slips.

Davenport

✕ **New Davenport B&B.** CA 1 and Davenport Ave.; 831-425-1818 $$$
Twelve rooms (with private baths) occupy a bathhouse ca. 1900 and the floor above the restaurant *(see below)*. Rooms are decorated with objets d'arts from the owners' travels.

✕ **New Davenport Cash Store.** *See above;* 831-426-4122 $$$
Locals gather in this lively room, with its beamed ceiling and decorative crafts, for New American cuisine. Great ocean views: lucky patrons see whales migrating during the season. Breakfast, lunch, dinner.

Del Mar

▦ **L'Auberge Del Mar.** 1540 Camino del Mar; 619-259-1515 $$$$
A posh, European-style hotel on beautifully landscaped grounds.

▦ **Best Western Stratford Inn of Del Mar.** 710 Camino del Mar; 619-755-1501 $$
A very comfortable, rather inexpensive spot. Nothing fancy, but the location's great.

✕ **Cafe Del Mar.** 1247 Camino del Mar; 619-481-1133 $$
Pasta dishes and brick-oven baked pizzas.

✕ **Epazote.** 1555 Camino del Mar; 619-259-9966 $$$
Epazote offers contemporary Southwestern cuisine and beautiful ocean views. Indoor and outdoor dining. There's often a bustling singles scene at the bar, which must have something to do with Epazote's signature margaritas.

✕ **Fish Market.** 640 Via de la Valle; 619-755-2277 $$
Unpretentious place with well-prepared fresh seafood, very popular with locals.

✕ **Kirby's Cafe.** 215 15th St.; 619-481-1001 $
Popovers on the patio at Kirby's has to be one of the best ways to start the day in Del Mar. The food's surprisingly imaginative. Lunch only.

✕ **Pacifica Del Mar.** 1555 Camino del Mar; (619) 792-0476 $$$
Atop the Del Mar Plaza, this stylish ocean-view restaurant specializes in Pacific Rim seafood: pan-seared marinated salmon garnished with ginger shrimp strudel and balsamic glaze, and the signature kimchee shrimp appetizer. Popular bar, too.

✕ **Stratford Court Cafe.** 1307 Stratford Court; 619-792-7433 $
A likeable cafe for vacationers, locals, dog lovers. Breakfast consists of granola, bagels, pastries, and enormous mugs of coffee. The lunch menu includes good sandwiches (especially the chicken salad), salads, and homemade soups. Outdoor patio.

El Segundo

✕ **Panama's Bar and Grill.** 221 Richmond St.; 310-322-5829 $
A popular blues bar (live music Thursday's through Sundays; no cover). A local hangout that serves good beer and features

bands too. Low-key, down-homey and very local. The food is standard American bar fare—but that's not why you came, is it?

Elk

☷ **Greenwood Pier Inn.** 5928 CA 1; 707-877-9997 $$$
Set on a lawn high above rocky, secluded beaches, this inn is comprised of a main house and a number of small, somewhat unusually designed cottages equipped with private baths, fireplaces, skylights, and views of the water. Gardens surround the little bungalows, and a country store and garden shop are onsite (707-877-3440). There's a wonderful cafe, too. *See below.*

☷ **Griffin House at Greenwood Cove.** 5910 CA 1; 707-877-3422 $$$
Next door to the Greenwood Pier Inn, Griffin House offers oceanview cabins at reasonable rates, as well as a cozy pub. Hot breakfast is brought to your room.

☷ **Harbor House.** 5600 CA 1; 707-877-3203 $$$-$$$$
This inn, beautifully and completely crafted from redwood, was built as a lumber executive residence in 1916 and overlooks a private piece of beach. Curl up with a book in the comfortable living room. Included in rates are breakfast and dinner in the dining room *(see below).*

✕ **Greenwood Pier Inn Cafe.** 5928 CA 1; 707-877-9997 $
Colorful seaside gardens and secluded rocky beaches surround this hotel eatery.

All breads and pastries served in the cafe are baked on the premises; most of the herbs used in the cooking come from the garden. Breakfast, lunch, dinner; open seasonally.

✕ **Harbor House.** 5600 CA 1; 707-877-3203 $$$
Menus in the dining room of this attractive inn *(see above)* emphasize local organic produce, fresh seafood, and free-range meats. Limited seating for non-guests.

Encinitas

☷ **Moonlight Beach Motel.** 233 Second St.; 760-753-0623 $
A plain but comfortable motel with balcony views of the beach.

✕ **Ki's Restaurant & Juice Bar.** 2591 US 101; 760-436-5236 $
Catering mostly to a health-conscious crowd, Ki's has built a statewide reputation for its smoothies.

✕ **La Bonne Bouffe.** 471 Encinitas Blvd.; 760-436-3081 $$-$$$
Despite its bland stripmall location, this small bistro has quite a sophisticated menu. Dinner Tuesday through Sunday; make reservations.

✕ **Roxy Restaurant & Ice Cream.** 517 N. US 101; 760-436-5001 $
A vegetarian favorite for decades, Roxy's offers hearty baked casseroles, interesting salads, pastas, and pizzas. Fish and chicken dishes are also on the menu, as well as the celebrated Niederfrank's ice cream.

Eureka

⊡ **Carter House.** 301 L St.; 707-444-8062
$$$-$$$$
This brown, four-story Victorian-style house was actually built in 1982. Rooms are sunnier than you'd think, judging from the exterior, and are furnished with antiques and contemporary local art. The restaurant *(see* Restaurant 301*)* is also good.

✕ **Lazio's Seafood.** 327 Second St.; 707-442-3767 $$
A local institution that's served fresh seafood since 1944. The Lazios know fish, and know how to run a fun dining room.

✕ **Lost Coast Brewery & Cafe.** 617 Fourth St.; 707-445-4480 $
A friendly local hangout with good beer and simple but tasty food.

✕ **Sea Grill.** 316 E St.; 707-443-7187 $$
An old-town eatery serving fresh fish prepared in multiple ways. Lunch during week, dinner every day but Sunday.

✕ **Restaurant 301.** Carter House, 301 L St.; 707-444-8062 $$$$
The "nouvelle continental cuisine" at this inn can be a bit precious, but it's just fine. This part of downtown is not necessarily safe after dark, but Carter House's popularity makes it safer.

Ferndale

⊡ **The Gingerbread Mansion.** 400 Berding St.; 707-786-4000 $$$-$$$$
About as fancy and elaborate as a Victorian can get. All rooms have private baths. Splendid breakfast in formal dining room overlooking the gardens.

✕ **Diane's.** 553 Main; 707-786-4950 $
Best breads, muffins, and pastries in town.

Fort Bragg

⊡ **Cleone Lodge Inn.** 24600 N. CA 1; 707-964-2788
A beautifully maintained place that was a small motel years ago, but has evolved into a comfortable inn over the last 20 years.

⊡ **Grey Whale Inn.** 615 N. Main St.; 707-964-0640
The former city hospital; now a very comfortable B&B. I like the story about the woman who was born here and came back to celebrate her wedding night

⊡ **Noyo River Lodge.** 500 Casa del Noyo; 707-964-8045 $$
Fireplaces, soaking tubs, private decks, sumptuous breakfasts, antique furnishings, landscaped gardens and paths; easy walk to Noyo harbor, the fishing docks, party boats, and restaurants.

⊡ **The Old Coast Hotel.** 101 N. Franklin St. (at Oak); 707-961-4488
1892 building in downtown Fort Bragg. The 16 rooms are done in Edwardian decor; private baths, off-street parking; beautifully landscaped grounds

⊡ **Surf and Sand Lodge.** 1131 N. Main St.; 707-964-9383 or 800-964-0184 $$
Rooms open onto the Old Haul Road,

with views of ocean and easy access to the blufftop trails.

⊞ **Vista Manor Lodge.** 1100 N. Main St.; 707-964-4776 $-$$
Not your standard motel, but a very comfortable lodge on he bluffs overlooking the Pudding Creek estuary. Tunnel to beach and easy access to Old Haul Road.

✗ **North Coast Brewing Company.** 444 N. Main St.; 707-964-3400 $$
Beer-matched fare; seafood; fresh pasta, chili, regional specialties like beer-batter red snapper fish 'n chips. Lunch, dinner.

✗ **The Old Coast Hotel.** *See above;* 707-961-4488 $$
Set in an 1892 building in downtown Fort Bragg, this hotel restaurant offers some very good, moderately priced Italo-California cooking, courtyard dining; and professional yet unpretentious service.

✗ **The Restaurant.** 418 N. Main St.; 707-964-9800 $$
This small storefront restaurant is one of Fort Bragg's culinary treasures: all of the food (except the bread) is prepared from scratch on the premises. The fare is seasonal and delicious, in the best California style. The formula works: The Restaurant has been very popular with locals for 25 years.Call ahead, as hours are quirky.

✗ **Schat's Bakery.** 360 N. Franklin (one block east of Main); 707-964-1929$
The place in Fort Bragg to pick up your breakfast pastry.

✗ **Viraporn's Thai Restaurant.** 500 S. Main (just off CA 1); 707-964-7931 $
No credit cards. Chef Viraporn Lobell has a special touch with classic Thai dishes which make them taste like new inventions. A very small and very friendly restaurant.

✗ **The Wharf Restaurant.** 780 N. Harbor Dr.; 707-964-4283 $-$$
This local hangout overlooking the harbor (with a glimpse of the ocean beyond the bluffs) serves very fresh fish cooked with just the right touch and sauced very lightly. For those who catch all of their own fish, try the steak or prime rib. The place has barely changed since it opened 40 years ago—except it's a lot less smoky.

Goleta

✗ **Beachside Bar Cafe** 5905 Sand Spit Rd.; 805-964-7881 $$
This Goleta Beach County Park Restaurant is a good place to sip a beer while eating a simple sandwich or fresh, expertly prepared local fish. Lunch and dinner.

Graton

✗ **Kitchen.** 8989 Graton Rd.; 707-824-0563 $$
With its wide veranda, this corner clapoard building on Graton's main drag looks like an old-fashioned American family restaurant. But the food is something else. Such dishes as turkey meatloaf, steak, bouillabaisse, and even vegetables and other

accompaniments are magically transformed here. Service is excellent. Make reservations: this is a western Sonoma hotspot.

Gualala

⌂ **Gualala Hotel.** Center of town on CA 1; 707-884-3441 $
Nineteen recently renovated, smallish rooms. Dining room, bar, wine shop.

⌂ **The Old Milano Hotel.** 38300 CA 1 (1 mile north of town); 707-884-3256 $$$
A Victorian country home overlooking Castle Rock Cove. Most rooms have shared baths, but a friend who owns a luxury inn says that this is the only place with shared baths he ever enjoyed—and he plans to stay here again. There's also a cliffside hot tub, and private cottages equipped with spas. Full breakfast is included in rates. Excellent small restaurant *(see below)*.

⌂ **St. Orres.** 36601 CA 1; 707-884-3303 $$-$$$
A lodge inspired by the Russian architecture of the first European settlers on this coast (it's hard to miss this spot as you drive up CA 1). The lodge has shared baths; the cabins are private. Close to a sheltered sandy cove. Great restaurant *(see below)*.

✕ **The Old Milano Hotel.** 38300 CA 1; 707-884-3256 $$$
Excellent small restaurant in the former living room of the country home. The hotel is a smidgen north of the Mendocino county line, but the menu will remind you of the best foods Sonoma County has to offer (prepared with a true California flair and exquisite skill): Sonoma lamb and duck, fresh seafood, the best local produce, and other seasonal fare. No credit cards.

✕ **St. Orres.** 36601 CA 1; 707-884-3303 $$-$$$
Regionally renowned restaurant with outstanding northern California wine list. No credit cards accepted in restaurant.

Guerneville

⌂ **Applewood Inn.** 13555 CA 116; 707-869-9093 $$$-$$$$
If you think a pink Mediterranean-style villa does not fit into a landscape of redwoods and apple trees, look again. Applewood is about as snug a fit as you can hope for. This is a truly great place, with splendidly comfortable rooms and inviolate privacy within walking distance from town. Fantastic breakfasts.

✕ **Applewood Inn & Restaurant.** 13555 CA 116; 707-869-9093 $$$$
The owners of this inn *(see above)* offer prix-fixe dinners Tuesday through Saturday. The food, prepared by chef David Frakes, is truly scrumptious.

Half Moon Bay

⌂ **Cypress Inn on Miramar Beach.** 407 Mirada Rd.; 650-726-6002 or 800-83-BEACH $$$-$$$$
A luxurious inn right on the beach.

⌅ **Mill Rose Inn.** 615 Mill St.; 650-726-8750 $$$-$$$$
This romantic inn is set amid lovely gardens. Guest rooms are furnished with Eastlake and Arts and Crafts antiques and have private entrances, as well as balconies that face the courtyard.

⌅ **San Benito House.** 356 Main St.; 650-726-3425 $-$$
This restored country inn is a local favorite. A sauna, redwood deck, and restaurant (see below) and reasonable prices add to its charms.

⌅ **Zaballa Inn.** 324 Main St.; 650-726-9123 $$-$$$
This 1859 building (Half Moon Bay's oldest) now houses 9 guest rooms, some with whirlpools and/or fireplaces.

✕ **Half Moon Bay Bakery.** 514 Main St.; 650-726-4841 $
This bakery offers sandwiches and salads in addition to pastries fresh from the 19th-century oven.

✕ **San Benito House Restaurant.** 356 Main St.; 650-726-3425 $$
Come here for a delicious Sunday brunch, or a weekend dinner of Northern Italian/French country cooking.

Healdsburg

⌅ **Camellia Inn.** 211 North St.; 707-433-8182 $$-$$$
This quiet, homey 1869 Italianate building once served as Healdsburg's first hospital.

The 50 varieties of camellias go all the way back to Santa Rosa horticulturist Luther Burbank. Innkeeper Ray Lewand is an accomplished winemaker—happy hour by the swimming pool is an education. Huge breakfast, private baths; several rooms have whirlpool tubs, gas fireplaces, private entrances. A splendid place.

✕ **Bear Republic Brewing Co.** 345 Healdsburg Ave.; 707-433-2337 $-$$
This wide open hall on the Healdsburg Plaza is one of the most fun places around. Uncommonly tasty beers, delicious food (especially the vegetarian sandwich and any soup), a jovial atmosphere, and friendly and fast service make this spot popular with locals. In warm weather there's outdoor seating with a view toward the creek.

✕ **Bistro Ralph.** 109 Plaza St.; 707-433-1380 $$
A very friendly, fun place, where the winemaker entertaining at the table next to you may offer you a glass of the latest, not-yet-released wine. The food is classy bistro fare, simple but tasty and very seasonal, since it's primarily made from fresh local ingredients. The menu changes regularly, but there's something for every palate: filet mignon with onion rings, lamb meatloaf, grilled Columbia River sturgeon, Dungeness crab ravioli. The wine list is excellent. Lunch on weekdays, dinner nightly.

✕ **Oakville Grocery.** 124 Matheson St.; 707-433-3200 $-$$
This specialty food store sells an amazing array of cheese, fruit, breads, wines, and

more for picnics. They also serve pizzas, salads, sandwiches, and wines by the glass, which you can enjoy at an outdoor table.

Hermosa Beach

✗ **Good Stuff.** 1286 The Strand (just north of Pier Ave.); 310-374-2334 $
The whole beach scene—body builders, strand skaters, volleyball players, and other folks come here for healthy, tasty, inexpensive dishes from omelets to sandwiches to burritos and fresh fish. Outdoor seating. On the beach close to the pier.

Imperial Beach

✗ **El Tapatio's.** 260 Palm Ave.; 619-423-3443 $
Quite authentic Mexican fare (shredded beef; flavorful salsa) near the pier.

Inverness

🛏 **Dancing Coyote Beach.** 12794 Sir Francis Drake Blvd.; 415-669-7200
Four cottages right on private beach in Tomales Bay. Cottages have fireplaces; breakfast included.

🛏 **Manka's Inverness Lodge.** Callendar Way, 3 blocks off Sir Francis Drake Blvd.; 415-669-1034 or 800-58-LODGE $$$
This former hunting and fishing lodge has become a romantic getaway, with a great restaurant to boot *(see below)*.

🛏 **Ten Inverness Way.** 10 Inverness Way; 415-669-1648 $$$
The redwood living room of this homey B&B features a large stone hearth and lots of bookshelves, and the simple but pretty guest rooms have hand-sewn quilts. Delicious breakfast menu.

✗ **Manka's Inverness Lodge.** *(See above)*; 415-669-1034 or 800-58-LODGE $$$
Set amid tall trees, this former hunting and fishing lodge has an intimate, wood-panelled dining room with a fireplace. The menu tends toward ambitious game dishes, but doesn't always succeed.

✗ **Vladimir's Czech Restaurant.** 12785 Sir Francis Drake Blvd.; 415-669-1021 $$$
Good Central European cooking—beef tongue, lamb shank seasoned with garlic, cabbage rolls, goulash, and other stick-to-your-ribs fare. Stay away on weekends when the place may be overrun and things may get a bit slack. No credit cards.

Jenner

🛏 **Murphy's Jenner Inn.** 10400 CA 1; 707-865-2377 or 800-732-2377 $$-$$$
Guest rooms in cottages and houses perched above the Russian River mouth.

✗ **River's End.** 11051 CA 1; 707-865-2484 $$$
Burgers to roasted baby pheasant, or fresh fish specials: this place has them all, plus great views of the mouth of the Russian River. Excellent Sonoma County wine list. Open seasonally.

Klamath

☎ **Requa Inn.** 451 Requa Rd.; 707-482-8205 or 888-788-1706 $-$$
A historic inn that was first established in 1885, burned to the ground in 1914, and rebuilt in the same year. All rooms have private baths; 4 have a view of the river. Breakfast is included in the room rate. Dinner nightly (reservations required).

La Jolla

☎ **La Jolla Cove Motel.** 1155 Coast Blvd.; 619-459-2621 $$
Comfortable motel; near Ellen Scripps Park, overlooking La Jolla Cove.

☎ **La Valencia.** 1132 Prospect St.; 619-454-0771 $$$
Beautiful old salmon-colored stucco hotel near the beach. Lovely views.

☎ **Sea Lodge.** 8110 Camino del Oro; 619-459-8271 $$$
Mexican-tiled courtyard, fountains, palm trees. Across the street from the beach. All rooms have balconies or lanais. Close to La Jolla Shores beach.

☎ **Sheraton Grande Torrey Pines.** 10950 N. Torrey Pines Rd.; 619-558-1500 $$$
A luxurious resort with beautiful ocean views; connected to the famous Torrey Pines Golf Course.

✕ **Bird Rock Cafe.** 5656 La Jolla Blvd.; 619-551-4090 $$
Reasonable prices help make Bird Rock a La Jolla favorite—even in a neighborhood where money's no object. Mussels (harvested locally) are served in a savory Thai curry; other seafood dishes are also well worth a visit, even at higher prices. A bustling, fun scene.

✕ **Brockton Villa Restaurant.** 1235 Coast Blvd.; 619 454-7393 $$
This converted, historic bungalow's got a comfortable, intimate dining room and a wide veranda facing La Jolla Cove. Lunch and dinner tend toward eclectic California cooking, but the kitchen is rarely overly ambitious, with dishes like grilled fish, meat loaf, pastas, and interesting salads. Be prepared to wait: this place is popular.

✕ **Carinos Restaurant.** 7408 La Jolla Blvd.; 619-459-1400 $
A neighborhood favorite for pizza and pasta.

✕ **The Cheese Shop.** 2165 Avenida de la Playa; 619-459 3921 $
The sandwiches at the Cheese Shop are made with all top-grade ingredients, from the roast beef and Black Forest ham, to the wide selection of imported cheeses. Cookies and other pastries are often fresh from the oven. A great place to get a picnic lunch for the beach.

✕ **Froggy's Bar & Grill.** 954 Turquoise St.; 619-488-8102 $
Innovative food with laid-back flair. Good seafood, for a great price.

✕ **George's at the Cove.** 1250 Prospect St.; 619-454-4244 $$$
A local favorite, with semi-formal indoor dining and more casual dining on the deck overlooking La Jolla Cove. In both places, the cuisine is California eclectic with an emphasis on seafood; one recent dish was applewood-smoked salmon with fennel, miso, and a Hawaiian pesto. Upstairs, **George's Ocean Terrace** ($$) is a rooftop aerie with stunning views and palate-tempting meals at a reasonable price. Lunch and dinner at both spots.

✕ **La Jolla Brewing Co.** 7536 Fay Ave.; 619-456-2739 $
After a day at the beach, this informal, shorts-almost-required brewery serves up good burgers and great beer. Try the Sea Lane Amber or the Pumphouse Porter.

✕ **Marine Room Restaurant.** 2000 Spindrift Dr.; 619-459-7222 $$$-$$$$
The Marine Room has long been loved for its seaside location, and now there's great food, too. The chef takes classic French and California cuisines to new heights of whimsy. Seafood is given a kick with surprising flavors (sambuca or candied endive, for instance). All this, with the same incredible ocean views the Marine Room's always had.

✕ **Mediterranean Room at La Valencia.** 1132 Prospect St.; 619-454-0771 $$$
Located near the beach (see hotel listings, above) this old favorite offers a seafood-oriented brunch. La Valencia also has the **Sky Room**, a formal continental-style restaurant with impressive views ($$$$), and the **Whaling Bar** ($$$).

✕ **Pannikin Coffee & Tea.** 7458 Girard Ave.; 619-454-6365 $
A cozy coffeehouse with a shady patio: great for a snack of sandwiches or pastries. There's a second location at 7467 Girard Avenue.

✕ **Porkyland Restaurant.** 1030 Torrey Pines Rd.; 619-459-1708 $
A no-frills eatery with first-rate carnitas, tacos al pastor, handmade tamales, and carne asada.

✕ **Trattoria Acqua.** 1298 Prospect St.; 619-454-0709 $$
Located in the Coast Walk complex (set into the hillside, steps down from Prospect Street), this appealing restaurant offers a variety of semi-outdoor seating: the "cupola room" has partial walls and an ocean view; or choose the breezy patio. Wonderful Italian cuisine—osso buco, an array of pastas, and flavorful grilled meats and fish.

Laguna Beach

🔲 **Hotel Laguna.** 425 S. Coast Hwy.; 949-494-1151 $$-$$$
Old Laguna Beach at its best—and surprisingly comfortable lodging, considering this place dates back to the very beginnings of Laguna Beach.

🔲 **Inn at Laguna Beach.** 211 N. Coast Hwy.; 949-497-9722 $$$-$$$$
Above Main Beach and next to the Las Brisas restaurant; the very comfortable rooms have private balconies with ocean view—a very seductive combination. Underground parking garage allows you to forget your car and *walk!*

☂ **Surf and Sand Hotel.** 1555 S. Coast Hwy.; 949-497-4477 or 800-664-7873 $$$$
You can hear the ocean from every room here; if you like the beach, and have the cash, it's the only place to stay. The restaurant Splashes is also very good *(see below)*.

✕ **Anastasia Cafe.** 470 Ocean Ave.; 949-497-8903 $-$$
A surprisingly inexpensive breakfast and lunch hangout for Laguna Beach's skinny fashion set. The fare is scrumptious and beautifully presented; dishes range from simple muffins to poached eggs with basil, tomatoes, and thyme.

✕ **Casa Olamendi.** 1118 S. Coast Hwy., South Laguna Beach; 949-497-4148 $
A local South Laguna Beach favorite for down-to-earth, low-cost Mexican food.

✕ **Five Feet.** 328 Glenneyre St.; 949-497-4955 $$$
Eclectic, Pacific Rim (accent on Chinese) cuisine is served in large portions at this hip bistro. Admirers love the catfish.

✕ **Laguna Beach Brewing Co.** 422 S. Coast Hwy.; 949-499-BEER $$
A winning combination: a restaurant with its own microbrews, food expertly prepared from fresh ingredients, and an ocean view. Lunch and dinner.

✕ **Las Brisas.** 361 Cliff Dr.; 949-497-5434 $$-$$$
Overlooks Main Beach, surf, and ocean from south end of Heisler Park. Seafood with Mexican flair.

✕ **Splashes.** Surf and Sand Hotel, 1555 S. PCH; 949-497-4477
Casual California/Mediterranean bistro fare is the order at this well-named spot (so close to the water the windows get splashed). Try to get a table at sunset.

✕ **242 Cafe.** 242 N. Coast Hwy. (north of Broadway); 949-494-2444 $$
Near the Laguna Museum of Art, this tiny upscale cafe right on the coast offers California/Mediterranean cuisine. Great for an after-museum snack.

✕ **Wahoo's Fish Taco.** 1133 S. Coast Hwy.; 949-497-0033 $
Locally famous fish taco and other *healthy* Mexican dishes.

Larkspur

✕ **The Lark Creek Inn.** 234 Magnolia Ave.; 415-924-7766 $$-$$$
Set in a small grove, this former home has been beautifully transformed into an excellent restaurant. Go for brunch, in fair weather, when the sun pours through the dining room skylight and onto the dining patio. American regional dishes like eggs with smoked salmon and chives are a perfect brunch; at dinner try the Yankee pot roast.

✕ **Left Bank.** 507 Magnolia Ave.; 415-927-3331 $$
At this pretty, upbeat eatery, chef Roland Passot serves French brasserie classics like steak and frites, steamed mussels, and roast chicken. Have brunch on the sunny patio.

Little River

⛏ **Heritage House.** 5200 N. CA 1; 707-937-5885 or 800-235-5885 $$$-$$$$
This classic coastal inn served smugglers of Chinese immigrants in the 19th century, when it was an isolated farmhouse, and rum runners during Prohibition. It's been steadily upgraded since 1949. There are 68 cottages, a lodge, and the old farmhouse, and it has a first-rate restaurant *(see below)*. Not bad for a little coastal hideaway. All room rates include breakfast and dinner

⛏ **Little River Inn.** 7751 CA 1; 707-937-5942 or 888-INN-LOVE $$-$$$
All of the 65 rooms have views of the ocean; some have fireplaces and Jacuzzis. The restaurant has what it calls ìscrumptious country meals in a beautiful garden setting. Oceanview bar. Special winter rates. There's an adjacent 9-hole golf course, plus championship tennis courts.

✕ **Heritage House Restaurant.** *See above;* 707-937-5885 or 800-235-5885 $$$$
A first-rate restaurant with an outstanding wine list. The kitchen serves the best local lamb, beef, fresh vegetables, and fish, prepared with integrity and style. As at many California restaurants, it's hard to tell whether French or California influence is stronger, since chefs from both places pride themselves on using local products. But the fresh flavors of the dishes and the kitchen's light touch are definitely California-style.

✕ **Little River Inn & Restaurant.** 7751 CA 1; 707-937-5942 or 888-INN-LOVE $$$
Delicious country meals are served in a pretty garden setting. Oceanview bar.

Long Beach

⛏ **Edgewater Beach Motel.** 1724 E. Ocean Blvd.; 562-437-3090 $
Inexpensive lodging near beach and downtown Long Beach; views of ocean and Catalina Island from deck.

✕ **Alegria.** 115 Pine St.; 562-436-3388 $-$$
This tapas restaurant is very popular, mostly for its fun decor and flamenco dancers. Food can be hit or miss, but the atmosphere makes up for unpredictability. Lunch and dinner.

✕ **555 East.** 555 E. Ocean Blvd.; 562-437-0626 $$$-$$$$
In an old San Francisco atmosphere, seafood and beef are served to the downtown set. A handsome place for a cocktail.

✕ **King's Fish House Pine Avenue.** 100 W. Broadway; 562-432-7463 $$$
The place in Long Beach for fresh fish, grilled or broiled, served with light but flavorful sauces.

✕ **L'Opera.** 101 Pine St.; 562-491-0066 $$$
Considered by many a real find in downtown Long Beach, this Northern Italian ristorante offers excellent food and service in

a sleekly renovated former bank. Flavorful goose prosciutto is paired with fresh mozzarella and drizzled with olive oil that's been infused with sun-dried tomatoes. The lobster-and-ricotta-stuffed mezzaluna pasta has loads of lobster flavor. The dessert collection is heavy on special-occasion sweets.

Malibu

⊤ Malibu Beach Inn. 22878 PCH; 310-456-6444 $$$-$$$$
On the beach, in a town that has virtually *no* hotel rooms of any kind, this place is a rare find—and can be hard to get into. Never mind the price, it's about the only way we peons can claim we spent a night in Malibu (unless you sleep in your car, as I did during my college days). Not to be confused with the **Malibu Inn** (22969 PCH), which is a surfer bar.

✕ Bambu Malibu. 3835 Cross Creek Rd.; 310-546-5464 $$
Caribbean-Asian cuisine is served at this crowded, see-and-be-seen eatery. Innovative cooking adds more punch to the experience.

✕ Beaurivage. 26025 PCH (2 miles north of Malibu Canyon Rd.); 310-456-5733 $$$-$$$$
A Malibu institution: the kitchen turns out superb southern French cuisine in formal surroundings. A cliffside setting adds to the charms here.

✕ Geoffrey's Malibu. 27400 PCH; 310-457-1519 $$$-$$$$
Gorgeous views, flashy artwork; very L.A.

crowd. A fun place to have a drink at the bar and watch the sunset.

✕ Granita. 23725 W. Malibu Rd.; 310-456-0488 $$$-$$$$
Trademark pizzas and baskets of delicious bread. The menu features Mediterranean seafood. As with all of Puck's restaurants, wife Barbara Lazaroff has put her flourish on the design, which has a colorful, Sea Worldy theme.

✕ Kay and Dave's Cantina. 18763 PCH; 310-456-8800 $
An old beachfront house with a few tables inside, more seating on a covered patio, and best of all, a few picnic benches outside, cradled at the foot of the Santa Monica Mountains. The "kitchen burrito" is stuffed with everything but the kitchen sink. All items are prepared with fresh ingredients, and without lard. Lunch and dinner.

✕ Neptune's Net. 42505 PCH, 1 mile north of Leo Carrillo Beach; 310-457-3095 $-$$
Great lobster, french fries, and jumbo shrimp heaped onto paper plates are the order of the day at this low-key, local-friendly seafood joint.

✕ Reel Inn. 18661 PCH; 310-456-8221 $$
New England–style fishhouse with an array of seafood cooking. Order at the counter and wait for chowder, fish tacos, even Cajun blackened fish dishes; dining at boardinghouse tables. There's a newer **Reel Inn** in Santa Monica at 1220 Third St. Promenade; 310-395-5538.

Manhattan Beach

✕ **Cafe Pierre.** 317 Manhattan Beach Blvd.; 310-545-5252 $$-$$$
A very friendly cafe with good, simple, but elegantly prepared food. A wonderful bistro for the local beach crowd.

✕ **The Kettle.** 1138 Highland Ave.; 310-545-8511 $
A truly great coffeeshop. An attractive, friendly spot, with a menu full of homemade American classics. Everybody in town shows up sooner or later; this is an excellent place for families. Open 24 hours.

✕ **Michi.** 903 Manhattan Ave.; 310-376-0613 $$-$$$$
A very trendy pan-Pacific restaurant opened by Michi Takahashi of Chaya Brasserie fame. Definitely Manhattan Beach's "in" place: reservations are essential.

Marina del Rey

⌶ **Ritz-Carlton Marina del Rey.** 4375 Admiralty Way; 310-823-1700 $$$$
Large and brilliantly colored guest rooms, private balconies, and a super-attentive staff characterize this deluxe hotel. Rather formal for the surroundings, but the hotel also offers plenty of recreational amenities—boats for rent, water sports, pools, etc.

✕ **Cafe del Rey.** 4451 Admiralty Way; 310-823-6395 $$$-$$$$
This pan-Asian restaurant has great views as well as a great chef, Katsuo "Naga" Na-

gasawa. The menu is eclectic, but the dishes are beautifully prepared and they work, whether the inspiration is American, French, Mexican, or Asian. Boats park just outside.

Marshall

✕ **Nick's Cove.** 23240 CA 1; 415-663-1033 $-$$
This old-fashioned waterfront restaurant near the boatyard serves standard fare and barbecued oysters—a trend in these parts. Oyster bash each weekend.

✕ **Tony's Seafood Restaurant.** 18863 CA 1; 415-663-1107 $$
Like Nick's but slightly more upscale, Tony's also has a deck from which you can watch the cooks grill your oysters.

Mendocino

⌶ **MacCallum House.** 45020 Albion; 707-937-0289 $$$
The town's oldest B&B (built in 1882) offers rooms in a Victorian house and garden cottages with quilts and comfortable furnishings. You can also stay in the barn, with its stone fireplaces, or in the water tower suite, equipped with a Franklin stove. Breakfasts are thoughtfully prepared.

⌶ **Mendocino Hotel & Restaurant.** 45080 Main St.; 707-937-0511 $$-$$$
1878 hotel, thoroughly updated with private baths in most rooms. Plush dining room; casual garden dining *(see below)*. In

the bar, you can sip drinks under the magnificent stained-glass dome or in front of the fireplace in a comfortable chair.

☨ **Whitegate Inn.** 499 Howard; 707-937-4892 $$-$$$
Beautifully restored, very comfortable Victorian; downtown Mendocino; close to everything; great gardens. All rooms have fireplaces and private baths.

✕ **MacCallum House Restaurant and Gray Whale Bar & Cafe.** 45020 Albion; 707-937-5763 $$$
Excellent creative California cuisine incorporating fresh local ingredients—organic vegetables, wild mushrooms, coastal huckleberries, fresh seafood. The **Gray Whale Bar & Cafe** offers lighter and less expensive fare in casual surroundings; the dining room and library are more upscale, with white linen and steep prices. The staff is knowledgeable and friendly.

✕ **Mendocino Cafe.** 10451 Lansing St.; 707-937-2422 $
Open daily for lunch and dinner. fresh seafood, vegetarian dishes. Oriental and Mexican food. Reasonably priced. Saturday and Sunday brunch from 10:00 A.M.

✕ **Mendocino Hotel & Restaurant.** *See above;* 707-937-0511 $$-$$$
At this 1878 hotel, California cuisine is served at breakfast, lunch, and dinner. Dining in the plush Garden Room is a memorable experience, and the wine list may be one of the finest on the North Coast.

✕ **Bayview Cafe.** 45040 Main St.; 707-937-4197 $
Not at all snooty, this restaurant has an amazing view of Mendocino—across the flower-covered bluffs to the cove and the wide ocean, across the street from the southern Headlands. The food is basic—hamburgers, burritos, sandwiches—and very inexpensive.

✕ **Cafe Beaujolais.** 961 Ukiah St.; 707-937-5614 $$$
Once known primarily for its lavish breakfasts, this cafe has expanded into other California-style fare influenced eclectically by the usual French, Italian, Asian, and Mexican suspects. Local, organic produce and free-range meats are used whenever possible. While the place is justly famous, the quality of food has slipped a bit since the owners have opened a place in Austria. Beautiful gardens.

Montecito

☨ **Four Seasons Biltmore.** 1260 Channel Dr.; 805-969-2261 $$$$
This top-of-the-line Mediterannean-style villa resort, spread out on 21 acres, opened in 1927. The elegant guest rooms boast Spanish balconies with views of the Pacific, the Santa Lucias, and of verdant gardens. Top-of-the-line and very expensive.

☨ **Miramar Resort Hotel.** 1555 S. Jameson Ln.; 805-969-2203 $$$$
The only hotel in Montecito directly on the beach.

☵ **Montecito Inn.** 1295 Coast Village Rd.; 805-969-7854 $$$$
An attractive if rather elaborate celebrity hangout established in 1928 by Charlie Chaplin and Fatty Arbuckle.

✕ **Four Seasons Biltmore.** *See above;* 805-969-2261 $$$$
In the opulent dining rooms, which overlook the Pacific, diners relish an impressive array of consistently delightful food. The eclectic culinary style is a California-style skip around the globe; you'll also find healthful "spa cuisine" dishes.

✕ **Stonehouse.** At the San Ysidro Ranch, 900 San Ysidro Ln. (3 miles east of CA. 101); 805-969-5046 $$$
Sited in an old granite farmhouse, this rustic but intimate dining room at one of California's most sumptuous resorts offers New American cuisine, sometimes with a Southern accent. Delicious dry-aged steak, perhaps served with an interesting horseradish sauce, and boldly prepared fresh fish.

Monterey

☵ **Hotel Pacific.** 300 Pacific St.; 831-373-5700 or 800-554-5542 $$$
A comfortable modern hotel designed to fit right in with Monterey's old adobes. Even though you're not right on the waterfront, you can hear the sea lions bark at night.

☵ **Jabberwock.** 598 Laine St.; 831-372-4777 $$-$$
At this whimsically run Victorian B&B, guests stay in spacious, antique-furnished rooms with names like Momerath and Borogrove. Breakfast might consist of delicious Snarkleberry Flumptious. The large wraparound porch has a view of the bay.

☵ **Old Monterey Inn.** 500 Martin St.; 831-375-8284 or 800-350-2344 $$$
This English Tudor house, set amid gardens, contains guest rooms decorated in themes: one room evokes an African safari, another a children's library from days past. Elaborate breakfasts are served course by course on gorgeous china.

☵ **Spindrift Inn.** 652 Cannery Row; 831-646-8900 or 800-641-1879 $$$
Right on Cannery Row and right on the water, where you can watch the sea otters float offshore from your window (if you get a room facing the water). The rooms are comfortable and elegantly appointed.

✕ **Cafe Fina.** 47 Fisherman's Wharf; 831-372-5200 $$
The Fisherman's Wharf restaurant most worth visiting. Good pasta and seafood.

✕ **Fresh Cream.** 99 Pacific St.; 831-375-9798 $$$-$$$$
This elegant room, up a spiral staircase, is the setting for French-California cuisine. Recent dishes have included lobster ravioli with two caviars, and roast duck with black currant sauce. Beautiful view of the bay.

✕ **Montrio.** 414 Calle Principal; 831-648-8880 $$-$$$
Bold flavors and hearty, Mediterranean-California cooking characterize the cuisine in this former firehouse, now done up in

modern rustic style, with brick wall, wrought iron, and leather. Specialties include risotto with artichokes.

Morro Bay

☲ **Inn at Morro Bay.** 60 State Park Rd.; 805-772-5651 $$-$$$$
This old inn has the kind of faded elegance that makes you feel warm and at home. Sit by the fireplace in the lounge when its cool, or on the deck in fair weather.

☲ **Tradewinds Motel.** 225 Beach St.; 805-772-7376 $$
A bit of surprise: on the outside this place looks like a small, standard-issue motel, but the rooms have been fixed up very nicely, with cciling fans and gas fireplaces. It's just a short walk down the hill to the Embarcadero and its restaurants.

✕ **Dorn's Original Breakers Cafe.** 801 Market St.; 805-772-4415 $$
On the bluffs overlooking the Embarcadero and the harbor, this is a favorite hangout for Morro Bay old-timers.

✕ **Galley Restaurant.** 899 Embarcadero; 93442 805-772-2806 $$-$$$
A very comfortable restaurant, right over the water, with beautifully prepared fresh seafood and very friendly and accomplished service.

✕ **Harada Japanese Restaurant.** 830 Embarcadero; 805-772-1410 $$$
Sushi in Morro Bay? You bet. And it's very popular, too. You can't miss this place: it's the only building on the Embarcadero that looks Japanese. Across the street from the waterfront.

✕ **Paradise.** At the Inn at Morro Bay, 60 State Park Rd.; 805-772-5651 $$$
Indulge in fresh food with Mediterranean accents in this elegant oceanview dining room. Sophisticated preparations of local seafood, especially sea scallops and salmon, often in rich, creamy sauces, or in paella.

✕ **Rose's Landing Restaurant and Lounge.** 725 Embarcadero; 805-772-4441 $-$$
Fresh seafood in the restaurant and in the bar. The bar has great happy hour with fish 'n chips and martinis.

Moss Beach

✕ **Moss Beach Distillery Restaurant.** Beach Way & Ocean Blvd.(follow signs); 650-728-5595 $$-$$$
This place has been popular since Prohibition, when it was said to have served alcohol anyway. A favorite Sunday brunch spot where patrons sit on low tables outside on a deck above the beach. In chilly weather the waitstaff hands out blankets.

Moss Landing

✕ **Moss Landing Cafe.** 421 Moss Landing Rd.; 831-633-3355 $
An inexpensive folksy place serving the area's trademark deep-fried artichokes, plus crab cakes, squid and eggs, and other simple but tasty fare.

Muir Beach

☼ **The Pelican Inn.** 10 Pacific Way (off Hwy 1, at entrance to Muir Beach); 415-383-6000 $$$
Built like a traditional inn with traditional guest rooms. The dining room serves traditional fare (beef Wellington, cottage pie, prime rib). Cozy and comfortable, especially on stormy nights: fireplaces in dining room and living room. Seven rooms on second floor, all with private baths. Full English breakfast included.

✕ **The Pelican Inn.** *See above;* 415-383-6000 $$-$$$
The dining room serves traditional fare (beef wellington, cottage pie, prime rib). Lunch, dinner, and late afternoon repasts.

Newport Beach

☼ **Newport Channel Inn.** 6030 W. PCH; 949-642-3030 $
Nothing posh, but clean, comfortable rooms in a motel on the off side of the Coast Highway, very reasonable rates, and staff who really know the area.

☼ **Portofino Inn.** 2306 Ocean Front; 949-673-7030 $$$
In Newport Beach, old surf shops don't die —they're turned into posh hotels. But it's close enough to the surf that, come the next hurricane, you can probably surf on the back stoop.

✕ **The Crab Cooker.** 2200 Newport Blvd.; 949-673-0100 $$
I remember reviewing this down-to-earth grilled and smoked fish place near the Newport Pier more than a decade ago. Having been in business for almost half a century, the Cooker is still going as strongly as ever. Maybe it's the proximity of the fresh fish of the Dory Fleet, handled by a genius in the kitchen. There's also great clam chowder. But no reservations are taken. If John Wayne and Richard Nixon could wait in line, so can you.

✕ **Newport Burger.** 6800 W. PCH; 949-642-5881 $
A different kind of burger joint: this place's specialty is an ahi (yellowfin tuna) burger.

✕ **Sabatino's Restaurant & Lido Shipyard Sausage Co.** 251 Shipyard Way on Lido Peninsula; 949-723-0621 $$
Southern Italian dishes and locally famous sausage. Takeout available.

Oakland Waterfront

☼ **Inn at the Square.** 233 Broadway; 510-452-4565 $$
Covered parking; easy access to Jack London Square, Produce Row, and Chinatown.

✕ **Oakland Grill.** 301 Franklin St.; 510-835-1176 $$
A pleasant cafe whose large doors open onto Produce Row. A family spot.

Oceanside

✕ **Beach Break Cafe.** S. Coast Hwy.; 760-439-6355 $
Diverse breakfast menu, or just go for bagels and croissants.

✕ **Johnny Mananas.** 308 Mission Ave.; 760-721-9999 $
Great, inexpensive Mexican food with take-out. BLT burrito and other non-traditional options as well as the standards.

✕ **Ruby's Diner.** 1 Oceanside Pier; 760-433-7829 $
Soup, salad, sandwiches, tacos, malts, meatloaf, and fish 'n chips are on the menu at this 1940s-style diner.

Olema

☖ **Olema Inn & Restaurant.** CA 1 and Sir Francis Drake Blvd.; 415-663-9559 $$
This 1876 New England–style inn is comfortable and convenient to Point Reyes. The dining room is attractive, too. Open seasonally.

✕ **Olema Farm House** 10005 CA. 1; 415-663-1264 $$
Famous for its bar and barbecued oysters.

✕ **Olema Inn & Restaurant.** *See above;* 415-663-9559 $$
Great barbecued oysters, and the straight-forward cooking is good, too. A few California-style dishes are also thrown in.

Pacific Grove

☖ **Beachcomber Inn.** 1996 Sunset Dr.; 831-373-4769 or 800-634-4769 $$
Just up from the beach at Asilomar. Free rental bikes for guests. Fishwife Restaurant adjacent *(see below)*, and within walking distance of the Links at Spanish Bay.

☖ **Gosby House Inn.** 643 Lighthouse Ave.; 831-375-1287 $$-$$$
This lovely 1887 Queen Anne has been an inn since 1894. Many rooms have fireplaces; most have private baths. Breakfast, as well as sherry in the afternoon.

☖ **Martine Inn.** 255 Ocean View Blvd.; 831-373-3388 or 800-852-5588 $$-$$$$
There are 22 rooms in this Victorian-style inn. Two sitting rooms overlook the ocean; rates include full breakfast.

☖ **Pacific Grove Lighthouse Lodge & Suites.** 1150 Lighthouse Ave.; 831-655-2111 or 800-858-1249 $$-$$$
A pleasant inn with rustic rooms tucked into the pines. One block from Point Pinos Lighthouse, 2 blocks from the beach, and 2 miles from Fisherman's Wharf (reached by a beautiful shore trail).

✕ **Fishwife Restaurant at Asilomar Beach.** 1996 1/2 Sunset Dr.; 831-375-7107 $-$$
Across the street from the Asilomar conference center and a short walk from Asilomar Beach, this plain restaurant has some of the freshest and best prepared seafood on the Monterey Peninsula. The daily specials from the grill use only the freshest seasonal

fish, like sand dabs; the seafood quesadilla is delectable. Lunch, dinner.

Pescadero

X **Duarte's Tavern.** 202 Stage Rd.; 650-879-0464 $$
Built in 1894 as a stagecoach stop, this old, comfortable building now serves as a tavern and restaurant regionally famous for its seafood dishes. Rock fish, sand dabs, and abalone (in season) are perfectly fresh and cooked just right. The fruit pies are made with fruit from the family garden.

Petrolia

☎ **Lost Inn.** Old Mattole Rd.; 707-629-3394 $$
No credit cards. Only one guest room, a large, two-room suite with double bed, kitchen, glassed-in porch, and private entrance. Call for directions.

Philo

X **Floodgate Store & Grill.** 1810 CA 128; 707-895-2870
The food here might best be described as California cuisine but specially tuned to Anderson Valley wines: fresh ingredients, etc., but seasoned to bring out the best in the local wines, which are more elegant, perhaps more nervy than wines from the hotter valleys. It all adds up to a very refreshing experience.

Pismo Beach

☎ **Shelter Cove Lodge.** 2651 Price St.; 805-773-3511 $$-$$$
Guests can walk to the cove from this beachfront lodging. All rooms have ocean views.

X **Shore Cliff Restaurant.** 2555 Price St.; (805) 773-4671 $$-$$$
This is a cliff-top place with an astounding view. Great food, presented in a light, California-continental style: there's a killer artichoke appetizer as well as perfectly fresh fish cooked to perfection. A great place for watching sunsets, and for observing the antics of shorebirds. The staff is friendly, relaxed and very professional. Sunday brunch is a local favorite.

X **Splash Cafe.** 197 Pomeroy; 805-773-4653 $
A great place for watching the parade of visitors en route to the pier, while enjoying a bowl of clam chowder or a hearty plate of fish 'n chips.

Point Arena

☎ **Coast Guard House Historic Inn.** Arena Cove; 707-882-2442 $$-$$$
Bed-and-breakfast with ocean views, full breakfast, outdoor hot tub.

X **Bookend.** 265 Main St.; 707-882-2287 $
Bookstore-cafe-coffeehouse. Breakfast, lunch, "and later." Slow service means more time to read the novel you've purchased.

X **The Galley at Arena Cove.** Arena Cove, at the foot of the pier; 707-882-2189
Fresh fish, sauteed with garlic, done as fish 'n chips, blackened Cajun-style. Fishermen's hangout. Breakfast, lunch, dinner.

X **Pangaea.** 250 Main St.; 707-882-3001 $$
Chef Shannon Hughes exceeded the reputation she made for herself at St. Orres and the Old Milano Hotel when she opened her own place. Eclectic cuisine, but her chicken-and-dumplings are dynamite! Art exhibits in the dining room. No credit cards.

Point Reyes Station

X **Station House Cafe.** 11180 CA 1; 415-663-1515 $$
Menu changes greatly but usually includes local seafood and locally raised organic beef; barbecued oysters. Shaded garden for summer dining.

X **Tomales Bay Foods.** 80 4th St.; 415-663-9335
The best place to get chow for your picnic.

Redondo Beach

T **Sunrise Hotel.** 400 N. Harbor Dr.; 310-376-0746 or 800-334-7384 $$
A plain, large, comfortable hotel across the street from the King Harbor marina, and in easy walking distance of restaurants, the Redondo Pier, and beaches.

X **Cucina Paradiso.** 1611 S. Catalina St.; 310-792-1972 $$-$$$

Elegant Italian cuisine and attentive service, with a menu that emphasizes Tuscan specialties. Impressive wine list.

X **Quality Seafood Inc. Fish Market.** 130 S. International Boardwalk; 310-374-2382 or 310-372-6408
A classic seafood market (live, fresh fish and shellfish) that's been around since 1953, and will cook your selection for you (broiled or steamed). Outdoor seating. Beware the gulls, pigeons, and sparrows. Yes, sparrows.

X **Tony's on the Pier.** 210 Fisherman's Wharf; 310-374-9246 $$
Old-fashioned fare prepared and served with flair. When the sliding glass doors to the water are open (watch how far you lean out), pigeons and sea gulls come to beg. Microbrews on tap.

X **Waterfront Brewery & Restaurant.** 230 ortofino Way; 310-379-8363 $$
This brewery-restaurant in King Harbor serves beef, pizzas, and seafood dishes designed to go with microbrews. The dining room has a view of the harbor entrance and of the South Bay all the way to Palos Verdes Peninsula. There's also an outside terrace for al fresco dining and sipping.

Samoa

X **Samoa Cookhouse.** Samoa Rd.; 707-442-1659 $$
Portions at this last lumber mill cookhouse in the West are huge. There's no menu. You eat what's set in front of you—as much of

it as you can anyway, because it's some of the best old-fashioned food you'll find anywhere. Bring a big appetite.

San Clemente

☂ **Casa Tropicana Bed & Breakfast.** 610 Avenida Victoria; 949-492-1234 $$$
Champagne, Jacuzzi, and full breakfast.

✕ **Fisherman's Restaurant & Bar.** 611 Avenida Victoria, San Clemente Pier; 949-498-6390 $$
Perfectly fresh, beautifully prepared and presented seafood in a very friendly, down-to-earth restaurant with great views. The bar across the pier is part of the same establishment and even more friendly. The menu changes daily. Good selection of local microbrews. Don't be surprised to see pelicans sitting on the roof: they know where the freshest fish is.

✕ **Beach Garden Cafe.** 618¹/₂ Avenida Victoria; 949-498-8145 $
Soups, sandwiches, pizza, fish 'n chips, omelettes.

San Diego

☂ **Catamaran Resort.** 3999 Mission Blvd., Mission Beach; 619-488-1081 $$$-$$$$
Six 2-story buildings and a highrise stand on a great spot, close to the beach. Rooms are done in a Polynesian theme, and tiki torches light the way between buildings.

☂ **Crystal Pier Motel.** 4500 Ocean Blvd., Mission Beach; 619-483-6983 $$$

The rooms are actually cabins attached to the pier.

☂ **Hotel Del Coronado.** 1500 Orange Ave., Coronado; 619-435-6611 $$$$
This ritzy old Victorian hotel is a relic that somehow works. All of the 689 rooms are comfortable (and different from each other—quite an achievement if you consider that 400 of the rooms were built in 11 months in 1887–88). On the grounds are two giant outdoor pools, six tennis courts, a croquet green, a gaggle of fancy shops, two formal dining rooms dishing up a variety of food from the opulent to the dietetic. *(see* **Crown-Coronet Room** and **Prince of Wales Room** *below),* and a central courtyard with palm trees and flowers. Some folks feel this place is perfectly down-to-earth; others prefer only a visit to one of the restaurants or bars.

☂ **Le Meridien.** 2000 Second St., Coronado; 619-435-3000 $$$$
New England–style buildings stand on a highly landscaped, 16-acre lawn, where flamingoes wander about. Rooms are large and decorated in a Provencal theme. Tennis courts, spas, pools, restaurants, and more.

☂ **Pacific Terrace Inn.** 610 Diamond St., Pacific Beach; 619-581-3500 $$$
This small and lovely hotel offers ocean views from the Pacific Beach cliffs.

✕ **Aesop's Tables Greek Cafe.** 8650 Genessee Ave., Pacific Beach; 619-455-1535 $$
Located in a shopping center, this cafe offers patio dining and a friendly staff, but it's

the great Greek food that'll make you come back. Specialties include the avgolemono soup, saganaki, and any lamb dish.

✕ **Anthony's Star of the Sea.** 1360 Harbor Dr.; 619-232-7408 $$$-$$$$
Young chef Jonathan Pflueger has turned Anthony's into a destination seafood restaurant. His contemporary seasonal cuisine includes such dishes as langoustines in cannelloni.

✕ **Bayou Bar and Grill.** 329 Market St. (at Fourth Ave.); 619-696-8747 $$
This longtime favorite for Cajun/Creole cooking has earned its popularity. On Monday nights, the kitchen serves toothsome plates of Cajun-style sausage and red beans and rice—the traditional Monday (or "wash day") dinner in New Orleans. Lively bar scene, too.

✕ **Cass St. Bar & Grill.** 4612 Cass St.; 619-270-1320 $
Local watering hole with best burgers in Pacific Beach.

✕ **Chez Loma.** 1132 Loma Ave., Coronado; 619-435-0661
This tiny cafe housed in a Victorian boasts sophisticated service and wonderful French classics such as roast duck and filet mignon with bleu cheese.

✕ **Croce's Restaurant.** 802 Fifth Ave.; 619-233-4355 $$
Most folks come here to hear jazz (seven nights a week) and have a drink or two, but the food at the restaurant downstairs can be quite good.

✕ **Crown-Coronet Room.** Hotel Del Coronado, 1500 Orange Ave., Coronado; 619-435-6611 $$$-$$$$
In this massive, 100-year-old landmark is the Crown-Coronet Room, which takes its name from the fact that is has served food to kings, queens, and assorted Middle Eastern sheiks. It's as long as a football field, with a 33-foot-high ceiling. The food is a standard but tasty version of "continental cuisine." Sunday brunch is popular with locals. Meals here are expensive, but not as steep as at the Prince of Wales Room.

✕ **Dockside Restaurant.** At the San Diego Princess Resort, 1404 W. Vacation Rd.; 619-274-4630 $$$
Spectacular views of Mission Bay from an elegant dining room where the food may best be described as eclectic continental. Seafood, chicken, pork beef; favorites include "scampi" (giant prawns) on a bed of angel hair pasta and topped with a garlic, tomato, and basil sauce. Filet mignon is available for those who've overdosed on seafood. The wine list runs heavily to California bottlings. Dinner only.

✕ **Guava Beach Bar & Grill.** 3714 Mission Blvd.; 619-488-6688 $-$$
Fish tacos, margaritas, and other Mexican fare in a relaxed setting.

✕ **Hodad's.** 5010 Newport Ave., Ocean Beach; 619-224-4623 $
Utterly unpretentious place with the best hamburgers in town.

San Diego *(cont'd)*

✕ **Laurel Restaurant & Bar.** 505 Laurel St.; (619) 239-2222 $$$
While not exactly on the beach, the highly talked-about Laurel is worth a visit: besides, it's one block from Balboa Park. The room exudes sophistication, but the friendly bartenders will put most anyone at ease. The impressive food—a combination of French, Mediterranean, and California cuisines—is never dull and always delicious.

✕ **Mission Cafe & Coffee Shop.** 3795 Mission Blvd., Mission Beach; 619-488-9060 $
This funky cafe has staggeringly good food for breakfast, lunch, and dinner. The menu (billed as Chino-Latino) includes such unusual, healthful specialties as Asian quesadillas, wok-fried brown rice with jalapeños, and a combo of brown rice, black beans, corn, and other vegetables wrapped in a whole-wheat/cilantro tortilla. For breakfast, try the banana blackberry pancakes.

✕ **Point Loma Seafoods.** 2805 Emerson St.; 619-223-1109 $
This seafood market on San Diego Bay offers a stunning selection of fresh fish and dependably good takeout fare.

✕ **Prince of Wales Grill.** Hotel del Coronado, 1500 Orange Ave.; Coronado; 619-435-6611 $$$$
A recent remodel here has lightened up this venerable dining room and brought more sun and sea into view, but the room retains its elegant, rather formal feel. Likewise, the kitchen has turned from its old approach to a hearty California/American regional style. Lamb chops are topped with a sweet, citrusy mustard; the exotic salsa frescas served with grilled meats are a nod to the local Mexican culinary influence.

✕ **Qwiigs Bar & Grill.** 5083 Santa Monica Ave., Ocean Beach; 619-222-1101 $$
The view from this second-floor restaurant (across the street from Ocean Beach) is enough to draw anyone in for a drink, but the food's good too. Simple, California-style preparations of grilled fish and burgers are especially tasty. Go to **Cecil's Cafe** downstairs (619-222-0501) for breakfast or lunch.

✕ **Sheldon's Cafe.** 4711 Mission Blvd., Pacific Beach; 619-273-3833 $$
A very popular place serving ever-popular traditional American fare: chicken-fried steak, soups, salads, et al. Popular breakfast buffet. Open 24 hours.

✕ **Thee Bungalow.** 4996 W. Point Loma Blvd.; 619-224-2884 $$
Fancy French-inspired fare—savory roast duck with a black cherry or a green peppercorn sauce, seafood almandine, and desserts such as Grand Marnier souffle—are served at this family-run, longtime favorite. The bungalow itself is an architectural landmark of Ocean Beach. Excellent wine list—perhaps one of San Diego's best.

San Francisco

Archbishops Mansion. 1000 Fulton St.; 415-563-7872 $$$
Once the official home of local Catholic prelates, this opulent B&B on Alamo Square is decorated in Belle Epoque style and is topped with a 16-foot-wide leaded glass dome. Some fireplaces, Jacuzzis.

Hotel Monaco. 501 Geary St.; 415-292-0100 or 800-214-4220 $$$$
With its playful, technicolor decor and chic atmosphere, the new hotspot in town attracts stylish out-of-towners; meanwhile, locals frequent the hyper Art Nouveau–style Grand Cafe restaurant and bar. Impressive sauna and gym.

Hotel Triton. 342 Grant Ave.; 415-394-0500 $$$
A comfortable hotel with quirky, almost surreal decor across the street from Chinatown Gate and within walking distance of the ferry building and the Embarcadero.

Ritz-Carlton. 600 Stockton St.; 415-296-7465 or 800-241-3333 $$$$
Actually a renovation of the neoclassical Metropolitan Life building, this superb hotel impresses visitors with a splendid lobby replete with crystal chandeliers and museum-quality oil paintings. Legendary afternoon teas, and excellent sports facilities to boot.

Tuscan Inn Best Western. 425 North Point; 415-561-1100 $$$
Easy walking distance to Fisherman's Wharf and to the Red-and-White ferry piers (Angel Island, Alcatraz, Vallejo).

Aqua. 252 California St.; 415-956-9662 $$$$
With its stylish, mirrored dining room and sophisticated menu, this restaurant has earned many kudos for delicious seafood dishes made from the freshest fish—some local and some flown in specially for dishes like black mussel soufflé, Idaho trout with foie gras and chanterelles, and smoked sturgeon ravioli. Heavenly desserts.

Caffe Macaroni. 59 Columbus Ave.; 415-956-9737 $$
The lively atmosphere and enthusiastic service here guarantee a delightful lunch or dinner. The jovial brothers who own this tiny Southern Italian spot serve up fabulous antipasti and tasty homemade pastas in record time. You won't leave hungry.

Enrico's. 504 Broadway; 415-982-6223 $$
Although this open air cafe (kept warm with floor- and space heaters) is better known for its history and jazz, the flavorful salads, pizzas, and cockles and mussels are great, too. Don't miss the sweet and sour Aviation, a 1930s cocktail; in summer try a mojito.

Eos. 901 Cole St.; 415-566-3063 $$$
With a spare, airy interior and lots of windows, this corner bistro offers Asian fusion cuisine that goes for broke. (Forgive the kitchen for their excessive garnishes.) Recent favorites have included skirt steak

San Francisco (cont'd)

marinated in Chimay ale; best appetizers are the wild mushroom potstickers and special spring rolls (with ahi or mango). Check out the adjacent wine bar while you wait.

✕ **Fog City Diner.** 1300 Battery St.; 415-982-2000 $$$
This always crowded (and noisy!) restaurant on the Embarcadero, at the foot of Telegraph Hill, resembles a 1940s train diner car—thanks to the chrome and paneling—and not a highway burger joint. But you *can* order a chili dog. The kitchen puts a spin on a range of American regional fare with dishes like Maryland crabcakes sauced with sherry-cayenne mayonnaise.

✕ **42 Degrees.** 235 16th St.; 415-777-5558 $$$
This China Basin restaurant feels industrial but cozy—concrete floors, yes, but giant, curvy banquettes too. The menu draws from European cuisines at 42° latitude (Provençal, Southern Italian, et al.). You'll see hearty dishes like grilled salmon with white beans and chanterelles, roasted potatoes with aioli, and frisée with gorgonzola.

✕ **Greens.** Fort Mason, Building A; 415-771-6222 $$-$$$
Affiliated with the Green Gulch Zen Center, this converted warehouse right on the water is the city's most established vegetarian restaurant. (Vegans note: dairy and eggs are used liberally.) Have a brunch of asparagus omelette with roasted potatoes and enjoy the lovely room with its view, but be prepared to wait, as service can be slow.

Prix-fixe dinners on weekends.

✕ **Harbor Village.** 4 Embarcadero Center, Suite 2420; 415-781-8887 $$$
Superb dim sum and, now that the Embarcadero Freeway has been torn down, a view. Even better at dinner time for banquets. Good wine list; great service.

✕ **Jardinière.** 300 Grove St.; 415-861-5555 $$$$
Chef Traci des Jardins opened this high-style restaurant near the opera, symphony, and ballet to rave reviews. The glittering interior (by Pat Kuleto) complements a largely French-influenced seasonal menu; specialties include the house foie gras with quince salad, perfectly crisped chicken, and flavorful (if a little too rich) soups. There's also a cheese-aging room just past the circular mahogany and marble bar.

✕ **John's Grill.** 63 Ellis St.; 415-986-0069 $$
This restaurant, with its dining room of dark wood paneling, has been doing business since 1908. It has literary significance, because here Sam Spade ate a hurried meal of "chops, baked potato, and sliced tomato," before taking a cab to Burlingame in pursuit of the Maltese Falcon. The menu hasn't changed much since Dashiell Hammet wrote in San Francisco.

✕ **Masa's Restaurant.** 648 Bush St.; 415-989-7154 $$$$
Invariably listed among the Bay Area's top restaurants, Masa's oozes indulgence. Each artfully presented course is complex and richly flavored—without making you feel

the chef is screaming to be noticed. Service is attentive in the extreme: leave the table to visit the bathroom, and your napkin will have been made into an origami flower by the time you return. Expensive, but worth every penny. Superb.

✕ **Rose Pistola.** 532 Columbus; 415-399-0499 $$ - $$$

At this popular trattoria, chef Reed Hearon serves what's best described as North Beach cuisine, based on the district's first Italian immigrants. Garlic, lemon, and olives are used. The menu offers neighborhood classics such as a hearty, delicious cioppino. Don't miss the cured fish (anchovies will never taste the same) or the rabbit. The bright dining room, done in wood and colorful tile, is open past 12 on weekends.

✕ **The Slanted Door.** 584 Valencia St.; 415-861-8032 $$$

The high-ceiling dining room of this haute Vietnamese/French/California restaurant is spare but warm, thanks to color-stained wood, velvet cushions, and a neo-French Colonial cast-iron balcony. Salads, like grapefruit and jicama, and curries, full of sweet potatoes and other vegetables, are wonderful. French-accented dishes such as an incredible roasted duck have vaulted this restaurant into the spotlight.

✕ **Thanh Long.** 4101 Judah St. (46th Ave.); 415-665-1146 $-$$

Local word-of-mouth recommendations for Vietnamese restaurants always include this family-run eatery not far from Ocean Beach. Dungeness crab, cooked with garlic and ginger, is the specialty here.

✕ **Thep Phanom.** 400 Waller St.; 415-431-2526 $-$$

Those in the know come here for "Weeping Lady," a fantastic eggplant dish, or almost anything else. Most local foodies'll tell you that this is the city's best Thai eatery.

✕ **Tommy Toy's Haute Cuisine Chinoise.** 655 Montgomery St.; 415-397-4888 $$$$

This extremely upmarket Chinese restaurant in the general area of the shoreline of gold rush San Francisco is famous for entrées like whole lobster with peppercorn sauce on angel-hair pasta. The elegantly presented food will cost you, but the gleaming surfaces and attentive service do exude luxury. You'll see lots of guests on cell phones here.

✕ **Zuni Café.** 1658 Market St. (Rose); 415-552-2522 $$-$$$

Excellent service, moderate prices, terrific cocktails, and an informal yet tony atmosphere make this a favorite spot for San Franciscans. A copper bar runs along one side of the front bar area toward the quieter dining room; two sides of the eatery are all window. The expertly prepared food is never precious: choose from an impressive list of oysters, then order Caesar salad or roast chicken with Tuscan bread salad.

San Gregorio

▦ **Rancho San Gregorio.** 5 miles inland of CA 1 on Hwy. 84; 650-747-0810 $$

A few miles from San Gregorio Beach is

this Mission-style retreat on 15 acres of ranch land. Terra-cotta tiles, wood-burning stoves, and private porches make for cozy appointments; breakfast is a full country spread of fruits and home-baked breads.

San Luis Obispo

Apple Farm Hotel. 2015 Monterey St.; 805-543-4000 $$$
Built around an old millhouse and farm, this Victorian is furnished with antiques and fireplaces; there's also a swimming pool, Jacuzzi, and restaurant *(see below)*.

Madonna Inn. 100 Madonna Rd.; 805-545-9802 $$-$$$
No doubt you've seen it on film or video. The Madonna is a hot-pink hodgepodge of 110 fantasy rooms: the Flintstones Suite is a mock cave with a rock waterfall shower; the Safari Room is filled with animal skins.

Apple Farm Hotel. *See above;* 805-543-4000 $$$
A pleasant, country-style restaurant specializing in grilled fish.

SLO Brewing Company. 1119 Garden St. ; 805-543-1843 $
Classic brews, pool hall, restaurant in downtown San Luis Obispo.

Big Sky Cafe. 1121 Broad St.; 805-545-5401 $$
A friendly downtown restaurant with terrific healthy food (the kitchen calls its cooking eclectic world cuisine). Tasty bagels, seafood, even burritos. Open for breakfast, lunch, and dinner.

San Rafael

The Panama Hotel. 4 Bayview St. (at the end of B St.); 415-457-3993 $$
A delightful, sprawling old hostelry with reasonable rates; some rooms share a bath.

The Panama Hotel Restaurant. *See above;* 415-457-3993 $$
A very good restaurant serving simply prepared, tasty classic American and Mediterranean dishes.

Santa Barbara

Santa Barbara Inn. 901 E. Cabrillo Blvd.; 805-966-2285 $$
A recently renovated, comfortable motel across the street from East Beach.

Bay Cafe Seafood Restaurant & Fish Market. 131 Anacapa St.; 805-963-2215
Fresh fish at the market and in the restaurant. Fresh spiny lobster, live or cooked.

Brophy Brothers Restaurant & Clam Bar. 119 Harbor Way; 805-966-4418
According to locals, this small restaurant in the harbor serves the freshest and best prepared fish in town.

The Brown Pelican. 2981 1/2 Cliff Dr., Arroyo Burro Beach; 805-687-4550 $-$$
Right on the beach, looking south toward the Channel Islands, this cozy dining room takes advantage of the views with 180 degrees of windows and outdoor tables. Fresh fish is a high point, as is breakfast on any sunny morning.

✕ **Citronelle.** At the Santa Barbara Inn, *see above;* 805-963-01111 $$$$
Opened by Michel Richard, this well-known, elegantly casual dining room boasts stunning views of the ocean from its large windows. Excellent Cal-French fare, as you'd expect; portions are smallish but artfully, even whimsically presented.

✕ **Downey's.** 1305 State St.; 805-966-5006 $$$$
A small restaurant that is among the best dining rooms anywhere in California (some say in the nation): chef-owner John Downey is a genius in the kitchen. The short but always exciting menu (venison sausage with blackberries and spinach was on a recent one) changes daily to keep up with freshest local foods. Dinner is consistently fresh and superb.

✕ **El Paseo Mexican Restaurant.** 10 El Paseo; 805-962-6050 $-$$
A large, fun courtyard place in the heart of Santa Barbara with good food and great service and ambience.

✕ **Palace Cafe.** 8 E. Cota St.; 805-966-3133 $$
Cajun fare in a festive, always packed cafe. Great blackened fish, wonderful martinis served in mason jars. Dinner only; singing patrons preferred.

✕ **Paradise Cafe.** 702 Anacapa St; 805-962-4416 $-$$
A popular, charming lunch spot with a nice patio. Great burgers, salads, and desserts.

✕ **Santa Barbara Brewing Co.** 501 State St.; 805-730-1040 $
A popular local hangout with good brews and very tasty bar food.

✕ **Wine Cask.** 813 Anacapa St.; 805-966-9463 $$$
Good food and good wine at the outer edge of El Paseo. Lunch and dinner.

Santa Cruz

▦ **Chaminade at Santa Cruz.** 1 Chaminade Ln.; 831-475-5600 or 800-283-6569 $$$
A conference center and resort perched on a hill overlooking the harbor, this retreat features hiking trails, tennis courts, and pool, as well as a completely outfitted fitness center.

✕ **Black's Beach Cafe.** 15th Ave. and E. Cliff Dr.; 831-475-2233 $$
Huge sandwiches and salads, plus more refined Pacific Rim dishes in an airy dining room near the beach. Ahi tuna might come with ginger and cilantro, a grilled chicken sandwich with plum sauce. Dinner weekdays; breakfast and dinner on weekends.

✕ **Casablanca Restaurant.** 101 Main St.; 831-426-9063 $$$
A romantic California cuisine restaurant, overlooking the pier and boardwalk. Excellent appetizers and fish dishes.

✕ **Costa Brava.** 505 Seabright Ave.; 831-423-8190
Good, inexpensive Mexican; fish tacos.

✗ **India Joze.** 1001 Center St.; 831-427-3554 $$-$$$

Lunch and dinner are served in the airy, plant-filled dining room. Excellent food: it's eclectic, pan-Asian cuisine, from spicy vegetarian dishes to seafood specials. In August the eatery hosts the Squid Festival, with calamari specials every night and great decorations.

✗ **Java House.** 120 Union St.; 831-459-9876 $

Big, funky coffee house, lots of plants and a nice patio in back. Live jazz most nights.

✗ **Oswald's.** 1547 Pacific Ave.;831-423-7427 $$-$$$

Probably Santa Cruz's most sophisticated eatery. A tiny spot serving French-inspired California cuisine. A recent menu included pork chops with roasted apples, and rack of lamb.

✗ **Pearl Alley Bistro & Wine Bar.** 110 Pearl Alley (bet. Pacific Ave. and Cedar St.), upstairs; 408-429-8070 $$$

Well-prepared, imaginative dishes and a long list of French and local wines by the glass are the draws here. Asian flavors accent some dishes (salmon with kim chee, risotto with burdock); other plates seem influenced by classic French cuisine.

✗ **Ristorante Avanti.** 1711 Mission St.; 831-427-0135 $$

A small trattoria frequented by students and faculty from nearby U.C. Santa Cruz. Best bets are bruschettas, simple fish dishes, and hearty pastas. Great breakfasts, too. Attractive wine bar.

✗ **Seabright Brewery.** 519 Seabright Ave.; 408-426-2739 $

A block or so from the beach, this popular, award-winning microbrewery serves California bistro cuisine—polenta, interesting pastas—and they also have one of the best burgers in town.

✗ **Stagnaro Brothers.** Municipal Wharf; 408-423-2180 $$

A restaurant with adjacent fish market. The fish at both is fresh, and the restaurant knows how to cook it.

Santa Monica

▥ **Hotel Carmel By the Sea.** 201 Broadway; (310) 451-2469 $$

A four-story hotel built in the 1920s; one block from the beach.

▥ **Miramar Sheraton.** 101 Wilshire Blvd.; (310) 576-7777 $$$

Housed in the former estate of Santa Monica's founder, John P. Jones, this elegant hotel has 32 bungalows and 240 rooms (many have balconies with oceanviews).

▥ **Shutters on the Beach.** 1 Pico Blvd.; 310-458-0030 $$$$

The only hotel in L.A. that sits right on the sand, the three buildings here are connected by trellises and awnings; simple rooms, many with balconies. Expensive and chic, with a big Hollywood following.

✗ **Chez Jay.** 1657 Ocean Ave.; 310-395-1741 $$-$$$

Sawdust covers the floor at this well-loved dive across from Santa Monica Pier. There are no more than 10 tables, and just about as many bar stools (usually occupied by regulars). Big steaks, good lobster, and a Sinatra-singing bartender are all part of the appeal. Lunch and dinner.

✕ **Chinois on Main.** 2709 Main St. (bet. Ocean Park Blvd. and Rose Ave.); 310-392-9025 $$$
Wolfgang Puck's highest-rated restaurant is always packed with L.A.'s in crowd. Specialties here include a rare duck with plum sauce and a Shanghai lobster with ginger and curry.

✕ **Drago.** 2628 Wilshire Blvd.; 310-828-1585 $$$
Many consider Celestino Drago's restaurant to have some of the best Italian food in California. Certainly the Sicilian Drago has brought the most authentic and sophisticated fare of his native land to his kitchen with dishes like pasta n' caciata—a timbale of eggplant surrounding hard-boiled eggs and arancine. The dining room is comfortably chic, the service, sharp and friendly, and the collection of grappas, staggering.

✕ **JiRaffe.** 502 Santa Monica Blvd.; 310-917-6671 $$
This California-French bistro is often praised for its understated yet skillful dishes. Selections include sauteed scallops with rock salt and garlic on a bed of braised endive; roast rabbit and rack of lamb are also wonderful. The attractive dining room and its upstairs loft feel light and spacious.

✕ **Gilliland's.** 2424 Main St.; 310-392-3901 $$
A pleasant cafe specializing in California-

Irish fare. Stellar bread basket. Lunch and dinner; brunch on Sunday.

✕ **I Cugini.** 1501 Ocean Blvd. 310-451-4595 $$
Well-prepared Italian fare served in an attractive, faux-Venetian room. The outdoor patio looks out across Ocean Boulevard to Pacific Palisades Park and the ocean. An oyster bar adds to the draw, and a small bakery counter inside displays irresistible cannolis, tiramisu, and biscotti.

✕ **Mäni's Bakery and Espresso Bar.** 2507 Main St; 310-396-7700 $
Low-fat, sugar-free bakery; several dairy free items, too. And the breads and pastries are *tasty,* believe it or not.

✕ **Ocean Avenue Seafood.** 1401 Ocean Ave.; 310-394-5669 $$$
Stylish seaview dining at one of the best seafood restaurants in Los Angeles. There's a fine oyster bar here and a wonderful variety of desserts, including excellent banana pie.

✕ **One Pico.** At Shutters on the Beach, 1 Pico Blvd.; 310-458-0030 $$$$
A slice of New England a la Hollywood is this chic bistro. "Close-up" views of beach and ocean are wonderful *(see* Shutters on the Beach, *above).* The food lives up to the surroundings, too. Seafood is always fresh and perfectly prepared; pastas (a bit pricey, perhaps) are flavorful.

✕ **Patrick's Roadhouse.** 106 Entrada Dr.; 310-459-4544 $$
Prepare to wait at this popular diner, especially for breakfast, unless you're part of the Hollywood crowd—both Roseanne Barr

and Arnold Swarzenegger are regulars.

✗ **Röckenwagner.** 2435 Main St.; 310-399-6504
Housed in a Frank Gehry–designed building on trendy Main Street, Hans Röckenwagner's justly celebrated restaurant offers wonderful eclectic California cuisine. Try the crab souffle or the lamb; in the morning try a fabulous European breakfast of bread and cheese.

✗ **2424 Pico.** 2424 Pico Blvd. (near 25th St.); 310-581-1124 $$
This unassuming cafe has a terrifically eclectic menu, hitting points all over the globe: Korean tacos with cubed grilled ribeye steak are accompanied by a habanero chili paste, a salad of ahi and greens is topped with goat cheese-filled won ton, and a duck b'stilla with dried cherry sauce.

Sausalito

⌃ **Casa Madrona Hotel.** 801 Bridgeway; 415-332-0502 $$$
A grand hotel, with modern theme rooms cascading down the hillside from an old 1880s mansion. Lots of stairways, lots of comfort; great views of the Bay. Superb service. One of the most enjoyable hotels on the entire California coast.

⌃ **Hotel Sausalito.** 16 El Portal; 415-332-0700 or 888-442-0700 $$$
Recent renovations to this Mission-style building (a bordello in the 1930s) have included an artsy interior styling that recalls the French Riviera, with warm terra-cotta

and earth tones. On the Plaza, within walking distance to most Sausalito attractions.

✗ **Cafe Tutti.** 12 El Portal Dr.; 415-332-0211 $
A pleasant, small, very informal cafe on the plaza. Great soups and delectable pizzas.

✗ **Mikayla.** 801 Bridgeway; 415-331-5888 $$
This elegant aerie, high above the Sausalito waterfront, has a retractable roof *and* walls, allowing diners to enjoy the food outdoors on warm evenings and indoors when it's cool outside (it never actually gets cold in Sausalito). The food is based on fresh local ingredients—Sonoma foie gras and locally grown vegetables—and is beautifully prepared and presented.

✗ **Sushi Ran.** 107 Caledonia St.; 415-332-3620 $$$
The best place for sushi in Sausalito. The restaurant has a hip feel, too.

Seal Beach

⌃ **The Seal Beach Inn and Gardens.** 212 Fifth St.; 562-493-2416 $$$
This restored 60-year-old inn has beautiful gardens. And it's within easy walking distance of the beach.

✗ **Walt's Wharf.** 201 Main St.; 562-598-4433 $$$
Fresh seafood and good beer—just the right combination for après-beach. Plus a great bar where the local nightlife congregates over drinks and appetizers.

Shelter Cove

⌂ **Shelter Cove Motor Inn.** 205 Wave St.; 707-986-7521 $
Basic motel lodging near the beach.

✕ **Shelter Cove Campground Store.** 492 Machi Rd.; 707-986-7474 $
Sit at the food counter and tables amid the merchandise. Great fish 'n chips; a very friendly spot.

Solana Beach

✕ **Fidel's.** 607 Valley Dr.; 619-755-5292 $$
Very popular and thus very crowded cantina with some great, rather authentic Mexican fare.

✕ **Belly Up Tavern & Cafe.** 143 S. Cedros Ave.; 760-481-8140 $$
A converted quonset hut that enjoys a great reputation as a night spot.

✕ **Roberto's Mexican Food.** 445 N. US 101 (and throughout S.D.); 619-259-0042
Popular, late-night Mexican restaurant.

Solvang

✕ **Bit O'Denmark.** 473 Alisal Rd.; 805-688-5426 $
Traditional, very tasty Danish fare: the gravlax and pickled herring alone are worth a trip. Try the meat balls, too. Breakfast, lunch, and dinner.

Stinson Beach

⌂ **Casa del Mar.** 37 Belvedere Ave.; 415-868-2124 800-552-2124 $$$
This inn is up the hill a bit and it looks very Mediterranean, with its beautiful terraced gardens. The rooms have views of the ocean, Mt. Tamalpais, or the garden. Flowers and artwork by local artists liven up the rooms. Breakfast is a special affair.

✕ **Parkside Cafe.** 43 Arenal Ave. (off Calle del Mar, next to park parking lot); 415-868-1272 $
Breakfast, lunch daily; dinners Thursday through Monday. Omelets, blueberry pancakes, burgers, mussel linguine, seafood pizza, and more. The snack bar has a take-out counter—burgers, fries, milkshakes.

Sunset Beach

✕ **Harbor House Cafe.** 16341 PCH; 562-592-5404 $
A place with a menu heavy on burgers, omelets, and fired seafood, with variations. But it works—the Harbor House has been around since 1939. Open 24 hours.

Tiburon

✕ **Guaymas.** 5 Main St. (at ferry); 415-435-6300 $$
A terrific dockside location and an action-packed bar scene make this trendy regional Mexican restaurant a festive place to eat, if a tad pricey. Flavors are generally mild, but

the mesquite-grilled seafood and the many tamales go well with the reliable margarita. If you take the ferry to Tiburon, you can't miss this place: you'll disembark here!

✗ **Tutto Mare Ristorante E Taverna.** 9 Main St.; 415-435-4747 $$
A very stylish local hangout where you can snack on oysters, steamed shellfish, or brick-oven pizzas in the downstairs bar or dine more formally upstairs on seafood and pasta. Beware the fishbowl-sized martinis.

Tijuana

✗ **Carnitas Uruapan.** 550 Blvd. Diaz Ordaz; 011-52-66-856181 $
Marinated pork is the specialty here, and it's sold by the kilo. Long wooden tables and benches; large and noisy.

✗ **Cien Años.** 1407 Calle Jose Maria Velazco (Zona Rio, off Avenida Paseo de los Heroes); 011-52-66-343039 $
A small, popular restaurant where generous portions of authentic Mexican food are served. Try an order of chile rellenos stuffed with shrimp. If you're feeling adventurous, try a Mexican delicacy such as ant eggs.

✗ **Guadalajara Grill.** 17 Paseo de los Heroes, Zona Rio; 66-34-30-87 $$
Reliably tasty dishes at this casual and lively eatery include the fajitas, chicken mole, and tequila shrimp.

Timber Cove

🛏 **Timber Cove Inn.** 217 N. CA 1; 707-847-3231 $$$

All 51 rooms have spas and wood-burning fireplaces.

Trinidad

🛏 **Bishop Pine Lodge.** 1481 Patrick's Point Dr.; 707-677-3374 $
Clean, relatively inexpensive motel on the road leading into town from the north.

🛏 **The Lost Whale Bed and Breakfast Inn.** 3452 Patrick's Point Dr.; 707-677-3425 or 800-677-7859 $$$
All rooms have private baths, five have balconies overlooking the ocean; a private stairway leads down the bluff to miles of rocky beach. Huge breakfasts. Playground for children.

✗ **Larrupin' Cafe.** 1658 Patrick's Point Rd.; 707-677-0230 $$
No credit cards. This place looks like a European country inn, though the fare is upscale American, with fresh seafood and barbecued pork ribs among the highlights.

✗ **Seascape Restaurant.** At the foot of the pier in the harbor; 707-677-3762 $$
A delightful place where local diners flock, and where the locals bring their visitors. Friendly, good service, fresh seafood prepared with flair has kept this dining room bustling for more than 35 years.

Valley Ford

✗ **Dinucci's Italian Dining.** 14484 Valley Ford Rd.; 707-876-3260 $$
Old-fashioned but excellent Italian fare.

Venice

✕ **A Votre Sante.** 1025 Abbot Kinney Blvd. 310-314-1187 $$
Serving stylishly prepared, healthy cuisine to a hip crowd. Menu includes vegetarian, chicken, and seafood dishes.

✕ **Chaya Venice.** 110 Navy St. (Main St.) 310-396-1179 $$$
A typically upscale Venice crowd patrons this trendy restaurant. Watch for filmmakers and leading artists hovering around the sushi bar or making deals in one of the comfortable banquettes. Brunch here is an elegant affair.

✕ **Hal's.** 1349 Abbot Kinney Blvd.; 310-396-3105 $$$
Venice's artsy crowd hangs out at this roomy, brick-walled bistro, home to the city's best Caesar salad and a number of fine grilled dishes.

✕ **Hama Sushi.** 213 Windward Ave.; 310-396-8783 $-$$
There isn't a sushi fanatic in West Los Angeles who hasn't sat blissfully at a cramped table or squeezed into the sushi bar at Hama Sushi. The wait may be long, but the people-watching is unbeatable.

✕ **James' Beach.** 60 N. Venice Blvd.; 310-823-5396 $$-$$$
This casual cafe, with its bright, art-filled interior, emphasizes American regional cooking, which proves both hugely satisfying and inventive. Calamari is served with chipotle chili mayonnaise, stuffed pork chops with brandied applesauce.

✕ **Joe's Restaurant.** 1023 Abbot Kinney Blvd.; 310-399-5811
Nothing like its name, this intimate bistro is one of L.A.'s top eateries. French-trained chef Joe Miller is known for his simple California menu that includes grilled fish, chicken, and roast pork. Entrees include a crisp chicken with creamy twice-baked Parmesan pototoes, and a fine saffron risotto with scallops and a frizz of carrots. Save room for the hazelnut crème brûlée. Lunch, dinner, and weekend brunch.

✕ **Sidewalk Cafe.** 1401 Ocean Front Walk.; 310-399-5547 $
A casual eatery with patio dining on the boardwalk.

✕ **26 Beach Cafe.** 26 Washington Blvd.; 310-821-8129 $
Adjacent to Venice Beach, this laid back little cafe serves giant and delicious hamburgers and sandwiches.

Ventura

▣ **Ventura Cliff House Inn.** 6602 W. PCH, Mussel Shoals; 805-652-1381 $$
Romantic getaway on the rocks above the beach where the roar of the surf often drowns out the roar of US 101.

✕ **Shoals Restaurant.** At the Ventura Cliff House Inn, *see above;* 805-652-1381 $$
Seafood, pork, lamb, filet mignon are usually offered here. Reservations are required; open for lunch, dinner, Sunday brunch.

HOTELS BY REGION

SAN FRANCISCO BAY

City/Town	Hotel/Inn	Phone	Price	Page
OAKLAND	Inn at the Square	510-452-4565	$$	362
SAN FRANCISCO	Archbishops Mansion	415-563-7872	$$$	369
	Hotel Monaco	415-292-0100	$$$$	369
	Hotel Triton	415-394-0500	$$$	369
	Ritz-Carlton	415-296-7465	$$$$	369
	Tuscan Inn Best Western	415-561-1100	$$$	369
SAN RAFAEL	The Panama Hotel	415-457-3993	$$	372
SAUSALITO	Casa Madrona Hotel	415-332-0502	$$$	376
	Hotel Sausalito	415-332-0700	$$$	376

MARIN COAST

City/Town	Hotel/Inn	Phone	Price	Page
INVERNESS	Dancing Coyote Beach	415-669-7200	$$	352
	Manka's Inverness Lodge	415-669-1034	$$$	352
	Ten Inverness Way	415-669-1648	$$$	352
MUIR BEACH	The Pelican Inn	415-383-6000	$$$	362
OLEMA	Olema Inn & Restaurant	415-663-9559	$$	363
STINSON BEACH	Casa del Mar	415-868-2124	$$$	377

SONOMA & MENDOCINO COUNTIES

City/Town	Hotel/Inn	Phone	Price	Page
ALBION	Albion River Inn	707-937-1919	$$$	339
BODEGA BAY	Inn at the Tides	707-875-2751	$$$	342
BOONVILLE	Boonville Hotel	707-895-2210	$$	342
ELK	Greenwood Pier Inn	707-877-9997	$$$	347
	Griffin House	707-877-3422	$$$	347
	Harbor House	707-877-3203	$$$-$$$$	347
FORT BRAGG	Cleone Lodge Inn	707-964-2788	$$	348
	Grey Whale Inn	707-964-0640	$$-$$$	348
	Noyo River Lodge	707-964-8045	$$	348
	The Old Coast Hotel	707-961-4488	$$	348
	Surf and Sand Lodge	707-964-9383	$$	348
	Vista Manor Lodge	707-964-4776	$-$$	349
GUALALA	Gualala Hotel	707-884-3441	$	350
	The Old Milano Hotel	707-884-3256	$$$	350
	St. Orres	707-884-3303	$$-$$$	350

GUERNEVILLE	Applewood Inn	707-869-9093	$$$ - $$$$	350
HEALDSBURG	Camellia Inn.	707-433-8182	$$–$$$	351
JENNER	Murphy's Jenner Inn	707-865-2377	$$ - $$$	352
LITTLE RIVER	Heritage House.	707-937-5885	$$$ - $$$$	356
	Little River Inn.	707-937-5942	$$ - $$$	356
MENDOCINO	MacCallum House	707-937-0289	$$$	358
	Mendocino Hotel	707-937-0511	$$ - $$$	359
	Whitegate Inn.	707-937-4892	$$ - $$$	359
POINT ARENA	Coast Guard House	707-882-2442	$$-$$$	364
TIMBER COVE	Timber Cove Inn.	707-847-3231	$$$ []	378

REDWOOD COAST

City/Town	Hotel/Inn	Phone	Price	Page
ARCATA	Hotel Arcata	707-826-0217	$	339
	Lady Ann	707-822-2797	$$	339
CRESCENT CITY	Crescent Beach Motel.	707-464-5436	$	345
EUREKA	Carter House.	707-444-8062	$$$-$$$$	348
FERNDALE	The Gingerbread Mansion.	707-786-4000	$$$-$$$$	348
KLAMATH	Requa Inn.	707-482-8205	$-$$	353
PETROLIA	Lost Inn.	707-629-3394	$$	364
SHELTER COVE	Shelter Cove Motor Inn.	707-986-7521	$	377
TRINIDAD	Bishop Pine Lodge	707-677-3374	$	378
	The Lost Whale B&B	707-677-3425	$$$	378

GOLDEN GATE TO SAN SIMEON

City/Town	Hotel/Inn	Phone	Price	Page
BIG SUR	Big Sur River Inn	831-667-2700	$$$	341
	Deetjen's Big Sur Inn	831-667-2377	$$$	341
	Post Ranch Inn	831-667-2200	$$$$	341
	Ventana	831-667-2331	$$$$	341
CAMBRIA	Sea Otter Inn	805-927-5888	**$$**	343
CAPITOLA	Venetian Hotel	831-476-6471	$$	343
	The Inn at Depot Hill	831-462-3376	$$$	343
CARMEL	Garden Court Inn	831-624-6926	$$$	344
	Carmel Highlands	831-624-3801	$$$$	344
	Cypress Inn	831-624-3871	$$$	344
	Lamplighters Inn	831-624-7372	$$$	344
	Sandpiper Inn	831-624-6433	$$-$$$	344
DAVENPORT	New Davenport B&B	831-425-1818	$$$	346

GOLDEN GATE TO SAN SIMEON *cont'd*

City/Town	Hotel/Inn	Phone	Price	Page
HALF MOON BAY	Cypress Inn	650-726-6002	$$$ - $$$$	350
	Mill Rose Inn	650-726-8750	$$$-$$$$	351
	San Benito House	650-726-3425	$-$$	351
	Zaballa Inn	650-726-9123	$$-$$$	351
MONTEREY	Hotel Pacific	831-373-5700	$$$	360
	Jabberwock	831-372-4777		360
	Old Monterey Inn	831-375-8284	$$-$$$	360
	Spindrift Inn	831-646-8900	$$$	360
PACIFIC GROVE	Beachcomber Inn	831-373-4769	$$	363
	Gosby House Inn	831-375-1287	$$-$$$	363
	Martine Inn	831-373-3388	$$-$$$$	363
	Pacific Grove Lighthouse	831-655-2111	$$-$$$	363
SAN GREGORIO	Rancho San Gregorio	650-747-0810	$$	371
SANTA CRUZ	Chaminade	831-475-5600	$$$	373

CENTRAL COAST RIVIERA

City/Town	Hotel/Inn	Phone	Price	Page
AVILA BEACH	San Luis Bay Inn	805-595-2333	$$	341
CAYUCOS	Cayucos Beachwalker	805-995-2133	$$	345
MONTECITO	Four Seasons Biltmore	805-969-2261	$$$$	359
	Miramar Resort Hotel	805-969-2203	$$$$	359
	Montecito Inn	805-969-7854	$$$$	360
MORRO BAY	Inn at Morro Bay	805-772-5651	$$-$$$$	361
	Tradewinds Motel	805-772-7376	$$	361
PISMO BEACH	Shelter Cove Lodge	805-773-3511	$$-$$$	364
SAN LUIS OBISPO	Apple Farm Hotel	805-543-4000	$$$	372
	Madonna Inn	805-545-9802	$$-$$$	372
SANTA BARBARA	Santa Barbara Inn	805-966-2285	$$	372

L.A. METRO & ORANGE COUNTY

City/Town	Hotel/Inn	Phone	Price	Page
CATALINA	Inn on Mount Ada	310-510-2030	$$$$	344
DANA POINT	Best Western Marina Inn	949-496-1203	$$	345
	Ritz-Carlton Laguna Niguel	949-240-2000	$$$$	345
LAGUNA BEACH	Hotel Laguna	949-494-1151	$$-$$$	354
	Inn at Laguna Beach	949-497-9722	$$$-$$$$	354
	Surf and Sand Hotel	949-497-4477	$$$$	355

LONG BEACH	Edgewater Beach Motel	562-437-3090	$	356
MALIBU	Malibu Beach Inn	310-456-6444	$$$-$$$$	357
MARINA DEL REY	Ritz-Carlton	310-823-1700	$$$$	358
NEWPORT BEACH	Newport Channel Inn	949-642-3030	$	362
	Portofino Inn	949-673-7030	$$$	362
REDONDO BEACH	Sunrise Hotel	310-376-0746	$$	365
SAN CLEMENTE	Casa Tropicana B&B	949-492-1234	$$$	366
SANTA MONICA	Hotel Carmel-by-the-Sea	310-451-2469	$$$$	374
	Miramar Sheraton	310-576-7777	$$$	374
	Shutters on the Beach	310-458-0030	$$$$	374
SEAL BEACH	Seal Beach Inn	562-493-2416	$$$	376
VENTURA	Cliff House Inn	805-652-1381	$$	389

SAN DIEGO COUNTY

City/Town	Hotel/Inn	Phone	Price	Page
CARLSBAD	Carlsbad Beach Terrace	760-729-5951	$$$	344
	Carlsbad Inn Beach Resort	760-434-7020	$$$	344
	Four Seasons Aviara	760-931-6672	$$$$	344
DEL MAR	Best Western Stratford Inn	619-755-1501	$$	346
	L'Auberge Del Mar	619-259-1515	$$$$	346
ENCINITAS	Moonlight Beach Motel	760-753-0623	$	347
LA JOLLA	La Jolla Cove Motel	619-459-2621	$$	353
	La Valencia	619-454-0771	$$$	353
	Sea Lodge	619-459-8271	$$$	353
	Sheraton Gr. Torrey Pines	619-558-1500	$$$	353
SAN DIEGO	Catamaran Resort	619-488-1081	$$$-$$$$	366
	Crystal Pier Motel	619-483-6983	$$$	366
	Hotel Del Coronado	619-435-6611	$$$$	366
	Le Meridien	619-435-3000	$$$$	366
	Pacific Terrace Inn	619-581-3500	$$$	366

RESTAURANTS BY REGION

SAN FRANCISCO BAY

City/Town	Restaurant	Phone	Price	Page
BERKELEY	Cafe Rouge	510-525-1440	$$-$$$	341
	Chez Panisse/Cafe	510-548-5525	$$$$/$$$	341
LARKSPUR	The Lark Creek Inn	415-924-7766	$$-$$$	355
	Left Bank	415-927-3331	$$	355
OAKLAND	Oakland Grill	510-835-1176	$$	362
SAN FRANCISCO	Aqua	415-956-9662	$$$	369
	Caffe Macaroni	415-956-9737	$$	369
	Enrico's	415-982-6223	$$	369
	Eos	415-566-3063	$$$	369
	Fog City Diner	415-982-2000	$$$	370
	42 Degrees	415-777-5558	$$$	370
	Greens	415-771-6222	$$-$$$	370
	Harbor Village	415-781-8887	$$$	370
	Jardinière	415-861-5555	$$$$	370
	John's Grill	415-986-0069	$$	370
	Masa's Restaurant	415-989-7154	$$$$	370
	Rose Pistola	415-399-0499	$$-$$$	371
	Slanted Door	415-861-8032	$$$	371
	Thanh Long	415-665-1146	$-$$	371
	Thep Phanom	415-431-2526	$-$$	371
	Tommy Toy's	415-397-4888	$$$$	371
	Zuni Café	415-552-2522	$$-$$$	371
SAN RAFAEL	The Panama Hotel	415-457-3993	$$	372
SAUSALITO	Cafe Tutti	415-332-0211	$	376
	Mikayla	415-331-5888	$$	376
	Sushi Ran	415-322-3620	$$$	376
TIBURON	Guaymas	415-435-6300	$$	377
	Tutto Mare Ristorante	415-435-4747	$$	378

MARIN COAST RESTAURANTS

City/Town	Restaurant	Phone	Price	Page
BOLINAS	Bolinas Bay Bakery	415-868-0211	$	342
	Smiley's Schooner Saloon	415-868-1311	$	342
INVERNESS	Manka's Inverness Lodge	415-669-1034	$$$	352
	Vladimir's	415-669-1021	$$$	352
MARSHALL	Nick's Cove	415-663-1033	$$	358
	Tony's	415-663-1107	$$	358

MUIR BEACH	The Pelican Inn	415-383-6000	$$-$$$	362
OLEMA	Olema Farm House	415-663-11264	$$	363
	Olema Inn & Restaurant	415-663-9559	$$	363
POINT REYES STN.	Station House Cafe	415-663-1515	$$	365
	Tomales Bay Foods	415-663-1277	$	365
STINSON BEACH	Parkside Cafe	415-868-1272	$	377
VALLEY FORD	Dinucci's Italian Dining	707-876-3260	$$	378

Sonoma & Mendocino Counties

City/Town	Restaurant	Phone	Price	Page
ALBION	Albion River Inn	707-937-1919	$$	339
BOONVILLE	Boonville Hotel	707-895-2210	$$	342
	Buckhorn Saloon	707-895-2337	$$	342
ELK	Greenwood Pier Inn	707-877-9997	$$$ Cafe,$	347
	Harbor House	707-877-3203	$$$	347
FORT BRAGG	North Coast Brewing Co.	707-964-3400	$$	349
	The Old Coast Hotel	707-961-4488	$$	349
	The Restaurant	707-964-9800	$-$$	349
	Schat's Bakery	707-964-1929	$	349
	Viraporn's Thai Rest.	707-964-7931	$	349
	The Wharf Restaurant	707-964-4283	$-$$	349
GRATON	Kitchen	707-824-0563	$$	349
GUALALA	The Old Milano Hotel	707-884-3256	$$$	350
	St. Orres	707-884-3303	$$-$$$	350
GUERNEVILLE	Applewood Inn	707-869-9170	$$$$	350
HEALDSBURG	Bear Republic Brewing	707-433-2337	$ - $$	351
	Bistro Ralph	707-433-1380	$$	351
	Oakville Grocery	707-433-3200	$-$$	351
JENNER	River's End	707-865-2484	$$$	352
LITTLE RIVER	Heritage House	707-937-5885	$$$$	356
	Little River Inn	707-937-5942	$$$	356
MENDOCINO	Bayview Cafe	707-937-4197	$	359
	Cafe Beaujolais	707-937-5614	$$$	359
	MacCallum House	707-937-5763	$$$	359
	Mendocino Cafe	707-937-2422	$	359
	Mendocino Hotel	707-937-0511	$$ - $$$	359
PHILO	Floodgate Store & Grill	707-895-2870		364
POINT ARENA	Bookend	707-882-2287	$	364
	The Galley at Arena Cove	707-882-2189		364
	Pangaea	707-882-3001	$$	365

RESTAURANTS BY REGION

REDWOOD COAST

City/Town	Restaurant	Phone	Price	Page
ARCATA	Abruzzi	707-826-2345	$$	339
	Humboldt Brewing Co.	707-826-BREW	$	339
	Tomo	707-822-1414	$$	341
Eureka	Lazio's Seafood	707-442-3767	$$	348
	Lost Coast Brewery	707-445-4480	$	348
	Restaurant 301	707-444-8062	$$$$	348
	Sea Grill	707-443-7187	$$	348
FERNDALE	Diane's	707-786-4950	$	348
SAMOA	Samoa Cookhouse	707-442-1659	$$	366
SHELTER COVE	Shelter Cove Camp. Store	707-986-7474	$	377
TRINIDAD	Larrupin' Cafe	707-677-0230	$$	378
	Seascape Restaurant	707-677-3762	$$	378
VALLEY FORD	Dinucci's Italian Dining	707-876-3260	$$	378

GOLDEN GATE TO SAN SIMEON

City/Town	Restaurant	Phone	Price	Page
APTOS	Cafe Sparrow	831-688-6238	$$	339
BIG SUR	Deetjen's Big Sur Inn	831-667-2378	$$	342
	Nepenthe	831-667-2345	$$	342
	Ventana Country Inn	831-667-2331	$$$$	342
CAPITOLA	Gayle's Rosticceria	831-462-1200	$	343
	Pizza My Heart	831-475-5714	$	343
CARMEL	Casanova	831-625-0501	$$$	344
	Crème Carmel	831-624-0444	$$$	345
	Hog's Breath Inn	831-625-1044	$$	345
	Pacific's Edge	831-624-3801	$$$	345
DAVENPORT	New Davenport Cash Store	831-426-4122	$$$	346
HALF MOON BAY	Half Moon Bay Bakery	650-726-4841	$	351
	San Benito House	650-726-3425	$$	351
MONTEREY	Cafe Fina	831-372-5200	$$	360
	Fresh Cream	831-375-9798	$$$-$$$$	360
	Montrio	831-648-8880	$$ - $$$	360
MOSS BEACH	Moss Beach Distillery	650-728-5595	$$	361
MOSS LANDING	Moss Landing Cafe	831-633-3355	$	361
PACIFIC GROVE	Fishwife Restaurant	831-375-7107	$-$$	363
PESCADERO	Duarte's Tavern	650-879-0464	$$	364

SANTA CRUZ	Black's Beach Cafe	831-475-2233	$$	373
	Casablanca	831-426-9063	$$$	373
	Costa Brava	831-423-8190	$	373
	India Joze	831-427-3554	$$	374
	Oswald's			374
	Pearl Alley Bistro	831-429-8070	$$$	374
	Ristorante Avanti	831-427-0135	$$	374
	Seabright Brewery	831-426-2739	$	374
	Stagnaro Brothers	831-423-2180	$$	374

CENTRAL COAST RIVIERA

City/Town	Restaurant	Phone	Price	Page
AVILA BEACH	Olde Port Inn	805-595-2515	$$$	341
CAMBRIA	Ian's	805-927-8649	$$	343
	Sow's Ear	805-927-4865	$$	343
CAYUCOS	Sea Shanty	805-995-3272	$	345
GOLETA	Beachside Bar Cafe	805-964-7881	$$	349
MONTECITO	Four Seasons Biltmore	805-969-2261	$$$$	359
	Stonehouse	805-969-5046	$$$	360
MORRO BAY	Dorn's Original Breakers	805-772-4415	$$	361
	Galley Restaurant	805-772-2806	$$	361
	Harada Japanese	805-772-1410	$$$	361
	Paradise	805-772-5651	$$$	361
	Rose's Landing	805-772-4441	$-$$	361
PISMO BEACH	Shore Cliff Restaurant	805-773-4671	$$-$$$	364
	Splash Cafe	805-773-4653	$	364
SAN LUIS OBISPO	Apple Farm Hotel	805-543-4000	$$$	372
	Big Sky Cafe	805-545-5401	$$	372
	SLO Brewing Company	805-543-1843	$	372
SANTA BARBARA	Bay Cafe	805-963-2215	$-$$	372
	Brophy Brothers	805-966-4418	$	372
	The Brown Pelican	805-687-4550	$-$$	372
	Citronelle	805-963-01111	$$$$	373
	Downey's	805-966-5006	$$$$	373
	El Paseo	805-962-6050	$-$$	373
	Palace Cafe	805-966-3133	$$	373
	Paradise Cafe	805-962-4416	$-$$	373
	Santa Barbara Brewing Co.	805-963-3090	$	373
	Wine Cask	805-966-9463	$$$	373
SOLVANG	Bit O'Denmark	805-688-5426	$	377

L.A. METRO & ORANGE COUNTY

City/Town	Restaurant	Phone	Price	Page
CAPISTRANO BEACH	Olamendi's	949-661-1005	$$	343
CATALINA	Avalon Seafood	310-510-0197	$	345
	Cafe Prego	310-510-1218	$$	345
DANA POINT	Jon's Fish Market	949-496-2807	$	345
EL SEGUNDO	Panama's Bar and Grill	310-322-5829	$	346
HERMOSA BEACH	Good Stuff	310-374-2334	$	352
LAGUNA BEACH	Anastasia Cafe	949-497-8903	$-$$	355
	Casa Olamendi	949-497-4148	$	355
	Five Feet	949-497-4955	$$$	355
	Laguna Beach Brewing Co.	949-499-BEER	$$	355
	Las Brisas	949-497-5434	$$-$$$	355
	Splashes	949-497-4477	$$$-$$$$	355
	242 Cafe	949-494-2444	$$	355
	Wahoo's Fish Taco	949-497-0033	$	355
LONG BEACH	Alegria	562-436-3388	$-$$	356
	555 East	562-437-0626	$$$-$$$$	356
	King's Fish House	562-432-7463	$$$	356
	L'Opera	562-491-0066	$$$	356
MALIBU	Bambu Malibu	310-546-5464	$$	357
	Beaurivage	310-456-5733	$$$-$$$$	357
	Geoffrey's Malibu	310-457-1519	$$$	358
	Granita	310-456-0488	$$$-$$$$	357
	Kay and Dave's Cantina	310-456-8800	$	357
	Neptune's Net	310-457-3095	$-$$	357
	Reel Inn	310-456-8221	$$	357
MANHATTAN BEACH	Cafe Pierre	310-545-5252	$$-$$$	358
	The Kettle	310-545-8511	$	358
	Michi	310-376-0613	$$	358
MARINA DEL REY	Cafe del Rey	310-823-6395	$$$-$$$$	358
NEWPORT BEACH	The Crab Cooker	949-673-0100	$$	362
	Newport Burger	949-642-5881	$	362
	Sabatino's & Lido	949-723-0621	$$	362
REDONDO BEACH	Cucina Paradiso	310-792-1972	$$-$$$	365
	Quality Seafood Inc.	310-374-2382	$	365
	Tony's on the Pier	310-374-9246	$$	365
	Waterfront Brewery	310-379-8363	$$	365
SAN CLEMENTE	Fisherman's Restaurant	949-498-6390	$$	366
	Beach Garden Cafe	949-498-8145	$	366
SANTA MONICA	Chez Jay	310-395-1741		374

	Chinois on Main	310-392-9025	$$$	374
	Drago	310-828-1585	$$$	375
	JiRaffe	310-917-6671	$$	375
	Gilliland's	310-392-3901	$$	375
	I Cugini	310-451-4595	$$	375
	Mäni's Bakery	310-396-7700	$	375
	Ocean Avenue Seafood	310-394-5669	$$$	375
	One Pico	310-458-0030	$$$$	375
	Patrick's Roadhouse	310-459-4544	$$	375
	Rockenwagner	310-399-6504	$$$-$$$$	375
	2424 Pico	310-581-1124	$$	376
SEAL BEACH	Walt's Wharf	562-598-4433	$$$	376
SUNSET BEACH	Harbor House Cafe	562-592-5404	$	377
VENICE	A Votre Sante	310-314-1187	$$	379
	Chaya Venice	310-396-1179	$$$	379
	Hal's	310-396-3105	$$$	379
	Hama Sushi	310-396-8783	$$-$$$	379
	James' Beach	310-823-5396	$$ - $$$	379
	Joe's Restaurant	310-399-5811	$$$	379
	26 Beach Cafe	310-821-8129	$$	379
VENTURA	Shoals Restaurant	805-652-1381	$$	379

SAN DIEGO COUNTY AND TIJUANA RESTAURANTS

City/Town	Restaurant	Phone	Price	Page
CARDIFF	Beach House	760-753-1321	$$$	343
	Las Olas	760-942-1860	$	343
	Miracles	760-943-7924	$	343
CARLSBAD	Harbor Fish South	760-729-4161	$	344
	Niemans/Niemans' Seagrill	760-729-4131	$$$	344
	Pelly's Fish Market	760-431-8454	$	344
DEL MAR	Cafe Del Mar	619-481-1133	$$	346
	Epazote	619-259-9966	$$$	346
	Fish Market	619-755-2277	$$	346
	Kirby's Cafe	619-481-1001		346
	Pacifica Del Mar	619-792-0476	$$$	346
	Stratford Court Cafe	619-792-7433	$	346
ENCINITAS	Ki's Restaurant	760-436-5236	$	347
	La Bonne Bouffe	760-436-3081	$$-$$$	347
	Roxy Restaurant	760-436-5001	$	347
IMPERIAL BEACH	El Tapatio's	619-423-3443	$	352

RESTAURANTS BY REGION

SAN DIEGO COUNTY & TIJUANA *cont'd*

City/Town	Restaurant	Phone	Price	Page
LA JOLLA	Bird Rock Cafe	619-551-4090	$$	353
	Brockton Villa Rest.	619 454-7393	$$	353
	Carinos Restaurant	619-459-1400	$	353
	The Cheese Shop	619-459-3921	$	353
	Froggy's Bar & Grill.	619-488-8102	$	353
	George's at the Cove	619-454-4244	$$$	354
	La Jolla Brewing Co.	619-456-2739	$	354
	Marine Room	619-459-7222	$$$-$$$$	354
	Mediterranean Room	619-454-0771	$$$	354
	Pannikin Coffee & Tea	619-454-6365	$	354
	Pannikin Coffee & Tea	619-454-5453	$	354
	Porkyland Restaurant	619-459-1708	$	354
	Trattoria Acqua	619-454-0709	$$	354
OCEANSIDE	Beach Break Cafe	760-439-6355	$	363
	Johnny Mananas	760-721-9999	$	363
	Ruby's Diner	760-433-7829	$	363
SAN DIEGO	Aesop's Tables	619-455-1535	$-$$	366
	Anthony's Star of the Sea	619-232-7408	$$$	367
	Bayou Bar and Grill	619-696-8747	$$-$$$	367
	Cass St. Bar & Grill	619-270-1320	$	367
	Chez Loma	619-435-0661	$$	367
	Croce's Restaurant	619-233-4355	$$	367
	Crown-Coronet Room	619-435-6611	$$$-$$$$	367
	Dockside Restaurant	619-274-4630	$$	367
	Guava Beach Bar & Grill	619-488-6688	$-$$	367
	Hodad's	619-224-4623	$	368
	Laurel Restaurant	619-239-2222	$$$-$$$$	368
	Mission Cafe	619-488-9060	$	368
	Point Loma Seafoods	619-223-1109	$	368
	Prince of Wales Grill	619-522-8819	$$$$	368
	Qwiigs Bar & Grill	619-222-1101	$$	368
	Sheldon's Cafe	619-273-3833	$$	368
	Thee Bungalow	619-224-2884	$$$	368
SOLANA BEACH	Belly Up Tavern	760-481-8140	$$	377
	Fidel's	760-755-5292	$$	377
	Roberto's Mexican Food	760-259-0042	$	377
TIJUANA	Carnitas Uruapan	01152-66-856181	$	378

I N D E X

Comments, suggestions, or updated information?
Please write:
Compass American Guides
5332 College Ave., Suite #201
Oakland, CA 94618

ACKNOWLEDGMENTS

A book is more than just the product of a single mind. I would, therefore, like to thank all of the many people who have made this book possible. Special thinks go to my editor, Kit Duane, for making me feel I could shoulder this demanding project, and for once again inspiring me to go beyond (what I thought were) my limitations. Thanks also go to Chris Burt and Julia Dillon at Compass American Guides, and especially to Debi Dunn who helped me tremendously with the beaches and beach folk of Southern California. I would also like to thank Nyna Cox for her help with lodging, Shari Dunn and Bill Burden for their insights into Los Angeles beach and California surfer culture, and Kelly Duane for the scoop on the Northern California surfer.

Last, but not least, I must thank all those beach companions, surfers, beach-combers, fishermen, oyster farmers, sailors, innkeepers, winery owners, and restaurateurs who have given me information about the coast, providing me with a continuous, Kaleidoscopic vision. And I must thank the gulls and pelicans, murres and guillemots, sanderlings, snowy plovers, ravens and hawks who were my companions whenever I could not entice any humans to join me at the shore. Nor should I neglect to mention the sea otters, seals, seal lions, and whales who have entertained me with their antics.

This is also the place to mention those writers who helped me understand the coast and its history: Richard Henry Dana, Robert Louis Stevenson, Jack London, Gertrude Atherton, Robinson Jeffers, Henry Miller, John Steinbeck, and Dan Duane.

COMPASS
AMERICAN
GUIDES

Available at your local bookstore,
or call (800) 733-3000 to order.

Alaska (1st Edition)
1-878-86777-6
$18.95 ($26.50 Can)

Arizona (4th Edition)
0-679-03388-2
$18.95 ($26.50 Can)

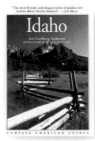

Idaho (1st Edition)
1-878-86778-4
$18.95 ($26.50 Can)

Las Vegas (5th Edition)
0-679-00015-1
$18.95 ($26.50 Can)

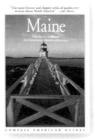

Maine (2nd Edition)
1-878-86796-2
$18.95 ($26.50 Can)

Manhattan (2nd Edition)
1-878-86794-6
$18.95 ($26.50 Can)

North Carolina (1st Edition)
0-679-03390-4
$18.95 ($26.50 Can)

Oregon (3rd Edition)
0-679-00033-X
$19.95 ($27.95 Can)

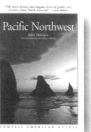

Pacific Northwest (1st Edition)
1-878-86785-7
$18.95 ($26.50 Can)

San Francisco (4th Edition)
1-878-86792-X
$18.95 ($26.50 Can)

Texas (2nd Edition)
1-878-86798-9
$18.95 ($26.50 Can)

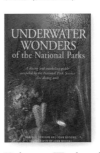

**Underwater Wonders of
the National Parks**
(1st Edition) 0-679-03386-6
$19.95 ($27.95 Can)

Utah (4th Edition)
0-679-00030-5
$19.95 ($27.95 Can)

Virginia (2nd Edition)
1-878-86795-4
$18.95 ($26.50 Can)

Boston (1st Edition)
1-878-86776-8
$18.95 ($26.50 Can)

Chicago (2nd Edition)
1-878-86780-6
$18.95 ($26.50 Can)

Colorado (4th Edition)
0-679-00027-5
$18.95 ($26.50 Can)

Hawaii (3rd Edition)
1-878-86791-1
$18.95 ($26.50 Can)

Minnesota (1st Edition)
1-878-86776-8
$18.95 ($26.50 Can)

Montana (3rd Edition)
1-878-86797-0
$18.95 ($26.50 Can)

New Mexico (3rd Edition)
0-679-00031-3
$18.95 ($26.50 Can)

New Orleans (3rd Edition)
0-679-03597-4
$18.95 ($26.50 Can)

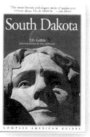
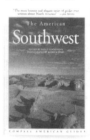

Santa Fe (2nd Edition)
0-679-03389-0
$18.95 ($26.50 Can)

South Carolina (2nd Edition)
0-679-03599-0
$18.95 ($27.95 Can)

South Dakota (2nd Edition)
1-878-86747-4
$18.95 ($22.95 Can)

Southwest (2nd Edition)
0-679-00035-6
$18.95 ($26.50 Can)

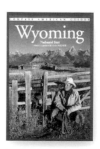

Washington (2nd Edition)
1-878-86799-7
$19.95 ($27.95 Can)

Wine Country (2nd Edition)
0-679-00032-1
$19.95 ($27.95 Can)

Wisconsin (2nd Edition)
1-878-86749-0
$18.95 ($26.50 Can)

Wyoming (3rd Edition)
0-679-00034-8
$19.95 ($27.95 Can)

■ ABOUT THE AUTHOR

John Doerper has been traveling the California Coast for more than 30 years, enjoying its beaches, inns, restaurants, and prime camping sites. He is the author of four books describing the pleasures of travel on the Pacific Coast, including *Wine Country* for Compass American Guides. He has acted as editor and columnist for several publications and has published articles in *Travel & Leisure* and *Pacific Northwest Magazine.* Mr. Doerper is the publisher and editor of *Pacific Epicure, A Quarterly Journal of Gastronomic Literature.*

■ ABOUT THE PHOTOGRAPHER

Galen Rowell, one of the most prominent nature photographers in the U.S. today, is the author and photographer of more than a dozen large-format books, including *Mountain Light: In Search of the Dynamic Landscape,* his valuable introduction to outdoor photography, and *Bay Area Wild.* A regular contributor to *National Geographic, Outdoor Photographer,* and *Life,* he is also a noted mountaineer, who has climbed in Nepal, Tibet, Alaska, and Patagonia, as well as making more than 100 first ascents in California's High Sierra. Major exhibitions of his work have been held at galleries across the United States, including the Smithsonian Institution in Washington D.C. and San Francisco's California Academy of Sciences.